AEROSPACE SCIENCE
A JOURNEY INTO
AVIATION
HISTORY

SACSCASI
Southern Association of Colleges and Schools
Council on Accreditation and School Improvement

PEARSON
Custom
Publishing

Pearson Custom Publishing Acquisitions Editor: Chris Will
Department of the Air Force Editor: Linda F. Sackie
Development Editor: Richard Gomes
Production Editor: Liz Faerm
Rights Project Editor: Jennifer Sczerbinski
Photograph Research and Licensing: Sarah Dowden
Cover Design: Chris O'Brien
Book Design: Mia Saunders
Manufacturing Buyer: Mary Beth Cameron
Printer/Binder: RR Donnelley

Cover photographs include "Wright Flyer," "WASPS," "Tuskegee Airmen," "Doolittle Raiders," "Robert H. Goddard," "TH-1H trainer helicopter," "C-17," "F-22A Raptor," "Charles Lindberg," "Gen. Daniel "Chappie" James," "KC-135 refueling an F-15," "Space Shuttle Atlantis," and "Colonel Eileen M. Collins," courtesy of the US Air Force; "International Space Station," courtesy of Getty Images, Inc; "US Army Balloon During the Battle of San Juan Hill," courtesy of the National Archives and Records Administration; and "Portrait of Galileo Galilei," courtesy of Nimatallah/Art Resource, NY.

Excerpts taken from various sources, which are referenced at the end of the book.

Grateful acknowledgement is made to the Civil Air Patrol for materials from *Aerospace: The Journey of Flight*.

Printed in the United States of America

10 9 8 7 6 5 4 3

ISBN 0-536-33383-1

2006420303

RG/SD

Please visit our web site at *www.pearsoncustom.com*

PEARSON CUSTOM PUBLISHING
501 Boylston Street, Suite 900, Boston, MA 02116
A Pearson Education Company

Contents

UNIT ONE

Imagining FLIGHT 3

CHAPTER 1 Ancient Flight 5

LESSON 1 Discovering Flight 6

How Humans Tried to Fly in Ancient Times 7
Key Aviation Devices Created During Ancient Times 7
Why Machines Do Not Fly the Way Birds Do 11

Lesson 1 Review 13

LESSON 2 The Early Days of Flight 14

Developments in Lighter-than-Air Flight From Da Vinci
  to the Wright Brothers 16
Why Balloons Were Used During the US Civil War 20
Ways the Balloon Contributed to US Victory in the Battle
  of San Juan Hill 21
Developments in Heavier-than-Air Flight From Da Vinci
  to the Wright Brothers 21

Lesson 2 Review 25

UNIT TWO

Exploring FLIGHT 27

CHAPTER 2 Pioneers of Flight 29

LESSON 1 The Wright Brothers 30

How the Wright Brothers Succeeded in the First Flight 31
The Anatomy of the *Wright Flyer* 38
The Principles of Airplane Flight 40
The History of the Wright Brothers' Involvement With the US Army 40

Lesson 1 Review 43

LESSON 2 Developing Aircraft 44

Key Individuals Involved in Early Aircraft Development 45
The Names and Anatomy of Period Aircraft 48
Other American Pioneers in Aviation Following the Wright Brothers 51

Lesson 2 Review 61

LESSON 3 Air Power in World War I 62

The Contributions of US Pilots During World War I 63
The Role of Air Power During World War I 72
How Air Power Expanded During World War I 76

Lesson 3 Review 79

CHAPTER 3 Expanding the Horizon 81

LESSON 1 The Barnstormers 82

The Barnstormers 84
The Barnstormers' Major Contributions 88
How the Barnstormers Contributed to Public Awareness of Aviation 90

Lesson 1 Review 91

LESSON 2   Flight Goes Mainstream   92

Charles Lindbergh's Famous Contribution to Aviation   94

The Significance of the First Transatlantic Solo Flight   94

Other Significant Contributions That Helped Flight Become Mainstream   99

Lesson 2 Review   105

LESSON 3   Commercial Flight, Airmail, and Helicopters   106

Early Developments in Commercial Flight   108

The Use of the Airplane in Delivering Mail   111

The Development and Use of Helicopters   112

Lesson 3 Review   115

UNIT THREE

Developing FLIGHT   117

CHAPTER 4   The Early Air Force   119

LESSON 1   The Army Air Corps   120

The Predecessors of the US Air Force   122

How the Army Air Corps Developed   129

The Air Force's Path Toward Independence   132

Lesson 1 Review   135

LESSON 2   Air Power in World War II   136

The Role Air Power Played in World War II and Its Significance   137

How Air Power Was Developed During World War II   143

The Significance of the Allied Air Campaigns   155

Lesson 2 Review   169

CHAPTER 5 Commercial Flight 171

LESSON 1 The Propeller Era in Commercial Flight 172

Key Developments in Commercial Aircraft 174

Key Developments in Commercial Flight Use 181

Key Contributors to the Expansion of Commercial Flight 182

Lesson 1 Review 187

LESSON 2 The Jet Era in Commercial Flight 188

The Significance of the Development of the Jet Engine 191

Key Developments in the Commercial Flight Industry 196

Pros and Cons of Commercial Flight Travel for Passengers 201

Lesson 2 Review 203

CHAPTER 6 The Modern Air Force 205

LESSON 1 Air Force Beginnings Through the Korean War 206

The Creation of an Independent Air Force in 1947 207

The Cold War and How It Began 209

The USAF Role in the Berlin Airlift 214

The Role of Air Power in the Korean War 221

Lesson 1 Review 227

LESSON 2 The Vietnam War and Other Military Operations 228

The Role of Air Power in the Cuban Missile Crisis 229

The Role of Air Power in the Vietnam War 232

How the USAF Gained an Increasingly Significant Role in Other US Military Operations During the Cold War 243

Key Developments in Aircraft, Missile Capability, and Nuclear Capability During the Cold War 249

Lesson 2 Review 253

LESSON 3   Global Interventions From 1990   254

The Significance of Stealth Aircraft   255

The Role of Air Power in the Gulf War (Operation Desert Storm)   257

The Role of Air Power in Operation Enduring Freedom   261

The Role of Air Power in Operation Iraqi Freedom   267

The Role of Air Power in Various Other US Military Operations   271

Lesson 3 Review   281

UNIT FOUR

Extending FLIGHT   283

CHAPTER 7 Astronomy and Space   285

**LESSON 1   The Solar System and
Some Early Astronomers   286**

The Objects in the Solar System   289

The Significant Contributions of Key Early Astronomers   295

Lesson 1 Review   301

LESSON 2   Rocketry and the Space Race   302

How Developments in Rocketry Made Space Exploration
Possible   303

How the Cold War Led to a Race in Space   311

Lesson 2 Review   315

CHAPTER 8 Exploring Space 317

LESSON 1 The Space Program 318

The Key Steps in the US and Soviet Space Programs 319

The Key Steps in the Development of Spacecraft 327

The Significance of the Phrase "One Small Step for [a] Man, One Giant Leap for Mankind" 332

Key Space Shuttle Missions 338

The Purpose of the International Space Station 348

Lesson 1 Review 349

LESSON 2 The Future of Air and Space Power 350

Current and Anticipated Developments in Manned Air Vehicles 351

Current and Anticipated Developments in Unmanned Systems 354

Current and Anticipated Developments in Cyber Warfare 356

Anticipated Air Force Plans for Integrating Air and Space Operations 358

NASA's Vision for the Future 361

Lesson 2 Review 364

McREL Standards 365

References 393

Glossary 413

Index 421

Preface

Aerospace Science: A Journey Into Aviation History is a course about aviation history focusing on the development of flight throughout the centuries. It starts with ancient civilizations, then progresses through time to modern days. It emphasizes civilian and military contributions to aviation, the development and modernization of the United States Air Force, and a brief history of astronomy and space exploration. The present edition is the first major revision of this course in more than two decades.

Our vision for this course is to bring alive the significant events that make up the exciting history of aviation. Along with the events, we focus on those people who accomplished them. This book tells their stories and shows why we are so proud of Air Force heritage—which lays the foundation for the Air Force Junior Reserve Officer Training Corps (AFJROTC) program. As our mission for AFJROTC is to "develop citizens of character dedicated to serving their nation and community," we know this course will meet one of our objectives—to provide instruction in air and space fundamentals.

New features of this book include *Flight Paths*—short profiles of famous people whose lives illustrate aspects of the lesson material; *Skynotes*—which provide brief information about a topic; and *Capsules*—interesting tidbits related to aerospace facts. Throughout the course, there are readings, video clips, hands-on activities, and in-text and student-workbook exercises. A student workbook and an instructor guide with lesson plans and slides supplement the text.

"Unit One: Imagining Flight" covers ancient flight. It includes how people discovered flight and the early days of flight. You'll read how the imaginative thinking of Leonardo da Vinci led people in following centuries to experiment with parachutes and gliders.

"Unit Two: Exploring Flight" deals with pioneers of flight. It begins with the Wright brothers and discusses the development of aircraft and air power in World War I. It continues with lessons on the barnstormers; flight goes mainstream; and commercial flight, air mail, and helicopters. You'll read about the Wright brothers' careful and logical experiments that led to the first controlled, manned, heavier-than-air flight. You'll study how aviation developed rapidly during World War I and how Charles Lindbergh captured imaginations with his trans-Atlantic solo flight.

"Unit Three: Developing Flight" focuses on the early days of the Army Air Corps through air power in World War II. It then goes on to the propeller and jet eras in commercial flight. The discussion of the modern Air Force includes US Air Force beginnings through the Korean War, the Vietnam War, and other military operations and global interventions from 1990. You'll read how brave Allied flyers helped liberate Europe and the Pacific region in World War II, about the birth of the independent US Air Force, and the role air power has played in US global interventions since then.

"Unit Four: Extending Flight" begins with astronomy and space, starting with the solar system and some early astronomers, then turning to rocketry and the space race. It goes on to discuss the space program and the future of air and space power. You'll read about the beginnings of the space program, the first men to reach the moon, the accomplishments and tragedies of the space shuttles, and possibilities of the future of air and space power.

This book is dedicated to everyone who enters the door into our AFJROTC program. We hope that as you go through this course, you will think about the possibilities that lie ahead and the great things that you can experience.

Linda Sackie

The subject matter in *Aerospace Science: A Journey Into Aviation History* was based on suggestions received from AFJROTC instructors around the world. The Air Force Officer Accession and Training Schools (AFOATS) Curriculum Division team involved in the production effort was under the direction of Dr. Charles Nath III, Director of Curriculum, at Maxwell Air Force Base, Alabama. His deputy, Major Chris Senkbeil and the Acting Chief of Junior ROTC Curriculum, Roger Ledbetter, completed an exceptional leadership team, resulting in a superb product for the AFJROTC program. Special thanks go to Curriculum's Linda Sackie, an instructional systems specialist and the primary editor, reviewer, and significant contributor for this project. We commend Linda's continued selfless dedication and outstanding efforts to produce the best academic materials possible for our units worldwide.

We are indebted to our academic consultants/reviewers who provided sustained leadership and guidance: Colonel John Gurtcheff (retired), AFJROTC Senior Aerospace Science Instructor at SC-873, Crestwood High School, Sumter, South Carolina, (and a former KC-135 pilot), and Dr. Nath. Special thanks go to Master Sergeant William Chivalette (retired), curator, Air Force Enlisted Heritage Hall, Gunter Annex in Montgomery, Alabama, for his invaluable historical expertise and insight, and to the Airman Memorial Museum in Suitland, Maryland, for their support of this project.

Our deepest gratitude goes to the people at Headquarters, Civil Air Patrol, for granting us permission to use all their curriculum materials. They were a significant resource and extensive source of information.

Other Curriculum Area Managers (CAM)/instructors from AFOATS/CR senior ROTC and Officer Training School curriculum development staff provided pivotal advice and subject-matter expertise: Captain Michael Collins, Captain Ben Harding, Kevin Lynn, and former CAM Major Gerald Cottrill.

We would like to express our gratitude to the Pearson Custom Publishing team for all its hard work in publishing this new book. That team consisted of subcontractors at High Stakes Writing, LLC—Lawrence J. Goodrich, W. Dees Stallings, John G. Birdsong, Katherine Dillin, Linda Harteker, and Ruth Walker; from Perspectives, Inc.—Philip G. Graham, Emily G. Haney, and Suzanne M. Perry; Mia Saunders (graphic design and page layout); Paul Lester (McREL standards); and numerous Pearson Custom Publishing personnel, including Christopher Will, Ed Perlmutter, Rich Gomes, Susan Kahn, Liz Faerm, Jennifer Sczerbinski, Sarah Dowden, Christopher O'Brien, and David Gehan.

Through the efforts of all the different team members identified, we believe this course continues our tradition of sustaining a "world-class" academic program.

UNIT ONE

1mag

An early German Zeppelin

ining FLIGHT

Unit Chapter

CHAPTER 1

Ancient Flight

CHAPTER 1

Union forces prepare a balloon
for use during the Civil War.

Ancient Flight

Chapter Outline

LESSON 1

Discovering Flight

LESSON 2

The Early Days of Flight

"The way in which we experience the irregularities of the wind while gliding through the air cannot be learned in any other way except by being in the air itself. . . ."

OTTO LILIENTHAL,
"The Father of Modern Aviation"

Discovering Flight

A stiff, 27-mile-an-hour wind roared across the dunes at Kill Devil Hills, North Carolina. Wilbur Wright reached out to steady the wing of his experimental flying machine. His brother, Orville, lay at the controls. For years the brothers had worked for this moment—both in their bicycle shop in Dayton, Ohio, and on these same coastal dunes. They'd tested kites. They'd tested gliders. They'd even built a small wind tunnel and learned how to control their craft in the air.

Now, on 17 December 1903, they were ready to find out: Would their heavier-than-air craft leave the ground and fly on its own?

Orville gunned the engine, and Wilbur let go of a wire that held the plane in place. The *Wright Flyer* rolled down a set of tracks on a trolley, with Wilbur's hand still steadying the wing. Suddenly, it happened: The *Flyer* lifted into the air, dropped the trolley, and flew for 12 seconds. Under Orville's control, it landed 120 feet away from the track's end. The Wright brothers had achieved a milestone: the first controlled, sustained, and powered heavier-than-air flight.

That flight and the three that followed on that raw December day changed the course of human history. After thousands of years of dreaming and trying, humans had mastered flight. But the Wrights' achievement was only the final step in centuries of attempts to learn how to fly. The brothers from Dayton built on the work of hundreds of others before them.

How Humans Tried to Fly in Ancient Times

Humans have dreamed of taking flight—of escaping gravity to fly "free as a bird"—for thousands of years. People told tales about flight—*the act of passing through the air on wings*—around the fire at night. Parents in early societies handed down these stories to their children.

One of the best known is the Greek story of Daedalus and his son, Icarus, who were imprisoned by King Minos on the island of Crete. To escape, they made wings from bird feathers and attached them to their bodies with beeswax. The wings did carry them off the island. But Icarus enjoyed his new freedom so much that he ignored his father's warning and flew too close to the sun. Its heat melted the wax. Icarus fell into the sea and drowned.

The story of Icarus and Daedalus is a myth. It isn't a true story. But people still tell it today because of what it says about the human quest for freedom—and about sons who disobey their fathers. The story, however, doesn't say much about how to build a good flying machine.

The first true stories of human attempts to fly, though, included things that today seem almost as strange as stick-on wings. Some of these early inventors made devices of lightweight material such as cloth or wood, in imitation of birds' or bats' wings. They strapped the devices onto their arms or legs, or both. Then they would jump from the top of a tower or tall building, hoping to glide or flap their way gently to earth.

Unfortunately, none of the devices succeeded. At best, they slowed their wearers' plunge to earth. These early inventors all made hard landings, resulting in serious injury or death.

History credits a Moor named Armen Firman with the first known human attempt to fly. In the year AD 852, he put on a huge cloak and jumped from a tower in Cordoba, Spain. He hoped the cloak would open wide like a bat's wings to slow him on the way down. But it didn't, and Firman fell to his death. His unfortunate experiment might be described as an early attempt at a jump by parachute—*a device intended to slow free fall from an aircraft or another high point.*

Key Aviation Devices Created During Ancient Times

Chinese Kites

A lot of ancient scientific progress took place in China. The Chinese invented the kite around 1000 BC. A kite *is a light framework covered with paper or cloth, provided with a balancing tail, designed to be flown in the air.* A kite may seem very different from an airplane, but kites were actually among the first man-made devices to take

Using Kites to Spot the Enemy

In 200 BC, a Chinese general named Han Hsin used kites to scout his enemy's position and movements by air. His soldiers attached long measuring ropes to the kites. They got the kites in the air and then let the wind carry them to a position over the enemy camp. By determining how much rope had been let out, the Chinese soldiers could figure how far away the enemy was. They wanted to tunnel under the enemy's walled fortress. The marks on the rope showed them how far they had to dig to reach the fortress.

flight. It's not clear that these early kites actually carried people at first. Evidence suggests, though, that they were quite large and strong. Within a few hundred years, people were using them in warfare.

Around AD 1300 the Italian explorer Marco Polo reportedly saw Chinese sailors attached to kites as "eyes in the sky," observing enemy actions during battle. In the seventeenth century, other Western observers reported seeing Chinese soldiers on kites serving as flying spies.

Chinese Gunpowder and Rockets

In the 800s AD, the Chinese made another important invention: gunpowder—*an explosive powder made of potassium nitrate, charcoal, and sulfur, used to shoot projectiles from guns.* And just 200 years later, the Chinese were using gunpowder to make the first simple rockets. A rocket *is a large, cylindrical object that moves very fast by forcing burning gases out one end of the tube.*

The Chinese used these devices mostly for celebrations, such as holiday fireworks. But they also used their rockets in battle to scare off the enemy.

There's even a Chinese legend, or *unverified story handed down from earlier times,* about a rocket trip into space. This legend says that a man named Wan Hoo fastened 47 rockets to a chair. He hoped his invention would take him to the moon. Not surprisingly, it didn't work. He went up in a ball of fire, and, the legend suggests, perhaps became the Man in the Moon.

It's obvious that this is just a story. But in a way, the legend foretold history. When the *Apollo* astronauts traveled to the moon in the 1960s and 1970s, they were strapped into special chairs in their spacecraft and then lifted away from Earth by rockets.

A Parachute and a Helicopter

The first person in the history of aviation who was also a real scientist was Leonardo da Vinci (1452–1519). Da Vinci produced the first known designs for a parachute and a helicopter, *an aircraft that gets its lift from spinning blades*. He apparently made models of both and may even have flown one of his helicopters.

Da Vinci's drawing of an "airscrew" looks a lot like a modern helicopter. And in fact, both devices are based on the same principle: a flat screw that, when turned, produces lift. What's more, today's parachutes are based on principles first described by Da Vinci. His invention, he wrote, would allow someone to "throw himself down from any height without sustaining any injury."

Flight Paths

LEONARDO DA VINCI

Courtesy of the Library of Congress

Leonardo da Vinci

Have you heard the term "Renaissance man?" It refers to someone who has many talents. Leonardo da Vinci was such a man. He's best known today as an artist—for example, he painted the *Mona Lisa*. But he was a scientist, too. He conducted the first scientific experiments in aviation.

Like other scientists, Da Vinci observed the world closely. Also like other scientists, he kept good records. He filled the pages of his notebooks with detailed drawings of things he had actually seen, as well as things he thought up. The notebooks included 160 pages of drawings of his projects for flight. The notebooks show that Da Vinci understood several key concepts in aviation, such as streamlining, *which is designing an aircraft to reduce resistance to motion through the air.*

His orderly way of working did a lot for science. But it could have done much more. Tragically, his notes were lost for about 300 years following his death. He left his drawings and papers in the care of a friend, who never published them. Scientists today wonder how much sooner human flight would have developed had Da Vinci's work been available during those "lost" years.

DA VINCI'S "AIRSCREW" HELICOPTER

Courtesy of Clipart.com

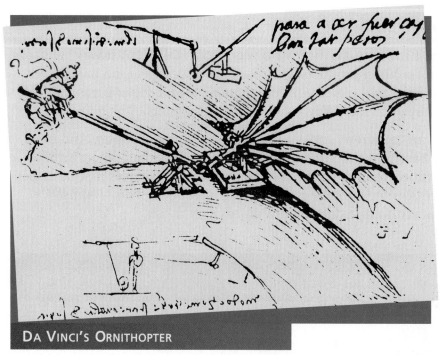

DA VINCI'S ORNITHOPTER

Courtesy of The Granger Collection, New York

Gliders

Da Vinci also researched the idea of a glider, *a light aircraft without an engine, designed to glide after being towed aloft or launched from a catapult.* Gliders were the first aircraft that had directional control.

Da Vinci was fascinated with birds, and he experimented with flapping-wing machines. He worked out structures and mechanisms intended to mimic the motions of a bird. These included some designs for ornithopters. An ornithopter *is an aircraft designed to get its support and forward motion from flapping wings.* (*Orni-* comes from a Greek word for bird.)

Da Vinci was a careful observer. But even he didn't understand how complex the movements of a bird's wing are. He also didn't realize that human muscle power could never be powerful enough to keep a person in the air. That realization didn't come until about 150 years after Da Vinci's death. At that time, the Italian biologist Giovanni Alfonso Borelli (1608–1679) concluded that a man's muscle power just wasn't great enough to lift his weight.

You may think of birds as "lightweights," and in many ways, they are. But it's relative proportions that matter. Birds are very powerful for their size. Their large wing muscles and hollow bones make them well suited to flight. Unfortunately, when it comes to being able to fly on their own muscle power, humans have more in common with elephants than with birds!

Why Machines Do Not Fly the Way Birds Do

The Principles of Bird Flight

A bird's flight is similar to an airplane's in some ways and different in others. Here's how Dr. Paul Fortin, author of *The Fantasy and Mechanics of Flight*, explains it:

> There are two phases of bird flight—a ground phase and a lift phase. The ground phase allows the bird to get started moving forward in order for the wings to provide the necessary lift. To be lifted by its wings, a bird . . . must be moving forward fast enough to make air pass over its wings. A bird can move forward by flapping its wings. Most of the flapping is done by the outer wing. The flight feathers work like the propeller of a plane: i.e., they push downward and backward, thereby driving the air backward and moving the bird forward. Once the bird's speed is adequate, lift over the wing is generated by the same principle as the flow of air over the wing of an airplane.

Dr. Fortin adds:

> Slow-motion pictures of birds in flight show that the wings move downward rapidly. The wing tips trace a figure eight as they move though the air. The downward beat of the wings moves the bird forward as the outer tips push against the air. Wing feathers are arranged much like shingles on a roof. They change position when the bird is flapping. On the downbeat of the wing, the feathers are pressed together so little air can pass through them. On the up stroke the feathers open.

Bird flight and the flight of human-made aircraft rely on two kinds of lift, each named for a famous scientist who never flew, but who made significant contributions to aeronautical science: Daniel Bernoulli and Isaac Newton.

DANIEL BERNOULLI

Courtesy of Photo Researchers, Inc.

SIR ISAAC NEWTON

Courtesy of Photo Researchers, Inc.

The Dutch-born scientist Daniel Bernoulli (1700–1782) made an important discovery about the relationship between pressure and fluids (liquids or gases) in motion. A fluid has a constant pressure, he found, but when a fluid starts to move faster, the pressure drops. Wings are designed to make air flow faster over their tops. This makes the pressure drop and the wings move upward, defying the force of gravity. This phenomenon is known as *Bernoullian lift* or *induced lift*.

Sir Isaac Newton, an Englishman who lived from 1643 to 1727, formulated three famous laws of motion. The third law states, "For every action, there is an equal and opposite reaction." This principle comes into play when an airplane is ascending, or flying higher. When a pilot angles the wing of the plane up against the oncoming wind, the action of the wind causes a reaction by the wing. This reaction provides some additional lift, known as *Newtonian* or *dynamic lift*. So with Bernoullian lift pulling from above and Newtonian lift pushing from below, a wing has no choice. It can only go up—whether it's attached to a bird or to an airplane.

By now you're beginning to understand that birds and airplanes don't work exactly alike. Here's another difference: Airplanes are fixed-wing aircraft. They don't flap their wings as birds do. Instead, airplanes rely on their propellers or jet engines to get them off the ground.

Timeline of Aviation History

1000 BC:	**Chinese invent the kite.**
200 BC:	**Chinese General Han Hsin uses kites for military surveillance.**
In the AD 800s:	**Chinese invent gunpowder.**
AD 852:	**In an unsuccessful attempt to fly, Armen Firman dons a huge cloak and jumps from a tower in Cordoba, Spain.**
AD 1100:	**Chinese start using gunpowder to make simple rockets.**
AD 1300:	**Explorer Marco Polo reportedly sees Chinese sailors flying on kites as "eyes in the sky," observing enemy actions during battle.**
1452–1519:	**Life span of Leonardo da Vinci, who pioneered the scientific study of aviation.**
1643–1727:	**Life span of Isaac Newton, who formulated three laws of motion.**
1700–1782:	**Life span of Daniel Bernoulli, who discovered the phenomenon of induced lift.**
17 December 1903:	**Wilbur and Orville Wright make the first controlled, sustained, and powered heavier-than-air flight.**

Why Ancient Inventors Tried to Mimic Bird Flight

At the beginning of aviation history, flapping wings seemed to be what flight was all about. People observed birds, bats, and insects flying this way. As you've now learned, some early inventors thought feathers might possess some lifting power of their own. And even a thinker as brilliant as Da Vinci got stuck on birds as the model for human flight. Some scientists think that if Da Vinci had focused on fixed-wing gliders, instead of ornithopters, he might have done even more for the progress of aviation than he actually did. Only when people stopped trying to fly as birds do did the way open for the Wright brothers' success on the North Carolina dunes.

CHECKPOINTS

Lesson 1 Review

Using complete sentences, answer the following questions on a sheet of paper.

1. What milestone did the Wright brothers reach in December 1903?

2. Who were Daedalus and Icarus?

3. Who was Armen Firman, and what was his role in aviation history?

4. What were some early military uses of kites?

5. Who made the first rockets? What were they first used for?

6. What kinds of flight devices did Leonardo da Vinci explore?

7. What are the two phases of bird flight?

Applying Your Learning

8. Flying squirrels don't have wings, but they do have flaps of skin between the legs on each side of their body. These flaps allow them to "fly" from tree to tree or from a tree to the ground. To which flying device would you compare a flying squirrel and why?

The Early Days of Flight

Learn About...

- **developments in lighter-than-air flight from Da Vinci to the Wright brothers**
- **ways balloons were used during the US Civil War**
- **ways the balloon contributed to US victory in the Battle of San Juan Hill during the Spanish-American War**
- **developments in heavier-than-air flight from Da Vinci to the Wright brothers**

It had been a tough trip for Lt Col Joseph E. Maxfield of the US Army Signal Corps. The year was 1898. The United States was at war with Spain.

Six years earlier, the Signal Corps had formed a balloon section. For the first time since the Civil War, the Army was back in the business of spying from the sky.

Now Lt Col Maxfield was in charge of a single balloon. It was the only one the Army had.

Maxfield traveled alone with the balloon from New York to Florida. Then with troops and some equipment, he sailed for Cuba. That country, then a Spanish colony, was one of the major theaters of the Spanish-American War.

Maxfield's party included three officers and 24 enlisted men. Only one man had ballooning experience—Sgt Will Ivy Baldwin—who had once worked as a stunt balloonist and had built a balloon with his wife the previous year. None of the others, including Maxfield, had ever even seen a balloon go up.

The party sailed into Santiago harbor 22 June. Because they lacked supplies, they would be able to inflate the balloon just once. They wouldn't be able to reinflate it.

The terrain was rugged. It took them a whole day to get from the harbor to their headquarters. And once they unpacked their balloon, they found that parts of it had stuck together in the heat. Other parts had disintegrated.

But somehow, they managed to inflate the balloon using hydrogen cylinders. And they got it into the air several times.

On 1 July 1898 during the Battle of San Juan Hill, Soldiers went aloft to scout the enemy position. They made an initial ascent at some distance from the battle. The leader of the Soldiers, Lt Col George M. Derby, then ordered the balloon forward. He got it to within 650 yards of the Spanish infantry trenches. Maxfield feared this was too close to the enemy.

In a way, he was right. By the end of the day, the balloon had been hit by so many enemy bullets that it was useless. But not before it gave observers aboard a totally different view of the battle. Because of what they'd seen, the balloonists suggested new ways to direct American troops advancing against the Spanish. They also identified new artillery targets.

The battle was a big US victory. Teddy Roosevelt's Rough Riders made a name for themselves in it. The "buffalo Soldiers," members of an all-African-American regiment, got to show what they were made of.

The Battle of San Juan Hill was a milestone in military aviation. The spies in the sky may have decided the battle.

It was a good day for Maxfield's balloon.

CUBA AND THE US GULF COAST

Courtesy of Maps.com

THE US ARMY BALLOON DURING THE BATTLE OF SAN JUAN HILL

Courtesy of the National Archives

Teddy Roosevelt's Rough Riders

The Rough Riders were a volunteer Army regiment. Theodore Roosevelt organized them to help Cuba win independence from Spain. He didn't have any military experience, so he asked a friend who did to be in charge. With the friend's help, Roosevelt, who would later become the 26th President of the United States, rounded up a group of 1,250 cowboys and Indians, as well as Ivy League athletes and sportsmen, to fight for a free Cuba.

Aviation developments in the 19th century followed two lines: lighter-than-air craft and heavier-than-air craft. Lighter-than-air craft include balloons and dirigibles. The story you've just read shows how far these craft had come by the end of the 19th century. Heavier-than-air machines include gliders, and later, airplanes and jets.

Whether their craft are lighter or heavier than air, all aviators face the same three problems:

- how to get up into the air
- how to stay up in the air
- how to control where they're going, including getting safely back to earth.

Developments in Lighter-than-Air Flight From Da Vinci to the Wright Brothers

Principles of Balloon Flight

A balloon operates on the principle of buoyancy. If the air or gas inside a balloon is lighter than the air around it, it will float. Hot air takes care of the first challenge of flight—getting up into the air.

A Jesuit priest, Laurenço de Gusmão, gets credit for inventing the hot-air balloon. In 1709 he demonstrated his invention before the King of Portugal. Word soon spread across Europe.

Skynotes

What do printing presses have to do with flying machines? Quite a bit. During the early years of aviation, the cost of printing fell sharply. Books and papers became cheaper. More people could afford to buy them. For the first time, scientists throughout Europe could read about one another's work. The printing presses were a big help in making the dream of flight come true.

Several people tried out balloons during the 18th century. The work of the Montgolfier brothers, Joseph and Étienne, led to the first balloon flight with humans aboard. On 21 November 1783, Pilatre de Rozier and François d'Arlandes made a historic 25-minute flight over Paris in a Montgolfier hot-air balloon.

The Montgolfiers' achievement was impressive. But there was still work to do. The brothers hadn't figured out how to achieve the second principle of flight— to keep the balloon up in the air. To do that, you need to keep the air inside the balloon hot. This meant having a fire under the balloon. That was dangerous. It also meant that balloons needed to carry fuel, and fuel was heavy.

A Big Idea Sparked in Front of the Fireplace

Joseph and Étienne Montgolfier were the first to achieve manned flight. The brothers were papermakers and amateur scientists in Annonay, France. They kept up with the work of other scientists around Europe.

One day in 1782 Joseph Montgolfier was sitting in front of his fireplace when he happened to notice the sparks and smoke rising.

This got him thinking—and experimenting. He made a small bag out of silk and held the bag upside down. Then he lit a fire under the opening at the bottom. The bag swelled and rose to the ceiling. Soon Joseph and his brother moved their experiments outdoors. They built and flew larger bags made of paper and linen.

The brothers thought they'd discovered a new gas. They even gave it a name: "Montgolfier gas." Today we know that they hadn't discovered a new gas. They'd simply observed a principle of physics: Hotter air rises above cooler air.

THE MONTGOLFIER BROTHERS' BALLOON

Courtesy of John Lienhard

The Montgolfiers' experiments attracted attention. French King Louis XVI and his Queen, Marie Antoinette, asked to see one of the balloons in action. Eventually this led to the first manned balloon flight, on 21 November 1783.

The Montgolfiers achieved a milestone in the history of flight. But Joseph Montgolfier's observation in front of the fire also has a lesson for creative thinkers of all kinds: You never know where you'll find a good idea. It may come as you sit in front of your fireplace.

While the Montgolfiers were testing their balloons, the young scientist J. A. C. Charles experimented with hydrogen. This gas is lighter than air. It provided much more lift than hot air, and the balloonists didn't need to carry a fire and fuel aloft to keep the air heated. Lift *is the upward force on an aircraft against gravity.*

But hydrogen could be risky, too, because it is very flammable—it catches fire easily. Many people were killed before a safer gas, helium, came into use. (Helium isn't as flammable as hydrogen.)

Despite the risks, Charles and a passenger made the first manned hydrogen balloon flight on 1 December 1783. Their flight lasted more than two hours and covered more than 27 miles.

In the years that followed, ballooning attracted interest across Europe. Benjamin Franklin, then an American diplomat in France, saw one of Charles's balloons in 1783. He immediately wrote home, stressing the military importance of the new invention. In 1793 the French Army started using balloons for aerial reconnaissance—*looking over battlefields from the sky.*

CAPSULES

Steam Engines

Steam engines were the main source of mechanical power in the 19th century—before the invention of the gasoline-powered internal-combustion engine and the electric motor. Water heated by fire (usually fueled by wood or coal) was used to create steam. The steam's force drove a piston or turbine blade that turned a wheel or—as in the case of the Giffard dirigible—a propeller. The discoverer of steam power, James Watt, coined the term *horsepower* as a measurement of mechanical power. One horsepower is 33,000 foot-pounds of work in one minute.

Dirigibles

Once balloonists started using lighter-than-air gases, they had solved two of the three problems of flight: getting up into the sky, and staying there. The days of bringing their flying fireplaces along with them were past. But the third problem of flight—control of the craft—was still a problem. That is, until inventors came up with the dirigible—*a steerable airship.*

A balloon in the sky is like an inner tube floating along a river. The inner tube follows the river currents, and a balloon follows the air currents. The balloon rides high or low, depending on how much gas it holds. You can't steer it.

The new dirigible airships had two things that helped pilots steer them. First, they had rudders. A rudder *is a movable flap or blade attached to the rear of a craft.* Pilots could use the rudder to turn the craft left or right. Second, like steamships or motorboats, the new airships had power sources that drove propellers. Equipped with propellers, the craft could move through the air much as ships move through water.

Scientists also thought an airship with pointed ends would fly better than a round balloon. In 1852 Henri Giffard of France built a cigar-shaped dirigible. It was 114 feet long and 39 feet in diameter. A three-horsepower steam engine pushed it through the sky at about five miles an hour. Most historians give Giffard credit for inventing the first successful dirigible.

Development of dirigibles continued. Some inventors tried out internal keels to improve these aircraft. A keel *is a structure that extends along the center of a craft from the front to the back.* A keel helps keep the craft rigid and fully extended. It also streamlines it. (A *rigid* craft has a frame that contains several balloons to provide lift. A *non-rigid* ship, on the other hand, holds its shape through gas pressure alone.)

The next breakthrough came in 1872, when German engineer Paul Haenlein built a dirigible with an internal-combustion engine, *an engine in which the fuel is burned inside, rather than in an external furnace.* (A gas-burning car engine is an internal combustion engine.) Two men made their names with these engines: Alberto Santos-Dumont and Count Ferdinand von Zeppelin.

Alberto Santos-Dumont

Santos-Dumont's first dirigible was 82 feet long. A three-horsepower gasoline motor (about half the power of a small lawn mower) powered it. It could reach an altitude of 1,300 feet. A pilot steered it with a rudder. Between 1898 and 1907 Santos-Dumont built and flew 14 of these non-rigid airships.

Santos-Dumont, a Brazilian, became famous in 1901. In that year, he flew an airship around the Eiffel Tower. He completed a nine-mile loop in less than half an hour. This won him a big cash prize from a rich oilman named Henri Deutsch. Santos-Dumont gave the money to his own workers and to the poor of Paris.

Santos-Dumont became a familiar sight in his frequent flights over the rooftops of the French capital. His generous and adventurous spirit won over the French people. He helped spark interest in aviation worldwide.

Count von Zeppelin

Zeppelin's machines were rigid dirigibles. In July 1900 this German inventor built and flew the first successful rigid dirigible, the LZ-1.

This led to the world's first commercial airships. The *Zeppelins*, as they were known, were luxurious. They had roomy, wood-paneled cabins. They carried 20 or more passengers. They flew at speeds exceeding 40 miles an hour. For a few years, they had a good safety record.

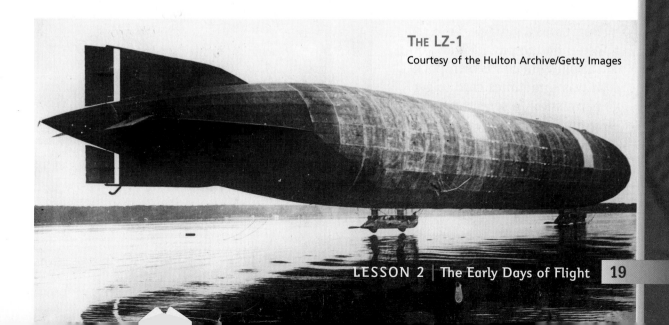

THE LZ-1
Courtesy of the Hulton Archive/Getty Images

But the days of airships were numbered. The first airplanes were beginning to hop off the ground. Within a few decades, airplanes would crowd airships almost completely out of the skies.

Ways Balloons Were Used During the US Civil War

The US armed forces first used balloons during the Civil War. But it took President Abraham Lincoln to make it happen.

After the Civil War began, many aeronauts—*people who travel in airships or balloons*—volunteered their services for the Union cause. They thought it would be a good idea to use balloons for aerial reconnaissance. After all, the French had done this more than half a century earlier.

One of these aeronauts was Thaddeus Lowe. He tried to interest Gen Winfield Scott, head of the Union Army, in balloons. But Scott saw no military need for them.

Lowe didn't give up, however. He was a friend of Joseph Henry, the head of the Smithsonian Institution. And Henry knew President Lincoln. Henry convinced the president to let Lowe demonstrate what a balloon could do.

Lowe launched a balloon from the National Mall, a short distance from the White House. A telegraph wire ran from the balloon, up into the sky, and down to the White House, where Lincoln could receive messages over it. From his balloon, the pilot described what he saw to the President. This demonstration made Lincoln realize how useful balloons could be for keeping an eye on Confederate forces. Lincoln sent General Scott a note asking him to reconsider Lowe's offer.

Lowe was finally allowed to organize the Balloon Corps of the Union Army, the first air arm of the United States military. The balloonists provided valuable information to Union forces during several battles.

But it was a struggle. Lowe often had to pay for staff and supplies out of his own pocket. It was sometimes hard to get permission to send the balloon aloft. Despite some success, the Army disbanded the balloon service in 1863, before the war ended.

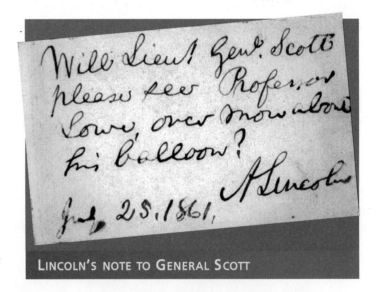

LINCOLN'S NOTE TO GENERAL SCOTT

The Confederates also tried to start a balloon force. Southern women even donated silk dresses to build a balloon. But the Southern balloon effort never really got off the ground.

Ways the Balloon Contributed to US Victory in the Battle of San Juan Hill

On 1 October 1890 the US Congress gave the Signal Corps the duty of collecting and transmitting information for the Army. At that point, the military had not conducted balloon operations for nearly 30 years. But several other countries—Britain, France, Germany, Italy, Japan, and Russia—had established balloon corps as part of their armed forces. Brig Gen Adolphus V. Greely, the chief signal officer, interpreted his assignment to include aerial navigation. In 1892 he established a balloon section in the Signal Corps.

A few years later, the United States was at war with Spain. The Battle of San Juan Hill gave the Army a chance to see what a balloon could do.

As shown in the story at the beginning of this lesson, Lt Col George M. Derby insisted on bringing the Army's single spy balloon as close to the action as possible during the Battle of San Juan Hill on 1 July 1898.

From that position, observers on board could see a new trail leading to the Spanish forces. This let US commanders divide their Soldiers into two forces to advance against the enemy. This relieved congestion on a main road where the Americans were more vulnerable to Spanish attack. The observers also suggested directing artillery fire from El Pozo Hill against the San Juan Hill trenches.

Historians say these actions may have turned the battle into a US victory.

Developments in Heavier-than-Air Flight From Da Vinci to the Wright Brothers

While balloons and dirigibles were enjoying success, other aviators were making progress with heavier-than-air craft.

Gliders

Sir George Cayley (1773–1857) picked up where Leonardo da Vinci left off in developing gliders. This Englishman's gliders resembled today's model gliders. They had the same design as most of today's airplanes, with wings up front and a tail behind.

Cayley also came up with the idea of using a fixed wing for lift and a separate system for propulsion. The fixed-wing idea seems simple now. But it was quite new at a time when many people still had flapping birds' wings as their model for flight.

Cayley identified three important forces in connection with aviation. The first force was lift. The second was drag, *the pull, or slowing effect, of air on an aircraft*. The third was thrust, *the forward force driving an aircraft*. In 1850 Cayley built the first successful full-size manned glider.

Cayley also recognized that a flying machine would need the right kind of engine to propel it. Steam engines were too heavy.

Flight Paths

SIR GEORGE CAYLEY'S GLIDER

Courtesy of The Granger Collection, New York

Sir George Cayley

Sir George Cayley was nine years old when the Montgolfiers made their first balloon flight. But even at that young age, he started experimenting with small paper balloons. Later he built model helicopters using Leonardo da Vinci's "airscrew" concept. In 1809 Cayley summarized his research in a scientific paper. It contained one sentence that laid the whole foundation for modern aeronautics. That sentence read: "The whole problem is confined within these limits, namely, to make a surface support a given weight by the application of power to the resistance of air." In other words, the problem was how to provide lift using wind resistance.

Work on gliders continued, even after the Wright brothers' flights in 1903. Two men were especially important.

The first was John J. Montgomery, an American. After 20 years of experiments, he unveiled his glider to the public in 1905. He thrilled people by performing sharp dives and turns in the air. His glider reached speeds of 68 miles an hour. Sadly, on 18 April 1906, Montgomery's gliders were destroyed in the San Francisco earthquake. He eventually started flying again. But on 31 October 1911, he was killed in a glider accident.

Otto Lilienthal of Germany was another famous aviator. In fact, he's often called the "Father of Modern Aviation." Between 1891 and 1896 he made more than 2,000 glides. He developed a powered biplane, *an aircraft with two main supporting surfaces, usually placed one above the other.* On the eve of the test flight, he decided to fly his glider one more time. He took off in a gusty wind. His glider stalled at 50 feet up and dropped like a rock. Sadly, Lilienthal was killed in the fall. But subsequent aviators, including the Wright brothers, made use of his data and experiments.

Failed Attempts to Construct an Airplane

In 1843, two Englishmen designed an aircraft theoretically capable of carrying a man. They were W. S. Henson, an inventor, and John Stringfellow, an engineer. The two received a patent—*a legal document protecting the rights of an inventor*—for their design. Their aircraft, the Ariel, was to be a monoplane—*an airplane with one set of wings.* It would have a 150-foot wingspan. It would be powered by a steam engine driving two six-bladed propellers. As it turned out, however, the Ariel was never built. But the plans were engineering masterpieces.

In 1848 Stringfellow built a steam-driven model that did fly. This was the first successful powered flight of a heavier-than-air craft.

OTTO LILIENTHAL'S GLIDER

Courtesy of Getty Images

JOHN STRINGFELLOW'S FLYING MODEL, 1848

Courtesy of Science Museum/
Science and Society Picture Library

SAMUEL LANGLEY'S AERODROME

Langley's Aerodrome prepares to take off from its launch track, but plunges instantly into the Potomac.

Courtesy of Time Life Pictures/Mansell/Time Life Pictures/Getty Images

The Contributions and Failures of Samuel Langley

Dr. Samuel Pierpont Langley was one of the first Americans to try to build a flying machine with a motor. He started experimenting with aerodynamics in 1885. Rubber bands powered his first models. In 1898 the US government gave him a $50,000 grant to continue his work.

On 7 October 1903 his aircraft, the *Aerodrome*, was ready for a test flight. Langley planned to launch it from a catapult on a barge on the Potomac River. The plane's engine worked well, but the aircraft caught on the launching car on takeoff. It fell into the river.

Two months later, Langley tried—and failed—again. His efforts got a lot of press coverage in Washington. Government officials read about them and withdrew their support. So Langley gave up his project. He donated his *Aerodrome* to the Smithsonian Institution.

Despite his failures, Langley made important contributions to aviation. For example, he explained how birds can soar in the sky with no apparent movement of their wings. (As you read in the last lesson, Bernouillian lift pulls the wings up from above, while Newtonian lift pushes them up from below.) Historians fault Langley for spending too much time on how to power his aircraft, and not enough on how to control it. Even so, for his contributions to aviation, Langley Air Force Base in southeastern Virginia is named after him.

CHECKPOINTS

Lesson 2 Review

Using complete sentences, answer the following questions on a sheet of paper.

1. What are the two basic types of aircraft?

2. What are the three problems of flight?

3. What is the principle behind a balloon?

4. What did printing presses have to do with the development of flying machines?

5. What kind of engine helped make dirigibles a success?

6. How did a balloon help the US Army win the Battle of San Juan Hill in Cuba?

7. What three important concepts did Sir George Cayley understand?

8. What do historians fault Samuel Langley for?

Applying Your Learning

9. Are dirigibles still in use today? What are they called? What are they used for?

UNIT TWO

Explo

The Wright Brothers' first flight

ring FLIGHT

Unit Chapters

CHAPTER 2

Pioneers of Flight

CHAPTER 3

Expanding the Horizon

CHAPTER 2

Capt Eddie Rickenbacker,
American ace in World War I

Pioneers of Flight

Chapter Outline

LESSON 1

The Wright Brothers

LESSON 2

Developing Aircraft

LESSON 3

Air Power in World War 1

"More than anything else, the sensation [of flying] is one of perfect peace mingled with an excitement that strains every nerve to the utmost—if you can conceive of such a combination."

WILBUR WRIGHT

The Wright Brothers

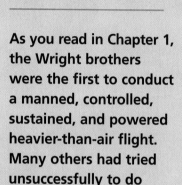
Learn About...

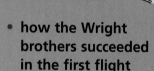

- how the Wright brothers succeeded in the first flight
- the anatomy of the *Wright Flyer*
- the principles of airplane flight
- the history of the Wright brothers' involvement with the US Army

It was 14 December 1903. Wilbur and Orville Wright stood on the sand dunes of Kill Devil Hills, North Carolina. Beside them was their aircraft, the *Wright Flyer*. It was ready for its first real test. Although their first successful manned flight of this craft would not come until three days later, on 17 December, they had high hopes. The two men had worked for years for this moment. One important question remained: who would fly the craft?

They tossed a coin. Wilbur won. He would pilot the *Flyer* on its first attempt at flight.

Choosing the pilot was a matter of chance. But it wasn't chance that brought the two brothers to this important day. It was years of work and study. Why did they succeed when others had failed?

First, they were intelligent men. They learned from the experiences of others. Second, they were also creative thinkers and great problem solvers. Third, and perhaps most important, they were patient.

A well-known proverb says, "Genius is patience." And the brothers' patience paid off. After making hundreds of flight trials between 1899 and 1903, the Wrights achieved what earlier men had only dreamed of.

How the Wright Brothers Succeeded in the First Flight

Vocabulary

- strut
- bracing
- warp
- lateral
- pitch
- elevator
- canard configuration
- airfoil
- center of pressure
- angle of attack
- relative wind
- spars
- ribs
- skids
- yaw
- bid

As you read in Chapter 1, all pilots face three challenges. They must *get up in the air, stay up,* and *control their craft.* The choice of craft was up to the pilot. And pilots had three choices to experiment in flight:

- manned and powered, full-size aircraft
- models
- full-size gliders.

The Wrights chose a glider as their starting point. By using a glider, they could focus first on balancing and controlling their aircraft. Power—an engine—could come later. This approach explains why they succeeded where Samuel P. Langley, who focused on power, failed.

But before they could build a full-size glider, they needed to experiment with other, smaller craft. This was a complicated process. The brothers applied what they learned at each step to make the next one go more smoothly.

Skynotes

Wilbur Writes to the Smithsonian

One reason for the Wright brothers' success was their patience. Another was that they asked lots of questions. They wanted to build on what others had learned. So Wilbur went to the experts. He wrote the following letter to Smithsonian Institution in Washington, D.C., on 30 May 1899:

Dear Sirs:

I am an enthusiast, but not a crank in the sense that I have some pet theories as to the proper construction of a flying machine. I wish to avail myself of all that is already known and then if possible add my mite to help on the future worker who will attain final success.

Wilbur Wright

Step One: An Unmanned Box Kite

The brothers began in July 1899 with an unmanned box kite. The kite had a five-foot wingspan and a biplane structure. It also had struts that connected the upper and lower wings. A strut *is a vertical post*. The kite also had bracing, *or support*, that was strung diagonally between the struts. The Wrights used steel for the bracing. They adapted their bracing design from a manned glider created by Octave Chanute and Augustus Herring in 1896.

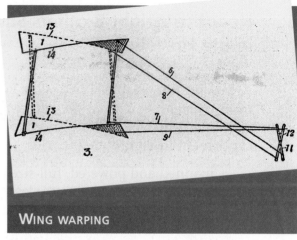

WING WARPING

Courtesy of the National Air and Space Museum, Smithsonian Institution (SI Neg. No. SI-2001-9902)

The brothers also had a unique approach to controlling the kite. They discovered that they didn't need to tilt an entire wing to turn the craft: They needed to twist only the ends of the wings. They called this process "wing warping." To warp, *or twist*, the wings, they removed the bracing between the front and rear struts. They attached four cords to the top and bottom of the front outer struts. Pulling on these ropes turned the craft.

In the summer of 1899, Wilbur successfully tested the kite in a field. The first step in the experiment for aircraft control was a success. The next step: man a glider.

Skynotes

An Absentminded Invention

Wilbur Wright was talking to a customer in the bicycle shop he owned with his brother in Dayton, Ohio. As he did so, he toyed with a long, empty carton. Twisting the carton this way and that, he made a discovery: the sides of the box retained their shape and strength. Wilbur figured this same principle would apply to the wings of a biplane kite. In other words, the tip could be twisted, but the wing would remain strong. Thus the brothers' groundbreaking wing-warping theory was born.

Step Two: Manned Gliders

The box kite taught Wilbur and Orville Wright how to control lateral—*sideways*—turns. But building a successful manned glider presented other challenges. Between 1900 and 1902, the brothers built three gliders. Before putting a man aboard, they flew each glider like a kite. They wanted to test it for control and lift. Only after doing this would they put a man aboard.

The early glider experiments were successful. They taught the brothers three important things:

- how to control climb and descent
- the best design for the shape of the wing
- how large the wing area had to be to sustain lift.

The First Glider (1900)

With a man on board the craft, knowing how to move up and down was essential. Otherwise, a sudden pitch—*a movement up or down*—could be fatal. For example, the German aviator Otto Lilienthal, whom you read about in the previous lesson, died when his craft made a downward pitch and crashed.

THE WRIGHTS FLYING ONE OF THEIR GLIDERS AS A KITE

Courtesy of the National Air and Space Museum, Smithsonian Institution (SI Neg. No. SI-2003-29083)

The Wrights studied Lilienthal's data. They used it to design a device that gave them greater control of pitch. In their experiments at Kitty Hawk in 1900, they had placed an elevator—*a movable, horizontal surface that controls motion up and down*—at the front of the glider. This was a unique idea: Earlier designers had mounted elevators behind the wings. But the Wrights found it easier to control climb and descent when the elevator was placed forward. This development saved the Wrights' lives on several occasions. A canard configuration *is another name for an elevator that sits in front of the wings.* (*Canard* is the French word for *duck*—early observers thought the canard configuration resembled a flying duck.)

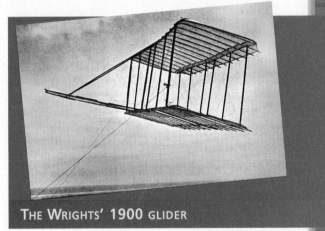

THE WRIGHTS' 1900 GLIDER

Courtesy of the National Air and Space Museum, Smithsonian Institution (SI Neg. No. SI-2002-23711)

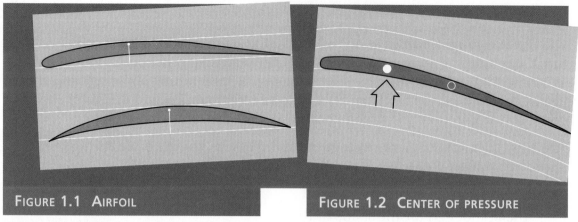

FIGURE 1.1 AIRFOIL

Courtesy of the National Air and Space Museum,
Smithsonian Institution

FIGURE 1.2 CENTER OF PRESSURE

Courtesy of the National Air and Space Museum,
Smithsonian Institution

Next, the Wrights tackled the challenge of how to shape the glider's wing. This took a couple years to figure out. In 1900 they focused on airfoil—*a wing's profile*. In particular, they zeroed in on the curve of a wing.

Wings have a lot to do with lift, which, as you've learned, is the upward force on an aircraft. The center of pressure *is the focal point of lift*. The Wrights tried to design a wing that shifted the center of pressure toward the front edge of the wing—the wing edge nearest the front of the aircraft. Earlier designers thought that the center of pressure should be in the middle of the wing. The Wrights placed the highest point of the wing's arc closer to the outer edge than to its center. They believed this would create greater stability and control.

The brothers test-flew their glider at Kill Devil Hills in 1900. It didn't crash. But clearly improvements were necessary. The Wrights left North Carolina and headed back to Ohio. During the winter, they would tinker with their craft and build the next version of their glider.

Skynotes

A Stitch in Time

A glider's wings need to be strong but not heavy. They need to be stiff but not inflexible. In 1900 Wilbur and Orville Wright hit on a way to get all of this: fabric. They covered the top of the glider's wings with French sateen. Pieces of the wings' framework slid into "pockets" sewn on the underside of the fabric. These skeleton-like pieces of the wings "floated" inside the pockets. The fabric took the role that heavier wires and bracing would otherwise have taken. The Wrights attached the fabric to the wing's frame on the bias, which is a 45-degree angle. This made the wing stronger.

The Second Glider (1901)

The Wrights' first glider had a wing area of 165 square feet. That glider didn't have nearly enough lift. So for their 1901 glider, the brothers increased the wing area to 290 square feet. This glider was also a big disappointment. The brothers couldn't control it well when they tested it at Kill Devil Hills. It flew less than 300 feet. Time to return to Dayton.

Wilbur and Orville built a wind tunnel in their bicycle shop in Ohio to test model-size wings. These wings came in many shapes—squares, rectangles, and semicircles. They ranged from perfect curves to arcs with their highest points at the outer edges. The Wrights made them of sheet steel. Over the winter, the brothers cut more than 200 model wings of different shapes.

A REPLICA OF THE WRIGHT BROTHERS' WIND TUNNEL

Courtesy of the Air Force Museum Foundation

MODEL AIRPLANE WINGS

The various model wing shapes the Wrights tested

Courtesy of the National Air and Space Museum, Smithsonian Institution (SI Neg. No. SI-2005-3452)

THE 1901 GLIDER

Wilbur Wright tries to fly the 1901 glider, as William and Dan Tate help.

Courtesy of the National Air and Space Museum, Smithsonian Institution (SI Neg. No. SI-86-3018)

THE WRIGHTS' 1902 GLIDER
Courtesy of the Library of Congress

Angle of attack

FIGURE 1.3 ANGLE OF ATTACK

The Third Glider (1902)

At this point, the brothers could have been tempted to try powered flight. After all, their model-wing tests had answered many questions. But remember—these two men were patient. They didn't want to rush the process. So in preparation for 1902, they applied what they'd learned to build a third glider.

This glider had two fixed, vertical rudders behind the wings. Test flights showed that this resulted in erratic behavior during turns. So the Wrights tried a single, movable, vertical rudder. This improved control. This aircraft, too, had a forward elevator, but it had a more elliptical shape, and longer, skinnier wings. Wing area was 305 square feet. In addition, the glider had a low angle of attack—*the angle between the* relative wind *(the flow of air) and the airfoil*. This also made the glider more stable and easier to control.

This design was a success. The brothers took to the air in the North Carolina dunes more than 700 times in the fall of 1902.

Winter arrived. It was time to head back to Ohio. It was also finally time to put an engine on the glider.

Step Three: A Manned, Powered Aircraft

One key to the Wright brothers' success was their countless test flights. Another was sticking with a core design. Their kites and gliders evolved from a single design into the manned, powered aircraft they eventually flew in 1903. They tinkered with the details, but didn't get distracted. For instance, they didn't attempt powered flight until they'd perfected other elements, such as the wings.

Once they'd resolved questions about control and lift, the brothers set out to fit their plane with an engine. They hoped they might buy one ready made. They sent out queries to a number of firms. But no one met their needs or price. So the brothers had their bicycle mechanic, Charles E. Taylor, build them a four-cylinder, 12-horsepower engine.

In September 1903 they returned to Kitty Hawk and Kill Devil Hills. The aircraft was ready. But they couldn't take to the skies quite yet. They had to build a trolley track to give their powered aircraft a running start. Bad weather also caused delays. So the first test flight of the *Wright Flyer* didn't take place until 14 December.

The brothers tossed a coin. Wilbur won the toss. He took the pilot's seat for the initial powered flight. He rolled down the trolley, launched into the air, and—crashed. That flight lasted only 3.5 seconds. The crash damaged the elevator. But the brothers were not discouraged. Quite the opposite—in a note to home, Wilbur wrote, "There is now no question of final success."

It took three days to repair the damaged craft. Then, on 17 December, Orville took the controls for this day's first flight. It was 10:35 a.m. The *Flyer* rose into the air. It stayed aloft for 12 seconds and traveled 120 feet. He had made the first controlled, sustained, heavier-than-air human flight with a powered aircraft.

On that momentous day, the brothers took turns piloting the *Flyer* for three more flights. Each launch was more impressive than the last. The fourth and final launch lasted 59 seconds. The craft traveled 852 feet.

THE WRIGHT BROTHERS' TRIUMPH AT KITTY HAWK
Courtesy of Bettmann/Corbis

The Anatomy of the *Wright Flyer*

Equipped with an engine and propellers, the *Wright Flyer* was larger than the aircraft the brothers built earlier. The biplane had a wingspan of 40 feet, 4 inches, and a wing area of 510 square feet. The *Flyer* was 21 feet, 1 inch long. It stood 9 feet, 4 inches tall. It weighed 605 pounds without a pilot and about 750 with a pilot on board.

The Parts of the Wright Flyer

The *Flyer's* wings had two main parts. The spars *were the main, lengthwise pieces of the wing*. Attached to the spars were ribs. The ribs *gave shape to the wings*. Muslin, a lightweight fabric, covered the wings. It reduced wind resistance and added strength as the wings warped during turns. Struts and bracing between the top and bottom wings further reinforced the plane.

Flight Paths

ORVILLE (LEFT) AND WILBUR WRIGHT

Courtesy of the National Air and Space Museum, Smithsonian Institution (SI Neg. No. SI-90-9558)

Orville Wright (1871–1948)

Orville Wright was the scientist of the family. He loved science and technology. He was also quite shy, although he was never timid about playing practical jokes on his family and friends. Later, he wrote about the support he and his siblings found at home:

> We were lucky enough to grow up in an environment where there was always much encouragement to children to pursue intellectual interests; to investigate whatever aroused curiosity. In a different kind of environment, our curiosity might have been nipped long before it could have borne fruit.

Wilbur Wright (1867–1912)

Wilbur, four years older than Orville, was outgoing. He excelled at writing and public speaking. He loved to read. Both Wilbur and Orville liked to tinker as children. When they had questions about anything mechanical, they would go to their mother, Susan. She was good at inventing. She made toys for her children and basic appliances for herself. Originally, Wilbur hoped to attend Yale University, but he was needed at home to help care for his mother. So he taught himself by reading a lot.

Two propellers sat behind the wings. They rotated in opposite directions and were made of two layers of spruce wood. Their job was to help move the craft forward. The plane also had a front elevator, which was covered by fabric. A rudder at the rear was also wrapped in fabric. The other important part of this plane was, of course, the engine. The *Flyer's* engine was water cooled like a car engine and fueled by gasoline. The engine and the propellers together weighed about 200 pounds.

Before the *Flyer*, two assistants hand-launched the brothers' gliders. Each assistant would hold a wing and help lift the craft in the air. But the new, powered *Flyer* was too heavy for that. Rather than the wheels that are so common on the airplanes you see today, the brothers used skids—*long, thin runners, like a pair of skis*. Before takeoff, the plane sat on a trolley that rolled along wooden rails.

How the Flyer Worked

The brothers controlled their craft through three main means they developed in their glider experiments: the forward elevator, the use of wing warping, and a single, movable rear rudder.

Surprisingly, the pilot did not sit upright. Instead, he lay on his stomach in a padded cradle on the lower wing. Because the engine was somewhat right of center, the pilot was placed slightly left of center to balance the weight.

To the pilot's left was a lever that he used to control the up-and-down movement of the elevator. By moving the lever with his hand, he could climb or descend. By moving his hips, he pulled on the cables connected to the wings and rudder. This movement could direct the plane left or right.

Before the brothers invented the single, movable rudder, their gliders often slid sideways rather than turned. *A sidewise movement is called a* yaw. With the new, flexible rudder, the plane finally turned in the intended direction. For instance, if the pilot moved his hips so the cable pulled down on the left wing, the plane would veer left. The cables attached to the wings from the cradle twisted one wing down while forcing the other wing up. If the aircraft began to yaw, the rudder corrected this by reacting to pressure from airflow.

To design the propellers, the brothers drew on their bicycle-shop experience. They made the propellers rotate by attaching them to the engine with bicycle chains. To rotate the propellers in opposite directions, they simply twisted one of the two chains into a figure 8.

Before launch, wires tethered the airplane to earth. Only when the engine had fully revved up did the trolley start to move down the tracks. The plane lifted off the trolley as it rose into the air.

The Principles of Airplane Flight

To get the *Wright Flyer* off the ground the brothers had to solve the principles of flight you have read about: *lift, drag, thrust, angle of attack, center of pressure, airfoil,* and *relative wind.* The combination of solutions they found is still used for modern airplanes.

An engine and propellers gave Wilbur and Orville the ability to use not only lift but also thrust to propel their plane through the air. Both these forces are necessary for powered flight. As you learned in Chapter 1, lift is an upward force, and thrust is a forward, or horizontal, force.

Principles of Flight

Lift

Drag

Thrust

Angle of Attack

Center of Pressure

Airfoil

Relative wind

When working on their gliders, the Wrights focused most of their attention on the lift exerted on the wings. Now that they had an engine and propellers, they could start to think more about thrust. They considered the propellers as extra wings on their airplane. But unlike wings, which are stable and horizontal, the propeller "wings" rotated and sat vertically. The propellers on the *Flyer* were eight feet in diameter.

If a horizontal, curved wing reacts to lift, the Wright brothers reasoned, vertically mounted propellers could provide the airflow for thrust. They calculated they needed 90 pounds of thrust to propel the *Wright Flyer.* Their 12-horsepower engine and the large propellers proved equal to the task.

The History of the Wright Brothers' Involvement With the US Army

After their first success, the Wright brothers continued refining their airplane. Once they had achieved powered flight, they no longer needed the wind conditions of the North Carolina coastline for their tests. In October 1905 they circled a field in Dayton for 38 minutes and traveled 24 miles. They decided it was time to cash in on their remarkable invention.

They'd already started their marketing effort. Back in January of 1905 they contacted their representative in Congress, R. M. Nevin, and asked him to try to interest the US government in buying their airplane. Mr. Nevin passed along their letter to the Board of Ordnance and Fortifications, which made military weapons purchases. The board was leery of wasting government money. It turned down the brothers' offer.

The brothers, patient as always, contacted the secretary of war later that year. Again, their offer was rejected. After all, as Chapter 1 related, the government had already invested $50,000 in Samuel Langley's flight experiments. The secretary didn't want to spend more money when the outcome seemed so uncertain.

Why the US Army Purchased the *Wright Flyer*

Meanwhile, the British and French governments got into the act. They were interested in buying the *Flyer*. Representatives from both countries made offers to the Wrights. But the brothers wanted the US government to have first crack at owning a *Wright Flyer*.

A turning point came on 22 May 1906. On that date, after three years of trying, the brothers received a government patent for their invention. This spurred the Aero Club of America, a group of aviation enthusiasts and scientists, to take action. They sent a clipping about the Wrights to President Theodore Roosevelt. The president ordered the Board of Ordnance and Fortifications to look again into the airplane.

After that, things started to happen. On 23 December 1907, Brig Gen James Allen, chief of the Army Signal Corps, sent out a request for bids to build a plane for the government. A bid *is an offer or a proposal, with a price attached.* The brothers received their copy of Brig Gen Allen's request on 3 January 1908.

The bid set forth the technical requirements for the craft. These requirements stated that the craft must:

- achieve a speed of 40 miles per hour
- carry two passengers for a total of 350 pounds
- have a fuel tank large enough to fly 125 miles nonstop
- be able to land without damage.

The government also required that the successful bidder train two Army pilots to fly the craft.

The *Wright Flyer* met these requirements. Orville Wright signed a contract on 10 February 1908 selling the *Flyer* to the US government.

Ways the Wright Brothers Contributed to Army Aviation

With the purchase of the *Wright Flyer*, the Army bought not only the military's first plane but also access to the Wright brothers' inventive minds. In the years that followed, the Wrights continued to improve their aircraft. For instance, they created wheels for the *Flyer*. The wheels enabled it to take off and land in a wider variety of settings.

Orville spent much of 1908 and 1909 improving the *Flyer*. He made more test flights and took up military passengers. One such flight tragically ended in a crash that seriously injured Orville and killed 1st Lt Thomas Selfridge—the first US military aviation casualty. Wilbur was often overseas giving demonstrations during this time.

The brothers switched roles in mid-1909. Wilbur trained two pilots for the Army—1st Lt Frank P. Lahm and 2d Lt Fredric E. Humphreys. In October 1909 both men made their first solo flights with less than a month's training. These were adventurous men: each had barely three hours' instruction in the air before going it alone.

A third pilot, 1st Lt Benjamin Foulois, got instruction late that month. One of the men initially picked for pilot training, he was delayed because of business in France. He took the *Wright Flyer* to Fort Sam Houston, Texas, where he continued teaching himself to fly. He corresponded with Wilbur and Orville whenever he had a question. On 2 March 1910 he took his first solo flight. By the time of his retirement a quarter-century later, Foulois had achieved the rank of major general. He was also chief of the Army Air Corps.

It took a while for the Army to decide how to use airplanes during war. At first, the Army thought that airplanes would be useful only for aerial reconnaissance, much as hot air balloons were used during the US Civil War and the Spanish-American War. But World War I brought about a change in strategy: soon, the warring sides were employing planes for bombing missions and to support troops on the ground. Before that could happen, however, airplanes needed improvements to make them faster, sturdier, and more reliable.

WORLD-RECORD FLIGHT, 1909

Orville Wright and 1st Lt Frank P. Lahm making a world-record flight at Fort Myer, Virginia, in 1909

Courtesy of Corbis Images

CHECKPOINTS

Lesson 1 Review

Using complete sentences, answer the following questions on a sheet of paper.

1. What three choices did pilots have to experiment in flight?

2. How did the Wright brothers' approach to building an aircraft differ from Samuel Langley's?

3. What three important points did Wilbur and Orville Wright learn from their gliders?

4. What did the Wright brothers do in Ohio to test for the perfect wing shape?

5. What role did fabric play in the anatomy of the *Wright Flyer*?

6. What kind of force do propellers provide?

7. Which powerful man in government sent out a request for bids to build a plane for the government?

Applying Your Learning

8. What process allowed the brothers to turn their box kite from side to side? How would you apply that process if you were building a biplane kite?

LESSON 2

Developing Aircraft

Quick Write

_____
_____
_____

Both the Wright brothers and Glenn Curtiss were heavily involved with bicycles before taking up flight. What similarities do you see between bicycles, early motorcycles, and early airplanes?

Learn About...

- **the key individuals involved in early aircraft development**
- **the names and anatomy of period aircraft**
- **the significance of other American pioneers in aviation following the Wright brothers**

Glenn Curtiss, born in Hammondsport, New York, in 1878, sped onto the aviation scene in the early 1900s. But he was riding a motorcycle, not an airplane. At Ormond Beach, Florida, in 1907, he set a world speed record for motorcycles: 136.3 miles per hour (mph). People called him the "fastest man on Earth." This was the same year the Wright brothers received their bid request for a military airplane from the Army Signal Corps chief, Brig Gen James Allen.

Much was happening all at once in the world of transportation. And any advance in one field sparked progress in another.

Curtiss's passion for speed began with bicycles. As a teenager, he raced at county fairs and often won. This experience led to his love of fast motorcycles. Curtiss liked to fiddle with the mechanical side of bicycles, motorcycles, and engines as well. Actually, he did more than tinker with them. He built gasoline engines for motorcycles. Barely out of his teens, he started his own motorcycle business, the G. H. Curtiss Manufacturing Company.

His work with motorcycle engines eventually caught the eye of people in the field of flight. Once they introduced Curtiss to aircraft, he was hooked for good.

Key Individuals Involved in Early Aircraft Development

In the first decade of the 1900s, when the Wright brothers were making aviation history, other people were also becoming aviation pioneers. Each person made developments in aircraft that earned him or her a place in aviation history.

Glenn Curtiss

Glenn Curtiss pushed aviation forward in several ways. Even before his record-setting motorcycle ride in 1907, Curtiss was dipping his toes into aviation. He'd begun racing with his bike motors in Florida in 1904. It was there that Thomas Baldwin discovered Curtiss.

Baldwin, an American balloonist, owned a dirigible. As you read in the lesson "The Early Days of Flight," a dirigible is a lighter-than-air craft filled with helium. By the early 1900s aviators in France and Germany were using engines to maneuver such aircraft in the sky. But balloonists in the United States hadn't yet taken that step. Baldwin was looking for a lightweight engine for his aircraft when he spotted Curtiss racing in Florida. He saw how well Curtiss's engine performed. He asked if he could buy one. The young mechanic agreed. He tweaked one of his engines for use in an aircraft.

Baldwin's aircraft, equipped with a Curtiss engine, was the first powered dirigible in America. Before long, other balloonists wanted Curtiss motors, too. And in 1908 the US government purchased one of Curtiss's engines for the US Army's first dirigible, SC-1. Later, the military would purchase Curtiss planes and engines for use in World War I. The Army used the Jenny airplane—or JN-4—for training pilots. Curtiss's Wasp engine broke records for speed and rate of climb.

GLENN CURTISS

Courtesy of Underwood & Underwood/Corbis

The Aerial Experiment Association

Glenn Curtiss was a busy man in 1907. In addition to working on some of the devices already mentioned, he joined the Aerial Experiment Association. Alexander Graham Bell, best known as the inventor of the telephone, formed this group. The inventors who belonged made some important design breakthroughs.

First, they built the first American plane equipped with ailerons. An aileron *is a small flap on the wing for controlling turns.* Ailerons replaced the Wright brothers' wing-warping technique, which used cables to pull on the ends of the wings. The aileron was a more effective means to move an aircraft left or right. It also provided lateral balance. This was critical whenever airplanes had rigid metal rings.

Although association members get credit for introducing this idea to America, none of them dreamed it up. The aileron was patented in Great Britain in 1868. In 1904 a Frenchman who was flying a glider used ailerons for the first time.

Second, members of the group built and flew the country's first seaplane. Curtiss would later win the first government contract with the US Navy for seaplanes.

Curtiss's Fame Grows

Curtiss continued to enter contests. In 1908, piloting an association plane called the *June Bug*, he won the Scientific American trophy. The award was for making the first public flight of more than one kilometer (0.6 miles). At the Rheims Air Meet in France in 1909, Curtiss picked up a prize for speed. He flew the fastest two laps over a triangular, 6.21-mile course. For this feat he took home the Gordon Bennett trophy. Curtiss won the trophy in his *Golden Flyer.* His average speed? An amazing 47 mph.

THE AERIAL EXPERIMENT ASSOCIATION

Members include Glenn Curtiss (left) and Alexander Graham Bell (center)
Courtesy of the Library of Congress

THE JUNE BUG

Courtesy of Bettmann/Corbis

THE GOLDEN FLYER

Two of Glenn Curtiss's award-winning planes: the June Bug and the Golden Flyer
Courtesy of Corbis Images

Never one to rest, Curtiss opened a flight school in 1910, the same year the Wright brothers opened their school. Also in 1910, a pilot named Eugene Ely flew a Curtiss biplane from the deck of a ship off Hampton Roads, Virginia. Later, Ely landed the plane on a wooden platform built on the armored cruiser USS *Pennsylvania*.

Curtiss's effect on aviation can still be felt today. To begin with, motorcycle engines were light and powerful. Aircraft also need light, powerful engines that won't weigh them down. Less weight puts less strain on the aircraft during takeoff, landing, and flight.

Louis Blériot

Across the Atlantic Ocean, the French pilot Louis Blériot was also pushing the limits of flight. He was the first man to cross the English Channel in a heavier-than-air craft. And what an adventure it turned out to be.

He took off from near Calais, in northern France, without a compass. Within 10 minutes, he was lost. He could see nothing but water and sky. He had no coastline in sight to guide him. Blériot piloted his aircraft as best he could toward England. He knew the journey was about 25 miles.

Finally he caught sight of the English cliffs of Dover. But then he encountered another hitch. His engine was overheating, and he was still above water and could not land. Then he spotted a small rainstorm. He veered toward it. The rain cooled his engine, and he landed safely. The flight took 37 minutes.

This flight took place in a powered monoplane that Blériot built. A *monoplane*, as you read in Chapter 1, is an airplane with one set of wings. The Wright brothers' aircraft were biplanes, or aircraft with two sets of wings. Louis Blériot was the first man to build a powered monoplane. He named the aircraft that brought him across the English Channel the *Blériot XI* because he'd built 10 others before it. He'd crashed nearly 50 times during test flights of those aircraft. The 11th plane brought him safely to England's shores.

Blériot achieved other accomplishments. Like Curtiss, he entered the first international air meet in Rheims in August 1909. While Curtiss won the two-lap contest for speed, Blériot snapped up a trophy for a one-lap contest by flying at 47.8 mph. Also like Curtiss, Blériot built planes for the war effort during World War I. But Blériot built aircraft for his own country, France.

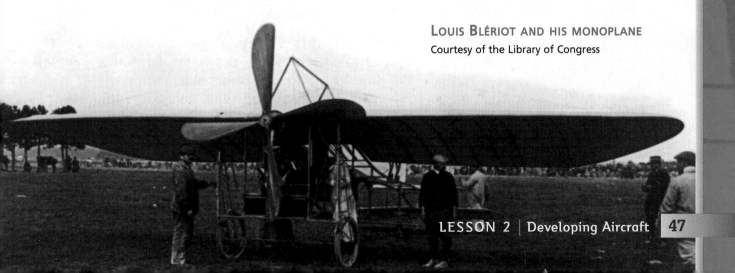

LOUIS BLÉRIOT AND HIS MONOPLANE
Courtesy of the Library of Congress

The Names and Anatomy of Period Aircraft

During the years between the Wright brothers' famous flight of 1903 and the start of World War I in 1914, aircraft continued to grow more sophisticated. The first man to use ailerons, Frenchman Robert Esnault-Pelterie, was also the first to fully enclose the fuselage. A fuselage *is the body of an airplane containing the crew and passengers (or cargo)*. Enclosed cabins protected pilots and passengers from the wind and rain.

Multiengine Planes

While Louis Blériot was experimenting with monoplanes, brothers Eustace, Howard, and Oswald Short of England were adding engines to their aircraft. A multiengine plane—*a plane with more than one engine*—had greater power, reliability, and safety than a single-engine plane. Just as two heads are supposedly better than one, two (or more) engines upped an aircraft's power. Safety increased, too. If one engine died during flight, the second could provide enough power to get the plane back to earth.

The Short brothers built the *Triple Twin*, a two-engine, three-propeller aircraft in 1911. They placed one engine in front of the cockpit—*a space inside the fuselage where the crew sits*. They mounted the second engine behind the cockpit. The forward engine ran the two propellers on the wings; the rear engine drove the third propeller.

Meanwhile a Russian pilot named Igor Sikorsky was designing a four-engine aircraft called *Le Grand*. He flew it on 13 May 1913. He used four 100-horsepower engines to lift the 92-foot-wingspan airplane. He mounted the four engines in two pairs in tandem—*two objects with one placed directly behind the other*—on the lower wings. The front engines powered the forward propellers, and the back engines drove the pusher propellers. Because the plane was so big, the landing gear had 16 wheels. The aircraft also had an enclosed cockpit. Each passenger could peer through a porthole—*a small, circular window*.

Passenger-friendly inventions such as portholes and enclosed cabins contributed greatly to the development of today's commercial airliners. Flying in a protected body and having viewing windows made air travel more attractive to paying passengers.

IGOR SIKORSKY

Courtesy of Corbis Images

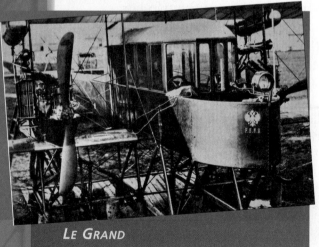

LE GRAND

Courtesy of the National Air and Space Museum, Smithsonian Institution (SI Neg. No. 85-18305)

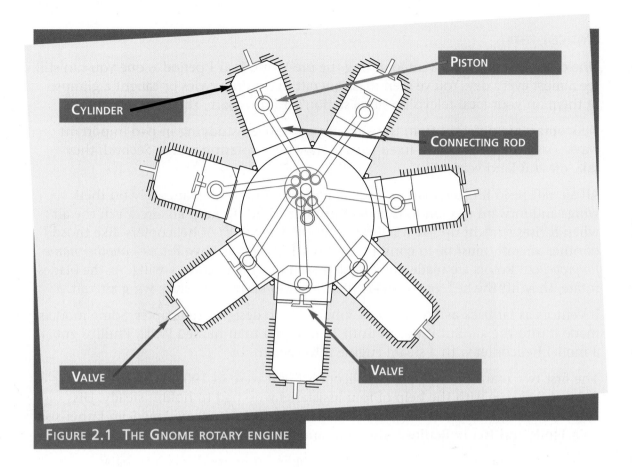

CYLINDER

PISTON

CONNECTING ROD

VALVE

VALVE

FIGURE 2.1 THE GNOME ROTARY ENGINE

Rotary Engines

Strong engines were essential for sustained flight. But the earliest engines were relatively heavy. The engine and propellers on the 1903 *Wright Flyer* weighed about 200 pounds. One reason for this heft was that these early engines used water as a coolant. They also weren't efficient: in 1907 every 10 pounds of engine generated just one horsepower.

Another set of brothers, Laurent and Gustav Seguin of France, set out to reduce the motor weight. Their solution? Rotary engines. Rotary engines used circulating air, rather than water, as a coolant. The Seguins placed the engine's cylinders in a radial, *or round*, pattern. They fitted each cylinder with a fin to draw out the heat as the plane flew.

With these changes, engines became more efficient. The number of pounds of engine weight needed to generate one horsepower dropped from 10 to three. The Seguins named their engine the Gnome.

But the Gnome was still a work in progress. The brothers needed to find a way to prevent the engine from overheating when the aircraft was revving up before takeoff. The brothers decided that the crankshaft—*a shaft that turns or is turned by a crank*—should no longer rotate the propeller and engine. Instead, the propeller and engine ought to rotate around the crankshaft. The Seguins bolted the crankshaft to the plane's frame. So even when the plane was at a standstill, air would circulate around the engine and keep it cool.

Helicopters

One of the last aircraft invented during the pre-World War I period is one you can still see almost every day. You've seen these aircraft in action movies or caught a glimpse of them on your local television news station's traffic report. They are helicopters.

Helicopters are different from the aircraft you've been studying in two important ways. First, they don't have fixed wings. They have rotating wings. Second, they take off and land vertically.

All aircraft need lift to remain in the air. Biplanes and monoplanes rely on their wings and forward motion to maintain lift. But what's to keep an aircraft in the air when it rises straight up like a helicopter does? The wings of helicopters, like those of other aircraft, must be in constant motion. Helicopters have rotors—*another name for propellers*. Rotors are made up of blades, each of which acts as a wing. As the blades rotate, they lift the helicopter. Helicopters are also known as rotary-wing aircraft.

Inventors as far back as Leonardo da Vinci tried to design a helicopter. Some models made it into the air. But it wasn't until 1842 that a man named W. H. Phillips got a model helicopter with a steam engine into the air.

The first two manned attempts at helicopter flight were in 1907. Frenchman Louis Bréguet flew one with the help of four assistants who had to hold it steady. His countryman Paul Cornu also got a helicopter to lift. In 1909 an American father-son pair, Emile and Henry Berliner, also built and piloted a helicopter.

All these men faced one common problem: helicopters are difficult to balance. Bréguet needed four assistants to steady the aircraft. They needed to do this because rotating blades create torque, *which is a twisting force*. Because of torque, while the blades are turning in one direction, the body of the aircraft spins in the other.

No one would find a solution for 30 years. But when they did, they came up with two possibilities. The first was to use two rotors and to make them spin in opposite directions. The second solution was to place a small rotor at the end of a long tail boom. A boom *is the section of the helicopter that connects the tail with the main body*. The tail rotor spins in a direction opposite that of the main rotor.

PAUL CORNU'S HELICOPTER
Courtesy of Branger/Getty Images

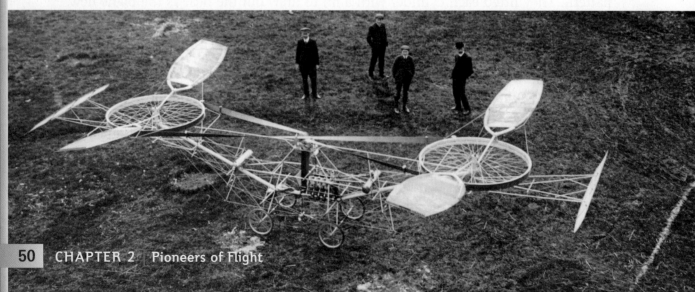

Other American Pioneers in Aviation Following the Wright Brothers

While some aircraft pioneers were achieving fame as inventors, others were breaking barriers as pilots. Those barriers ranged from distance to altitude to gender and race. Calbraith Perry Rodgers made the first cross-country flight in the United States. American Bessie Coleman was the first black woman in the world to get a pilot's license. Blanche Stuart Scott was the first woman to fly solo. The early 20th century was a time when all kinds of records could be broken.

Other American Aviation Pioneers

All these aviation pioneers needed great courage. They were flying in an age when planes were, frankly, quite flimsy. They also had to be very curious. They were exploring a new frontier. And like Glenn Curtiss, they shared a passion for flight and speed—for soaring into the sky. Each one faced challenges—crashes were many, and all pilots knew the possible consequences. But they dared to continue flying.

The *Vin Fiz Flyer*

Could Calbraith Perry Rodgers fly across the United States in 30 days? That was his goal in 1911. Newspaper publisher William Randolph Hearst was offering a $50,000 prize to the first pilot who made the journey in that timeframe. Rodgers wanted to give it a try. But he had no money. Like today's NASCAR drivers, he needed a sponsor.

Rodgers asked soft drink manufacturer Vin Fiz if it would provide financial support for his flight in exchange for nationwide publicity. The company agreed. It bought him a Wright airplane (the *Vin Fiz Flyer*) and made sure he had all the spare parts he'd need. Rodgers hired mechanic Charles Taylor away from the Wright brothers to help him out on his adventure.

Rodgers took off on 17 September 1911 from Sheepshead Bay, on New York's Long Island. Vin Fiz, with publicity in mind, mapped his route. The flight plan called for stops in major cities such as New York City, Chicago, Kansas City, San Antonio, El Paso, and Yuma. The destination was Pasadena, California.

THE VIN FIZ FLYER

Courtesy of the National Air and Space Museum, Smithsonian Institution (SI Neg. No. 2006-25765-640)

A VIN FIZ ADVERTISEMENT

Showing the route of Calbraith Perry Rodgers' cross-country flight

Taken from Aerofiles.com

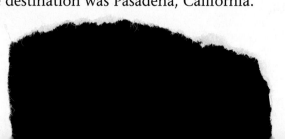

Rodgers's biggest worry was getting over the Rocky Mountains with a 40-horsepower engine. Head winds and weather would slow him down. As the flight progressed, his shortest laps were around 40 miles, and his longest was 133 miles. He averaged around 52 mph. He made 68 landings. The plane needed countless repairs along the way. In fact, by the time it got to Pasadena, the *Vin Fiz Flyer* had only two original parts—the rudder and one strut.

The trip turned out to be 4,251 miles long, rather than the anticipated 3,390. It took 49 days. Rodgers didn't win the award because the flight took too long. But he'd earned a place in aviation history— he made the first airplane crossing of the United States from coast to coast.

The First Enlisted Pilot Gets His Wings

Private First Class (PFC) Vernon Burge was the first enlisted man to become a pilot. The US Army Signal Corps' Aeronautical Division, created in 1907 to take charge of ballooning and air machines, had a general rule that only officers could be pilots. Enlisted men trained as mechanics. And as late as 1908, the bulk of the "flying" done in the Aeronautical Division was done in balloons. The mechanics had to know how to work with balloon fabric, to control the aircraft, and to prepare the gases for the balloons.

Burge was one of eight enlisted men who joined the division in 1907. In 1909 he and nine other enlisted men joined 1st Lt Benjamin Foulois and a civilian mechanic at Fort Sam Houston in San Antonio, Texas. This was when Foulois was teaching himself how to fly. Burge and another private, Glenn Madole, assisted by the civilian mechanic, built a landing system for Foulois' airplane. During this time, Burge learned as much as he could about repairing and flying airplanes.

COL VERNON BURGE

Col Vernon Burge on the eve of his retirement, right before his final flight

Courtesy of the Airmen Memorial Museum

ENLISTED MEN LEARNING THE BALLOON TRADE

Courtesy of the Airmen Memorial Museum

By the time Burge became a pilot in 1912, the Army had 11 aircraft, 14 officer pilots, and 39 enlisted men. But it wasn't until 18 July 1914 that the US House of Representatives passed a bill that authorized enlisted men to fly. The bill limited the number of enlisted pilots to 12. That bill was also important because it gave official status to the Army's aviation arm—it created the Aviation Section of the Army Signal Corps, which replaced the corps' Aeronautical Division.

Flight Paths

A Private's Persistence

PFC Vernon Burge knew he wanted to be a pilot from the moment he laid eyes on an airplane. When he volunteered for balloon duty in August 1907, he began a five-year journey as ground crewman, balloon handler, and airplane mechanic. He and his fellow mechanics spent a good deal of those five years at air shows around the country, helping prepare aircraft and keep them fit for flight. Burge absorbed all he could about balloons and airplanes.

In early 1912 Burge, by now a corporal, shipped with a *Wright B* airplane to the Philippines. Brig Gen James Allen had ordered that an air station be established at Fort McKinley. Burge reported to 1st Lt Frank P. Lahm, who was setting up a flight school at the station. Aware of the shortage of officers, Burge took the plunge. He asked Lt Lahm whether he could train to be a pilot.

SGT VERNON BURGE IN UNIFORM

Courtesy of the Airmen Memorial Museum

Lahm agreed, and Burge began his instruction 8 April 1912. He already knew a good deal about flying. As a mechanic, he'd taxied a good many airplanes along runways to make sure the engines were running right and repairs were correctly done. He passed his flight test 14 June 1912.

Burge's hard work, love of flying, and persistence eventually earned him a place in the Army as an officer. He retired 31 January 1942 at the rank of colonel. He'd spent 35 years in military aviation and had served as a pilot for 30 of those years. He'd logged 4,667 hours and 55 minutes in the air—quite a career.

Europe Versus America

Although the Wright brothers invented the airplane in America, Europe had more pilots than the United States did in those early days. France was the leader; by 1911 it boasted 353 pilots. Great Britain had 57, Germany 46, Italy 32, and Belgium 27. The United States had 26, giving it a sixth-place ranking in the world.

Tearing Down the Barriers

Bessie Coleman faced two obstacles to becoming a pilot—her race and her gender. She overcame both. In 1921 Coleman became the first black woman to get a pilot's license. She had to go to France for training because no flight school in the United States would accept her. She died in an airplane crash only four years after getting her license. You'll read more about Coleman in Chapter 3.

Opportunities for Women in Aviation

Before Bessie Coleman got her license in 1921, other women found it difficult to realize their dream of joining men in the skies. Even the most successful female pilots felt the strain.

Blanche Stuart Scott, the first American woman to solo in a plane, said, "There seemed to be no place for a woman engineer, mechanic, or flier. Too often people paid money to see me risk my neck, more as a freak, a woman freak pilot, than as a skilled flier." Because of this public pressure and a few severe accidents in the air, Scott retired from flight in 1916 when she was only 27 years old.

Despite the obstacles, many women thrived on the thrill of lifting and looping and diving through the air. They broke records and paved the way for women in the future to enter careers in commercial and military aviation.

BESSIE COLEMAN AND HER PILOT'S LICENSE

Courtesy of the National Air and Space Museum, Smithsonian Institution (SI Neg. No. SI-99-15416)

BLANCHE STUART SCOTT

Blanche Stuart Scott was used to setting records. She became the first woman to drive a car across America in 1910. And she didn't do it on a highway, or even on a state route. At that time, there were fewer than 300 miles of paved roads in the entire United States.

When men started setting records in aviation, Scott wanted to be part of the action. She was Glenn Curtiss's only female student in 1910. In fact, she was Curtiss's first student ever, and he never took on another. In addition, Scott was the only female student pilot in the United States at that time. Curtiss worried about this. If Scott crashed, he feared he'd be blamed for putting a woman in harm's way. What's more, she'd be using a single-engine plane that Curtiss designed, and some people might think the plane was faulty. For these reasons, he did what he could to keep Scott from being able to take off.

Scott would taxi back and forth across the runway in Curtiss's plane. But she could never get into the air. Frustrated, on 2 September 1910, she got out of the plane and took a close look at the engine. She was, after all, a curious person. She noticed a small piece of wood lodged under the throttle lever. She deduced this hindered the lever's motion. And she also concluded that Curtiss had placed the wood there to make sure the aircraft wouldn't be able to get off the ground when she sat at the controls.

Scott removed the wood, climbed back into the cockpit, and asked a mechanic to crank the propeller. The plane lifted off the runway. Scott was airborne.

Scott had become the first American woman to solo in a fixed-wing airplane. To solo *is to fly with no one else on board.* She flew with exhibition groups for six years, although she never got her pilot's license. She was known for two stunts. In one, she flew under bridges upside-down. Her other stunt was the "death dive." She would climb to 4,000 feet, and then plunge the plane toward earth, leveling off only when she reached 200 feet.

Scott was adventurous, but even daring people get their fill. After a number of accidents, she retired in 1916 at the age of 27. She died in 1970 at the age of 81. She'd lived to see the first man land on the moon.

BLANCHE STUART SCOTT
Courtesy of the National Air and Space Museum, Smithsonian Institution (SI Neg. No. SI-72-4803-A)

BESSICA MEDLAR RAICHE

Some aviation historians think Bessica Medlar Raiche was really the first woman to go solo. She made that flight on 13 October 1910. They contend Scott got into the air purely by accident. But Raiche herself gave Scott credit for the event.

"Blanche deserved the recognition," Raiche said, "but I got more attention because of my lifestyle. I drove an automobile, was active in sports like shooting and swimming, and I even wore riding pants and knickers. People who didn't know me or understand me looked down on this behavior. I was an accomplished musician, painter, and linguist. I enjoyed life, and just wanted to be myself."

Raiche never got a license. But flying excited her. She and her husband, François, formed a lightweight airplane company called the French-American Aeroplane Company. They did two important things to make their planes better than other lightweight aircraft. They took off some pounds by exchanging heavier fabrics, such as muslin, for silk. They also used piano wires instead of iron wires.

Raiche eventually left flying. She entered medical school and became a doctor.

BESSICA MEDLAR RAICHE
Courtesy of the National Air and Space Museum, Smithsonian Institution (SI Neg. No. SI-2007-5475)

HARRIET QUIMBY

Quimby was the first American woman to earn her pilot's license. A journalist, she wrote for a popular magazine called *Leslie's Weekly*. But she wanted to make more money to support herself, her parents, and her ambition to become a creative writer.

In 1910 she watched aviator John Moisant fly around the Statue of Liberty in New York harbor. The sight thrilled her. She signed up for flying lessons. She got her license on 1 August 1911, after completing a two-part test. The first part of the test required her to make five left and right turns around pylons—*tall, thin towers*. She also had to fly five figure eights. Quimby passed this part with ease. For part two, she had to land within 100 feet of her takeoff point. Quimby failed this part first time around. She took the test again the next day. This time she succeeded. She landed within 7 feet, 9 inches, of her takeoff point. What was so remarkable was that in those days, planes did not have brakes. Quimby set a record with her mark.

HARRIET QUIMBY
Courtesy of the National Air and Space Museum, Smithsonian Institution (SI Neg. No. SI-2002-23705)

Quimby set other records: She was the first woman to fly at night (1911) and the first woman to cross the English Channel in the pilot's seat (1912).

She broke a fashion barrier, too. The long dresses that women wore at that time weren't practical for a pilot. Most of the planes were open to the elements, and long pieces of fabric might get caught in a propeller or other mechanism. Quimby designed an outfit for female pilots. Her tailor sewed a one-piece uniform made of purple satin. Quimby had invented the jumpsuit, *a one-piece outfit.*

Despite the progress, flight was still a dangerous business. Quimby entered the Boston Air Meet on 1 July 1912 in a Blériot monoplane. She and her passenger, William P. Willard, took off over Boston Harbor in hopes of making a record 58 mph flight over a body of water. At 5,000 feet, the plane flipped and nosed downward. As horrified spectators watched, Quimby and Willard fell from the plane and plunged into the waters. Both perished. Amazingly, the monoplane—now with no pilot or passenger—righted itself and landed in the harbor with a light crash.

In 1991, the US Post Office created a stamp in Quimby's honor.

**HARRIET QUIMBY
IN A PURPLE JUMPSUIT
OF HER CREATION**
Courtesy of the Library of Congress

CAPSULES

Dressed for Success

Harriet Quimby was a good friend of Matilde Moisant, John's sister. The two women decided to sign up for flight training together. When they did, both dressed as men. Why? Women were discouraged from learning how to fly, so they figured they'd need a disguise. Somehow, newspapers found out. They'd uncovered a fascinating story about two determined women.

MATILDE MOISANT

MATILDE MOISANT
Courtesy of the National Air and Space Museum,
Smithsonian Institution (SI Neg. No. SI-73-3564)

Matilde Moisant didn't buy into the superstition that the number 13 is unlucky. Her achievements proved how wise she was to ignore such beliefs. To begin with, she was born Friday, 13 September 1887. That was a good day for her and her parents.

Nearly 24 years later, on 13 April 1911, Moisant became the second woman in America to get a pilot's license. She won the Rodman Wanamaker Trophy for flying at an attitude of 2,500 feet. This was amazing in a day when planes weren't as stable as they are now. She also got a court to acknowledge it was legal to fly on Sundays. This happened after a sheriff in Long Island, New York, tried to arrest her for flying on a Sunday. Moisant's response was to hop in her plane and fly to another field.

One tragedy did strike: her brother, John Moisant, also a pilot, died in a crash in 1910. Matilde crashed a number of times herself, but she continued flying. Her brother's death deeply affected her, and on 13 April 1912, she said she'd make her last flight the next day. It turned out to be a very dangerous flight. The fuel tank sprang a leak, and by the time Moisant landed, her clothes were on fire.

Fortunately, the thickness of her clothing and her leather helmet protected her. Matilde Moisant died in 1964 at the age of 77.

European Women in Aviation

Women in Europe also turned their eyes to the sky during the early days of flight. Thérèse Peltier was the first European woman to fly as a passenger in a powered airplane in July 1908. The first European woman to pilot a plane was French baroness Raymonde de la Roche. The date was 22 October 1909. Soon after, she attained another first. On 8 March 1910 she became the first woman to earn a pilot's license.

RAYMONDE DE LA ROCHE
Courtesy of the National Air and Space Museum,
Smithsonian Institution (SI Neg. No. SI-81-3423)

JULIA CLARK

On 19 May 1912, Julia Clark was the third American woman to gain her pilot's license. Sadly, she achieved an unfortunate other first: she was the first woman pilot to die in a crash.

Clark had a fascinating life. She emigrated to the United States from London and became an American citizen. She learned to fly at the Curtiss Flying School at North Island in San Diego. After soloing in a Curtiss plane, she joined an exhibition group. On the evening of 17 June 1912, she decided to take a test flight. It was dark, and she couldn't see that one of her plane's wings was about to hit a tree limb. The aircraft crashed. She died only about two weeks before Harriet Quimby.

KATHERINE AND MARJORIE STINSON

Flying was a family affair for the Stinsons. Katherine, her two brothers, and her sister all became pilots.

Katherine earned her pilot's license on 24 July 1912. She was the fourth American woman to do so. And at age 16, she was also the youngest. She would eventually become one of the most successful women in aviation.

For example, Katherine was the first pilot of either gender to take part in a parade. She covered her plane with roses for the 1913 New Year's Day Tournament of Roses Parade in California and flew over the parade route. Later, she set a distance record for both genders in a nonstop cross-country flight.

Her younger brothers, Eddie and Jack, became pilots. Jack was a test pilot. Her younger sister, Marjorie, graduated from the Wright Flying School in August 1914 (Wilbur Wright had her mother sign a waiver because of Marjorie's age). At 17, Marjorie became the first woman authorized to fly the experimental airmail service.

KATHERINE STINSON
Courtesy of the National Air and Space Museum, Smithsonian Institution (SI Neg. No. SI-2007-5474)

All four siblings had the support of their mother, Emma. She even went so far as to move the family to San Antonio, Texas, so her daughters could open a flying school. When World War I began, the sisters tried to enlist as pilots in the Army, but they were rejected. So the sisters opened a school to train Americans and Canadians as pilots for the war. A supporter, New York Congressman Murray Hulbert, tried unsuccessfully to get Congress to pass a bill allowing women to join the Flying Corps. But women were allowed to do little more than serve as nurses during the war. Katherine went to France to work as an ambulance driver because, in her own words, "I didn't feel I was doing enough for the war effort."

That war would lead to revolutionary developments in aviation.

MARJORIE STINSON
Courtesy of Corbis Images

CHECKPOINTS

Lesson 2 Review

Using complete sentences, answer the following questions on a sheet of paper.

1. Who was the famous founding member of the Aerial Experiment Association?

2. Which of Glenn Curtiss's effects on aviation are felt today?

3. What did Louis Blériot do when his engine overheated as he was crossing the English Channel?

4. What type of "wing" does a helicopter have that gives it lift?

5. When did the first enlisted man become a pilot? What was his name?

6. Who was the first black woman to get a pilot's license? What two obstacles did she have to overcome?

7. What did Blanche Stuart Scott remove from her plane's engine to get it to fly?

8. Why was it remarkable that Harriet Quimby landed her plane 7 feet, 9 inches from her takeoff point?

Applying Your Learning

9. What are the advantages of multiengine planes?

Air Power in World War 1

Quick Write

_____

_____

_____

Faced with seven German planes against his one, Eddie Rickenbacker knew he must remain calm. Why do you think that was important? What lesson do you think you can learn for use in emergencies you might face?

Learn About...

- **the contributions of US pilots during World War I**
- **the role of air power during World War I**
- **how air power expanded during World War I**

Edward Rickenbacker was an American combat pilot during World War I. He shot down 26 German airplanes in just five months. He was the only surviving pilot of that war to receive the Congressional Medal of Honor during his lifetime.

Rickenbacker earned his medal for an act of bravery on 25 September 1918. He was flying alone when he came across seven German planes—five Fokker D-VIIs and two Halberstadt CL-IIs. When facing such situations, he knew a pilot must remain calm. And he certainly must have done so. Defying the huge odds, he shot down two of the seven enemy planes.

Rickenbacker was one of the American "aces" in the war. The French came up with the title of ace for any pilot who had knocked five or more enemy planes out of the sky over the course of the war. The Germans, however, insisted their ace pilots bring down at least 10 aircraft to earn the title. An "ace of aces" was the pilot from each country who had taken down the most enemy aircraft. France's ace of aces was René Fonck. He had 75 kills, or planes shot down. Edward Mannock, with 73 kills, took the prize in Britain. And Baron Manfred von Richthofen of Germany (known as the "Red Baron") shot down 80 airplanes. Rickenbacker, with 26 kills, was America's ace of aces.

EDWARD RICKENBACKER was America's ace of aces. He shot down 26 planes during World War I.
Courtesy of Bettmann/Corbis

The Contributions of US Pilots During World War I

Vocabulary

- **Allies**
- **Central Powers**
- **U-boat**
- **escadrille**
- **machine gun**
- **stalemate**
- **appropriate**
- **strategic**
- **zeppelin**
- **dogfight**
- **strafe**

Despite the contributions of brave pilots on both sides, most World War I battles were fought on land or at sea. Airplanes were still fragile when the war started in 1914. After all, the Wrights didn't make their historic flight until 1903.

But during the war, aviation engineers made tremendous advances. Some American commanders in the field had great faith in the capabilities of the Aviation Section of the Army's Signal Corps. In a few key instances, aircraft contributed to the Allied victory. Aircraft had important functions—from doing aerial reconnaissance to shooting down enemy aircraft.

The Outbreak of World War I

World War I began in Europe, when a Serb assassinated Archduke Franz Ferdinand on 28 June 1914. Ferdinand was next in line to the Austro-Hungarian throne. Because of alliances among different nations in Europe, one country after another soon declared war.

First Austria-Hungary declared war on Serbia. Then Russia entered the fray on Serbia's side. Germany, which had ties to Austria-Hungary, was the next to step into the conflict by declaring war on Russia. Soon *Russia, France, Serbia, and Britain*—the Allies—were at war against *Germany, Austria-Hungary, and Turkey*—the Central Powers. (Many other countries later joined the fight, including the United States and Italy on the side of the Allies. Russia withdrew from the war after the Russian Revolution at the end of 1917.)

When Germany invaded France on 4 August 1914, the war started in earnest.

American President Woodrow Wilson vowed that the United States would remain neutral. But over time, that proved impossible. German U-boats—*German submarines*—attacked American ships in the Atlantic because the United States was sending goods to Britain. Wilson asked Germany to stop sinking American ships. And for a while, Germany did.

But in early 1917 two things happened. Germany once again targeted all American ships headed toward Britain. And in a telegram discovered by British intelligence, Germany asked Mexico to make war with the United States if the United States did not remain neutral. If Mexico joined the war and the Central Powers won, Germany promised Mexico it could have Texas, Arizona, and New Mexico.

President Wilson asked the US Congress to declare war on Germany. Congress agreed. The United States entered World War I in April 1917.

The use of airplanes as weapons took major leaps forward during that war. The heroic central figure in air power was the pilot.

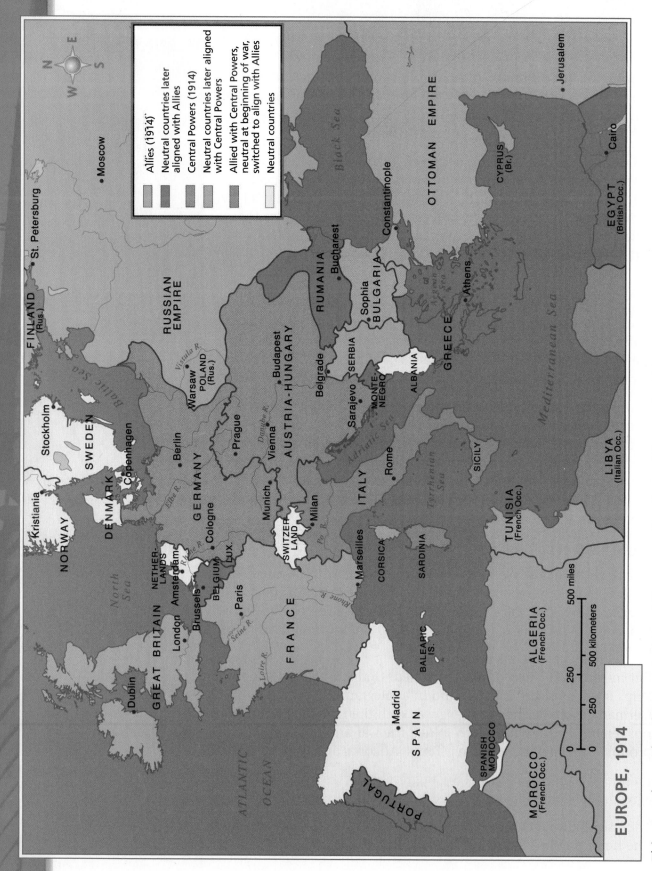

EUROPE, 1914

This map shows the alignment of the Allies versus the Central Powers in 1914. Turkey would join the side of the Central Powers in October of that year.
Courtesy of Maps.com

Legend:
- Allies (1914)
- Neutral countries later aligned with Allies
- Central Powers (1914)
- Neutral countries later aligned with Central Powers
- Allied with Central Powers, neutral at beginning of war, switched to align with Allies
- Neutral countries

The Contributions of World War I Pilots

Four American pilots in particular made their marks during World War I, also known as the Great War. But it all began with a group of US pilots who together formed the Lafayette Escadrille in France.

THE LAFAYETTE ESCADRILLE

Some American pilots didn't wait for the United States to join the war. They tried to enter the military services of the Allies. For legal reasons, most countries couldn't accept the men's offers. But France, with its French Foreign Legion made up entirely of fighters from outside France, could sign up these volunteers.

In April 1916 seven American pilots formed a fighting group that they called *Escadrille Américaine*. An escadrille *is a small squadron of planes.* The pilots were wealthy young men who had been living in Paris. In the next few days seven more Americans, then serving in French units, joined the squadron.

When the men of *Escadrille Américaine* began racking up German kills, Germany protested. It said that the United States was breaking its promise of neutrality. The men had to change their group's name. They decided to call it the Lafayette Escadrille. Its name honored the Marquis de Lafayette, who fought for the 13 American colonies during the Revolutionary War. Now individual Americans were fighting on behalf of France and the Allies in the war against the Central Powers.

In the escadrille's first five months, its pilots fought in 156 air battles and shot down 17 enemy planes. By the time the United States Air Service brought the unit under its supervision in 1918, its pilots had made 199 kills. Six members were aces. Forty died by the war's end. The escadrille included Eugene Bullard, the only African-American to serve as a pilot in the war.

THE LAFAYETTE ESCADRILLE, 1916
Members of the Lafayette Escadrille with their mascots, which included a lioness and a lion cub.
Courtesy of Bettmann/Corbis

RAOUL LUFBERY

Raoul Lufbery was the most famous pilot of the Lafayette Escadrille. He had 17 combat victories during the war. A native of France, he came to the United States as a child and became an American citizen. As a young man, he tried the US Army but didn't care for the discipline. During travels abroad, he met Marc Pourpe, a French pilot. Pourpe took him on as his mechanic. Together they traveled to India, China, and Japan.

The pair was in France when war broke out. Lufbery followed Pourpe into the military by way of the French Foreign Legion. He continued working as Pourpe's mechanic. No doubt he was also listening to the pilots talk about effective combat maneuvers and flying techniques. When Pourpe died in action in 1914, Lufbery trained to be a pilot. He signed up with the Lafayette Escadrille shortly after it was established.

RAOUL LUFBERY

Raoul Lufbery flew with the Lafayette Escadrille.
Courtesy of the Library of Congress

Lufbery used to give two pieces of advice to new combat pilots. First, he said, don't lunge headfirst into combat. Take stock of the scene before committing yourself. Second, he cautioned that a pilot in a burning plane would have a better chance of survival if he tried to bring it in for a landing. Parachutes were not standard equipment in those days, so pilots couldn't safely jump from a damaged aircraft.

Sadly, Lufbery was not able to follow his own advice. When a German aircraft shot Lufbery's plane on 19 May 1918, his aircraft became engulfed in flames. Lufbery jumped to his death.

EDWARD RICKENBACKER

America's ace of aces started out as a professional racecar driver. He competed in the Indianapolis 500 three times. Rickenbacker learned a lot about automobiles through an engineering correspondence course. He also worked at a car-manufacturing company. Like Glenn Curtiss, who'd broken speed records on motorcycles, Rickenbacker set a record in a racecar. His top speed was 134 mph.

Although he was making excellent money as a racer, Rickenbacker wanted to be a part of the war effort. In 1917, he asked the US Army to consider forming a squadron of pilots made up of racecar drivers. The military didn't take him up on his offer, but they did ask whether he would like to enlist and serve as a staff car driver.

Rickenbacker said yes, and fate stepped in. One day while Rickenbacker was driving a member of Gen John J. Pershing's staff, they passed the broken-down car of Col William "Billy" Mitchell, chief of the US Air Service. Rickenbacker pulled over to the side of the road. Drawing on his expertise in engine repair, he fixed the car. Col Mitchell was impressed. Later he asked Rickenbacker to be his driver. Before long, Rickenbacker had Mitchell's permission to train as a pilot.

Rickenbacker rose from an enlisted Soldier to the rank of captain and took command of the 94th Squadron. He did two important things for his men. He got them equipped with parachutes. And he figured out how to keep an airplane's machine gun—*an automatic rifle that uses belt-fed ammunition*—from jamming.

The Ace Who Became an Airline President

American ace of aces Edward Rickenbacker (1890–1973) didn't slow down when World War I ended. He remained in the reserves and worked his way up to colonel. He also returned to one of his first loves—cars. Rickenbacker founded an automobile manufacturing company.

The personal side of his life flourished, too. He got married and had two children. In 1927, the pace picked up. Rickenbacker, who'd once raced in the Indianapolis 500, bought the Indianapolis 500 Speedway. He sold it after World War II.

Rickenbacker remained engaged in engines, cars, and planes in other ways as well. He was an aviation advocate. He managed General Motors Fokker Aircraft Company. Next he took on the job of vice president of American Airlines. He eventually left that job to go back to Fokker, where he became manager of its Eastern Airlines division.

1ST LT EDWARD RICKENBACKER

A former racecar driver, 1st Lt Rickenbacker of the 94th Squadron is shown here in his Spad airplane on a French field.
Courtesy of Corbis Images

Then in 1938, Rickenbacker bought Eastern Airlines. Friends gave him financial support for the purchase. He worked at Eastern for more than 20 years and retired in 1959 as president. He remained as chairman of the board until 1963. Rickenbacker spent the last 10 years of his life promoting aviation, both military and civilian.

FRANK LUKE

Frank Luke was a wild card. He didn't have the discipline of a Rickenbacker or a Lufbery. But he did have their guts. He was tough—he came from the Arizona mountains and had worked in copper mines.

As soon as the United States entered the war, Luke volunteered. He chose the Army Signal Corps and completed his nine-week flight training in seven weeks. In March 1918 he went to France as a second lieutenant. After more training, he began to go out on patrols. But he never saw any German aircraft. Running out of patience, he flew solo over a German airfield in August 1918. He met up with six Albatros fighters (a German biplane) and shot one down.

One month later Luke asked permission to go after a German balloon that another squadron had tried unsuccessfully to shoot down. Balloons were always heavily guarded because they were so vulnerable. Another plane went along with Luke to watch his back. Luke got his balloon.

Luke still sometimes went off by himself. Once he disappeared overnight. When Luke returned, his commander grounded him. Luke took off again anyway, even though he risked court-martial. This time he downed three balloons. He also shot some German soldiers on the ground.

He landed his plane later to get a drink of water from a stream. A German foot patrol surrounded him. When he drew his revolver, they killed him.

Luke's career as a combat pilot was short: he died just 17 days after his first kill. In that time, he shot down 15 balloons and three airplanes. It was one of the records of the war.

2D LT FRANK LUKE

Frank Luke once shot down three German balloons within 35 minutes. Balloons were among the most heavily guarded aircraft during World War I and were, therefore, extremely dangerous to attack.

Courtesy of Corbis Images

EUGENE BULLARD

Only one African-American served as a pilot during World War I. His name was Eugene Bullard. Bullard was also one of the few enlisted men to fly an airplane.

Bullard carved his own path throughout his life. When he was only eight years old, he ran away from his home in Georgia. His goal was to get to France. He'd heard France was a wonderful place for people of all races. It took him 11 years, but he finally got there.

Like other Americans wishing to join the fight in World War I, Bullard signed up with the French Foreign Legion in October 1914. He was wounded four times while with an infantry unit whose members called themselves the "swallows of death." After his fourth wound, he transferred to the French Air Service and became a pilot. He was the first black man to get a pilot's license and the first black American fighter pilot. He tried to join the US Air Service, but the Army turned him down. He shot down two German aircraft while in the French Air Service. Finally, he got into a tussle with a French officer—rather than court-martial him, the French military transferred him back to the infantry, where he served the rest of the war.

Bullard eventually returned to the United States, where he lived in Harlem, New York. The French government awarded him a *Croix de Guerre* (War Cross) medal, which it gave to individuals who displayed heroism during fighting with enemy forces. Bullard also received several other medals for his contributions to the war effort, both in the air and in the infantry. In 1954, France asked him to visit to help light the Eternal Flame of the Tomb of the Unknown French Soldier in Paris at the Arc de Triomphe. This was a great honor.

EUGENE BULLARD
Eugene Bullard was the only African-American combat pilot during World War I.
Courtesy of the US Air Force

When Eugene Bullard (1894–1961) hung up his infantry boots at the end of World War I, he returned to Paris. This was the city that felt like home to him. Before the war he'd been a boxer. But now he was a war veteran who'd suffered many wounds. He needed work that exercised his mind more than his body. He went into the nightclub business and met many famous people such as authors Ernest Hemingway and F. Scott Fitzgerald. He also got married. His wife was the daughter of a countess. They had two children. Years passed and another war was brewing—World War II.

During all his time in Europe, the former war pilot had picked up language skills. In addition to English and French, Bullard spoke German quite well. Because Bullard had great affection for his adopted country of France, he agreed to help when the French government asked him to spy on Germans living in France. War broke out in 1939 and with the German army about to take the city of Paris in 1940, Bullard knew he had

to leave. He did this because if he were captured he'd be charged as a spy and because he wanted to protect his two children. Bullard and his wife had separated years before but when she died, Bullard gained custody of their children.

After fleeing Paris, Bullard went with his children to the city of Orleans, south of the French capital. He joined a group of uniformed troops defending that city, and was once again wounded. A woman spy smuggled him and his children into Spain. The family was later sent back to the United States, where Bullard recovered.

Bullard spent the rest of his life in Harlem, New York, working as an elevator operator at the Rockefeller Center. The US military didn't recognize his wartime achievements until after his death, when the US Air Force commissioned him as a lieutenant.

But the grateful French never forgot him. French President Charles de Gaulle even praised Bullard on a visit to New York City in 1960.

MANFRED VON RICHTHOFEN, THE RED BARON

Courtesy of the National Archives and Records Administration

Baron Manfred von Richthofen was Germany's ace of aces. He made 80 kills. He came from a wealthy military family. By age 20, he was a lieutenant in a Prussian Army cavalry regiment. But once the fighting moved to the trenches, the horse cavalry no longer had an important role in combat.

So Von Richthofen joined the German Imperial Air Service. He soon commanded a group with scarlet-colored planes. Because of his record of conquests in the air and the color of his planes, he became known as the Red Baron. Allied fire killed Von Richthofen in 1918, three years after he became a pilot.

US Contributions to the Air War

By 1917, after years of bloody fighting which cost both sides terrible casualties, the war in Europe was at a stalemate. A stalemate *is a situation in which further action is blocked.* The French Army was demoralized. The British tried to reinforce France, but inexperienced replacements composed the bulk of British troops by this point. Germany was also weakening. A force was needed to tip the balance one way or the other. The Allies hoped that force would be the United States, which joined the effort in April.

In August 1917 the US Congress vowed to "darken the skies over Europe with US aircraft." It voted to appropriate—*to set aside for a specific use*—$64 million to build airplanes.

Congress had good intentions, but it had made an empty promise. The United States lacked both the engineers to design planes and the manufacturers to assemble them. Even by the end of the war, all American pilots were still flying British or French planes.

Britain and France had entered the war in 1914 with 450 aircraft. Germany at that time had 200. All three countries had working aviation industries in those years. By 1917 France and Germany each boasted more than 2,000 aircraft. Britain was continually flying patrols along the North Sea, but the Allies were running out of steam. At that time, the United States had just one manufacturer: Curtiss Aircraft.

While the United States never built more than a handful of airplanes during the war years, it did provide considerable manpower in the air. It entered the European conflict with 100 pilots and trained 10,000 more before the war's end in November 1918. In all, 781 enemy planes fell to US aircraft. US pilots took part in 150 bombing raids.

It may have taken America the better part of a year to ramp up its effectiveness in the war, but its support of the Allies was crucial. In one of the most significant air battles of World War I—the Battle of Saint Mihiel—America's Billy Mitchell led the Allied air attack. That battle determined the war's outcome.

CAPSULES

Weakness in the Air: Congress Responds

August 1917 wasn't the first time Congress tried to pump up the country's air power. On 18 July 1914 the US House of Representatives authorized the Army's Signal Corps to create an aviation branch with 60 officers and 260 enlisted men. When in March 1916 the 1st Aero Squadron took to the field to help Gen John J. Pershing secure the US–Mexico border, the squadron had eight biplanes. But these planes were not nearly powerful enough to get over Arizona's Casa Grande mountains. Recognizing the need, the Congress appropriated $13.2 million to build up the Aviation Service.

Enlisted Pilots

The United States entered the war in 1917 with 100 pilots. Billy Mitchell and another officer, Hap Arnold, had done their best to build up the number of pilots by training enlisted men. Both officers thought highly of the enlisted men in the Army's Signal Corps. The enlistees knew aircraft engines inside and out. Mitchell, an outspoken advocate of air power, helped ensure that the National Defense Act of 3 June 1916 included language that authorized the training of enlisted men as pilots.

The Role of Air Power During World War I

Until World War I, most people thought the role of aircraft in combat was limited to aerial reconnaissance. Countries won wars based on the strength of their infantries and the power of their navies. That's how it had been for centuries.

When the US Army bought its first *Wright Flyer*, even Brig Gen James Allen didn't think of an airplane as a potential offensive weapon. Dropping bombs from the sky seemed an unlikely idea. Conducting battles between squadrons of planes also seemed far-fetched. After all, planes of those days were built of plywood, and their wings were wrapped in fabric. But World War I would alter the military's views.

While many improvements were still needed to make the airplane the fierce weapon it is today, battlefield strategy evolved dramatically over the course of the Great War. The airplane reshaped the way countries fight wars more quickly than any other weapon in military history. A motto emerged by war's end: "If you control the air, you cannot be beaten; if you lose the air, you cannot win."

The Significance of Air Power in World War I

You've read that air power was essential to winning World War I. But where was its impact the greatest?

The Long-Range Raid and the Machine Gun

London, 1915: German airships floated over the city and dropped bombs with great accuracy. They destroyed buildings and killed many people. Through 1917 the Germans worked on perfecting these long-range strategic raids. Strategic means *designed to strike at the sources of an enemy's military, economic, or political power.* The British were really the first to attempt a long-range raid. In 1914 they targeted hangars housing German aircraft.

A GERMAN ZEPPELIN

World War I German airmen dropped bombs on French and English cities from German zeppelins.

Courtesy of the Library of Congress

The Germans flew hydrogen-filled zeppelins. A zeppelin *is a German dirigible with a rigid frame used for observation and bombing raids.* Zeppelins, invented by the German Count Ferdinand von Zeppelin, had one major weakness: they easily burst into flames when hit by antiaircraft fire. So the Germans built a twin-engine bomber called the Gotha IV. The Gotha IV went on bombing raids over many British cities in 1917.

As a result of these raids, Britain had to take new measures to protect its own shores. English fighter squadrons were ordered to return from France so that they could guard British soil.

CAPSULES

Bombs on Britain

It wasn't a zeppelin that dropped the first bombs on Britain. It was a German FF-29 seaplane. The date was 21 December 1914, and the target was Dover, a city in southeast England. The FF-29 missed its target that day. But three days later it raided Britain a second time. Its bombs hit Dover this time, but no one was killed. The next day the aircraft invaded British airspace a third time. It dropped two bombs on nearby Kent. Over the course of the war, Germany hit London alone with 56 tons of bombs. German aircraft dropped 214 tons of bombs on the rest of the country.

Skynotes

The First Independent Flying Force

In response to German air raids on English cities and factories, the British formed their own bombing unit. Although the British were the first to conduct a long-range raid, they hadn't established a new arm of their military to do so. But in 1917 the British Royal Flying Corps (RFC) founded its first bombing wing. Unlike American and other Allied aviation units, the RFC did not answer to an infantry officer. It was independent. In 1918 the RFC merged with the Royal Naval Air Service and became today's Royal Air Force.

THE GERMAN *ALBATROS* D-II

The German *Albatros* D-II had two machine guns mounted toward the front.

Courtesy of the EAA/Jim Koepnick

Another innovation dreamed up by the Allies and picked up by the Germans was the airplane-mounted machine gun. Machine guns had been around since the late 19th century, and they were in full use by infantryman from the start of World War I. They weren't used right away in the air, however. Until 1915 pilots shot at one another with pistols and rifles. French pilot Roland Garros first bolted an automatic rifle to his plane so he could shoot straight through the propeller. To keep from shooting his propeller off, he attached steel plates to the backs of the blades.

The Germans got to see Garros's deadly invention up close when they downed his plane in April 1915. They asked a Dutchman, Anthony Fokker, to take the design a step further. Fokker built an interrupting gear. He hooked the machine gun to the plane's engine. In this way, the gun would not fire while the propeller was in the way. For the next year, the Germans ruled the skies.

But if the Germans could capture and copy Garros's design, it was only a matter of time before the Allies captured a German aircraft and copied Fokker's interrupting gear. In April 1916 the Allies did just that. Soon the Allies and the Central Powers were again on equal footing. The famous dogfights commenced. A dogfight *is a battle between fighter planes.* The fighter aces came out of these aerial battles. Sometimes squadrons with as many as 50 planes faced off.

The Battle of Saint Mihiel

In September 1918 the Battle of Saint Mihiel in France finally turned the tide in favor of the Allies. Air power played a tremendous role in this offensive. Brig Gen Billy Mitchell commanded nearly 1,500 Allied airplanes—American, French, British, Italian, and Portuguese—to drive the Germans out of France. This was the largest assembly of aircraft ever gathered for a single mission.

The Allied pilots had two goals. The first was to destroy German planes in the air. The second was to destroy German aircraft in hangars on the ground. Mitchell committed 1,000 planes to this portion of the mission. The rest of the planes protected the Allied ground troops. They scouted out enemy positions. Mitchell wrote that the Allied planes were "to be put into a central mass and hurled at the enemy's aviation, no matter where he might be found, until complete ascendancy had been obtained over him in the air."

The four-day Battle of Saint Mihiel established the role of mass movements of air power during wartime. It weakened the Central Powers and destroyed enemy supply lines. This offensive helped lead to Allied victory two months later.

How the Airplane Revolutionized War

When World War I began in 1914, pilots flew everything from balloons and dirigibles to airplanes. They soared over enemy positions to spot troop movements and artillery positions. They also took photos of what they'd seen.

Each side wanted to do something to counteract this use of aircraft. Both sent up airplanes to shoot down observation aircraft, first with pistols and rifles and later with machine guns, as you read in the previous section.

Whether the enemy was using pistols or machine guns, another countermeasure was now necessary. Each side had to protect its observation aircraft. Aerial combat was born.

Furthermore, once machine guns were mounted on planes, pilots could use them to strafe soldiers on the ground. To strafe *is to attack with a machine gun from a low-flying aircraft*. Planes also delivered bombs behind enemy lines. At first pilots carried small bombs in their laps and dropped them by hand. Once aircraft could carry heavier loads, some ferried thousands of pounds of bombs. Accuracy of bombing, however, remained an issue.

A PILOT USES A GRAFLEX CAMERA

A pilot takes pictures of enemy troop positions circa 1917–1918.
Courtesy of Corbis Images

A GERMAN PILOT

A German pilot drops a bomb on an Allied position.
Courtesy of Corbis Images

Airplanes now offered possibilities that challenged age-old warfare strategies. In traditional battles, troops dug trenches. They tried to hold their own lines and break through the enemy's trench lines. Assaults were from the front. But airplanes changed that. Planes could fly over an enemy's trenches, bomb from overhead, and strafe troops. What's more, they could hit important targets behind enemy lines, such as factories. This provided the element of surprise as well.

Planes didn't come into their own until World War II. Nevertheless, their use during World War I set the stage for the next worldwide conflict.

How Air Power Expanded During World War I

Airplanes flew a whopping 64 mph when the first shots of the Great War rang out. Most European nations had a few hundred planes. America had only about 20. But no one had aircraft that were combat worthy.

Over the next four years, the technology of the Allied and Central Powers' air power would continually leapfrog one over the other. Speeds picked up. Aircraft became stronger and sturdier. Maximum altitudes climbed from 10,000 feet to 24,000 feet.

As the saying goes, "Necessity is the mother of invention." And if survival in war isn't a necessity, what is?

New Developments in Aviation During World War I

When Louis Blériot crossed the English Channel in 1909, some thought his quick, 37-minute passage from one country to another suggested the face of future wars. If a friendly aircraft could travel that fast from Calais to Dover, couldn't an enemy do the same? Many countries built small armies of planes. Once war broke out, the pace of invention picked up.

By 1918 three specialized types of aircraft had emerged: the fighter, the observation aircraft, and the bomber. Observation aircraft were in use from the start. Most of them were dirigibles and balloons. Some planes even had extra seats for photographers.

The fighter came into its own with the birth of the dogfight. This era had the biggest impact on small-craft development. Once both the Allies and the Central Powers had mounted machine guns with interrupting gear on their airplanes, quick, easy maneuvers became essential. A pilot wanted to get out of the way of the bullet spray.

A British *Sopwith Triplane*

A British *Sopwith Triplane* was one of the aircraft
designed during the war to engage in dogfights.

Courtesy of the EAA/Jim Koepnick

These fighter aircraft needed three qualities: they had to be lightweight, fast, and
maneuverable. Both sides designed their own memorable fighters. The British built
the Sopwith Camel and the SE-5A. The French had the Spad VII and Nieuport 28.
The Germans crafted the Fokker Dr-I and D-VII.

Seven months before the war ended, a German designer named Hugo Junkers made
a breakthrough. He built an all-metal, low-wing monoplane fighter, the Junkers D1.
No longer would a pilot have to fly a plywood-and-fabric contraption that easily
caught fire. Fortunately for the Allies, the Germans assembled only 45 of these planes.

During the war, airplanes became faster. By early 1918 fighters zipped along
at a cool 130 mph. When Igor Sikorsky flew his four-engine, 92-foot-wingspan
Le Grand in 1913, he probably couldn't have imagined that in just five years
100-foot-wingspan bombers would be carrying loads that weighed thousands of
pounds. As the Germans learned with their zeppelins, bombs were best delivered
by planes sturdy and large enough to carry heavy loads. The British, for example,
designed the Super-Handley Page bomber. The first model had two engines;
later models had four. The four-engine model could carry six men and 30
260-pound bombs.

Any breakthrough in design gave the side that had it an edge. Ground soldiers,
pilots, commanders, and engineers—all contributed to the war effort.

Why War Sped Up Aviation Development in the United States

When Congress appropriated $64 million for airplanes in 1917, the United States was far behind other nations in air power. Curtiss Aircraft was the only aviation manufacturer in the country. Army staff officers still had their eyes focused on the infantry. They had no plans for their aviation section. The United States could never again be so unprepared.

Brig Gen Billy Mitchell believed strongly in the future of aviation as an instrument in warfare. He saw its possibilities, including as a weapon against navies. Mitchell didn't learn to fly until he was 36—that's old for a beginning pilot. But he was one of the freshest thinkers in air warfare.

After consulting with other officers, Mitchell devised a three-pronged theory to fight wars from the sky:

1. Air superiority over the battlefield must be completely assured.

2. Air power may then be employed offensively against the enemy's ground troops.

3. Finally, aerial bombardment may be directed against the enemy's supplies, railroads, communications, and airdromes.

BRIG GEN BILLY MITCHELL

As chief of the Air Service, Mitchell held great sway with Airmen. But the aviation arm still fell under the command of the Army. And the Army saw airplanes as nothing more than extensions of ground forces. Mitchell, on the other hand, always pushed for an independent air service. He considered new strategies, such as the mass use of airplanes in the Battle of Saint Mihiel. For these reasons, today's US Air Force still considers Mitchell one of its founding fathers. You'll read more about him in a later lesson.

Chief of the Air Service Brig Gen Billy Mitchell drew up the plan for the 1,500-plane movement in the Battle of Saint Mihiel.

Courtesy of the Wisconsin Aviation Hall of Fame

CHECKPOINTS

Lesson 3 Review

Using complete sentences, answer the following questions on a sheet of paper.

1. How many planes did an Allied pilot have to shoot down to earn the "ace" title? How many did a German pilot have to down?

2. What type of soldiers made up the French Foreign Legion?

3. What two important things did American ace of aces Edward Rickenbacker do for his men?

4. Who was the only African-American pilot during World War I? Which air service accepted him?

5. Did Americans ever fly their own planes during the Great War? Whose planes did they fly?

6. What motto regarding air power emerged by war's end?

7. What two good ideas concerning combat aircraft did the Germans borrow from the Allies?

8. What was the average airplane speed in 1914, and what was the average speed by 1918?

9. What three specialized types of aircraft had emerged by the end of World War I?

Applying Your Learning

10. Explain how the airplane revolutionized war.

CHAPTER 3

Wing walking,
a favorite barnstormer stunt

Courtesy of Museum of Flight/Corbis

Expanding the Horizon

Chapter Outline

LESSON 1

The Barnstormers

LESSON 2

Flight Goes Mainstream

LESSON 3

Commercial Flight, Airmail, and Helicopters

"Ours is the commencement of the flying age, and I am happy to have popped into existence at a period so interesting."

AMELIA EARHART

Quick Write

If you're trying to reach a goal, it helps to have a supporter, as Bessie Coleman did—someone who has confidence in you and convinces you that you can achieve your dream. Describe an experience when you or someone close to you got support in reaching a goal.

Learn About...

- the barnstormers
- the major contributions of the barnstormers
- how the barnstormers contributed to public awareness of aviation

Bessie Coleman was an unlikely pioneer.

She was one of 13 children born to a former slave in Texas sometime in the 1890s. Her father was part African-American and part Cherokee and Choctaw Indian. Her mother, an African-American, didn't know how to read. But she had big ideas for her little girl. She made Bessie want to "become somebody."

It took a while, but Coleman figured it out. The "somebody" she wanted to become was an airplane pilot.

Coleman managed to graduate from high school. She even had a semester of college in Oklahoma. She loved to read. One of the things she read about was aviation. During World War I, she was living in Chicago, working as a manicurist. The newspapers were full of stories about the air war in Europe.

Coleman decided she didn't want to remain on the ground. She didn't want only to read about aviation. She wanted to fly.

When she went to sign up for lessons, doors closed in her face. Yes, there were a few women pilots— but a black woman? No one she talked to could imagine such a thing.

But she had a powerful friend—Robert S. Abbott. He was the editor of the *Chicago Weekly Defender*. His newspaper had sponsored a contest to find the best manicurist in black Chicago. Coleman won that contest.

So Coleman had an "in" with Abbott. She went to see him. He liked her idea of flight lessons. And he had an idea of his own. Go to Europe, he said. People there will be more accepting of you. He had another tip: Learn French before you go!

So Coleman went back to school—night school this time. She learned French and traveled to Europe.

After a few months, she ran out of money. So she returned to the United States. She went back to work. She saved as much money as she could. Finally she had enough to return to Europe. She looked for the best flight teacher she could find. She ended up studying with the chief pilot for Anthony Fokker, the famous aircraft manufacturer.

Fokker saw Coleman's talent and encouraged her. He became her mentor. A mentor *is a trusted coach or guide*.

On 15 June 1921, Bessie Coleman got her license. She was the first licensed black woman aviator in the world.

BESSIE COLEMAN

Bessie Coleman was the first black woman to get a pilot's license.

Courtesy of the Smithsonian Institution/Corbis

The Barnstormers

Bessie Coleman's story is inspiring to anyone striving to make a dream come true. Her story is also important because of the kind of aviator she was. Coleman earned fame as a barnstormer—*a pilot who travels around the country giving exhibits of stunt flying and parachuting.* The term barnstorming comes from the time pilots would fly over a small rural town to attract attention, then land at a local farm. In the 1920s, the term became attached to stunt flying. Historians give stunt pilots like Bessie Coleman credit for sustaining the aviation industry during its early years.

Significance of the Barnstormers

Barnstorming shows drew crowds of spectators—*people who come to see an event or show*—during and after World War I.

These daredevil pilots, along with the stuntmen and parachutists who worked with them, entertained people in the days before there were theme parks or television. Some pilots worked in teams. Their acts were called "flying circuses." Once the war was over, these pilots became the public face of American aviation.

The aircraft industry had boomed during the war. Britain, France, Germany, and Italy produced tens of thousands of planes. And the United States was catching up. By the war's end, it had almost 4,000 planes and about 9,500 men in the air service.

But on 14 November 1918, three days after the war ended, the US government canceled $100 million worth of airplane contracts. The country's leaders didn't yet see how important aircraft could be for national security in peacetime.

THE CURTISS JN 4 "JENNY"

The Curtiss "Jenny" became available as Army surplus after World War I and was popular with barnstormers.

Courtesy of the EAA/Jim Koepnick

Within three months, 175,000 workers in the aircraft industry lost their jobs. Aircraft production dropped by 85 percent. The Army dumped its surplus warplanes onto the market. That was a big blow to the aircraft companies. Who would buy their new planes when Uncle Sam was selling old ones at bargain prices?

Commercial and private aviation did not exist. There were no regularly scheduled flights for business or vacation travelers. Cars weren't yet popular either. Most people traveled from one city to another by train. In fact, even though aviation had been important during the war, by 1918 most Americans had still never seen an airplane.

The barnstormers changed that. Many of them were former Army pilots. Since military aviation had been cut back, a large number lost their jobs. They leaped at the opportunity to keep flying.

These pilots enjoyed showing off the skills they had mastered in combat. They excelled at tight turns and daring maneuvers. And they often flew the same aircraft—planes such as the Curtiss JN-4 ("Jenny")—that they had trained on in wartime.

Significant Barnstormers

Bessie Coleman was just one of several Americans who gained fame as barnstormers and helped move aviation into the public eye. Like the pilots of World War I, the barnstormers were a special breed.

For the barnstormers, flying was in some ways less risky than it had been for combat pilots. No enemy guns fired on them as they performed maneuvers over fields and county fairgrounds. But flying, especially stunt flying, was still dangerous. Many of the barnstormers died in air accidents. Among them were Bessie Coleman and another pilot named Lincoln Beachey.

LINCOLN BEACHEY

Courtesy of Corbis Images

Born in San Francisco, Beachey (1887–1915) was one of the top barnstormers. At one point, Orville Wright called him "the greatest pilot of all time." In his Curtiss biplane, Beachey thrilled crowds with his dives. He could snatch a scarf or a handkerchief off the ground using the tips of his wings. For an exhibition at Niagara Falls, New York, he drew 150,000 spectators.

WING-WALKING

Wing-walking was a favorite stunt barnstormers performed to demonstrate to the public the thrill of flying.

Courtesy of Museum of Flight/Corbis

Someone on the ground would first notice it as a buzz or a whine. Much too loud for an insect, they said. It sounded like an engine. But what was an engine doing up in the sky? Could it be one of those newfangled flying machines?

Or maybe a farmer would see a shadow fall across his field—a shadow much too big to be that of a bird.

It's an airplane! A barnstormer had come to town!

The pilot would typically circle over a village or a small town to get people's attention. Then he'd land in a nearby field. Word would spread. People would gather to get a look at the aircraft. The pilot would offer rides. Some hardy souls would volunteer to go up. They would typically get a five-minute flight for $5—the equivalent of about $50 today.

Barnstormers liked to show what they could do wherever crowds gathered at places like county fairs and carnivals. Flying circuses, conducted by teams of pilots, became a popular form of entertainment.

Pilots who weren't part of the circuses often teamed up with stuntmen. The stuntmen had an amazing bag of tricks. "Wing walking," for example, was a real crowd pleaser.

With the pilot flying a biplane in a circle, the stuntman would leave the cockpit. He or she would walk out on the edge of the lower wing, then climb to the upper wing and walk back toward the cockpit. To give viewers an extra thrill, some wing walkers would stand on their heads.

Even Charles A. Lindbergh, best known for his 1927 solo flight across the Atlantic Ocean, was a barnstormer at the beginning of his career. (You'll read more about Lindbergh in the next lesson.)

As you read earlier, most barnstormers were former military aviators. But a number of women also were taking to the skies. Among them was Phoebe Fairgrave Omlie. She ran her own flying circus. She was the first woman in the United States to become a licensed transport pilot. In 1933, she also became the first woman appointed to a federal government job in aviation—special assistant for air intelligence for the National Advisory Committee for Aeronautics, the agency that eventually became the National Aeronautics and Space Administration (NASA).

Skynotes

Omlie's Air Markers

In 1935, Phoebe Fairgrave Omlie made one of her biggest contributions to American aviation when she developed the "air marker" system. This was a network of black and orange navigational markers in which names of towns were painted in 12-foot letters on the roofs of buildings all across the country. These markers identified the location, showed which direction was North, and indicated the distance and direction of the nearest airport. Eventually 16,000 markers—one every 15 miles—guided pilots along every air route in the United States.

Phoebe Fairgrave Omlie (center), special assistant to the intelligence division of the National Advisory Committee for Aeronautics, with Edna Gardner, a leading speed pilot, greet Elly Beinhorn, Germany's foremost woman flyer, in her low-wing monoplane.

PHOEBE FAIRGRAVE OMLIE

Courtesy of Underwood & Underwood/Corbis

For pilots such as Coleman and Omlie, as well as for women across the nation, it was an exciting time. Opportunities were widening. With passage of the 19th Amendment to the US Constitution, women won the right to vote. Many cast ballots for the first time in the 1920 presidential election.

Margery Brown, another female barnstormer, wrote about why women wanted to fly: "Halfway between the Earth and sky one seems to be closer to God. There is a peace of mind and heart, a satisfaction that walls cannot give. When I see an airplane flying I just ache all over to be up there."

The Barnstormers' Major Contributions

Historians call the years between 1919 and 1939 the "golden age of aviation." Pilots set one record after another. They flew faster. They attained greater altitude— *the height above Earth's surface.* They served as test pilots. (It's probably fair to say that in those early days, every pilot was a test pilot.)

During this period airplanes evolved from slow-moving, cloth-and-wood structures to faster aircraft made of metal. These planes were more aerodynamic—*designed with rounded edges to reduce wind drag.*

Engines became more reliable. This was another key advance. Soon wealthy aviation enthusiasts—*strong supporters or fans*—began to offer prizes for the first pilot to achieve a certain goal.

In 1911, for instance, newspaper owner William Randolph Hearst offered $50,000 to the first pilot who could fly across the United States in 30 days or less. As you read in Chapter 2, Calbraith Rodgers was the first to fly the distance. But he didn't win the prize. He took almost three weeks too long. Engine trouble, among other problems, slowed him down.

Another wealthy aviation enthusiast was Raymond Orteig. In the early 1920s he offered $25,000 for the first nonstop flight from New York to Paris. Again, the engines weren't up to the task.

But within a few years, engines had improved enough to make transatlantic flight possible. Some pilots then turned to a new challenge: polar exploration.

From childhood, Rear Adm Richard E. Byrd had longed to explore the North and South Poles. Trained as a flier, he advanced both aviation and polar exploration. In 1926 he and his pilot were the first to fly over the North Pole. Their aircraft was a Fokker monoplane with three Wright Whirlwind engines.

In 1929 Byrd flew to the South Pole. His expedition included three Loening amphibian planes—*aircraft designed to take off and land on either water or land.*

Rear Adm Richard E. Byrd, Polar Aviator

After World War I, barnstormers brought the magic of flight to the American heartland. And beginning in the 1920s, Richard E. Byrd helped direct attention to the ends of the earth—the North and South Poles.

Born in 1888 to a famous Virginia family, he graduated from the United States Naval Academy in 1912. He was a naval aviator in World War I. Eventually he rose to the rank of rear admiral in the US Navy.

He developed plans and navigational aids for the Navy's first transatlantic flights. He also helped Charles Lindbergh prepare for his solo flight across the Atlantic Ocean.

Byrd's polar adventures began with an assignment in western Greenland, in the North Atlantic. On 9 May 1926 he and his pilot, Warrant Officer Floyd Bennett, were the first people to fly over the North Pole. For their feat, both men received the Medal of Honor, not usually given in peacetime. Finally, Byrd turned his attention south. For the next three decades, he did more than anyone else to direct exploration of Antarctica.

RICHARD E. BYRD

Courtesy of George Silk/
Time Life Pictures/Getty Images

On 28 November 1929, Byrd and his pilot Bernt Balchen flew to the South Pole. It was the first of many trips. The team carried out scientific research. They studied meteors, cosmic rays, weather, and Earth's magnetism.

In 1934 Byrd spent five months living alone in a hut 123 miles away from his main base. It was as far south as any human had ever lived.

He was a celebrity, and he liked being famous. He knew that interest in his exploits helped build public support for scientific exploration. He raised a great deal of money for research, too.

By the 1950s he was the senior US government official in charge of South Pole research. He was an active explorer until the last months of his life. He died in 1957 at the age of 68.

How the Barnstormers Contributed to Public Awareness of Aviation

Since most Americans had never even seen an airplane, whatever ideas they had about flying probably included many fears. The barnstormers' demonstrations didn't do away with people's fears. After all, spectators sometimes saw dreadful accidents. But the barnstormers' air shows certainly created an interest in flight, even in rural areas and small towns. They publicized the airplane and brought romance to flying. Some people believe that without the barnstormers, aviation might have died altogether in the United States.

Stanford University historian Joseph Corn describes the importance of the barnstormers in his book, *The Winged Gospel*:

> Crowds assembled at the smallest airfield to watch planes take off and land, while the public voraciously consumed the many stories about aviation in newspapers and magazines. . . . So central was the airplane in the American imagination, in fact, that many people expected that they would soon take to the sky, flying their own family plane or helicopter. But more than anything, the airplane symbolized the promise of the future.

As the people around the world would soon find, that future was closer than most of them realized.

A 1919 NEWSPAPER ADVERTISEMENT FOR A BARNSTORMER EXHIBITION

Courtesy of the National Air and Space Museum, Smithsonian Institution (SI Neg. No. 85-12327)

CHECKPOINTS

Lesson 1 Review

Using complete sentences, answer the following questions on a sheet of paper.

1. How did Bessie Coleman learn about aviation?

2. Why did Robert Abbott suggest that Bessie Coleman go to Europe?

3. Why did aircraft manufacturers have a hard time after World War I ended?

4. What background did many barnstorming pilots share?

5. What was Phoebe Fairgrave Omlie's "air marker" system?

6. What did wealthy aviation enthusiasts offer that advanced progress in flight?

7. What technical improvements in aircraft made possible Richard Byrd's polar flights?

8. How did the barnstormers contribute to public awareness of aviation?

Applying Your Learning

9. Why do you think the barnstormers' air shows changed people's ideas about aviation?

LESSON 2

Flight Goes Mainstream

Quick Write

_____

_____

_____

Give some examples of the equipment aboard modern transatlantic aircraft that Charles Lindbergh did not have when he made his famous New York-to-Paris flight.

Learn About...

- **Charles Lindbergh's famous contribution to aviation**
- **the significance of the first transatlantic flight**
- **other significant contributions that helped flight become mainstream**

Charles A. Lindbergh was one of many young men and women learning to fly in 1922.

He toured as a wing walker and parachutist in a barnstorming act, and then a pilot. He joined the Army in 1924 and graduated first in his flying class in 1925, but did not receive a regular commission. He joined the Army Reserve and returned to civilian life. He then spent a year as a pilot for the new airmail service.

In September 1926 he decided to try to fly across the Atlantic. He had his eye on the Orteig prize—$25,000 for the first pilot to fly solo nonstop from New York City to Paris, France.

Lindbergh knew that other pilots were after the same prize, so he moved fast. He had $2,000 of his own savings, plus $13,000 he'd collected from businessmen in St. Louis. He struck a deal with Ryan Aircraft Inc. to build him a plane. He wanted a high-wing monoplane with a single air-cooled 220-horsepower Wright Whirlwind engine.

Just 60 days after the contract was signed, Ryan delivered the aircraft. After a few weeks of test flights, Lindbergh was ready. He named the aircraft the _Spirit of St. Louis_, in honor of the men who had supported him.

On 10 May 1927, he flew nonstop from San Diego to St. Louis. After a brief stop, he flew on to New York City. He made it in 21 hours and 20 minutes of flying time. No one had ever flown across the country so fast. He had set a record before he even took off for Paris. On 20 May, after waiting a while for the weather to clear, he took off from a rain-soaked runway at Roosevelt Field.

Lindbergh had no radio. He had only a compass to guide him as he flew above the stormy skies over the North Atlantic. And he was alone.

But 27 hours after taking off, he saw a promising sight: the green western edge of the British Isles. Circling low, he spotted some boats in the water. He leaned out of his plane and called down to the fishermen: "Which way is Ireland?"

He was on course. And he was ahead of schedule. He crossed the Irish Sea and the English Channel. Finally he entered the French skies.

He touched down 21 May 1927 at Le Bourget Airport outside Paris. He'd flown 3,600 miles in 33½ hours. He won the Orteig prize for the first pilot to fly solo nonstop from New York to Paris.

Vocabulary

- **milestone**
- **apprentice**
- **transcontinental**
- **autogiro**
- **circuit**
- **equator**
- **blind flight**
- **spatial disorientation**
- **mainstream**
- **flight simulator**
- **aerial refueling**

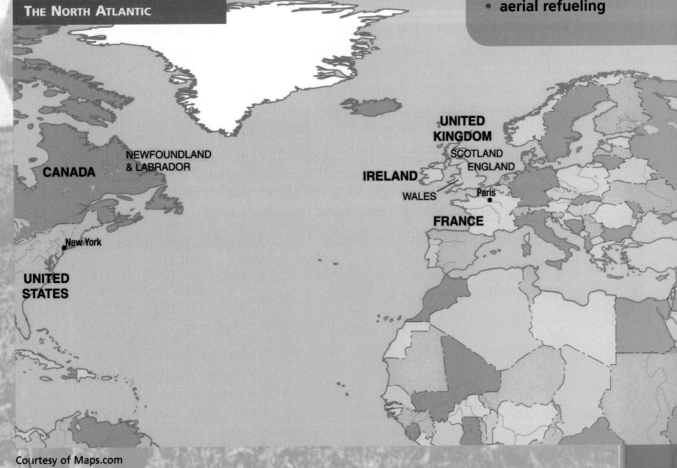

THE NORTH ATLANTIC

CANADA

NEWFOUNDLAND & LABRADOR

UNITED KINGDOM

SCOTLAND

ENGLAND

IRELAND

WALES

Paris

FRANCE

New York

UNITED STATES

Courtesy of Maps.com

Charles Lindbergh's Famous Contribution to Aviation

The minute his plane touched down in Paris, Lindbergh became an international hero. Newspapers and magazines around the world reported on his achievement.

The barnstormers had built public interest in aviation by giving farmers five-minute spins over their cornfields. Lindbergh's transatlantic flight opened people's minds to larger possibilities of air travel.

In July 1927, still piloting the *Spirit of St. Louis*, Lindbergh embarked on a tour of the country. A high-level kind of barnstorming, you might call it. In a little more than three months, he flew 22,350 miles back and forth across the United States. He made speeches in 72 cities. Lindbergh encouraged people to get pilot training. His efforts to promote civil aviation led to the construction of hundreds of airports. He was a true goodwill ambassador for aviation.

In December Lindbergh capped off a historic year with a 3,200-mile all-American tour. He began with a nonstop flight from Washington, D.C., to Mexico City. He then continued southward to a dozen other Latin American countries.

Over the next several years, Lindbergh and his wife, Anne Morrow Lindbergh, worked in civil aviation. They made survey flights to determine the best routes for new airlines.

The Significance of the First Transatlantic Solo Flight

In times past, travelers would often see big stones or slate tablets along the road. These stones marked the distance to the next town. These were called milestones. Today people use the word milestone to describe *an important event, such as a breakthrough in the advancement of knowledge in a field.*

The Wright brothers' flight on 17 December 1903 was a milestone flight. So was Lindbergh's transatlantic solo flight, which opened the door to the daily international air travel we enjoy today. In the early 20th century, the golden age of aviation, such milestone flights came one after another.

Today, jumbo jets fly from New York to Paris in less than one-third the time Lindbergh took. But his flight—which demonstrated the potential of the airplane as a safe, reliable mode of transportation—still stands as one of the greatest individual achievements of all time.

Charles A. Lindbergh

Charles Lindbergh—"Lucky Lindy"—appeared to lead a charmed life in many ways, but his life was not without controversy or tragedy.

He and his wife suffered personal tragedy when their infant son was kidnapped and murdered in 1932. The case was one of the most sensational crimes of the first half of the 20th century. Weary of life in the public eye, the Lindberghs moved to England.

But Europe wasn't all that peaceful in the 1930s. War was brewing. Lindbergh assessed the strength of the air forces of different countries in Europe. As a result, he called for the United States and its Allies to make an agreement with the Germans that would end the war. He thought the Germans were too strong to defeat in battle.

Lindbergh returned to the United States in 1939 and made a survey for the War Department. He gave speeches for the America First Committee, a group that opposed the US entry into World War II. For this, some people branded him pro-Nazi, and he resigned his Army Reserve commission.

But in 1941, when the United States entered World War II, he offered his services to the Army Air Force. Later, he went on several missions as a civilian consultant to the Ford Motor Company and the United Aircraft Corporation. Although officially an "observer," he flew 50 combat missions during a tour of duty in the Pacific.

In 1954, President Eisenhower and the US Senate returned Lindbergh to the Air Force Reserve as a brigadier general. Lindbergh died in 1974.

CHARLES A. LINDBERGH

Courtesy of AP Photo

Anne Morrow Lindbergh—Aviator and Writer

ANNE MORROW LINDBERGH

Courtesy of the National Air and Space Museum,
Smithsonian Institution (SI Neg. No. 80-438)

In 1927 Anne Morrow was in Mexico City when Charles Lindbergh showed up for Christmas dinner at her parents' house.

He was on the goodwill tour of Latin American countries that he made after his historic transatlantic flight. Anne's father, Dwight Morrow, was the US ambassador to Mexico. Lindbergh had stopped to spend the holiday with him and his family.

Anne and Charles fell in love, and in 1929 they married. They formed a remarkable partnership. She learned to fly. The sky was the one place they could be alone together, away from hero-worshipping crowds.

She referred to herself as "Charles's faithful page." Her husband said of her, "No woman exists or has existed who is her equal."

As an aviator, Anne Lindbergh is best known for her 1931 flight to China via the "Great Circle Route." She accompanied her husband, serving as his copilot, navigator, and radio operator. The Lindberghs showed it was possible to reach Asia from the United States by flying over Canada and the North Pole, rather than across an ocean.

She wrote about the trip in a book called *North to the Orient*. Writing was a way for her to establish her own identity and to step out of her husband's shadow. She also wrote *Listen: The Wind* and *Gift from the Sea*.

Amelia Earhart's Record Flights

Amelia Earhart also made two milestone flights across the Atlantic. The story of her achievement sheds light on the state of aviation at the time.

Lindbergh's historic solo crossing did not lead to routine air travel right away. Flying was still dangerous. In 1927, the year Lindbergh achieved fame, 19 men and women died in unsuccessful attempts to fly across the Atlantic.

Amelia Earhart was the first woman to fly across the Atlantic. But she went as a passenger, not a pilot. She'd had some flight training. But Earhart hadn't yet devoted her life to aviation.

In April 1928, however, aviator Wilmer Stultz asked her a favor. He and his navigator, Louis Gordon, wanted Earhart to accompany them as they crossed the Atlantic. They were seeking a prize offered by Pittsburgh heiress Amy Phipps Guest. She wanted to get a woman across the ocean in the air—even if only as a passenger.

The plane Stultz, Gordon, and Earhart flew was the *Friendship*—a Fokker C-2 trimotor with a gold and flame-red paint job. It was a long, cold, dangerous trip. They lost radio contact on the way. They had only a gallon of fuel left when they landed. And they landed in the wrong country—Wales instead of Ireland. But they made it across the Atlantic.

Stultz got a $20,000 award. Gordon got $5,000. Earhart received no money. After all, she had gone along, as she later indicated in the title of her autobiography, "for the fun of it."

But the flight was a great opportunity for her to be an apprentice—*a person who works with a skilled master to learn by practical experience.*

Stultz was one of the best pilots of that day. And Earhart, even though wedged between two gas tanks for most of the trip, didn't miss a thing. She watched every move Stultz made. She saw how he maneuvered through fog and storms. And she got it all down in her notebook.

The press hailed her as "Lady Lindy." Like Lindbergh, Earhart gained fame overnight. And like him, she toured the country.

But not everyone accepted Earhart as a hero. Some critics said she'd gotten a free ride. They said she'd depended on the luck and the skill of her male pilot. She struggled with self-doubt. But finally she proved her courage: she made more milestone flights. She set the altitude record for an autogiro, *an early, helicopter-like aircraft,* reaching 18,415 feet. Then she became the first woman, and second person, to make a transcontinental—*coast-to-coast*—flight in an autogiro.

But Earhart still wasn't content. For her, the milestone that mattered most was a solo crossing of the Atlantic. She wanted to be the first woman to do it.

On 20 May 1932 she took off in her Lockheed Vega from Harbour Grace, Newfoundland. It was the fifth anniversary of Lindbergh's famous flight.

Fifteen hours later, she touched down at a farm outside Londonderry in Northern Ireland. She had covered 2,065 miles, braving storms, heavy clouds, and strong winds. She had coped with iced-up wings, instrument problems, and a broken weld in the exhaust system.

But she made it. No free ride this time. She proved she was a skilled and brave aviator.

Earhart reached another milestone in 1935 as the first pilot to fly from Honolulu to Oakland, California. That trip took 18 hours and 16 minutes.

At that point, she felt the only goal left was a "true" round-the-world flight. Other pilots had flown around the world by that time. But they'd made their circuits in the northern hemisphere, where there is more land. A circuit *is a route that passes through one or more points and then returns to the starting point*. Pilots could make a circuit of the globe by "island hopping"—making periodic stops to refuel. Earhart's goal was to circle the globe as close as possible to the equator— *the imaginary circle that divides Earth into northern and southern halves*.

Earhart took off 2 June 1937. With her was copilot Frederick Noonan. All went well for 40 days. They racked up 22,000 miles. But on the longest leg of the trip, from Lae, New Guinea, to Howland Island in the Pacific, the plane disappeared. President Franklin D. Roosevelt ordered a massive search. It was not successful. On 18 July 1937, the US Navy declared Earhart and Noonan lost at sea.

Flight Paths

AMELIA EARHART

Courtesy of Topham Picturepoint/
The Image Works

Amelia Earhart—Aviation Pioneer

Amelia Earhart (1897–1937) is one of the most outstanding women in aviation. Had she lived longer, she probably would have accomplished even more. Sadly, she disappeared at the peak of her career.

She was born in Kansas. She learned to fly, but didn't have a clear career goal. She was a teacher and social worker in Massachusetts. She thought about becoming a doctor.

But after becoming the first woman to fly across the Atlantic, she knew what she wanted to do with her life: she wanted to be an aviator.

Earhart encouraged other women pilots. Like some other early aviators, she was also a writer. She published two books and even married her publisher, George Putnam, in 1931. She continued her career under her own name, however.

Earhart disappeared two-thirds of the way into an around-the-world flight in 1937. How she met her fate in the South Pacific remains a mystery.

Other Significant Contributions That Helped Flight Become Mainstream

1st Lt James Harold Doolittle made another milestone flight on 24 September 1929. His milestone was the first successful blind flight—*the act of taking off and landing relying solely on instruments inside the cockpit for guidance.* He took off, flew five miles, and landed safely—all without looking out of the plane. Because of his work, manufacturers started equipping planes with instruments and two-way radios.

Doolittle's blind flight built on the work of Sgt William C. Ocker, the third enlisted man in the Army to become a pilot.

Ocker worked with Capt David A. Myers, the flight surgeon at Crissy Field, California, to solve the problem of spatial disorientation. Spatial disorientation *is a condition in which a person's sense of direction does not agree with reality.* A pilot who is spatially disoriented literally doesn't know which end is up.

In the early days, even experienced pilots could get confused when visibility was poor. They sometimes thought they were banking left when they were banking right. This happened because they'd lost sight of the horizon, which they used to orient themselves.

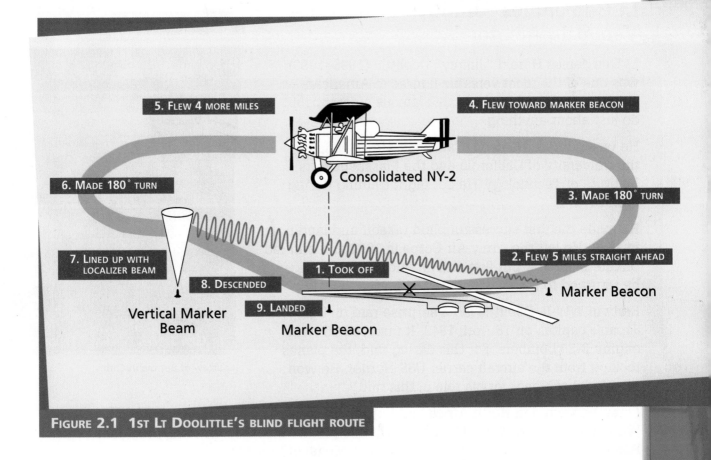

FIGURE 2.1 1ST LT DOOLITTLE'S BLIND FLIGHT ROUTE

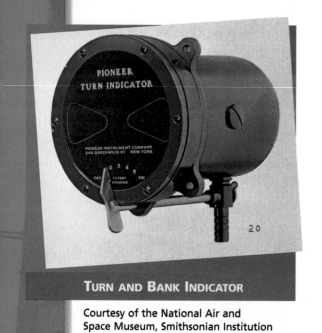

TURN AND BANK INDICATOR

Courtesy of the National Air and
Space Museum, Smithsonian Institution
(SI Neg. No. 83-7649)

This problem had to be solved if aviation was to be part of the mainstream—*the current of most people's life and activities*. If airlines were to be a part of the nation's commerce and transportation, planes needed to be able to fly at night. They also had to be able to fly during fog and storms as well as in good weather.

Ocker knew about spatial disorientation. He'd struggled with it himself. For years he had used a turn-and-bank indicator, a device created by his friend Elmer Sperry, to help him stay oriented while flying. But the device never seemed to work in bad weather. At such times, it often gave a reading at odds with what Ocker's instincts were telling him.

Flight Paths

Lt Gen James "Jimmy" Doolittle— Versatile Aviator

Lt Gen James Harold "Jimmy" Doolittle (1896–1993) was one of the most versatile figures in American aviation. Despite his name, this famous aviator could do just about anything.

He was born in Alameda, California. He attended the University of California and the Massachusetts Institute of Technology. He got flight training during World War I.

He made the first successful blind takeoff and landing in 1929. He left the Army Air Corps in 1930 and entered private business, But first and foremost a Soldier, he returned to the Air Corps in 1940.

Early in WW II, Doolittle led a surprise raid on Tokyo, Japan's capital, on 18 April 1942. It involved 16 twin-engine B-25 bombers. For this daring raid, the planes took off from the aircraft carrier USS *Hornet*. He won the Medal of Honor for his role in this raid.

LT GEN JAMES "JIMMY" DOOLITTLE

Courtesy of Bettmann/Corbis

Later, he served in North Africa and Europe. He became a lieutenant general in 1944. When the war ended in 1945, he returned to private business. In 1989, President Ronald Reagan awarded him a Presidential Medal of Freedom.

Ocker's "lightbulb" moment came when he realized that the times when the indicator seemed wrong were exactly the times when he needed it most. When he was disoriented, the indicator was correct.

Ocker failed an orientation test when Capt Myers spun him around in a special chair designed to simulate the conditions that gave pilots so much trouble. But Ocker passed when he brought along and used his trusty turn-and-bank indicator.

Many early pilots took pride in their ability to "fly by the seat of their pants." But Ocker and Myers realized that pilots of the future would have to rely more heavily on instruments. Their work led to Doolittle's successful blind flight.

Ocker developed a number of devices that became critical to pilot training and aviation in general. These inventions are forerunners of today's flight simulators. A flight simulator *is a training device that simulates, or imitates, the experience and sensation of flight.* It lets pilots train without having to go up in the air.

Flight Paths

Katherine Sui Fun Cheung— First Asian-American Woman Pilot

Katherine Sui Fung Cheung (1904–2003) left China at 17 to study music in Los Angeles. At age 26, she started flying lessons. She made her first solo flight after only 12 1/2 hours of instruction. She became the first licensed Asian-American woman pilot in the United States. A member of the exclusive "Ninety-Nines" club—an organization of 99 women pilots, such as Amelia Earhart and Phoebe Fairgrave Omlie, who worked to further women's interest in aviation and aviation in general—she took part in air shows and air races. (The Ninety-Nines organization continues today.) Cheung amazed crowds with her rolls and loops in the air.

KATHERINE SUI FUN CHEUNG

Courtesy of the Los Angeles Public Library

Cheung planned to go to China to train pilots there. But a tragic crash that killed her cousin ended those plans. At 38, she promised her dying father she would give up flying. She kept her promise and in later years went into the flower business.

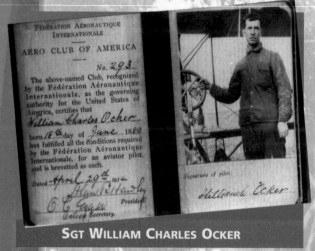

SGT WILLIAM CHARLES OCKER

Courtesy of the Airmen Memorial Museum

Sgt William C. Ocker— A Flying Hero Moves Up Through the Ranks

When William Charles Ocker enlisted in the US Army in 1898, most Soldiers were still on the ground. Ocker helped give the Army wings.

He became an excellent pilot. When he took the test for his license, the examiner wrote, "It was the most remarkable series of landings ever made by a student flying for a pilot's license. Ocker's mastery of the machine was superb. . . ." He got his license on 29 April 1914.

But his great achievements were in laying the foundation for blind flight and developing testing and training equipment.

Ocker was born in Philadelphia. He left school at the end of seventh grade. He enlisted during the Spanish-American War. He saw action in that conflict and the Philippine Insurrection as well.

On guard duty in Fort Myer, Virginia, in 1909, he'd seen the Wright brothers demonstrate their aircraft. From then on, he knew he wanted to fly. He became the third enlisted man allowed to serve as a pilot.

Later Ocker became an officer. Among his many aviation inventions was the 1938 development of a new type of airplane propeller that made less noise and vibrated less. This meant less stress on the propeller blades.

His ambition, he often said, was to be not the best pilot, but the oldest pilot. He was indeed one of the oldest pilots in time of service in the Army Air Corps. He retired as a colonel and died in 1942 at age 62. His contributions to aviation safety helped countless aviators live longer, saving many lives during World War II. In 1955, the Air Force presented the Legion of Merit medal to his widow, Doris Ocker.

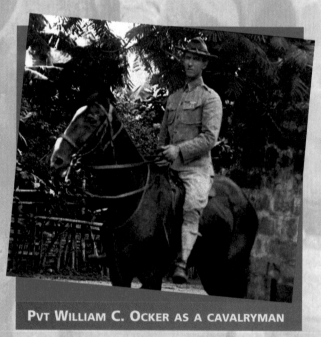

PVT WILLIAM C. OCKER AS A CAVALRYMAN

Courtesy of the Airmen Memorial Museum

The First Air Refueling of the *Question Mark*

Another hurdle to mainstream aviation was providing enough fuel for long-distance runs. Pilots needed a system for aerial refueling, *which is taking on more fuel in flight.* Two Army lieutenants, 1st Lt Lowell H. Smith and 1st Lt J. P. Richter, achieved this in 1923. They tanked up by running a 50-foot hose from a supply aircraft to a plane making a long trip. They could pump about 50 gallons of fuel each time. They were able to stay aloft for 37 hours and 15 minutes.

On New Year's Day 1929, Maj Carl Spaatz took off in the *Question Mark*, a Fokker C-2 Trimotor. By the time he landed—almost a week later—he had set an endurance record. Spaatz and his crew—Capt Ira C. Eaker, 1st Lt Harry A. Halverson, 2d Lt Elwood R. Quesada, and SSgt Roy W. Hooe—stayed up 150 hours, 40 minutes, and 15 seconds. They had refueled 37 times.

Two Douglas C-1 aircraft, each with a three-man crew, provided the fuel for the *Question Mark*. Capt Ross G. Hoyt, 1st Lt Auby C. Strickland, and 2d Lt Irvin A. Woodring served as one tanker crew. Members of the second crew were 1st Lt Odas Moon, 2d Lt Andrew F. Solter, and 2d Lt Joseph G. Hopkins. Their feat demonstrated the practicality of in-flight refueling.

REFUELING THE QUESTION MARK
Courtesy of the US Air Force

The Birth of Airmail and Airlines

Aerial refueling was important for the Army. But other, everyday things brought aviation into the mainstream for most Americans. Two of the most important were airmail service and commercial airlines.

The Post Office Department started the first airmail service on 15 May 1918. It used a few planes borrowed from the Army. Regular airmail service started 1 July 1924.

Airmail not only sped up mail delivery—it contributed a great deal to the development of the airlines. The Airmail Act of 1925 allowed private companies to carry mail under contract with the US government. This was a big boost for the aviation industry. Government contracts ensured a steady flow of money to the new airlines. In fact, the money from carrying the mail was so good for the airlines that their planes often had hardly any room for people. Most mail planes carried only two or three passengers.

That changed with the passage of the Air Commerce Act on 20 May 1926. The act provided for the first federal safety regulation of aviation for pilots and aircraft. It also sparked the growth of commercial airlines.

In 1934 Congress passed another airmail act. It separated the air-transport companies from the aircraft manufacturers. It also set the stage for a well-organized air-transport system using government payments for carrying mail by air.

CHECKPOINTS

Lesson 2 Review

Using complete sentences, answer the following questions on a sheet of paper.

1. Why did Lindbergh want his plane built quickly?

2. Where did Lindbergh get the money for the plane?

3. What record did Lindbergh set before he took off for Paris?

4. What record did Lindbergh set when he landed in Paris?

5. What milestone did Earhart achieve on the five-year anniversary of Lindbergh's record?

6. Why was blind flight important to aviation?

7. Why does a pilot want to see the horizon?

8. Who was the first licensed Asian-American woman pilot in the United States?

9. What was the importance of refueling the *Question Mark* in the air?

10. Why was airmail service important?

Applying Your Learning

11. What were the roles of heroes such as Lindbergh and Earhart in developing aviation? What was the role of the US government?

Commercial Flight, Airmail, and Helicopters

Unlike most other pioneers of flight, William E. Boeing came to aviation as a businessman. He was the son of a wealthy Detroit businessman. He left Yale University in 1903 to start a timber business in the Pacific Northwest.

A few years later, Boeing saw a public exhibition of flying in Los Angeles. He became fascinated with aviation. He made his first flight in 1914. He decided he wanted to build his own planes. He thought he could build better planes than those in use at the time.

He hired his friend George Conrad Westervelt, an engineer, to design and build a twin-float seaplane. A twin-float *is an airplane with floats for landing on or taking off from a body of water.*

It was a success. Boeing launched the Boeing Airplane Company, later called Boeing Air Transport. In 1917 he sold the US Navy 50 of his Model C seaplanes for use in World War I.

Like other airplane builders, Boeing lost his government contracts at the end of the war. He kept his business going by making furniture, cabinets, and boats.

But Boeing didn't lose interest in aircraft. Soon he built the Boeing-1, or B-1, a commercial biplane. On 3 March 1919, he and his pilot, Eddie Hubbard, opened the first international airmail route. They flew between Seattle, Washington, and Vancouver, British Columbia. A one-way trip was 140 miles.

Soon Boeing won the contract for the San Francisco–Chicago airmail route. He served the route with a Boeing 40-A mail plane. Air, not water, kept the plane's engine cool. This made the plane hundreds of pounds lighter. Boeing 40-As, he said, were designed to carry mail and people, not radiators.

In 1934 Congress made it illegal for airmail carriers and aircraft builders to be part of the same company. Boeing had to break up his firm. But his reputation was assured. In that same year, he won the Guggenheim Medal for his contributions to aviation.

Vocabulary

- **twin-float**
- **subsidy**
- **incentive**
- **stressed skin**
- **retractable**
- **cowling**
- **scheduled airlines**
- **amendment**
- **tail rotor**
- **outrigger**
- **tethered flight**

William E. Boeing was a businessman who became fascinated with aviation.

WILLIAM E. BOEING

Courtesy of Getty Images

Early Developments in Commercial Flight

As you read in Lesson 1 of this chapter, many aircraft companies fell on hard times when the government canceled their contracts at the end of World War I. William Boeing owned one such company. Despite the setback, he saw a future in aviation. He kept his company going. As a result, Boeing was in a good position when the government began to support aviation again.

This time, opportunity came in the form of the new airmail service. In 1925 the government decided to let private firms carry the mail. New companies sprang up to do the job. To help these firms, the government offered subsidies. A subsidy *is government money paid to a person or company that serves the public.*

After a few years, the rules changed again. The government began to support passenger service, too. New rules gave airlines an incentive—*a motivating reward*—to fly larger planes with more passenger space. The rules also encouraged the use of planes that could fly in all types of weather.

Soon Boeing Air Transport won a contract to build a two-engine aircraft for United Airlines. In 1933 Boeing rolled out the Boeing 247.

The Boeing 247 was the first all-metal airliner. Its wings were placed low on the plane's body. It had a stressed skin—*an outer covering that can stand up to the push-and-pull forces of flight.* Its landing gear was retractable—*it folded into the aircraft.* Each of its two engines had a cowling—*a covering to protect and streamline the engine.*

The B-247 could carry 10 passengers and 400 pounds of mail. It could cruise at 189 miles an hour (mph). "Same-day" service between New York and San Francisco was now possible. Modern airline service had begun.

THE BOEING 247

With the Boeing 247, same-day service from San Francisco to New York became possible.

Courtesy of the EAA/Jim Koepnick

THE C-47

The government ordered 10,000 of these planes during World War II.

Courtesy of the EAA/Jim Koepnick

The First Airlines

By the late 1920s, Charles Lindbergh's vision of civil aviation was taking form. Within a year of his 1927 flight, the number of licensed pilots in the country grew from 1,500 to 11,000. The number of licensed planes also rose sharply. Building and flying airplanes became the country's most profitable business. By 1929 there were 44 scheduled airlines. These are *airlines that have flights that depart and arrive at set times*.

Competing for passengers, the airlines worked with aircraft companies to build them better and better planes. Shortly after United introduced the B-247, a second airline got into the act.

Transcontinental and Western Airlines (TWA) signed a contract with Douglas Aircraft of Santa Monica, California, to build an even bigger plane.

The result was the Douglas Commercial-2, or DC-2. It came out in May 1934. It cruised at 192 mph. It could carry 14 passengers and several thousand pounds of mail up to 900 miles.

Meanwhile, a third airline—American Airways—was flying foreign-built aircraft. American was also losing money. It asked Douglas Aircraft to improve on the DC-2. The result was the DC-3. The DC-3 could carry 24 passengers, or 5,000 pounds of cargo, a distance of 1,200 miles.

American Airways rolled out the first DC-3 in June 1936. It became one of the most successful planes ever built. By 1938 it was carrying 95 percent of all commercial traffic in the United States. A year later, 90 percent of all commercial traffic worldwide was flying the DC-3.

Later, during World War II, Douglas developed a military version of the DC-3—the C-47. Douglas built some 10,000 of these planes for the Army Air Force. The C-47's official name was the *Skytrain*. But pilots called it the *Gooney Bird*. ("Gooney bird" is another name for albatross, a large sea bird. Albatrosses are superb fliers. They can fly long distances without tiring.) Some C-47s are still in use.

THE PAN AMERICAN CLIPPERS

The Pan American Clippers were named for the swift sailing ships of the 19th century. Their crews wore naval-style uniforms and bore naval ranks.

Courtesy of the National Air and Space Museum, Smithsonian Institute (SI Neg. No. 89-1216)

Another important advance was Pan American Airways' seaplane Clippers. The Clippers came to represent a way of traveling in style and luxury. But they also marked a major step forward in aircraft development.

Pan Am started out in 1927. It flew the first airmail route between Key West, Florida, and Havana, Cuba. In time the route extended down the Atlantic coast of South America.

Pan Am pilots soon found themselves flying over water more often than over land. And in remote areas, seaplane bases were easier to build than land airports for ordinary airplanes.

So Pan Am decided that the kind of "bigger and better" plane it needed was an advanced seaplane. The company hired Igor Sikorsky. (He later won fame for helicopter design, as you'll soon read.) Sikorsky designed a four-engine "flying boat"—the S-40. It could fly 125 mph and carry 40 passengers. Pan Am used the S-42, a successor to the S-40, for survey flights to find routes across the Pacific.

Other airplane makers got into the flying-boat business. In 1934 Pan Am received a larger boat, the Martin 130, built by the Glenn L. Martin Company. The airline called it the *China Clipper*. On 29 November 1935, the *China Clipper* completed the first airmail flight between San Francisco and Manila, in the Philippines. By 1937 the route went all the way to Hong Kong. By that time, Pan Am was flying a round trip across the Pacific every seven days.

Regular passenger and airmail service across the Atlantic began on 20 May 1939 with the Boeing 314. Many considered this the "ultimate flying boat."

There were only about two dozen seaplane Clippers. But they defined an era in air travel. They had an excellent safety record during their six and a half years in service. Pan Am used the name "Clipper" for other aircraft until the company went out of business in 1991. The name of its famous aircraft lives on because some other companies have adopted it.

The era of passenger-carrying seaplanes was short. During World War II, aircraft design made great strides. Four-engine land planes improved. New runways appeared around the world. As a result, seaplanes lost their competitive edge. They gave way to new types of land-based aircraft.

The Use of the Airplane in Delivering Mail

As you have read, the need to deliver mail by air led to many changes in aviation. During the 1920s and 1930s, Congress passed several laws on civil aviation. The first was the Air Mail Act of 1925, also known as the Kelly Act. It let private airlines carry mail. The Air Commerce Act of 1926 provided the first safety regulation for pilots and aircraft.

In 1930 Postmaster General Arthur F. Brown got Congress to pass the McNary-Watres Act. This act was an amendment—*a revision or change*—to the Air Mail Act of 1925.The McNary-Watres Act led to United's contract to build the B-247 and other aircraft. Such contracts played an important role in air service across the seas as well. The seaplanes Pan Am needed to fly the mail over water led to regular passenger service across the Atlantic and Pacific oceans. The act also encouraged airlines to fly bigger planes that held more passengers.

Lighting the Way for the Mail

The first airmail pilots in the 1920s had a tough job. They flew in rebuilt warplanes with open cockpits. They flew through rain, fog, and high winds. They had no radios, weather stations, instruments, or beacons.

One of the most important early airmail routes went between New York and Chicago. These planes flew over the Allegheny Mountains. The route was so dangerous that pilots called it "the graveyard run."

What's more, the airmail service wasn't holding its own against the railroads. The trains, after all, rolled on day and night. To meet the competition, postal authorities introduced night flights.

At first, Post Office staff, farmers, and other people built bonfires to light the pilots' way at night. Then came electric beacons. These were powerful rotating lights mounted on 50-foot towers. Towers were built every 10 to 15 miles along a cross-country route. Emergency landing fields were built about every 30 miles. Lights for landing and navigation were soon added to planes as another safety feature.

The government launched regular airmail service on 1 July 1924. At that time, the United States had the world's first regular night service on a lighted airway. The route ran between New York City and the West Coast. From this "trunk" airway, branch lines grew all over the country. This was a major advance in aviation.

BONFIRES AND ELECTRIC BEACONS
During the early days of airmail service, bonfires lit the way for pilots. Electric beacons soon replaced the bonfires.

The Air Mail Act of 1934 made air carriers responsible to three federal agencies. The Post Office Department awarded airmail contracts and set routes. The Bureau of Air Commerce, within the Department of Commerce, was in charge of operating airways. It also regulated the licensing of planes and pilots. And the Interstate Commerce Commission's Bureau of Air Mail set the rates for payments to mail carriers.

Through the Air Mail Act of 1938, Congress created the Civil Aeronautics Authority. This law moved civil aviation responsibility from the Commerce Department. It increased government control over the airline industry. It limited competition between airlines and protected the routes of established carriers.

The Development and Use of Helicopters

The Wright brothers get most of the credit for developing the airplane. Developing the helicopter was another story. It involved several inventors in different countries and even in different centuries.

As you read earlier, Leonardo da Vinci (1452–1519) designed a rotary flying machine. In 1842 W. H. Phillips built a model of a steam-powered helicopter. But many improvements were needed to create a practical helicopter.

Rotary flight is different from fixed-wing flight. The early inventors didn't understand the forces facing the helicopter. They didn't know how to design devices to address these forces.

Some inventors who experimented with helicopters early in the 20th century gave up on them for a time. But 9 January 1923 marked another milestone flight. On that day, a Spanish Army pilot made the first successful flight in an autogiro. Juan de la Cierva of Spain built this aircraft. It looked like an airplane but had an overhead rotor instead of wings. An engine and a propeller made the autogiro move.

But Cierva's machine had serious drawbacks. For example, it couldn't move in all directions. So during the 1930s, Cierva and other designers in Spain, France, and Germany continued to experiment.

Frenchman Louis Bréguet was one experimenter. He'd turned away from helicopters, despite some early success. But by the early 1930s, he was thinking about them again. He established the Syndicate for Gyroplane Studies and hired a young engineer named René Dorand.

Bréguet didn't want to get people's hopes up too soon. He named his new aircraft the *Gyroplane-Laboratoire*. Using the French word for *laboratory*, he thought, would let people understand that the helicopter was experimental. His was another attempt to solve the problems of stability and control.

The Problem of Control

The early experimenters struggled with how to control the helicopter in flight. As you read in Chapter 2, Lesson 2, their challenge was to find a way to overcome the torque of the rotor blade.

A helicopter gets lift from its rotor's spinning blades. But when the rotor turns, the rest of the machine tends to spin in the opposite direction.

One way to overcome torque is to have two rotors that move in opposite directions. Another way is to use a tail rotor, *a small propeller at the end of a long tail boom.* The small propeller's thrust offsets the main rotor's torque.

The first helicopter a pilot could completely control was the Focke-Achgelis (FA-61). A German, Dr. Heinrich Focke, built it in 1937. Its two rotors were mounted side by side on outriggers from the fuselage. An outrigger *is a frame extending laterally beyond the main structure of an aircraft.* It stabilizes the structure.

The world's first female helicopter pilot, Hanna Reitsch, demonstrated the FA-61 in 1938. She flew it inside a stadium in Berlin, Germany. She was able to hover and make 360-degree turns. She could fly backward, forward, and sideways.

The first practical helicopter, however, was Igor Sikorsky's VS-300. It was equipped with one main rotor and a tail rotor. It made its first vertical takeoffs and landings in September 1939. The helicopter could carry a useful load and perform work. The pilot could control it well. The early experiments were tethered flight, *or flights in which the aircraft was tied to the ground by cables.* The helicopter's first free flight was 13 May 1940. Its top speed was 50 mph. It weighed 1,150 pounds.

Sikorsky worked hard to overcome problems with vibration and control. At first, his helicopter flew "like a bucking bronco," according to an Army project officer. Nevertheless, all later Sikorsky helicopters have been refinements of the VS-300. From this small aircraft, the helicopter has developed into the workhorse of the skies.

THE VS-300, Sikorsky's first successful helicopter
Courtesy of Bettmann/Corbis

Military and Civilian Use of Helicopters

The military first used helicopters in World War II. But the helicopter came into its own during the Korean and Vietnam Wars. In both wars the US military used it to carry the wounded and rescue downed pilots. It was well suited for the jungle warfare of Vietnam. There, the military used helicopters to place ground troops in battle areas and to outmaneuver enemy ground forces. Since that time, helicopters have been an important part of US military tactics.

In civilian life, helicopters are crucial to search-and-rescue work. The US Coast Guard relies on them to save fishermen and sailors in distress at sea. In the floods after Hurricane Katrina that hit the Gulf Coast in 2005, the Coast Guard and other agencies used helicopters to rescue more than 30,000 people.

Helicopters are used for medical transport, civilian police work, and to broadcast news and highway-traffic reports. Helicopters also play important roles in other sectors, such as the construction, timber, and offshore oil industries.

Flight Paths

Igor Sikorsky and the First Practical Helicopter

A Russian who moved to France before settling in the United States, Igor Sikorsky (1889–1972) is best known as the man who developed the first practical helicopter. But that wasn't Sikorsky's first claim to fame. He'd already made two other contributions to aviation.

A mosquito—yes, an insect—led to Sikorsky's first breakthrough. While a young flyer in the Russian Army, he produced a plane—the S-6A—that won the highest award in the Moscow air show. But on a later flight, a mosquito got caught in the fuel line, causing the engine to fail. Sikorsky had to make an emergency landing. That experience gave him the idea for an aircraft with more than one engine. This led him to build and fly the first successful four-engine aircraft, *Le Grand* (See Chapter 2, Lesson 2).

Sikorsky left his native country in 1918, after the Russian Revolution. In France, he won a contract to build a bomber for the Allies. But World War I ended soon after that. His bomber was not needed.

Sikorsky arrived in New York City in 1919. Unable to find a job in aviation, he lectured for a while. Then some friends and students who knew of his work in aviation pooled their funds to launch him in business. He formed the Sikorsky Aero Engineering Corporation.

Within a few years Sikorsky made his second major achievement. As you read earlier, he designed a flying boat for mail service.

But Sikorsky still cherished a lifelong dream: to build a helicopter. When Igor was a child in Kiev, Ukraine (then part of Russia), his mother told him about Leonardo da Vinci's helicopter designs. He became fascinated by the idea of rotary-wing flight. People told him it was an impossible dream. Some of his own staff called it "Igor's nightmare."

In 1940 he achieved his dream. Today, the name Sikorsky stands for excellence in helicopters.

CHECKPOINTS

Lesson 3 Review

Using complete sentences, answer the following questions on a sheet of paper.

1. What development saved hundreds of pounds on Boeing's 40-A mail plane?

2. How successful was the DC-3?

3. Why did Pan American Airways need a new type of advanced seaplane?

4. What brought the era of the Pan Am Clippers to an end?

5. Why did manufacturers start building planes with more passenger space after 1930?

6. In the early days of airmail service, what prompted postal authorities to add night flights?

7. How did Igor Sikorsky solve the problem of control with his helicopter?

8. How are helicopters used today in civilian life?

9. A mosquito led to which important development in aviation?

Applying Your Learning

10. Describe how competition among airlines and among manufacturers led to new developments in aircraft.

UNIT THREE

Devel

B-52G Stratofortress bomber

Courtesy of the US Air Force

oping FLIGHT

Unit Chapters

CHAPTER 4

The Early Air Force

CHAPTER 5

Commercial Flight

CHAPTER 6

The Modern Air Force

CHAPTER 4

C-47 Skytrain transport plane

Courtesy of the US Air Force

The Early Air Force

Chapter Outline

LESSON 1

The Army Air Corps

LESSON 2

Air Power in World War II

"Allied air power was decisive in the war in Western Europe.... In the air, its victory was complete. At sea, its contribution, combined with naval power, brought an end to the enemy's greatest naval threat—the U-boat; on land, it helped turn the tide overwhelmingly in favor of Allied ground forces."

The United States Strategic Bombing Survey, 1945

The Army Air Corps

Quick Write

_____
_____
_____

The Army, Navy, and Congress were reluctant to create an equal branch of the military dedicated to air power. Why did Brig Gen Billy Mitchell want to do so and how did he draw attention to air power's potential?

Learn About...

- the predecessors of the US Air Force
- how the Army Air Corps developed
- the Air Force's path toward independence

After World War I Brig Gen William "Billy" Mitchell wanted to find a way to get military leaders and the US Congress to pay attention to his calls for an independent air service. He'd seen how air power helped turn the war in the Allies' favor. This included the major role of aircraft in the Battle of Saint Mihiel in 1918.

Air power was emerging as an offensive weapon and a powerful defensive tool. Mitchell thought the Army Air Service ought to be under its own command. But the Army, Navy, and Congress saw things differently. To them, air power was auxiliary—_functioning as a branch of another military organization_—to the Army's ground forces. In their view, aircraft played secondary roles. For example, they thought the role of aircraft was to provide reconnaissance and ground-troop support, not to lead attacks.

THE BOMBING OF THE _OSTFRIESLAND_
Brig Gen Billy Mitchell's pilots bomb the German battleship _Ostfriesland_.
Courtesy of the US Air Force

In 1920 Mitchell proposed a test to challenge prevailing notions about the country's defense. He suggested that his Airmen sink ships. (At that time the Navy's battle fleet was America's first line of defense.) The test would show how planes could defend the country against an attack from the sea.

In 1921 the Navy reluctantly agreed to the test. It provided several German vessels captured during World War I. One of the ships was the "unsinkable" battleship *Ostfriesland*.

On 13 July Mitchell's pilots sank a destroyer off the coast of Virginia with light bombs. On 18 July they hit a cruiser. It went under, too. They tried to sink the *Ostfriesland*, but even 1,000-pound bombs couldn't do the job. So on 21 July the pilots dropped 2,000-pound bombs. The "unsinkable" battleship rolled over and sank in about 20 minutes. But the Army and Congress still weren't convinced. They didn't believe an independent air service could help the armed forces. Navy admirals disagreed, however. They immediately ordered that aircraft carriers be built. The United States had its first aircraft carrier within eight months of the *Ostfriesland*'s sinking.

Vocabulary

- **auxiliary**
- **grades**
- **ordnance**
- **incompetent**
- **treasonable**
- **insubordination**
- **bombsight**
- **overhaul**
- **corps**
- **pursuit aircraft**
- **annex**
- **logistics**
- **autonomy**

THE SINKING OF THE *OSTFRIESLAND*
Using 2,000-pound bombs, Mitchell's pilots sank the *Ostfriesland* on 21 July 1921.
Courtesy of the Library of Congress

The Predecessors of the US Air Force

Most changes come in small steps. So air power in the United States went through a number of makeovers. The major changes occurred between 1907 and 1947, a stormy period that saw the flowering of aviation and two world wars.

Even before the US government bought the *Wright Flyer* in 1909, it had set up the Aeronautical Division within the US Army Signal Corps. The Signal Corps started with balloons, and then added planes. The division existed from 1907 to 1914. Many consider its creation the birth of the US Air Force.

Next came the Aviation Section, US Army Signal Corps (1914 to 1918). It was up and running during World War I. The number of pilots grew to 10,000 by the end of the war. These pilots took on many roles. They went on reconnaissance missions after the United States joined the war in 1917. By 1918 they were taking part in dogfights and bombing runs.

The Creation of the Army Air Service

One of the first major steps toward an independent air service took place around the time the Great War ended. President Woodrow Wilson used his executive powers to create the Army Air Service in May 1918. Under this order, the Air Service became a combat arm of the Army. The Army Air Service existed between 1918 and 1926. Although it was still part of the Army, it was a step closer to separate-but-equal footing with the Army and Navy.

With the Army Reorganization Act of 1920, Congress wrote the change into law. The Army Air Service was no longer auxiliary to the ground forces. It was its own branch within the Army. This change gave the Air Service more control. But it still answered to the Army.

The Different Stages of the US Air Arm From 1907 to Present

Aeronautical Division, US Army Signal Corps	**1 August 1907 – 18 July 1914**
Aviation Section, US Army Signal Corps	**18 July 1914 – 20 May 1918**
Division of Military Aeronautics, Secretary of War	**20 May 1918 – 24 May 1918**
Army Air Service	**24 May 1918 – 2 July 1926**
Army Air Corps • **General HQ Air Force**	**2 July 1926 – 17 September 1947** **1 March 1935 – 1 March 1939**
US Army Air Forces	**20 June 1941 – 17 September 1947**
US Air Force	**18 September 1947 – Present**

PRESIDENT WOODROW WILSON

President Woodrow Wilson used his executive powers to create the Army Air Service in 1918.

Courtesy of The Granger Collection, New York

The National Defense Act, also passed in 1920, established the number of men and ranks in the Air Service. The service could have 16,000 enlisted men. But Congress had cut back on defense spending after World War I. So the Air Service didn't have enough funds to enlist 16,000 men. Today's Air Force still uses the grades—*ranks*— authorized under that act.

The Creation of the Army Air Corps

Funds were in short supply after the war. Congress no longer emphasized national defense. It was more concerned with needs at home. As a result, the Army was tightfisted in how much it passed along to its air arm. This only increased the Air Service's desire for separate-but-equal footing with the Army and Navy.

Brig Gen Billy Mitchell believed that air power would be crucial to winning any future wars or to defending American soil. He believed it would be easier to direct air power if the Air Service were equal in stature to the Army and Navy. An independent service would also get a larger share of government money.

The US Department of War disagreed with Mitchell. It believed in a three-pronged national defense based on:

1. the Navy's battle fleet
2. the Navy's coastal defenses
3. the Army's coastal defenses.

But based on what he'd seen in Europe during 1917 and 1918, Mitchell believed air power was a necessary tool. First, casualties from trench warfare would decrease if bombers could cross enemy lines to hit supply routes and factories. Soldiers would no longer be stuck in one place. They would no longer die in waves of assaults. Second, as the Battle of Saint Mihiel showed, a mass of aircraft could overwhelm the enemy and bring the battle to him. Finally, planes could now carry heavier loads and fly greater distances. Before long, the Atlantic and Pacific oceans would no longer guarantee safety for the US coasts. Mitchell thought US air power could thwart an enemy arriving by sea better than sea power could. So he launched a major public relations campaign for an air force independent of the Army and Navy.

CAPSULES

Enlisted Men After the Great War

At the end of World War I, the Army Air Service had 195,000 enlisted men. Of these, 74,000 were overseas. What would these men do once the fighting stopped?

The Army worked with the government to find jobs for some. In other cases, commanders wrote letters of recommendation for their enlistees. For instance, they would do this for their mechanics. They kept other Airmen in the service, even after discharge, until they could find work.

Demonstrations to Gain Independence

Mitchell's biggest, splashiest campaign maneuver was the sinking of the German battleship *Ostfriesland* in 1921. Although that event convinced the Navy to build aircraft carriers, not much else happened after that. So Mitchell tried new tactics. His goal was to draw the public's attention to the wonders of flight. If he got the public eye, he thought, people might ask their congressmen to support air power.

In 1922 Mitchell arranged for two pilots, 1st Lt Oakley Kelly and 1st Lt John Macready to fly nonstop across the United States. Their first two tries didn't succeed. They finally made it on the third try, in 1923. Kelly and Macready flew from New York to San Diego in 26 hours and 50 minutes. The flight was 2,520 miles long. Their Fokker T-2 aircraft had a 400-horsepower engine. They took advantage of a tailwind during the flight. Plus, they hoped having little fuel left by the end of their voyage, and therefore less weight, would help them cross the Rocky Mountains.

In 1924 Mitchell tried an even bigger stunt—an around-the-world trip. He started out with four airplanes. Two of them—the *Chicago* and the *New Orleans*—finished the 26,345-mile journey. The trip took 175 days. The pilots visited cities around the globe, starting and finishing in Seattle, Washington. Also in 1924, Mitchell sent 1st Lt Russell Maughan in a Curtiss PW-8 from New York to San Francisco. To people's astonishment, Maughan finished the trip in a single day. This showed that if the country were attacked, airplanes could fly in one day to defend the area under attack.

AROUND THE WORLD

One of the Douglas Aircraft that completed Mitchell's around-the-world trip in 1924

Courtesy of E. Bacon/Topical Press Agency/Getty Images

THE USS *NEW JERSEY*

The USS *New Jersey* after Sgt Ulysses Nero's hit on 5 September 1923

Courtesy of the Airmen Memorial Museum

In 1923 Mitchell conducted a second series of bombing tests against ships. This time, the Navy let him use two World War I battleships, the USS *New Jersey* and the USS *Virginia*. Ten of Mitchell's 11 bombers missed the *New Jersey*. But one pilot, Sgt Ulysses S. Nero, had two hits. Mitchell wouldn't let Nero continue, because the pilot hadn't followed instructions. But when the other pilots couldn't sink the ships, Mitchell gave him another chance.

From 6,900 feet in the air at 85 miles per hour, Nero released his first ordnance through the *New Jersey*'s smokestack. Ordnance *is military supply such as weapons, ammunition, combat vehicles, and equipment.* The ship sank. Next he dropped a bomb on the deck of the *Virginia*. It, too, sank to the bottom of North Carolina's coastal waters.

Mitchell pushed in other ways for an independent air force. He gave talks. He wrote articles. Meanwhile, the US House of Representatives and the Army General Staff formed committees to study possible directions for the Army Air Service.

In 1925 President Calvin Coolidge instructed a group of experts to find the "best means of developing and applying aircraft in national defense." This group, the Morrow Board, made three proposals:

1. Rename the Army Air Service the Army Air Corps
2. Give the Army Air Corps a seat on the Army General Staff
3. Appoint an assistant secretary of war for air power.

Congress adopted these recommendations. The Air Corps Act became law on 2 July 1926.

PRESIDENT CALVIN COOLIDGE

Courtesy of Bettmann/Corbis

Brig Gen Billy Mitchell's Stamp on Air Power

Brig Gen William "Billy" Mitchell (1879–1936) was a controversial figure in US air power. He played a vital role in the creation of the US Air Force. He believed the bomber should be a key weapon of warfare. He thought it could bring the battle to the enemy and shorten wars.

BRIG GEN BILLY MITCHELL IN 1922

Courtesy of the Airmen Memorial Museum

Mitchell got off to a great start in life. ` He was the son of a US senator from Wisconsin. In 1895 he entered George Washington University in Washington, D.C. He was only 16 and the youngest student at that time to enter that school. By age 18, he was a second lieutenant in the Wisconsin Volunteers. At 19, he was promoted to first lieutenant. By 23, he was a captain in the US Army.

Mitchell graduated from the Army Staff College in 1909. At age 32 he was assigned to the Army General Staff. The General Staff oversees the Army and makes any decisions on major policy changes. Mitchell was the youngest person ever posted to it.

During World War I Mitchell was chief of the Air Service for American forces in Europe. Experiencing battlefield action helped persuade him of the great possibilities of air power. The battles also convinced him that the air arm needed its independence.

After World War I Mitchell was named deputy chief of the Air Service. During those years, he conducted bombing tests such as the one against the *Ostfriesland*. He also spoke publicly and wrote about the need for a separate air force.

But in 1925 Mitchell got into trouble. He harshly criticized senior officers in the military. A Navy plane had recently disappeared during a flight to Hawaii. And a Navy dirigible had crashed, killing 13 crew members. Referring to these events, Mitchell said, "The high command of both the Army and the Navy are guilty of incompetency, criminal negligence, and almost treasonable administration of the national defense." Someone who is incompetent *is lacking the qualities needed for effective action.* A treasonable act is one that *involves a violation of allegiance towards one's country.*

Because he so openly criticized military officers, Mitchell was court-martialed for insubordination under the 96th Article of War. This article forbids "all conduct of a nature to bring discredit upon the military service." Insubordination *is a refusal to submit to authority.*

Mitchell was convicted. Rather than face a five-year suspension, he resigned from service in 1926. But he continued to speak for an independent air force. Unfortunately, Mitchell died in 1936. He never got to see the advent of powerful bombers such as the B-17 that played crucial roles in World War II.

In 1946, 10 years after Mitchell's death, Congress awarded him the Medal of Honor. The award recognized his insightful air-power theories.

Mitchell and Pearl Harbor

Some people are not only smart. They're also imaginative. They can put what they know in a new perspective. Brig Gen Mitchell was such a person. He predicted, as early as 1924, the Japanese attack on Pearl Harbor.

Mitchell visited Japan in 1924. He noticed the country seemed bent on expanding its territories. He wasn't sure when that would be. But he figured if Japan went to war to expand its influence in the Pacific, it would attack US bases in Hawaii and the Philippines from the air and sea. He wrote:

> Attack will be launched as follows:
> Bombardment, attack to be made on Ford Island [at Pearl Harbor in Hawaii] at 7:30 a.m. . . . . Attack to be made on Clark Field [in the Philippines] at 10:40 a.m.

Seventeen years later, on 7 December 1941, the Japanese attacked Pearl Harbor in Hawaii. They struck Ford Island at 7:55 a.m. They hit Clark Field at 12:35 p.m.

ULYSSES S. NERO

Ulysses S. Nero in the 13th Cavalry, I Troop, Fort Riley, Kansas, in 1917

Courtesy of the Airmen Memorial Museum

Col Ulysses S. Nero: Bombardier, Inventor, Engineer

Col Ulysses S. Nero (1898–1980) spent most of his career in the US military. He was an intelligent, confident, yet modest, man. His family sent him to work in a shipyard when he was 14. He completed high school at age 15 by taking night classes.

Nero enlisted in the US Army in 1917 as a private. He retired in 1952 as a colonel. In between, he served in World War I, World War II, and the Korean War. His contributions to the military were extraordinary. They included 12 patents for military equipment.

Nero's adventure in the military began in the Army's 13th Cavalry. His unit performed the US military's last horse-cavalry mission. It pushed Mexican bandit Pancho Villa back to his homeland. (In late 1917 artillery units replaced horse cavalry.)

Nero then transferred to the US Army Signal Corps. He served in France in the Great War. He joined the Aviation Section of the Signal Corps in 1918, the same year it became the Army Air Service. In 1919, he returned to civilian life. But he felt he could do better in the military. So he reenlisted in 1921.

Nero became an expert bombardier. He made two important advances during his early years with the Air Service. In 1922 he invented a wireless means for pilots and ground crews to communicate. This brought him to the attention of Brig Gen Mitchell. Second, Nero invented a bombsight—*a device that helps determine when to drop a bomb*—that let bombardiers place their loads more accurately. He dropped nearly 10,000 bombs while running tests at the Aberdeen Proving Grounds in Maryland.

In 1923 Nero sank the USS *New Jersey* and the USS *Virginia* during tests arranged by Mitchell. This led Mitchell to promote him. The two men became good friends.

Over the next 30 years or so, Nero developed more inventions. For example, he designed bomb fuses. He entered World War II as a master sergeant and became well known not only for his combat skills but also for his ability to maintain aircraft. During the Korean War, he was the first to overhaul a jet engine. To overhaul *is to go over carefully and make needed repairs.*

Many people today call Nero the "father of US Air Force precision bombing."

ULYSSES S. NERO

Ulysses S. Nero as an officer (around 1942–1951)

Courtesy of the Airmen Memorial Museum

How the Army Air Corps Developed

Changing the name of the Army Air Service to Army Air Corps was significant. It boosted the idea that the air arm was no longer only in "service" to ground troops. The corps could conduct independent missions. A corps *is a branch or department of the armed forces having a specialized function.*

The Army Air Corps wouldn't gain full independence for another 21 years. It got off to a slow start for several reasons. First, many people felt that World War I was the "war to end all wars." They thought the world would never again fight such an all-out battle. As a result, Congress drastically reduced defense spending. Most Airmen returned to civilian life. Furthermore, when the Great Depression hit in 1929, neither people nor countries had cash to spare.

But important changes would soon take place. By the late 1930s many people feared that war was about to break out in Europe. This helped lead to a growth spurt in the Air Corps. In addition, the years between World War I and World War II saw major advances in bombers and pursuit aircraft, or *fighter planes.*

The Growth of the Army Air Corps

The fear of war was well founded. War shadows grew in Europe during 1938. Germany annexed Austria that year. To annex *is to incorporate territory into an existing political unit such as a country.* Austria didn't resist when German troops marched across its borders. Meanwhile, Italy waged war in Africa, and Japan had invaded China.

On 12 January 1939, President Franklin D. Roosevelt spoke to Congress about the need to rebuild the US military. US forces, he said, were "utterly inadequate." Three months later, Congress approved increasing the number of Army Air Corps pilot officers from 1,200 to 3,203.

Civilian Flight Schools

Meanwhile, the chief of the Air Corps, Maj Gen Henry "Hap" Arnold, knew the corps didn't have the facilities to train more than 550 pilots a year. If a second world war broke out, the United States would need to train thousands of pilots a year—far more than the 3,203 pilots authorized by Congress.

Arnold had a great idea. Why not train military pilots in civilian schools? He asked Congress for the funding, but lawmakers turned down his request.

Arnold went ahead with his plan anyway. He approached eight World War I and civilian pilots. He asked them if they would train pilots for the Army. Although he offered no guarantee of pay, all eight agreed to do it. Congress finally authorized contracts for civilian flight schools in July 1939.

Under this plan, volunteers would check in with the Army for a physical and a psychological test. If they passed, they'd attend a civilian flight school close to home. Once a volunteer graduated, a military pilot would take him for a "check ride." If it went well, the volunteer would report for combat training at an Army base.

Arnold's idea eventually produced some 110,000 pilots per year. But more were needed.

Civilian Reserve Pilots

In 1939 the Air Corps tried another idea: the Civilian Pilot Training Program. Under this program, civilians could volunteer to train as civilian pilots. This reserve of civilian pilots would be available in case of a national emergency. Congress set aside $7 million a year for the program. In 1942 the name was changed to the Civil Aeronautics Authority War Training Service. About 300,000 reserve pilots earned their private-pilot certificates by the time the program ended in 1944.

Black Pilots

Black men were not permitted in the Army Air Corps or in the Civilian Pilot Training Program. But two African-American pilots—Dale White and Chauncy Spencer—refused to accept this. They wanted to draw attention to the exclusion of black pilots from the military. So they made a 3,000-mile flight across the United States in May 1939 that brought them through Washington, D.C. While in D.C., they met Senator Harry Truman of Missouri. They told him about their mission. He was impressed and got Congress involved. On 22 March 1941 the all-black 99th Pursuit Squadron of Tuskegee, Alabama, was born. It was made part of the Civilian Pilot Training Program.

THE TUSKEGEE AIRMEN
Courtesy of AP Photo/USAAF

All three of these steps—civilian flight schools, civilian reserve pilots, and acceptance of black pilots—greatly increased the number of pilots available to the Army Air Corps and helped the United States prepare for war.

Significant Missions Conducted by the Army Air Corps

In the 1930s Army Air Corps officers focused on aircraft development. They believed that if they could get the aviation industry to build a powerful, fast aircraft that could travel long distances, they could fulfill Billy Mitchell's dream of a long-range bomber.

Airplane manufacturers at that time were focusing on commercial aircraft—because that's where the money was. To get the manufacturers' attention, the Army Air Corps held a design competition for a multiengine bomber.

As you read in the previous lesson, Douglas Aircraft came out with two commercial aircraft, the DC-2 (1934) and the DC-3 (1936) about this same time. These aircraft put Boeing's commercial 247 out of date. Army officers gave Boeing a suggestion for its entry in the design competition. Instead of using a typical two-engine plane, they said, why not design a four-engine aircraft? Boeing did just that—building the Boeing 299.

Boeing's 299 flew to the contest site at Wright Field in Dayton, Ohio, in July 1935. It won the Army competition easily. The aircraft had speed, range, and altitude. The Air Corps ordered 13 of them. It renamed the plane the B-17. The corps could now finally fly long-range strategic bombing missions using one of the most important aircraft of this era.

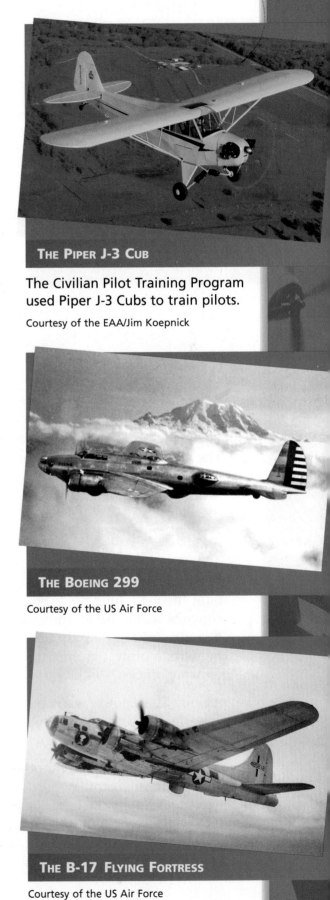

THE PIPER J-3 CUB

The Civilian Pilot Training Program used Piper J-3 Cubs to train pilots.

Courtesy of the EAA/Jim Koepnick

THE BOEING 299

Courtesy of the US Air Force

THE B-17 FLYING FORTRESS

Courtesy of the US Air Force

THE CURTISS P-36 HAWK

Courtesy of the Air Force National Museum

The B-17 was faster than any pursuit aircraft in the United States. This made the Army realize that it now needed better pursuit planes. It signed contracts for the Curtiss P-36 and the Seversky P-35. (The "P" stands for "pursuit.") These aircraft could guard American bombers and attack enemy bombers. It developed other important pursuit aircraft, as well. When the United States entered World War II, it had Lockheed P-38s, Bell P-39s, and Curtiss P-40s in its pursuit arsenal.

One more important invention took place during these years. The Army borrowed the Norden Mark XV bombsight from the Navy to use in B-17s. This allowed the Air Corps to conduct precision daylight bombing by just a few aircraft in a tight formation instead of raids by a large number of planes saturating a wide area.

The Air Force's Path Toward Independence

The Army Air Corps officially became the Army Air Forces on 20 June 1941. The new Air Force remained under the command of the Army. But it could now oversee its own functions in combat, training, and maintenance. Maj Gen "Hap" Arnold took command of the Army Air Forces.

The Rationale of Advocates for an Independent Air Force

After Brig Gen Mitchell's resignation in 1926, others carried his ideas forward. The foundation of his air-power theory was the long-range bomber. Once Boeing built the B-17, long-range bombing missions could become a reality. Here was a concrete reason for an independent air service. Air power was an offensive weapon. It could strike at military bases and factories in enemy lands. It could do much more than protect ground troops. And it didn't need to be under the command of Army officers.

As long as air power was a part of the Army, air advocates believed it would remain underfunded and underdeveloped. They were right—air power was suffering. As late as 1928, the Army placed greater emphasis on observation aircraft than on bombers.

In 1934, air power faced another setback. President Roosevelt turned over airmail delivery to the corps. Within short order, nine fatal crashes occurred. The crashes were not entirely the corps' fault. It didn't have enough money, for one thing. Its aircraft weren't outfitted with night instrument panels and other equipment. Pilots weren't well trained for night flight. These things made it clear to such people as Mitchell that air power needed to go its own path to grow.

The Rationale of Objectors to an Independent Air Force

The Army General Staff was the biggest proponent of keeping the Air Corps in the Army. The Army was, after all, steeped in history. Ground forces had been a part of war for thousands of years. Many in the Army saw air power as no more than long-range artillery. They wanted the Army to keep total control of its air arm, just as the Navy controlled its own air arm. But major advances in technology such as the B-17 would make the old ways more difficult to maintain.

Flight Paths

Maj Gen Benjamin Foulois: From Army's First Pilot to Air Chief

Benjamin Foulois (1879–1967) started his military career as an enlistee. He spent the last four years of his career as chief of the Air Corps—quite a leap. Like Brig Gen Billy Mitchell, he spoke out for an independent air force.

Foulois was only 5 feet, 6 inches, tall. But he loved adventure. And he loved to fly. Even when he was chief of the Air Corps, he spent more time in the air than many of his junior officers.

MAJ GEN BENJAMIN FOULOIS

Maj Gen Benjamin Foulois (left) was chief of the Air Corps from 1931 to 1935.

Courtesy of the US Air Force

Even in his early years of service, Foulois achieved several milestones. He became the Army Signal Corps' first pilot when he flew Dirigible No. 1 in 1908. He rode with Orville Wright in 1909. With the Wrights' help, he learned to pilot a plane while stationed at Fort Sam Houston, Texas.

Foulois served in World War I at home and abroad. After the war, he testified before the Senate Military Affairs Committee. He suggested that the committee sponsor a bill to create an air department.

Foulois held strong opinions, which helped and hurt him throughout his career. In oral and written statements, he criticized the Army and Navy for failing to support an independent air force. Nonetheless, he ended up as chief of the Air Corps from 1931 to 1935. He resigned in 1935 when he came under attack for the Air Corps' mishandling of the airmail mission.

Creation of a Separate Air Corps Headquarters

When two sides can't agree, a compromise is often necessary. In 1933, Maj Gen Hugh Drum headed an Army board that explored possible changes in the structure of the Air Corps. The board recommended that the War Department form a General Headquarters Air Force (GHQ). The GHQ would command the aerial combat arm. The Air Corps would retain training and logistical duties. Logistics *is the aspect of military operations that deals with the procurement, distribution, maintenance, and replacement of materiel and personnel.* Secretary of War George H. Dern endorsed the plan. But nothing happened for a few years.

In 1934, the War Department set up another board. Former Secretary of War Newton Baker chaired this group. It, too, proposed a combat group separate from training and logistical duties.

The recommendations of the Drum and Baker boards were implemented in March 1935, when the GHQ set up camp at Langley Field, Virginia. GHQ remained within the Air Corps and answered to the Army. Brig Gen Frank Andrews was senior officer of GHQ. In the past, Air Corps commanders had shared responsibility for tactical units. Now all combat aircraft would fall under Andrews's command. During peacetime, Andrews would answer to the Army chief of staff. In war, he'd report to a regional combat commander.

With the formation of the Army Air Forces in June 1941, the Air Corps and GHQ now fell under unified control. Maj Gen Arnold was in charge of the Air Forces. Under him was Maj Gen George Brett, who was chief of the Air Corps. Lt Gen Delos C. Emmons headed the new Air Force Combat Command (formerly known as the GHQ).

This last change came not a moment too soon. By the end of the year, the United States would find itself fully engaged in war in both Europe and the Pacific. The experiences gained during that war, and the performance of the Army Air Forces, would finally lead to complete autonomy—*independence*—of the US Air Force with the passage of the National Security Act of 1947.

CHECKPOINTS

Lesson 1 Review

Using complete sentences, answer the following questions on a sheet of paper.

1. What was the name of the captured German battleship that was supposed to be unsinkable?

2. Which American president established the Army Air Service in May 1918?

3. What is the name of the Army air branch that Congress created in 1926?

4. What happened to Brig Gen Billy Mitchell when he criticized senior officers in the Army and Navy?

5. What is Col Ulysses Nero considered the father of?

6. Why did President Roosevelt ask Congress in 1939 to increase the number of officers in the Army Air Corps?

7. When the Army Air Corps didn't have enough facilities to train pilots, what was one of the programs the corps set up?

8. What was one of the most important aircraft the Army Air Corps ordered during the 1930s?

Applying Your Learning

9. Why do you think it took so many years to convince Congress that the Air Force should be independent, rather than a branch of the Army?

Air Power in World War II

Quick Write

_____

_____

_____

Explain why SSgt Henry Erwin earned the Medal of Honor.

SSgt Henry Erwin

Courtesy of the Air Force Heritage Research Institute

SSgt Henry E. Erwin (1922–2002) was a radio operator on a B-29 bomber in the Pacific. On 12 April 1945 he and his crewmates were targeting a chemical plant in Koriyama, Japan. Erwin's other duty on board was to light and drop phosphorus smoke bombs.

One of the bombs he lit blew back up the bomb chute and struck him in the face. The bomb's flare was 1,100 degrees. It burned off his nose and one of his ears, and temporarily cost him his sight. In terrible pain, Erwin knew he had to get the fiery bomb canister out of the plane. For one thing, he was afraid the canister would burn through the metal floor into the bomb bay. For another, the smoke was making it impossible for the pilot to navigate. The aircraft was diving toward earth.

Although gravely injured and on fire, Erwin carried the burning bomb canister to the front of the aircraft. He tossed it out of the copilot's window. The smoke cleared enough for the pilot to level out at 300 feet and make an emergency landing on Iwo Jima.

No one thought Erwin would live. Senior Army Air Force officers approved awarding him the Medal of Honor so they could give it to him while he was still alive. But he survived. Gen Curtis LeMay himself presented the medal. Erwin went through 30 months of surgery and rehabilitation. He received a disability discharge as a master sergeant in 1947. He went on to work for 37 years for the Veterans Administration. He was the last enlisted man in the US Army Air Forces to receive the Medal of Honor. Erwin died in 2002 at age 80.

In 1997, the Air Force created the Henry E. Erwin Outstanding Enlisted Aircrew Member of the Year Award. It is given each year to an airman, noncommissioned officer, and senior noncommissioned officer in the active-duty or reserve forces. It is only the second Air Force award named for an enlisted person.

The Role Air Power Played in World War II and Its Significance

"To! To! To!" (Japanese code for "Charge! Charge! Charge!"). With that order, Japanese pilots plunged from the skies over Pearl Harbor in Hawaii at 7:55 a.m. on 7 December 1941. Fifty fighters and 140 bombers strafed and bombed the US base. Less than an hour later, 40 more Japanese fighters and 130 more bombers dropped their deadly loads.

The Americans were caught off guard. They weren't prepared for an attack from the air. The Army and Navy thought any assault on Pearl Harbor would come by foot. Only a little more than a week before, they'd ordered all planes and ships grouped in clusters. They placed guards around the aircraft. The officers wanted to protect against sabotage—*the destruction of property by enemy agents in time of war*. This move proved disastrous for the American forces. For Japanese pilots, the clusters of planes must have looked like bull's-eyes.

In all, the Japanese destroyed 96 Army planes and 92 Navy aircraft. They crippled 159 more. They sank three US battleships—the *Arizona*, *California*, and *West Virginia*. They capsized the battleship *Oklahoma*. They also damaged four other battleships, three cruisers, three destroyers, and a seaplane. The casualties—*military persons lost through death, wounds, injury, imprisonment, or missing in action*—were high. The Navy and Marine Corps lost 2,117 members. Another 960 were missing and 876 wounded. The Army and Army Air Forces suffered losses, too: 226 killed and 396 wounded.

PEARL HARBOR UNDER ATTACK
Courtesy of the National Archives and Records Administration

Learn About...

- the role air power played in World War II and its significance
- how air power was developed during World War II
- the significance of the Allied air campaigns

Vocabulary

- sabotage
- casualty
- Allies
- Axis Powers
- Holocaust
- theater
- Luftwaffe
- occupation
- isolationist
- infantry
- squadron
- flight
- blitzkrieg
- combined arms
- tactical
- interdiction
- transport
- materiel
- escort
- paratrooper
- embargo
- incendiary bombs

During the raid, the Army got just six fighters into the air. The Navy sent up 36 airplanes. But the Japanese lost only 28 planes and 64 men. The only real break for US forces was that the enemy did not touch a single aircraft carrier of the US Pacific fleet. All four ships were out on exercises.

The United States declared war on Japan on 8 December 1941. Three days later, on 11 December, the United States declared war on Japan's allies, Germany and Italy. England and its allies had already been fighting Germany and Italy for two years. The British joined America in declaring war on Japan.

The Japanese attack on Pearl Harbor is a fitting place to begin a discussion of America's entry into World War II. In many ways, this attack was symbolic of this major war. Another name for World War II is the "air war." For Americans, the air war began with the Japanese air attack on Pearl Harbor. The war ended in 1945, when American aircraft dropped atomic bombs on the Japanese cities of Hiroshima and Nagasaki. The air war began for Britain and Europe in 1939, when Germany invaded Poland.

There were two sides during World War II. The Allies included *Britain, France, the United States, the Soviet Union, and China.* (The Soviet Union was the new name for Russia after the Russian Revolution overthrew the czar in 1917.) The Axis Powers included *Germany, Italy, and Japan.* Many other countries contributed to the Allies' effort, and a few others fought for the Axis Powers. In Chapter 2, Lesson 3, you read that during World War I, a slightly different group of countries referred to themselves as the Allies; they were Russia, France, Britain, the United States, and Italy. A country's loyalties can shift as circumstances change.

The War's Causes

World War II was the most horrific war in history. As the chart nearby shows, more than 50 million people died.

The roots of the war lay in the end of World War I. After that war, Japan was the biggest power in the Far East. But it had few of the natural resources, such as oil, that a modern economy needs. So it was looking for ways to expand. Germany was also hurting. Britain and France had forced it to pay huge sums of money for war damage, which hurt Germany's economy.

In 1932 the Great Depression threw millions of workers out of work around the world. It hit Germany especially hard. The people wanted change. So Adolf Hitler's National Socialist Party—the *Nazis*—won the 1933 elections. The Nazis preached a vicious brand of racism. They believed that other ethnic groups, such as Jews and Slavic peoples, were less human than Germans. They wanted to remove these groups—or even kill them—to make "living space" for a German master race. They wrongly blamed Jews for Europe's economic problems. They imprisoned or murdered anyone who disagreed with their teachings. The Nazis were responsible for the Holocaust, *or the mass murder of some six million Jews, mostly in death camps.*

Meanwhile, in Italy, dictator Benito Mussolini led his country into a series of wars. This included taking over Ethiopia, in Africa. Mussolini was a Fascist. The Fascists held views like those of the Nazis.

In the Far East, Japan was fighting in China and elsewhere for control of other people's countries and resources.

The final major player was Joseph Stalin, the dictator who headed the Communist Party in the Soviet Union. The Communists believed that the state should own all the means of production. They permitted no private ownership of land, factories, or businesses. Like the Nazis, they imprisoned or murdered those who disagreed with them.

Most Europeans and Americans rejected the Communists' views. The Nazis and Fascists particularly hated them. This didn't stop Hitler and Stalin from signing a treaty that allowed Germany to conquer most of Poland. The Soviet Union got the rest. It also took over the Baltic countries of Lithuania, Latvia, and Estonia.

But in 1941 Hitler double-crossed Stalin. He attacked the Soviet Union. Millions of Soviet civilians died in the fighting. In the siege of Leningrad (now St. Petersburg) alone, 900,000 people starved.

After the German invasion, the Soviet Union joined the Allies. With the United States and Britain, they helped defeat the Nazis.

CAPSULES

Estimated Military and Civilians Killed in World War II, by Country

Allied Powers

Australia	30,000
Belgium	112,000
Britain	460,000
Canada	42,000
China	10,300,000
Denmark	3,000
France	270,000
Greece	490,000
India	36,000
Netherlands	264,000
New Zealand	10,000
Norway	16,000
Poland	2,630,000
South Africa	9,000
United States	300,000
U.S.S.R. (Russia)	28,000,000
Yugoslavia	305,000

Axis Powers

Bulgaria	60,000
Finland	104,000
Germany	5,500,000
Hungary	320,000
Italy	400,000
Japan	2,100,000
Romania	900,000
TOTAL	**54,226,000**

Compiled by Professor Joseph V. O'Brien, Department of History, John Jay College of Criminal Justice, New York, NY

Gen Carl A. Spaatz:
First Chief of Staff, US Air Force

Gen Carl A. ("Tooey") Spaatz (1891–1974) flew in World War I. He was also commander of air forces in several regions during World War II. He remained in the military between the wars. During the Battle of Britain, he spent time in Britain, where he observed German tactics.

GEN CARL A. "TOOEY" SPAATZ

Courtesy of Getty Images

The West Point graduate served in every theater—*a large geographic area in which military operations are coordinated*—during World War II. He headed the Eighth Air Force in England. While the British conducted nighttime bombing raids over Germany, Spaatz had his pilots fly during the day. He was also responsible for the 12th Air Force in North Africa.

After the Allies defeated the Germans in Africa, Spaatz led the 12th and 15th Air Forces as well as the Royal Air Force in Italy. In 1944 he was put in charge of the US Strategic Air Forces in Europe. He oversaw air power there until Germany's collapse. In July 1945 he was sent to the Pacific. His pilots delivered the atomic bombs on Japan. Although he did not agree with using atomic weapons, he carried out his orders.

After the war, Spaatz served for about a year as the first chief of staff of the new US Air Force. He retired in 1948. He earned many awards, including the Distinguished Service Cross. Spaatz was one of the foremost military leaders of World War II.

The Strategic Role Air Power Played in World War II

Many decisive battles of World War II were fought in the air. After Germany surrendered in 1945, all its military commanders and civilian leaders who'd been held prisoner conceded that air power had won the war for the Allies.

Air power played a strategic role in determining the outcome of World War II at several points. As you read in the lesson on World War I, *strategic* means designed to strike at the sources of an enemy's military, economic, or political power.

Germany began World War II using its Luftwaffe—*the German air force*—in combination with ground troops. The Germans broke through Poland's borders on 1 September 1939. In less than a month, they crushed Poland's army, which was the fifth largest in Europe. Poland surrendered in just 20 days. Germany then rolled over a number of other countries in short order. They included Norway, the Netherlands, France, and Belgium. All these countries faced German occupation—*invasion, conquest, and control of a nation or territory by foreign armed forces.*

But Germany's good luck changed when it struck Britain. Britain's air power put a stop to German air power. This clash, which began in August 1940, was called the *Battle of Britain*.

Britain was in a fight for its life. For a year, it stood alone against the Axis onslaught. But it had a few advantages over Germany. First, its Royal Navy was superior to Germany's navy. Second, German aircraft weren't equipped to fly the long distances needed to cross the English Channel and conduct missions in Britain. Even so, Germany continued to strike Britain from the air through much of the war. But its strategy and air power were never able bring the British to their knees. The British kept the Germans from grabbing their island nation.

On 20 June 1941, Hitler invaded the Soviet Union. The Japanese air strike on Pearl Harbor brought America into the war six months later. Pearl Harbor is a second example of the importance of air power in World War II. Following the attack, America declared war on Japan and on the other two Axis Powers, Germany and Italy.

Now Britain had two powerful new allies. Had Japan not attacked Pearl Harbor, it's difficult to say how much longer the United States would have maintained its isolationist stance. An isolationist country *is a nation that does not enter alliances with other countries.*

The D-Day invasion on 6 June 1944 was a third punch delivered through air power. It prepared the Normandy beaches for the infantry—*soldiers armed and trained to fight on foot*. It helped drive the Germans back to their own country. While all the armed forces contributed to the D-Day mission, air power was an essential element in that battle.

Finally, the atomic bombs dropped on Japan in August 1945 ended the war in the Pacific. Those bombs, delivered by American aircraft, broke the will of the Japanese government and people.

The Role of Air Power in World War II Versus World War I

Air power had a much larger role in World War II than it did in World War I. During World War I, air power was still a novel concept. This was especially true in that war's earliest years. All-metal planes were still new. Bombs were so light that pilots could carry them on their laps and drop them by hand. The pilots' work was mainly to observe enemy locations and support ground troops.

But by the end of World War I, things were changing. All-metal planes were becoming the norm. Bombs weighed as much as 2,000 pounds. Pilots engaged in dogfights. Some 1,500 planes fought in the Battle of Saint Mihiel in France in 1918.

Even so, much of World War I took place in the trenches. Infantrymen died in huge numbers. No country wanted its Soldiers to suffer such losses ever again. That's one reason the use of air power morphed so quickly between 1914 and 1918. It's also why air power was used so heavily in World War II. During this second war, fought between 1939 and 1945, long-range bombers saw lots of action. These aircraft could fly over trenches and enter enemy territory. Not only could fighters protect bombers and transports, they could also drop bombs.

Flight Paths

The Foresight of Gen Henry Arnold

Gen Henry ("Hap") Arnold (1886–1950) served in both world wars. He learned how to fly from Orville Wright. Arnold was a West Point graduate. He first served in the infantry. In 1911 he transferred to the Aeronautical Division of the US Army Signal Corps.

Arnold thought air power was essential to the future of the military. When troubles began brewing in Europe in 1938, he asked Congress for more funding for the Army Air Corps. He was especially interested in developing aerospace technology to give the United States an edge in achieving air superiority. He fostered the development of jet aircraft, rockets, rocket-assisted takeoff, and supersonic flight.

During the war, Arnold had a couple of jobs. He was commanding general of the US Army Air Forces. He also was the air representative on the US Joint Chiefs of Staff. In 1944 the Army made Arnold a five-star general. He is the only air commander to achieve that rank.

GEN HENRY "HAP" ARNOLD

Gen Henry "Hap" Arnold was the first five-star general in the US Army Air Forces.

Courtesy of Underwood & Underwood/Corbis Images

The Allies and Axis Powers used their aircraft to destroy airfields, supply lines, and military posts. They also used aircraft to try to break the will of the people. In fact, during World War II, civilians were often targets. This strategy had been used throughout history. But in World War II it greatly widened the scope of destruction. German bombs killed more than 40,000 civilians in and around London, for instance. The United States firebombed Tokyo and dropped atomic weapons on Hiroshima and Nagasaki, Japan, killing hundreds of thousands.

Victory in World War II relied on contributions from all forces—land, sea, and air. Each was indispensable. But for the first time in history, air power was the key to victory.

How Air Power Was Developed During World War II

Now that air power was more reliable, military leaders began to think ever more seriously about its prospects. Even in Brig Gen Billy Mitchell's day, visionaries knew aircraft would some day serve in more than a supporting role. With World War II, that day arrived. Both the Allies and the Axis Powers soon developed new strategies for waging war in the air.

The Development of Strategic Air Warfare

When World War I ended, both sides signed a peace treaty. It was named the Treaty of Versailles. Among other points, this treaty stated that Germany could not build a military air force. It was free, however, to develop commercial aircraft.

Germany used the progress it made in commercial planes as a cover for the advances it was secretly making in military aircraft. It was also quietly training pilots in South America. By 1932 Germany's military air force had three bomber squadrons, four fighter squadrons, eight observation squadrons, 1,500 trained pilots, and 3,000 pilots in training. A squadron *is an air force unit consisting of two or more flights.* A flight *is a unit that has two or more elements.*

In 1933 Adolf Hitler became chancellor of Germany. In 1935 Germany unveiled its Luftwaffe. In 1939 the German Army and Air Force invaded Poland. Germany was once again a power to be contended with.

Wanting to avoid getting bogged down in trench warfare as it had in World War I, Germany perfected a new strategy to invade and control Poland. The Germans called it *Blitzkrieg*, which in English means "lightning war." A blitzkrieg *is a war conducted with great speed and force.* In a blitzkrieg, the offense attempts to overwhelm its enemy. Because the fighting is quick, it supposedly results in fewer deaths and less damage to the invaded country. A blitzkrieg uses combined arms, *the coordinated efforts of different military branches, such as air and ground.*

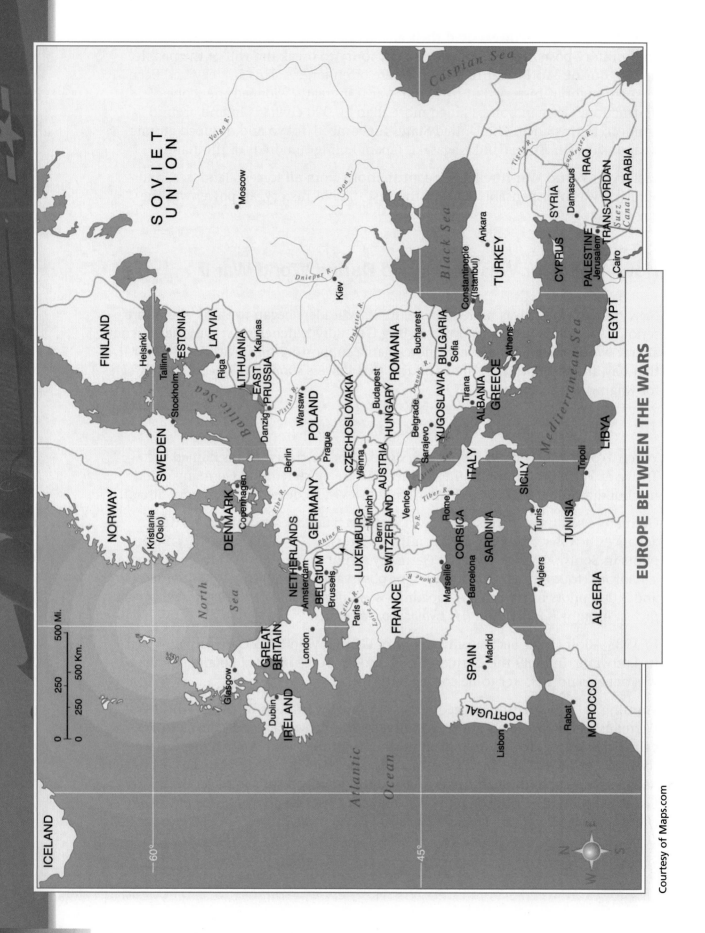

EUROPE BETWEEN THE WARS

Courtesy of Maps.com

In a World War II blitzkrieg, the Luftwaffe would strike first. Its pilots would fly behind enemy lines to take out an enemy air force, often before it could even get in the air. Then the German Army, using tanks to get its infantry safely across trench lines, would blow up railroads and strike at enemy troops. Combined arms were used a bit at the end of World War I, when the tank was developed. But they came into their own during World War II.

Tactical Operations: The Three-Point Plan

German and Italian forces were also in North Africa. From this base, they attacked British positions in the Mediterranean and along the Suez Canal. The Axis Powers needed Middle Eastern oil. To get it, they had to gain control of the canal, through which oil was shipped. The fight between the Allies and the Axis Powers in North Africa began in 1941, when the Germans targeted the British on Malta, an island in the Mediterranean.

In Africa, the United States and Britain used the same air policy at first. When the Luftwaffe attacked an Allied air base, only the aircraft at that base would respond. Each base commander was in charge of his planes. He did not coordinate with any other base commander. As a result, very few Allied planes were going up. They were always outnumbered by German aircraft. It became clear that if the Allies didn't change tactics, their huge losses would continue.

So Britain's Royal Air Force (RAF) and then the US Army brought all their planes under centralized control. This way, if a base were attacked, all Allied bases could defend it or retaliate together.

It worked. By 1942 the German Afrika Korps under Field Marshal Erwin Rommel was crumbling. The Germans' supplies were cut off. By 1943 the Allies controlled the skies. That meant the infantry could now control the ground. The Allies had won the battle of Africa. The US Air Force still uses this strategy of centralized control.

A new plan for tactical operations also grew out of the experience in Africa. Something that is tactical *involves military operations that are smaller, closer to base, and of less long-term significance than strategic operations.* The theory had three points:

1. Air superiority, achieved by destroying opposing airfields, aircraft, fuel tanks, and manufacturers of aircraft and spare parts
2. Interdiction, or *the act of cutting or destroying an enemy's advance through firepower.* As part of interdiction, aircraft hit supply routes, railroads, bridges, highways, warehouses, troops, and means of communication
3. Close ground support. Aircraft bombed and strafed within enemy territory and provided an aerial shield for Allied infantry

Lt Gen Pete Quesada: An Advocate of Close Air Support

LT GEN PETE QUESADA

Courtesy of the US Air Force

Lt Gen Pete Quesada (1904–1993) realized as early as the 1930s that "future war will require all sorts of arrangements between the air and the ground, and the two will have to work closer than a lot of people think or want." As commander of the First Air Defense Wing in North Africa, he put close air support into practice. He refined his idea as commander of the 12th Fighter Command, also in North Africa, in 1943.

Close air support has three major features:

1. Making ground and air commanders equal
2. Using centralized control
3. Establishing air superiority before committing ground troops

Another name for close air support is "tactical operations."

Quesada later commanded the Ninth Fighter Command, which saw action on D-Day in 1944. It provided close air support. Later, he was the first commander of the Tactical Air Command. He retired from the Air Force in 1951. In 1958 President Dwight Eisenhower named him the first director of the Federal Aviation Agency.

Strategic Operations: Long-Range Bombing

One of the Allies' air-warfare strategies was long-range bombing. The Allies used this strategy a great deal since they had more long-range bombers than Germany did. Germany's manufacturers produced mostly short- and medium-range bombers. Hitler had figured most of his battles would be in continental Europe, and therefore close to Germany.

Long-range bombing was an Allied air *strategy*; the approach used in North Africa involved Allied air *tactics*. Tactical operations apply to a specific fight. Strategic operations encompass the entire philosophy of a military's plan to win the war. The Allies relied heavily on long-range bombers to hit deep inside Germany and Japan and to destroy their ability to wage war.

Between the German blitzkrieg and Allied tactical and strategic plans, air power was taking shape. Both sides fine-tuned operations throughout the war. And that fine-tuning continues today.

The Tuskegee Airmen and President Harry Truman

Neither the Army Air Corps nor the Civilian Pilot Training Program (CPTP) accepted African-Americans at first. It was Senator Harry S. Truman, a future US president, who got Congress to admit blacks into the CPTP. The Tuskegee Airmen were born. They flew fighters.

The men, all African-Americans, got basic flight training at the Tuskegee Institute in Alabama. Those who passed went on for combat flight training at Tuskegee Army Air Field. Tuskegee pilots formed the 99th Fighter Squadron, which saw action in North Africa. Pilots also joined the 332nd Fighter Group. The 332nd and the 99th fought side by side in Italy later in the war.

By the end of the war, the Tuskegee program produced 992 black pilots. Of those, 150 lost their lives in training or combat.

When Truman became president, he vowed to push for more rights for blacks in all branches of the military. His overall goal was to end racial segregation in the armed forces. In July 1948 he signed Executive Order 9981. It said: "It is hereby declared to be the policy of the President that there shall be equality of treatment and opportunity for all persons in the armed services without regard to race, color, religion, or national origin."

The Tuskegee Airmen's service during World War II helped make this new order possible.

THE TUSKEGEE AIRMEN

Members of the Tuskegee Airmen during World War II

Courtesy of the US Air Force

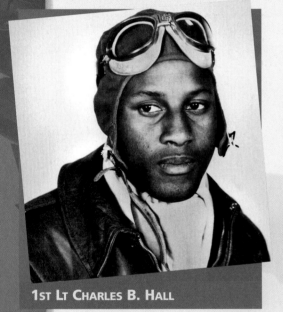

Lt Col Benjamin O. Davis Jr.

Lt Col Benjamin Davis Jr., commander of the 99th Fighter Squadron, prepares to lead a bomber escort mission during World War II.

Courtesy of the US Air Force

1st Lt Charles B. Hall

1st Lt Charles B. Hall was a fighter pilot with the 99th Fighter Squadron. He was the first African-American pilot to score a kill.

Courtesy of the National Air and Space Museum, Smithsonian Institution
(SI Neg. No. 99-15449)

Gen Benjamin O. Davis Jr.: All in the Family

The military was in Benjamin Davis Jr.'s blood. His father was an Army general. The younger Davis (1912–2002) would become the first African-American brigadier general in the US Air Force.

Davis trained in the Tuskegee program. In 1941 he led the all-black 99th Pursuit Squadron. He saw action in 1943 in North Africa. He also commanded the all-black 332nd Fighter Group. This group fought in 15,000 air battles in Europe during World War II. It destroyed 260 enemy planes.

Davis flew 60 combat missions and logged 224 combat hours. He earned the Distinguished Flying Cross, the Silver Star, the Croix de Guerre, the Star of Africa, and more. In 1998, Davis became a four-star general.

Charles Hall: A First for the 99th Fighter Squadron

1st Lt Charles Hall was a fighter pilot with the all-black 99th Fighter Squadron. On 21 July 1943, he was flying a P-40 over Italy as part of the escort for a B-25 bomber. He saw two German Focke-Wulf 190s coming his way. He zipped this way and that, intent on stopping the enemy aircraft. Hall let off a spray of bullets. One of the German fighters went down. Hall was the first African-American to score a kill during the war. He had two more by war's end. The US government awarded Hall the Distinguished Flying Cross.

The Combat Box Formation and Formation Pattern Bombing

It was 1943. Brig Gen Curtis LeMay's bombers were coming under heavy fire. US losses were staggering. During the US Eighth Air Force's first flight into Germany in July, the enemy shot down 92 American bombers. A month later it destroyed 60 more. In October antiaircraft fire and German fighters downed another 148 US bombers. Such losses could not continue.

Part of the problem was that the US bombers were flying into Germany unaccompanied. They had no protection. Normally fighters accompany bombers. But Allied fighters didn't yet have the range that Allied bombers had. By the end of the war, at least one fighter, the P-51 Mustang, would be developed to escort bombers. In the meantime, bombers' only defense was gunners all around the aircraft. But gunners weren't as helpful as a protective flank of fighters.

Furthermore, US pilots were conducting their precision-bombing missions during daylight hours. The RAF had lost many planes trying this. So they switched to night bombing. Americans were responsible for daytime runs. They had the Norden bombsight, which helps them hit targets during the day.

LeMay knew he had to do something to cut losses. He came up with two tactics: the combat box formation and formation pattern bombing.

LeMay instructed his bombers to fly close together. He called it the combat box formation. By sticking together, the gunners on the aircraft could more effectively protect against enemy fighters. This tactic helped somewhat until long-range escort fighters became available later in the war.

Formation pattern bombing is what results when bombers fly in a combat box formation. Bombs dropped from aircraft flying close together will land closer together and can have a big impact in a small area.

THE P-40 WARHAWK

Courtesy of the EAA/Jim Koepnick

The Development of Bombers, Fighters, and Transports

Between the end of World War I and the start of the second world war, both the United States and Britain cut defense spending drastically. The Axis Powers were doing just the opposite. So when Germany invaded Poland in 1939, the Axis nations were well prepared for war. The Allies were not.

In 1939 the US had 1,500 airplanes. At the time of the Pearl Harbor attack, it had 2,900 aircraft. Many weren't fit for combat duty. Furthermore, in 1939 US manufacturers could build no more than 2,100 aircraft per year. By 1940 they increased that to 570 a month. And by 1941 they could build 1,900 airplanes a month. Requests from Britain and France, as well as the US military, spurred the factories to ramp up production.

Pilots flew three key kinds of aircraft in World War II: the bomber, the fighter, and the transport.

Flight Paths

Gen Curtis E. LeMay and His Bombers

Gen Curtis E. LeMay (1906–1990) rose from flying cadet to many leadership positions. He worked with fighter planes. He moved to bombers in 1937. He charted routes to Africa and England before World War II.

In 1942 LeMay was in charge of the 305th Bombardment Group in the European theater. These pilots flew B-17s. It was with this group that he developed the combat box formation and formation pattern bombing. Later, when placed in charge of B-29s in the Pacific, he adapted those bombing theories to the new theater.

LeMay was a tough commander, but he was also tough on himself. He had a theory about war: "If you are going to use military force, then you ought to use overwhelming military force. Use too much and deliberately use too much. . . . You'll save lives, not only your own, but the enemy's, too." He applied this philosophy when his B-29s firebombed Tokyo in the most destructive air raid in history.

GEN CURTIS LeMAY

Courtesy of the US Air Force

After the war, LeMay had a number of leadership roles. Among them was command of the US Air Force in Europe during the Berlin airlift, an operation in Germany that followed World War II. Back in the United States, he commanded the Strategic Air Command, which oversaw atomic-bomb operations.

In 1961 LeMay became the fifth chief of staff of the Air Force.

Bombers

America had the long-range B-17 Flying Fortress bomber as early as 1935. This, along with the B-24, saw a lot of action in Europe. The B-24 Liberator was developed by 1938 and was in production by 1941. It had a 2,850-mile range and could fly 303 miles per hour (mph). Some 18,000 were built during the war. An Army Air Force report from 1944 nicely expresses the reasons for designing the B-24:

> The Liberator was the result of the Army Air Forces' desire for a long-range running mate for the Flying Fortress. In football language, we sought a good ball carrier who was just as good at long end runs as he was at off-tackle smashes. We thought of the B-24 in terms of patrol and transport as well as bombardment, and it has performed all three functions splendidly.

The B-29 Superfortress was the long-range bomber of the Pacific theater. It was bigger than the B-17 and the B-24. It could also fly greater distances—5,830 miles, with a top speed of 365 mph. It was designed for bombing runs over Japan.

Medium-range bombers included the B-25 Mitchell (1938) and the B-26 Marauder (1939). Both were in mass-production by February 1941. Lt Col Jimmy Doolittle used the B-25 in the 1942 Tokyo raid. This attack showed Japan that Allied planes could reach the home islands. The B-25 had a range of 1,200 miles and flew 275 mph. The B-26 Marauder flew mostly in England and the Mediterranean. It could fly 1,100 miles at a top speed of 285 mph. This bomber claimed the distinction of having the fewest of its numbers shot down of any Allied aircraft.

B-17 Flying Fortress

Courtesy of Betttman/Corbis

B-24 Liberator

Courtesy of the US Air Force

B-29 Superfortress

Courtesy of the EAA/Ken Lichtenberg

B-26 Marauder

Courtesy of the US Air Force

P-38 Lockheed Lightning

Courtesy of the US Air Force

P-51 Mustang

Courtesy of the EAA/Jim Koepnick

F-4F Wildcat

Courtesy of the EAA/Jim Koepnick

F-4U Corsair

Courtesy of the EAA/Jim Koepnick

Fighters

Among the American fighters that saw action in World War II were the Lockheed P-38 Lightning, Bell P-39 Airacobra, Curtiss P-40 Warhawk, and Republic P-47 Thunderbolt. Perhaps the most famous fighter was the North American P-51 Mustang.

Both the P-51 Mustang and the P-38 Lightning escorted long-range bombers. These fighters protected the bombers on missions deep into Germany. The P-38 gained a reputation among the German Luftwaffe in North Africa. They called it the "fork-tailed devil."

P-39 pilots went on many strafing runs. And the P-40 was a tough, sturdy plane. It saw action from the very start, going up against Japanese fighters at Pearl Harbor. The ranges on these fighters reached from 650 miles (the P-39) to 1,100 miles (the P-38). The P-51 had a top speed of 437 mph while the P-40's fastest pace was 362 mph.

The Navy, meanwhile, enjoyed success in the Pacific with the P-38, as well as with the carrier-launched Grumman F-4F Wildcat, the Grumman F-6F Hellcat, and the Chance-Vought F-4U Corsair.

F-6F Hellcat on the USS Yorktown

Courtesy of the National Archives and Records Administration

Developing any new aircraft was costly. The P-38, for instance, cost $852,000 to design. It would be considerably more in today's dollars. Unlike other countries at the time, the United States held design competitions for its military aircraft. The Army Air Forces believed this resulted in better aircraft. The designers came up with unique features that furthered advances in air combat capabilities.

Other fighters of note included the British Supermarine Spitfire (range 395 miles; maximum speed 355 mph), the Hawker Hurricane (700 miles; 325 mph), and the twin-engine De Havilland Mosquito (1,400 miles; 378 mph). Germany's main fighters were the famed Messerschmitt 109 (405 miles; 292 mph), the Messerschmitt 110 (1,305 miles; 342 mph), and the Focke-Wulf 190 (560 miles; 408 mph). Significantly, Germany also launched the world's first operational jet fighters at the end of the war, the Messerschmitt 262 Schwalbe (650 miles; 540 mph) and the Heinkel 162 Volksjaeger (606 miles; 562 mph). Fortunately for the Allies, these jets appeared too late in the war to affect the outcome. Japan's premier fighter was the Mitsubishi Zero (1,930 miles; 331.5 mph), which completely dominated its American counterparts at the beginning of the war.

SUPERMARINE SPITFIRE

Courtesy of the EAA/Phil High

MESSERSCHMITT 109

Courtesy of the EAA/Jim Koepnick

MESSERSCHMITT 262

Courtesy of the National Air and Space Museum, Smithsonian Institution (SI Neg. No. 79-4620)

MITSUBISHI ZERO

Courtesy of the Museum of Flight/Corbis

C-47 Skytrain transport

Courtesy of AP Photo

Transports

Transports were built to move people and cargo. They were less comfortable than commercial aircraft. As applied to all branches of the military, a transport *is a vehicle—aircraft, ship, or other—that carries people, supplies, tanks, and artillery.* The best-known air transport was the C-47 Skytrain. It was based on the Douglas Aircraft DC-3. It could fly 1,513 miles. It could reach 232 mph but generally cruised around 175 mph. Besides ferrying ground troops and equipment, it moved paratroopers and towed gliders. Some 9,348 C-47s were built by the end of the war.

CAPSULES

Enlisted Pilots

Before World War II, the United States had more pilots than planes. But once the United States entered the war and the war-manufacturing industry heated up, there were more planes than pilots. This meant that more enlistees would get a chance to fly. Congress passed a bill on 3 June 1941 to encourage enlistee pilots.

There were 3,000 enlisted pilots from 1912 to 1942. Cpl Vernon Burge, whom you read about in a previous chapter, was the first. The main differences between noncommissioned and commissioned pilots were age and education. Enlisted pilots were between 18 and 22 years old. They had to graduate in the top half of their high school classes. They didn't have to attend college. Commissioned pilots were 20 to 27 years old. They had college degrees. Most enlistees who became pilots eventually did receive commissions.

Army command intended to use enlisted pilots for transport duties, not for combat. But the needs of war often meant that the enlistee pilots saw action. These pilots fought most of the air battles over North Africa, for instance. In the Mediterranean, officers who had started out in the military as enlisted men were in charge of all the troop carrier groups in the region. Troop carrier groups flew Soldiers in transports. Enlisted pilots contributed mightily to Allied victory.

The Significance of the Allied Air Campaigns

Germany resumed hostilities in Europe in 1938 to take lands it felt belonged to it: Austria, Czechoslovakia, and later, Poland. Most of Europe caved quickly before German aggression. Britain was an exception. This small island nation was about all that stood between Germany and total conquest.

Before the United States joined Britain in its campaign to free Europe, the military and civilian leaders of the two countries met many times. They talked strategy. The United States was already supplying Britain with ships, planes, and parts. The Allies considered the chance Japan would one day attack the United States. They asked themselves how this would affect the Allied strategy.

The United States and England came to some important conclusions. They decided that even if Japan struck the United States, the first objective of the Allies would still be to defeat Germany. Germany was in Britain's backyard. Its factories churned out excellent planes and tanks. It had been hammering Britain for two years. As of 1941 the combined forces of the US and England would have been hard pressed to fight all-out war on two fronts. But by 1944 that was no longer true. Helped by the Soviets' battle with the Germans on the Eastern Front, they could take on Germany and Japan full force.

Once the United States entered the war, air power had a big part in the European and Pacific theaters. It played both its old support role and its new offensive role of strategic bombing.

Significant Allied Air Campaigns in the European Theater

All Allied air actions in Europe had a single goal: to shut down the German offensive. The first great clash was the Battle of Britain.

The Battle of Britain

The Battle of Britain was one of the most important of the war. This was a defensive battle for the British. The British were the first to stop the Nazi war machine.

The battle began in August 1940. The Germans did small-scale raids to test British strength. England relied on its fighters for defense. Both British resolve and poor German planning helped Britain hold out. As you read above, the Germans had only short- and medium-range bombers. They needed long-range bombers to hit Britain effectively.

Germany made another big mistake. It didn't count on British radar. Radar let the British spot German squadrons heading toward them across the English Channel. Because of radar, the RAF didn't have to waste fuel patrolling in the air. And it didn't have to waste manpower or put unnecessary wear and tear on its planes. Having radar was a bit like being able to see into the future. It allowed the RAF to send its fighter pilots where and when they were needed.

Even so, German bombers did manage to get through to bomb London and the surrounding areas. They inflicted serious death and damage. But German efforts grew weak by 1941. The Luftwaffe had lost too many planes and crews to British fighters. British air power had saved Britain.

The Allies Versus the Axis Powers in Europe

When the United States declared war on Germany and Italy, a new phase of the air campaign began. Britain now had active allies in the United States and the Soviet Union. Before America's entry, Britain had been on the defensive. With America by its side, Britain mounted an offensive campaign.

Between 1942 and 1945, the Western Allies went hard after Germany. The US Eighth Air Force went on its first strategic bombing run over Germany on 17 August 1942. It used B-17 bombers with Norden bombsights for daytime precision strikes. The RAF hit Germany at night. The Allies' strategy was threefold:

1. Protect Allied supply routes between the United States and Britain to stop the Germans from blowing up Allied ships carrying materiel—*the equipment and supplies of a military force*

2. Bomb the German war industry (factories and warehouses)

3. Destroy German roads, bridges, and communication lines.

THE RAF HAWKER HURRICANE FIGHTER

The RAF Hawker Hurricane fighter played a huge role in the Battle of Britain.

Courtesy of the EAA/Phil High

THE GERMAN STUKA DIVE-BOMBER

A German Stuka dive-bomber used during the early years of World War II

Courtesy of ullstein bild/The Granger Collection

The Allied plan had one big hitch. Until 1944 most bombers flew without fighter escorts. The fighters weren't equipped to make the long flight to Germany. The Allies suffered huge losses, especially in 1943 over Germany. Not until March 1944 would bombers reach Berlin. Fighters eventually accompanied the bombers. In the meantime, the Allies also focused on German positions in France from 1942 to 1943. The hop across the English Channel was just more than 20 miles.

In mid-1943 the Ninth and Twelfth Air Forces of the US Army became free for European theater duty. They'd been fighting in North Africa. Now the Ninth and Twelfth provided support in Italy. The Allies invaded the island of Sicily in July 1943 and Italy in September 1943. Upon Italy's surrender soon after, the Ninth and Twelfth turned their attention to support actions against Germany, including the D-Day invasion.

Flight Paths

Maj Glenn Miller: Morale Booster

Back in the states, Glenn Miller was a successful bandleader. At 38, he was too old to be drafted into the war. So he volunteered. He started as a captain in the Army Air Corps. Miller felt that his swing music could cheer up Allied troops overseas.

Miller put together the 418th Army Air Forces Band in 1943. Fifty Airmen—almost all enlisted—played for it. Many thought that this wartime band was even better than Miller's civilian band. The band played all over Europe. It made weekly radio broadcasts and often gave live shows every night. The musicians also did everyday military duties, such as playing Reveille and Taps.

On 15 December 1944 Maj Miller took off from England for Paris. The aircraft never made it. No one ever found the wreckage. However, even without its leader, the 418th Army Air Forces Band continued to lift the troops' spirits throughout the remainder of the war. Miller's goal of helping his countrymen lived on. The band evolved into today's USAF premier jazz band, "The Airmen of Note."

CAPT GLENN MILLER

Courtesy of Hulton Archive/Getty Images

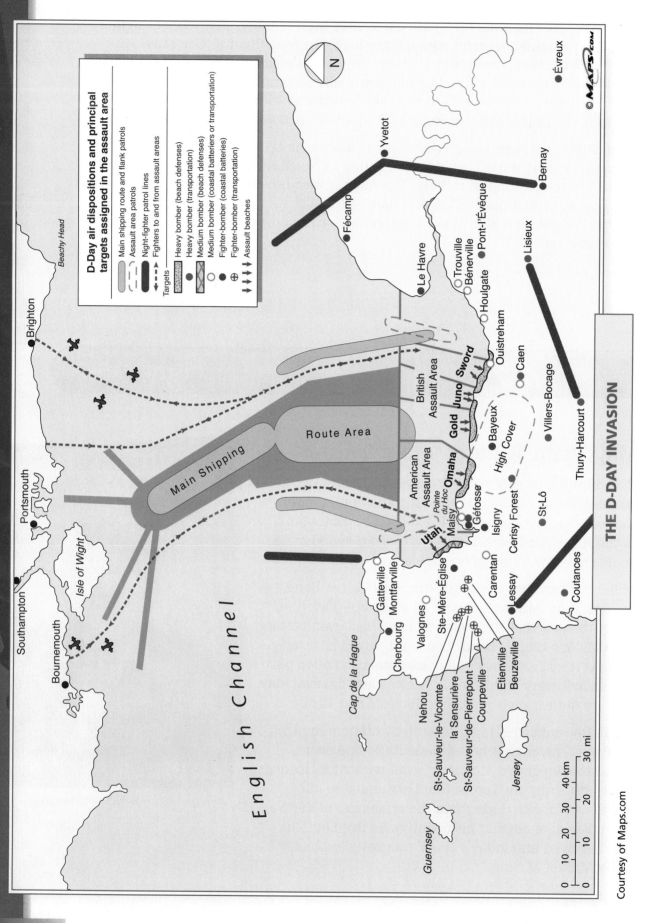

D-Day air dispositions and principal targets assigned in the assault area

Main shipping route and flank patrols
Assault area patrols
Night-fighter patrol lines
Fighters to and from assault areas

Targets

- Heavy bomber (beach defenses)
- Heavy bomber (transportation)
- Medium bomber (beach defenses)
- Medium bomber (coastal batteries or transportation)
- Fighter-bomber (coastal batteries)
- Fighter-bomber (transportation)
- Assault beaches

N

Évreux

Yvetot

Bernay

Fécamp

Le Havre

Pont-l'Évêque

Trouville
Bénerville

Houlgate

Lisieux

Ouistreham

Sword

Juno

Caen

Villers-Bocage

British Assault Area

Gold

Bayeux

High Cover

Thury-Harcourt

Beachy Head

Brighton

Route Area

Main Shipping

American Assault Area

Omaha

St-Lô

Cerisy Forest

Isigny

Géfosse

Pointe du Hoc

Maisy

Utah

Coutances

Portsmouth

Isle of Wight

Carentan

Lessay

Southampton

Bournemouth

Gatteville

Montfarville

Ste-Mère-Église

Valognes

Cherbourg

Étienville

Beuzeville

Courpeville

St-Sauveur-de-Pierrepont

la Sensurière

St-Sauveur-le-Vicomte

Nehou

Cap de la Hague

E n g l i s h   C h a n n e l

Guernsey

Jersey

0   10   20   30 mi
0   10   20   30   40 km

THE D-DAY INVASION

Courtesy of Maps.com

D-Day

The Western Allies delivered a backbreaking blow to Germany in 1944. They called it Operation Overlord. The purpose of this invasion, which would take place on "D-Day," was to retake Western Europe once and for all.

The D-Day invasion began on 6 June 1944 at Normandy, on the northern coast of France. But preparations had begun much earlier. For two months, bombers and fighters of the Army Air Forces and RAF had been striking at German positions in and around Normandy. They wanted to soften the German defenses. They hit airfields, railroads, and coastal barriers. They downed Luftwaffe planes. They wiped out as much as they could within a 130-mile radius of the Normandy beaches where American, British, and Canadian Soldiers would land.

The night before the invasion, the Allies hit German forces extra hard. Hundreds of bombers, which normally flew at an altitude of 20,000 feet, raced through the air just 100 feet to 1,000 feet above ground. After dropping their bombs, the aircraft strafed targets on the ground.

On D-Day, fighters played a critical role. They, too, conducted bombing missions. The P-38 Lightning could carry two 1,000-pound bombs. One group of fighters flattened a German command center. In addition, fighters strafed German infantry. They protected ships crossing the English Channel en route to the Normandy shoreline. They were also used to escort, *or accompany*, bombers and air transports.

The first wave of transports that crossed the channel on D-Day was breathtaking. It was nine aircraft wide in a line extending for 230 miles. Many of the Soldiers arriving on the beach by air transport were paratroopers. A paratrooper *is an infantry Soldier who is trained to parachute, often behind enemy lines.* Transports also towed gliders carrying men and materiel. Most of these gliders were made of wood and fabric, just as the earliest planes were. The maneuver was huge. On the evening of 6 June one glider took off from England for France every 15 seconds.

A B-17 CREW PRAYING BEFORE TAKEOFF FOR D-DAY

Courtesy of the 91st Bomb Group Memorial Association

The D-Day invasion and the Battle of Normandy cost 57,000 Allied Soldiers and Airmen their lives. But it was a major turning point in the war. It gave the Allies a foothold in Europe. More than 1 million men landed along 60 miles of beaches within seven weeks of D-Day. But there was still more to be done to achieve final victory in Europe.

Paul W. Airey: From POW to the First Chief Master Sergeant of the Air Force

In July 1944 Paul W. Airey was flying his 28th combat mission in the European theater. He was a technical sergeant and radio operator. He was flying on a B-24 over oil refineries around Vienna, Austria. Antiaircraft fire severely damaged the bomber. The pilot ordered everyone to jump. Airey parachuted from 18,000 feet into a field. Austrian farmers beat him and held him until German forces arrived. Airy became a prisoner of war (POW).

The Germans sent him to a POW camp called Stalag Luft IV. Later, when Allied forces approached the region, the Germans made all the prisoners march 400 miles to a camp in Berlin. British forces arrived in Berlin in May 1945 and freed the POWs.

CMSGT PAUL W. AIREY IN THE 1990S

Courtesy of the US Air Force

Despite his experience as a prisoner, Airey loved the Air Force. On 3 April 1967, Paul Wesley Airey became the first Chief Master Sergeant of the Air Force (CMSAF). Now he was in the highest NCO position and the enlisted advisor to the secretary of the Air Force and Air Force Chief of Staff.

CMSAF Airey helped produce the Weighted Airman Promotion System. This system included clear, weighted criteria for promotion, including test scores and time-in-grade, and is still in use today. He noted that "WAPS is the most equitable promotion system for enlisted personnel in any of the US armed services." Airey considered this his most important contribution as the CMSAF. He retired on 1 August 1970.

The Women's Airforce Service Pilots

Shortly after Europe went to war in 1939, two Americans tried to find a way for more women to get into the air. The result of their efforts was the Women's Airforce Service Pilots program (WASP).

This program didn't come about overnight. Jacqueline Cochran contacted First Lady Eleanor Roosevelt about setting up a training program for women pilots in September 1939, the month Germany invaded Poland. Nancy Harkness Love got in touch with Lt Col Robert Olds about forming an all-women's ferrying squadron in 1940. These women's job would be to fly military aircraft from factories to bases.

It took a while to grant either request. First, America hadn't even entered the war as of 1939. Second, the country at that time had more pilots than planes.

But eventually the women got their wishes. Once the United States entered the war, the Army Air Forces needed to free men for combat duty. Cochran was in charge of training women through the Women's Flying Training Detachment (WFTD). Some 1,879 female pilots passed through her program. Love became director of the Women's Auxiliary Ferry Squadron (WAFS). In 1943 the Army Air Forces merged the two units into WASP. While Cochran was in charge of WASP, Love headed its ferrying-operations arm. WASP pilots were not members of the military but civil-service employees. By the time WASP was broken up in December 1944, its female pilots had flown 60 million miles and ferried 77 kinds of aircraft.

WOMEN'S AIRFORCE SERVICE PILOTS

Pilots in the Women's Auxiliary Ferrying Squadron fly aircraft from factories to bases. Behind them is a B-17E.

Courtesy of the US Air Force

Jacqueline Cochran: From Foster Care to the Air

Jacqueline Cochran (1906–1980) had grit. She was in foster care as a child. Cochran said she didn't get her first pair of shoes until she was 8 years old. She trained to be a beautician. She liked to make people happy through her work. But along the way, she caught the flying bug.

It started in 1932, when she met millionaire Floyd Bostwick Odlum in New York City. She told him she'd like to start a cosmetics company. Odlum said that in that case, she'd need to find a way to fly her goods to many markets. Cochran saved up money for flying lessons. Rather than cosmetics, flying became her career.

JACQUELINE COCHRAN

Courtesy of the US Air Force

In 1938 Cochran broke a record with a nonstop flight from Los Angeles to Cleveland in eight hours, 10 minutes, 31 seconds in a P-35 fighter. This won the cross-country Bendix Race. Around this time, she reached an altitude of 33,000 feet—a new women's record. She performed other feats as well. Cochran liked to say: "I might have been born in a hovel, but I was determined to travel with the wind and the stars."

As early as 1939 she tried to get the US government to let her train women pilots to help with the war effort. The women couldn't take on roles in fighting, but they could fill support roles and allow more men to enter combat, she figured. The government turned her down.

But later President Franklin D. Roosevelt asked her to study ways to use female pilots in the Army Air Corps. Things went better this time. Cochran, with 25 other women, went to London and served in the British Air Transport Auxiliary in 1942. At Maj Gen Hap Arnold's request, Cochran later established the Women's Flying Training Detachment within the Army Air Forces.

After the war, Cochran kept on flying. In 1953 she became the first woman to break the sound barrier.

Nancy Harkness Love's Early Love of Flight

Nancy Harkness (1914–1976) came from a wealthy Philadelphia family. She attended excellent schools: the Milton Academy in Massachusetts and Vassar College in New York. Early on, she fell in love with flying. She once buzzed her college campus and was suspended from her classes for two weeks.

As a young woman, Nancy fell in love with another pilot, Robert Love. He was an Air Corps Reserve officer. The two married in 1936. They founded an aviation business in Boston. Nancy Love got more flight time in other ways. Through the Bureau of Air Commerce, she was a test pilot for new landing gear with three wheels.

Nancy Love is best known for getting the Women's Auxiliary Ferrying Squadron set up. Maj Gen Hap Arnold turned down her first proposal in 1940. Then in 1942 Robert Love talked to Col William Tunner, who was in charge of the stateside division of the Army Air Forces Ferry Command. Robert Love told Tunner about Nancy Love's piloting skills. Tunner desperately needed more pilots.

Nancy Love got her Women's Auxiliary Ferry Squadron. It had 25 female pilots. She was its director. After the war, she was awarded an Air Medal.

NANCY HARKNESS LOVE

Courtesy of the US Air Force

The Ninety-Nines

Female pilots faced all sorts of barriers at the start of the 20th century. For example, they weren't allowed to compete in air races with men. Nor were they allowed to work as commercial pilots.

In 1929 there were only 117 licensed, American female pilots. A few of them decided to form an all-women pilots' club. They sent letters to all the licensed women pilots. Ninety-nine of the women replied. So Amelia Earhart proposed the group be named The Ninety-Nines. Earhart was the first president.

At first, the women mostly discussed air races. But they gradually took on a more important role. They began to lobby for rights for women pilots. During World War II, members joined the Women's Airforce Service Pilots. Those with nursing training became flight nurses and treated Soldiers wounded in battle. And before the war, they worked on the National Air Marking Program to create a navigation guide visible to the naked eye for pilots without instrument panels or radios.

The Ninety-Nines organization still exists. It has more than 5,500 members. And it continues the air-marking program to this day.

The Final Push

Despite these gains, the Allies had not yet won the war in Europe. From the beaches in Normandy, the Western Allies pushed through the rest of France, then Belgium, and Luxembourg. Meanwhile, on the Eastern Front, the Soviets pushed the Germans out of the Soviet Union and through Eastern Europe. In September the first US patrols entered Germany.

At the end of December 1944, the Germans made a desperate surprise counterattack in Belgium. They wanted to divide the Allied armies and force a negotiated peace. The epic battle in the Ardennes Forest is known as the Battle of the Bulge. Allied air power provided crucial help to the brave ground troops in beating back this attack. Luftwaffe planes attempted to support German forces by attacking US troops on the ground. But in most cases Allied fighters stopped them short of their targets. Although poor weather limited flying on several days, Allied bombers seriously hampered German efforts. They bombed roads, railroads, and bridges behind the lines. This made it more difficult for the Germans to move up supplies and troops.

German defeat in the Battle of the Bulge not only sealed the Nazis' fate on the ground, it also destroyed German air power. The commander of the Luftwaffe fighter arm, Lt Gen Adolf Galland, wrote, "The Luftwaffe received its death blow at the Ardennes offensive."

The strategic bombing of Germany went on. The Allied bombers and escorts hit airplane factories, oil refineries, and roads. Allied manufacturers poured out thousands of airplanes and other supplies. The intensity of air battles grew. By 1945 most bombing runs over Germany involved between 1,000 to 1,500 bombers. The Eighth and Fifteenth Air Forces conducted these missions.

The Army Air Forces and RAF ran out of targets by 15 April 1945. They had unloaded 2.5 million tons of bombs on the Axis Powers in Europe. The United States and Britain lost 8,000 bombers and 7,000 fighters. But the Luftwaffe, despite its initial advantage, lost 33,000 airplanes. On 7 May 1945 the Germans surrendered. The European chapter of the war was closed.

Significant Allied Air Campaigns in the Pacific Theater

Having defeated Germany, the Allies could turn their full attention to Japan. In 1931 Japan reached beyond its borders for more and more resources like oil. It invaded Manchuria and China. In 1940, after France fell to Germany, Japan snatched French Indochina. (French Indochina is today the three countries of Vietnam, Cambodia, and Laos.)

The United States and Britain wanted to put an end to these land grabs. They imposed a trade embargo on Japan. An embargo *is a legal ban on commerce.*

In response, Japan went after its biggest naval threat in the region: the US Pacific fleet at Pearl Harbor in Hawaii. If Japan could defeat this fleet, it could place bases on islands in the Pacific to protect its imports.

As it entered war with America, Japan knew it must maintain its navy. And even though the navy wasn't especially strong in the beginning, it was successful. It surprised the Americans at Pearl Harbor. It drove the Allies all the way to Australia by mid-1942.

The US and Britain were up to their elbows with the war in Europe in 1942. Yet they began a Pacific offensive. It started with two important battles.

Maj Arthur T. Chin: Early Ace of World War II

MAJ ARTHUR CHIN IN 1944

Courtesy of the American Airpower Heritage Museum

Maj Arthur T. Chin (1913–1997) was born in Portland, Oregon. He was a Chinese-American. He took flying lessons as a teenager. Chin started the Portland Chinese Aero Club when still a teen with some of his friends. When Japan invaded China in 1931, they all wanted to go help China fight the Japanese.

When Japan again invaded China in 1937, Chin headed overseas to join the Chinese Air Force. The Chinese thought he was such a good pilot that they sent him to Germany for extra training. When Chin returned to the Chinese Air Force, he flew the Gloster Gladiator and the Curtiss P-40 Warhawk. He made 5 kills and got half credit for another. This made him an ace. He was one of the first American aces of World War II.

In 1939 Chin was shot down and badly burned. As he fell from his airplane, with his hands on fire, he managed to pull the ripcord to his parachute. Nearby Chinese peasants rescued him. He spent several years in recovery. In 1944 he flew again, now as a member of the US military. He delivered supplies over the Himalayan Mountains to Chinese troops. This was necessary because Japan had cut off land and sea routes to China. Chin remained in China until 1949, when the Communists took over the country. At that time he returned to Portland.

The Battle of the Coral Sea and the Battle of Midway

The Battle of the Coral Sea and the Battle of Midway put the brakes on the Japanese advance through the Pacific. These were air battles fought at sea. Air power didn't play a supporting role; the US Navy's ships did. During these battles the aircraft carrier became the principal ship in the navy.

The Battle of the Coral Sea took place from 7 May to 8 May 1942. This was the first naval battle in history in which the opposing ships never saw each other. It was fought entirely by aircraft. US and Japanese planes dive-bombed each other's aircraft carriers off the east coast of Australia. Japan lost two carriers, three heavy cruisers, one light cruiser, two destroyers, and 100 airplanes. The United States lost the aircraft carrier USS *Lexington*, one destroyer, one tanker, and 50 airplanes.

The two sides fought the Battle of Midway from 3 to 6 June 1942. Both sides launched planes from their carriers. The US knew where the Japanese ships were because it had broken the Japanese Navy's secret code. The Japanese suffered greater losses in this clash. They lost four aircraft carriers, one heavy cruiser, three destroyers, and 275 airplanes. In addition the Japanese Navy left the battle site with many damaged vessels, including three battleships, three heavy cruisers, one light cruiser, and a handful of destroyers. By contrast, the United States lost only one aircraft carrier (the USS *Yorktown*), one destroyer, and 150 airplanes. With this battle, the tide of the Pacific war turned in favor of the United States. The Japanese never recovered from their losses at Midway.

The Battle for the Pacific Islands

Less than a month before the Battle of the Coral Sea, America had delivered its first blow to Japan, with the famed Doolittle raid. Lt Col Jimmy Doolittle led 16 B-25 bombers over Japan on 18 April 1942.

Until that day, Japan had promised its people their island nation was safe. Doolittle's raid proved otherwise. The bombers took off from the US Navy aircraft carrier *Hornet*. They hit Tokyo, Kobe, and other cities. Japan didn't shoot down a single B-25. There wasn't enough fuel to return to the *Hornet*, so most of the crews landed in China. One outcome of this raid was that Japan brought some of its air forces home for defense.

Two years later the United States made more strategic bombing attacks over Japan. On 15 June 1944 American B-29s took off from China. Later that year they took off from the Mariana Islands. Many Japanese civilians died in these raids. One reason was that the Japanese placed their factories in the middle of residential neighborhoods. Furthermore, in February 1945 the bombers switched from explosive bombs to incendiary bombs—*bombs designed to start fires*. The incendiary bombs created huge firestorms on the ground. Americans dropped such bombs on the cities of Tokyo and Kobe. An estimated 100,000 civilians died.

Many US bombers also met their end in these raids because they had to fly unescorted from the Marianas, some 1,500 miles away. To reduce their losses, the US forces fought long and hard for the island of Iwo Jima in 1945. Once they captured it, their new air base was only 750 miles from Japan.

A B-25 BOMBER

A B-25 bomber like the one Lt Col Jimmy Doolittle flew during the Tokyo raid

Courtesy of the EAA/Jim Koepnick

The Atomic Bomb

By mid-1945 Germany had surrendered. A few weeks earlier, Harry S. Truman became president of the United States when Franklin D. Roosevelt died. The firebombing of Tokyo and Kobe was weakening Japanese resolve. But more was needed to break the Japanese military government's will. President Truman didn't want to risk hundreds of thousands of US casualties—and the lives of millions of Japanese—on an invasion of Japan.

COL PAUL W. TIBBETS JR.

Enola Gay pilot Col Paul W. Tibbets Jr. shortly before takeoff with the atomic bomb that was dropped on Hiroshima, Japan.

Courtesy of the National Archieves/Getty Images

So Truman asked the military to use its newest weapon, the atomic bomb. The United States had two of them. Col Paul W Tibbets Jr. piloted the *Enola Gay* B-29 bomber. It took off from Tinian Island in the Pacific with the first of the atomic bombs. The crew dropped it on the city of Hiroshima on 6 August 1945. The US dropped the second bomb on Nagasaki, another major Japanese city, on 9 August. Tens of thousands died in the blasts. Tens of thousands more would die of radiation poisoning. Japan surrendered on 14 August 1945.

World War II ended with the utter defeat of Germany, Italy, and Japan. But developments during the war set the stage for much of the next 40 years. The nuclear arms race, jet airplanes, and humanity's first steps in space all happened because of developments during the war. The war also ended in a new rivalry between the Western democracies and the Soviet Union.

At the same time, however, the US economy and the recovering economies of Europe would grow rapidly after the war. And advances in commercial aviation were at the forefront of that growth.

CHECKPOINTS

Lesson 2 Review

Using complete sentences, answer the following questions on a sheet of paper.

1. What is the date of the Japanese attack on Pearl Harbor?

2. Who were the leaders of Italy and Germany?

3. What was the name of the German Air Force?

4. Define the word *blitzkrieg*.

5. What are the three major features of close air support?

6. In what year did President Harry Truman desegregate the armed forces?

7. Who was the first African-American brigadier general of the US Air Force?

8. What is the name of the general who thought up the combat box formation?

9. Name three long-range bombers used by the Allies during World War II.

10. On what day did the D-Day invasion begin?

11. What was the name of the battle that first put a stop to the German advance across Europe?

12. Name two important battles in the Pacific theater during World War II.

13. What was the name of the US bomber that delivered the atomic bomb on Hiroshima?

Applying Your Learning

14. Why was the long-range bomber so important to the United States and Britain in winning World War II?

CHAPTER 5

NASA uses a DC-8 as a flying science laboratory.

Commercial Flight

Chapter Outline

LESSON 1

The Propeller Era
in Commercial Flight

LESSON 2

The Jet Era
in Commercial Flight

"Flying has torn apart the relationship of space and time;
it uses our old clock but with new yardsticks."

Charles Lindbergh

The Propeller Era in Commercial Flight

_____

_____

_____

When Howard Hughes needed a new plane for TWA, why did he turn to Lockheed?

Learn About...

- **key developments in commercial aircraft**
- **key developments in commercial flight use**
- **key contributors to the expansion of commercial flight**

Howard R. Hughes Jr., son of a Texas oilman, was born in 1905. Young Hughes learned to fly at age 14. He quickly became a skilled pilot. When his father died, Howard Jr. inherited the family business, Hughes Toolco. He was a millionaire before he was out of his teens. He soon expanded Toolco to include a division called Hughes Aircraft.

He also gained fame as a pilot, setting many records for speed and distance.

In 1939 Hughes became the principal stockholder of Transcontinental and Western Air (TWA—later known as Trans World Airlines). A stockholder *is a person who owns shares of a public company.* This gave Hughes a voice in running the airline.

TWA had a fleet of state-of-the-art Boeings. They attracted attention—and passengers. They could fly coast to coast in 14 hours. But that wasn't fast enough for Hughes. He wanted a new type of plane.

THE LOCKHEED CONSTELLATION, WITH ITS TRIPLE-FIN TAIL
Courtesy of the EAA/Jim Koepnick

But TWA couldn't build it. New antitrust laws—*laws intended to prevent concentrations of power in business*—now kept TWA and other airlines from building their own planes. Hughes had to look elsewhere. He turned to Lockheed, a company he'd worked with before.

Hughes told the designers that he wanted a really fast passenger plane. So they chose a different type of engine, an 18-cylinder Wright R-3350. The plane's propellers were more than 15 feet in diameter. To enable the props to clear the ground, the plane needed very tall landing-gear *struts*, or braces. For better control, the plane needed a large tail surface. That led to a distinctive triple-fin tail design.

Hughes demanded that his new plane be built under strict secrecy. He got his wish until World War II. At that point, the government took over commercial planes for wartime service. The secret project was out in the open.

The new plane was the L-049 Constellation. Although designed for passengers, it was first used as a military plane (the Lockheed C-69 Constellation). The L-049 flew faster than the fighter planes of its day.

When the Constellation was ready for a test flight in 1944, Hughes was at the controls. The new plane, painted in TWA's distinctive red, flew nonstop across the country in less than seven hours. Hughes broke his own speed record with that flight.

TWA wasn't ready to offer regular nonstop cross-country service. But the Constellation cut about eight hours off the trip from coast to coast.

The Constellation and its counterparts from Douglas Aircraft, the DC-6 and DC-7, were the stars of air travel during the 1940s and 1950s. They were the fastest, safest, and most comfortable propeller-driven airliners ever built. Until the passenger jet came along in the late 1950s, they were the highpoint of air travel.

HOWARD HUGHES AND JACK FRYE

Howard Hughes (left) and TWA's Jack Frye (right, rear) after setting a speed record in the Lockheed Constellation

Courtesy of the Hulton Archive/Getty Images

Howard Hughes—Moviemaker and Aviator

Howard Hughes Jr. (1905–1976) learned to fly in his early teens. But before earning fame in aviation, he was a well-known movie director and producer. One of his movies was a World War I epic called "Hell's Angels." He wrote and directed it himself. Filming began in 1928. He got 87 combat planes together and directed combat scenes in the skies over Mines Field. (The Los Angeles International Airport is there now.)

Years later, Hughes made another war movie, "Jet Pilot," starring John Wayne. Hughes started filming in 1949 but didn't release the movie until 1957. He kept tinkering with the combat scenes to get them just right. This was long before the days of computer-generated special effects. He needed real planes for his action scenes.

The Air Force was grateful for Hughes's pioneering work in aviation. So it let him use military planes.

Hughes's movie included a scene with superstar pilot Chuck Yeager at the controls of a Sabre jet. It also showed Northrop's XF-89 Scorpion prototype which appeared as a Russian fighter plane.

But Hughes is better known for another case of cooperation with the US armed forces. In 1942 German submarines were sinking US troop transports. Shipbuilder Henry Kaiser had an idea—why not build a fleet of flying boats? They would be made of wood because of a wartime shortage of metal.

Key Developments in Commercial Aircraft

As you read in Chapter 4, air power helped the Allies win World War II. The war also exposed millions of Americans to aviation, often for the first time. More than 2 million Americans worked in the aircraft industry in the 1940s. More than 16 million served in uniform and saw air power firsthand. Hundreds of thousands of them flew for the first time during the war.

After the war, interest in aviation was keen. People who wanted to start airlines could buy military-surplus planes at bargain prices. Many people wanted to work in the field. Many more now saw air travel as a great way to get across a vast country. Americans were ready to fly.

When Kaiser got an $18 million government contract, Hughes signed on. The partnership didn't last long. Things didn't move fast enough for Kaiser. And so he pulled out.

Hughes renamed the aircraft the H-4 Hercules. But most people called it the "Spruce Goose" because of its wooden frame. Hughes hated the nickname. For one reason, the H-4 was made of birch, not spruce. He also thought the nickname belittled a good design and the workers who'd built it.

The H-4 was eventually the world's largest flying boat. Hughes flew it once for 60 seconds. It never flew again. It still holds the record for the largest wingspan in aviation history: 319 feet, 11 inches.

As time passed, Hughes became more and more isolated and eccentric. Some people think he may have been mentally ill. The man who was once a public figure lived his final years in seclusion.

THE H-4 HERCULES, OR "SPRUCE GOOSE"

Courtesy of AP Photo

The war did more for aviation than just make people aware of it. It also spurred many technical advances. New kinds of planes came into use. New airports appeared around the world. Weather forecasting got better. Navigation aids improved. These things made flying safer. Better fuel— 100-octane aviation gas—gave aircraft engines more power. This meant planes could carry heavier loads and fly farther.

Radar, which helped the British keep an eye out for German bombers during the war, came into use in civil aviation, making air travel safer. And pressurized cabins—*cabins with normal air pressure even at high altitudes*— made air travel more comfortable.

No matter how strong or large their planes, people who flew in the early days had one big problem: flying could literally make you sick. One reason was that there wasn't enough oxygen in the cabins.

The higher you go above sea level, the less oxygen is in the air. Mountain climbers deal with this problem all the time. If planes flew much higher than 10,000 feet in the early days, people on board got dizzy. Some even fainted.

One solution might be to fly low. But below 10,000 feet, planes often hit rough weather. That led to airsickness—motion sickness associated with flying. Airlines knew if they could make passengers more comfortable, more people would want to fly.

The big breakthrough was the Boeing 307B Stratoliner. It made its first flight 8 July 1940. It had a pressurized cabin. As the plane rose, air was pumped into the cabin. Even well above 10,000 feet, air pressure inside the cabin was the same as it is on the ground.

The 33-seat Stratoliner could fly at an altitude of up to 20,000 feet. It reached speeds as great as 200 miles per hour.

BOEING 307 STRATOLINER

The Boeing 307 Stratoliner took air travel comfort to new heights.

Courtesy of the National Air and Space Museum, Smithsonian Institution
(SI Neg. No. SI-2007-4592)

Important Commercial Aircraft

The DC-3 (See Chapter 3, Lesson 3) was the most widely used aircraft right after the war. But before long the airlines wanted to fly longer routes. They also wanted to carry heavier traffic. They turned to the civilian versions of two planes that first saw service in the war.

The four-engine Douglas DC-4 was the civilian version of the C-54. And as you read earlier, the Lockheed Constellation started out as the C-69.

The Constellation had a pressurized cabin, so it could fly higher. It could also fly about 100 miles an hour faster than the DC-4. But the DC-4 won the first round of competition between the two. One reason is that DC-4s were easier to come by. More than 1,000 of them were built during the war. Soon almost every airline was flying DC-4s.

But when the supply of surplus DC-4s ran out, the Constellation became the top seller.

Meanwhile, Douglas and Lockheed kept developing bigger and better planes. Douglas had the DC-6, the DC-6B, DC-7, DC-7B, and DC-7C. The DC-7C was known as the "Seven Seas" because of its great range.

DC-4

DC-4s such as this one were in great demand right after World War II.

Courtesy of the Lake County Museum/Corbis

DOUGLAS DC-7C

Courtesy of Boeing

LOCKHEED SUPER CONSTELLATION
Courtesy of Bettmann/Corbis

LOCKHEED STARLINER

Courtesy of R.M. Petersen

MARTIN 2-0-2

Courtesy of Thomas D. Mcavoy/Time Life Pictures/
Getty Images

Not to be outdone, Lockheed developed the Super Constellation and the Starliner. These planes eventually had 100 seats. They flew at around 300 mph. They could cross the country nonstop in nine hours or less. They could also fly from New York to London.

By 1947 airlines flying shorter routes could choose between the Martin 2-0-2 and the Convair 240. These planes were faster than the DC-3. They were pressurized. They offered the same passenger comforts as the DC-6 and Constellation did.

Another development at this period was the rise of all-cargo airlines—*airlines that carried freight, not passengers.* Like early passenger planes, the first all-cargo planes were developed for the military. They included C-47s and C-69s.

CONVAIR 240

Courtesy of Bettmann/Corbis

Donald Wills Douglas Sr.— Aviation Pioneer

DONALD WILLS DOUGLAS SR.

Courtesy of Bettmann/Corbis

Donald Wills Douglas Sr. (1892–1981) was born in Brooklyn, New York. He entered the US Naval Academy at Annapolis, Maryland, at 17. He spent much of his time there working on model planes. His family and professors thought this interest would pass. But Douglas was hooked on planes. He left the academy before graduation to look for work as an aeronautical engineer.

Douglas enrolled in the Massachusetts Institute of Technology. He finished a four-year course in two years. The school offered him a job as assistant professor immediately.

After that, he lived in Connecticut, California, and Ohio. He served briefly as a civilian in the Army Signal Corps Aviation Section in Washington, D.C.

But Douglas's goal was to make it on his own in the aircraft business. In March 1920 he returned to Los Angeles, with $600 and a family to support. He hoed potatoes and washed cars to provide for his family.

And then he got his first aircraft order. It was from millionaire sportsman David R. Davis. They got together and formed the Davis-Douglas Co. The company built the Cloudster. It was the first aircraft to lift a useful load exceeding its own weight.

DAVIS-DOUGLAS CLOUDSTER

Courtesy of Boeing

Davis soon lost interest in the company. He sold out to Douglas, who incorporated the Douglas Company in July 1921. Douglas landed his own Navy contract— to build torpedo bombers, starting with the DT-1. By 1928, the company was worth $25 million.

Douglas kept going through the Great Depression by building military aircraft. Soon after, he started building his famous airliners. By 1940 sales of DC-2 and DC-3 aircraft reached nearly $61 million.

Douglas remained president of his company until 1957.

THE CRASH OF THE *HINDENBURG*

Courtesy of Arthur Cofod/Pictures Inc./
Time Life Pictures/Getty Images

Between the world wars, another kind of aircraft had a moment of glory. This was the rigid airship, or zeppelin. (Airships were a type of lighter-than-air flying machine you read about in Chapter 1.)

The German maker Zeppelin was the most successful builder of airships. The Germans used them during World War I. At the end of the war, they had to surrender their airship fleet to the Allies. According to terms of the Treaty of Versailles, the Germans could no longer build military aircraft.

But by 1926 the Germans could once more build zeppelins. One of them, the *Graf Zeppelin*, flew more than a million miles, made 590 flights, and carried more than 13,000 passengers before it was retired.

But the most famous zeppelin was the *Hindenburg*. It was the largest and most luxurious airship ever built. It made 10 round trips between Germany and the United States. But on 6 May 1937, as it prepared to land in New Jersey, it exploded, crashed, and burned. Thirty-five passengers and crew members died. They were the first fatalities in scheduled airship operations.

The US Navy also flew airships. In 1923 it built the *Shenandoah*. It was a flying public relations machine. It flew around the country visiting air shows and county fairs.

On 3 September 1925, however, the *Shenandoah* was caught in a storm over southern Ohio. It broke up. Part of the airship landed in a cornfield. Lt Cmdr Charles E. Rosendahl brought the nose section to a safe landing. But 14 of the 43 crew members died.

Later, Goodyear Tire and Rubber Company won a contract to build zeppelins in the United States. It built two airships for the Navy—the *Akron* and the *Macon*.

USS *SHENANDOAH*

USS *Shenandoah* flying over the New York City area around 1923

Courtesy of the US Navy Historical Center

Both met with disaster. The *Akron* crashed off the New Jersey coast in 1933, killing 73. The *Macon* plunged into the Pacific Ocean in 1935. Fortunately, Navy ships nearby saved all but two of the 83 on board.

After these accidents, the United States lost interest in airships. The *Hindenburg* disaster marked the end of efforts to use airships for commercial travel.

Key Developments in Commercial Flight Use

Many features of air travel today had their roots in these early years. Among them were flight attendants, frequent-flier discount programs, travel credit cards, and airline agents who could reissue tickets after a missed connection or a delayed flight. The airlines even offered a telephone reservation service.

Growth of Commercial Flight Use

The 1930s were a time of enormous growth in passenger air travel. The number of air passengers in the United States rose from 474,000 in 1932 to 1,176,858 in 1938. The number of air-passenger miles increased 600 percent between 1936 and 1941. The DC-3 was responsible for much of this growth. Still, long-distance travel was mostly by rail.

TWA began the first cross-country passenger air service between New York and Los Angeles on 25 October 1930.

The first regular passenger and airmail service across the Atlantic began 20 May 1939. But as you read earlier, that was seaplane service—Pan American's "flying boats."

In October 1945 an American Airlines plane took off from New York and touched down at Hurn Airfield in England. This was the first commercial flight by a land-based plane from North America to Europe.

Development of Federal Regulation of Commercial Flight

In 1938 a new federal agency, the Civil Aeronautics Authority, took charge of civil aviation. It set airfares. It also set airlines' routes.

In 1940 President Franklin Roosevelt split this agency in two. Both new agencies were part of the Department of Commerce.

Roosevelt put one new agency, the Civil Aeronautics Administration (CAA) in charge of air traffic control—*the ground-based system for keeping aircraft safely separated from one another*. The CAA licensed pilots and planes. It enforced safety rules. It also developed airways, *the routes that planes must follow through the sky.*

Eventually CAA air traffic controllers would take over responsibility for takeoffs and landings at airports. After the war, radar helped CAA controllers keep up with the airline boom. In 1946 Congress gave the CAA the task of promoting development of the nation's civil airports.

The second agency, the Civil Aeronautics Board (CAB) made safety rules. When an accident occurred, the CAB tried to find out what happened. The CAB also regulated airlines as businesses.

Key Contributors to the Expansion of Commercial Flight

Aviation progressed during this period because leaders of the major airlines were competing with each other for passengers. The companies' executives demanded more and more of aircraft manufacturers. This led to more competition among manufacturers vying with one another for contracts.

Major Commercial Airlines

Four airlines dominated this period—American, Eastern, TWA, and United.

American Airlines

American Airlines grew from several companies launched in the 1920s to fly airmail. These companies joined to form the Aviation Corporation. AVCO, as it was called, quickly bought several small airlines.

In 1930, to streamline its operation, the company's board of directors voted to form a new company, American Airways. In 1934 the company's name became American Airlines.

The company's new president, Cyrus R. Smith, wanted a new plane to match his vision. American flew 18-passenger Curtiss Condors at that time. Smith wanted something bigger. He worked out a deal with Douglas Aircraft to build 20 DC-3s. The DC-3 became one of the most successful aircraft ever built. By 1939 American was flying more passenger miles than any other domestic airline.

Smith retired in 1968. He was a true pioneer of commercial flight.

CLEMENT KEYS

Clement Keys helped launch two of the "big four" airlines in the United States.

Courtesy of the National Air and Space Museum, Smithsonian Institution (SI Neg. No. SI-2004-51803)

Eastern Air Transport

Clement Keys, a former editor at *The Wall Street Journal*, promoted commercial aviation in the 1920s and 1930s. He eventually bought a small Philadelphia airline called Pitcairn Aviation.

Pitcairn became Eastern Air Transport on 17 January 1930. It served Boston, Atlanta, and Miami. It soon reached Richmond, Virginia. Eastern specialized in the East Coast. Its "Great Silver Fleet" connected the big cities of the Northeast with Florida vacation spots.

EDDIE RICKENBACKER

World War I ace Eddie Rickenbacker had a long career at Eastern Airlines.

Courtesy of the Library of Congress

Eddie Rickenbacker, the World War I ace, was Eastern's general manager. Later he and some associates bought the airline from Keys and his investors.

Transcontinental and Western Air Inc. (TWA)

TWA, like Eastern, had a connection with Clement Keys. Also like other major airlines, TWA started out carrying mail. Keys and other investors launched Transcontinental Air Transport (TAT) in 1928 to carry mail. But he thought the time was right for air-passenger travel. He offered a coast-to-coast service combining air and rail. Passengers rode in Pullman sleepers at night. By day, they flew in Ford Trimotors. But even with the support of Charles Lindbergh, the service lost money.

TAT merged with Western Air Express in July 1930 to form Transcontinental and Western Air, Inc. (TWA). TWA received its first mail contract immediately. It began coast-to-coast flights on 25 October 1930. The planes made overnight stops in Kansas City.

FORD TRIMOTOR
Courtesy of Neil Rabinowitz/Corbis

Like many other airlines, TWA attracted strong and colorful personalities. Its first director of operations was William John Frye (1904–1959), a former Hollywood stunt flier.

One day when Frye was a teenager, three Army Curtis Jennies (See Chapter 3, Lesson 1) made emergency landings near a pond where he was ice skating. He forgot his skates to go help the fliers. By the end of the day he'd picked up pneumonia and a fascination with flight. He recovered from the first. The second stayed with him the rest of his life.

He became president of TWA at age 30. A licensed pilot, Frye kept TWA on the leading edge of technical advances. He helped set the specifications for the Douglas DC-1 and DC-2 as well as other planes.

WILLIAM JOHN (JACK) FRYE (LEFT)

TWA president William John (Jack) Frye was a former stunt flier.

Courtesy of AP Photo

When Frye wanted 33 Boeing Stratoliners built in 1938, he convinced a quirky millionaire named Howard Hughes to finance the deal. He later persuaded Hughes to buy a controlling interest in TWA.

United Airlines

United Airlines began as part of the United Aircraft and Transport Corporation. This was a partnership between Boeing Airplane Company and Pratt and Whitney, the engine maker. United Airlines began as an operating division of the partnership on 1 July 1931. It advertised itself as the "world's largest air transport system."

New antitrust legislation soon required Boeing to sell the company off. But United remained important. On 30 March 1933 it introduced the Boeing 247 (See Chapter 3, Lesson 3). Many people call this the world's first modern passenger plane. Soon United was flying coast to coast in a little less than 20 hours.

Other Developments in Commercial Airlines Operations

Transatlantic Service

From the time commercial aviation began, fliers dreamed of connecting North America and Europe.

It was a real challenge. North Atlantic skies are often stormy. Natural stopping places are few. Partly for that reason, some of the first transatlantic services crossed the South Atlantic. These routes connected West Africa and South America.

British Imperial Airways and Pan American Airways tried out transatlantic service in 1936. Before then, the British hesitated to give Americans landing rights.

In June 1945 the CAB allowed three carriers to operate regular air service across the Atlantic. They were American Export, Pan Am, and TWA.

That ended Pan Am's role as the sole US carrier. It also led to a boom in air travel.

Freight Airlines

In November 1910 a department store in Dayton, Ohio, shipped a bolt of silk by air to Columbus, Ohio—a distance of less than 100 miles. This was the first practical demonstration of freight shipping by air. Even for short routes, air express was already faster than the railroad.

But all-cargo airlines didn't emerge until after World War II. Companies found it hard to get into the cargo business. Passenger airlines tried to keep them out of airports. Passenger lines feared that freight carriers would upset the aviation industry with cheap rates and irregular service. Through the 1940s passenger airlines, freight carriers, and the government regulators struggled for a solution. They needed to find a way to award contracts and set rates.

In August 1949 the CAB gave four all-freight airlines the go-ahead. They were Slick, Flying Tiger, U.S. Airlines, and Airnews. Only Slick and Flying Tiger lasted through the propeller era of aviation.

Freight airlines never grew as expected. They accounted for only a small share of air cargo. The big four passenger carriers and other passenger lines continued to carry freight. The passenger carriers had better facilities at airports and lower costs.

Not until 1973, when Fred Smith launched Federal Express, with a guarantee of overnight delivery, did an all-freight carrier come into its own.

Throughout the 1950s manufacturers worked on the jet aircraft that would eventually replace planes such as the Lockheed Constellation. On 2 May 1952 the world's first jet airliner, the British-made De Havilland Comet, made its first public demonstration flight in London. On 4 October 1958 a British Comet IV with 31 passengers made the first transatlantic commercial jet flight. On 10 December 1958 National Air Lines began the first jet passenger service in the United States. The aircraft was a Boeing 707. It flew between New York City and Miami, Florida.

The propeller era had ended. The jet age had begun.

PIPER CUB

Courtesy of Bettmann/Corbis

CESSNA 140

Courtesy of the EAA/Jim Koepnick

BEECHCRAFT 35 BONANZA

Courtesy of the National Air and Space Museum, Smithsonian Institution (SI Neg. No. 75-1021-55)

The Taylor E-2 Cub made its first flight on 10 September 1930. This plane led to the famous Piper Cub. It came out in 1938. The Piper Cub was one of the world's most popular general aviation planes. General aviation *is all civil aviation other than flights by scheduled airlines and government agencies.*

During the early 1930s the US government tried to get ordinary people to buy planes. It even came up with a plan for a "poor man's plane," to sell for $700. That would be about $10,000 in today's dollars.

But manufacturers thought that price was too low. The government's idea fell through.

In the 1940s general aviation was part of the war effort. The Civil Air Patrol, begun in 1941, trained men as military pilots. Manufacturers built small planes for use in military training and as observation aircraft.

After the war thousands of former military pilots wanted to keep flying. So they bought small planes. Thousands of other veterans learned to fly with government help.

Surplus aircraft were widely available after the war. But manufacturers soon started bringing out new planes as well.

In 1946 Cessna Aircraft launched its C-120 and C-140. Both planes were all-metal high-wing monoplanes. Both were very successful. They led to the Cessna 150/152 and the Cessna 182.

Piper continued its Cub series with the PA-28 Super Cub.

In 1947 Beech, the third of the "big three" manufacturers, introduced the Bonanza. It was an all-metal low-wing craft with retractable landing gear. It could fly at 200 mph, at night, and in all kinds of weather.

The Bonanza was as close as the public could get to a "fighter" plane. Beech had 500 orders for the Bonanza before the plane made its first flight.

CHECKPOINTS

Lesson 1 Review

Using complete sentences, answer the following questions
on a sheet of paper.

1. Why did the Air Force give Howard Hughes help with his movie "Jet Pilot"?

2. Why did Hughes hate the nickname "Spruce Goose"?

3. How did pressurized cabins make it easier for people wanting to fly?

4. Why did the DC-4 win the first round of competition against the Constellation?

5. What was the Cloudster's claim to fame?

6. Why did the United States lose interest in zeppelins?

7. Which four airlines dominated the postwar propeller era?

8. What coast-to-coast service did TAT offer unsuccessfully?

9. Why was it a challenge for early fliers to cross the North Atlantic Ocean at first?

10. Why did freight airlines not grow as expected?

Applying Your Learning

11. How did World War II make Americans more aware of aviation? How might things have been different had there been no war?

LESSON 2

The Jet Era in Commercial Flight

Learn About...

- **the significance of the development of the jet engine**
- **key developments in the commercial flight industry**
- **pros and cons of commercial flight travel for passengers**

The jet engine is the technology that shrank the world. Jets fly faster and higher than propeller planes. That cuts down travel time and brings distant places closer.

And 1958 was the year of the commercial jet. In that year US airlines introduced jet service on both overseas and domestic flights.

Jet engines developed through the 1930s and 1940s. World War II and the Korean War saw the deployment of military jets. But commercial airlines took their time in adopting the new technology.

Why hesitate? Because jet engines were very different from the engines in propeller aircraft. These differences made jets an expensive investment. Jet engines burned much hotter than the engines in propeller aircraft. So they had to be made of alloys. An alloy *is a combination of different metals— or of metal and nonmetal— fused for strength, resistance to corrosion, or other desired qualities*. Alloys cost more than single metals.

Jet engines also used more fuel. Planes with jet engines had higher takeoff speeds. So they needed longer runways.

In view of these differences, airlines understandably took a wait-and-see attitude toward the new technology.

But Juan Trippe, chief executive of Pan American Airways, didn't want to wait. He'd already pioneered transoceanic air service with the "flying boats" known as Pan Am Clippers.

Trippe wanted to see Pan Am fly nonstop across the oceans. Some people thought that Comet jets would achieve this goal. A British manufacturer, De Havilland, built the Comet. But after a couple of crashes, the Comet's promise faded.

Who would now take the lead? Trippe decided to play Douglas and Boeing off against each other. These companies were two of America's largest airplane manufacturers. They competed for Pan Am's business. Douglas offered the DC-8 and Boeing the 707.

In October 1955 Pan Am signed on to buy 20 of the 707 jets and 25 of the DC-8s.

Two years later, Boeing rolled out its first 707. And on 26 October 1958 Pan American introduced jet service from New York to London, with a stop in Newfoundland.

The first flight had 111 passengers. That was more people than had ever boarded a single regularly scheduled flight.

The fare was about the same as for a propeller plane: $272. It sounds like a good deal, but in 2007 dollars, that ticket would cost about $1,500.

The new service was a huge success. Several other airlines quickly adopted the 707. Pan Am continued to forge ahead. Within a year, it was able to get rid of the Newfoundland layover. It introduced nonstop service on Boeing 707-320s. Pan Am set the standard for the industry.

The era of passenger jet travel had a slow start. But once it took off, it soared. Around the world, airlines moved quickly to replace propeller planes with jets.

Vocabulary

- alloy
- metal fatigue
- turbine engine
- reciprocating engine
- propulsion
- weight
- tri-jet
- consortium
- configuration
- jet lag
- free market

DE HAVILLAND COMET
Courtesy of AP Photo

Juan Trippe—Pan Am's Pioneering Chief

Juan Terry Trippe (1899–1981) was the founder and longtime chief executive of Pan American Airways.

Trippe was born in Sea Bright, New Jersey. His ancestors were English seafarers who came to Maryland in the 17th century.

While in his 20s, Trippe used some inherited money to launch Long Island Airways in New York. That venture failed. He tried again. This time he invested in Colonial Air. It flew mail routes between New York City and Boston.

But Trippe had bigger things in mind. He wanted to develop air routes in the Caribbean and South America. In 1927 he launched Pan Am. Under his leadership, it became the largest and most successful international airline in the world.

Trippe understood that success in the airline business meant knowing both economics and politics. So he reached out to aircraft builders and politicians as well as the public.

Trippe greatly improved Pan Am's passenger service. He helped develop new aircraft, from the Boeing 707s and DC-8s to the 747. He was president of the airline until 1968.

JUAN TRIPPE

Juan Trippe,
founder of Pan Am

Courtesy of the Library of Congress

The Significance of the Development of the Jet Engine

AEOLIPILE

About 100 BC, Hero of Alexandria developed this simple engine called an aeolipile.

Courtesy of DK Images

A Greek named Hero of Alexandria invented a type of jet engine around 100 BC.

But the history of modern jet engines begins with Frank Whittle. An engineer, he was also an officer in the British Royal Air Force.

On 16 January 1930 Whittle got a patent for his design of a jet aircraft engine. This gave the British a head start in jet aircraft. They kept the lead for a number of years.

In September 1941 the US Army Air Forces decided to build their own version of Whittle's engine. On 1 October 1942 Robert Stanley made the first flight of the Bell XP 59-A Airacomet, at Muroc, California. It had General Electric engines based on Whittle's design.

On 2 May 1952 the British Overseas Airways Corporation started the first regular jet airline service. It flew De Havilland Comets between London and Johannesburg, South Africa.

The Comet transformed air travel. It flew at 500 mph. It soared at altitudes of up to 30,000 feet.

But in 1954 two Comets had fatal accidents. Structural failure was the cause. Aircraft flying at high speeds and high altitudes are subject to enormous stress and pressure. This can lead to metal fatigue—*a slow weakening of strength in metal caused by repeated deformation, vibration, or other stress*. It's like what happens when you bend a paper clip back and forth. Eventually it breaks.

That's what happened to the British jets. The two Comets couldn't take the stress and pressure. They broke up in the air. The accidents were setbacks for British aviation. But manufacturers learned a lot from them. The result was much safer aircraft.

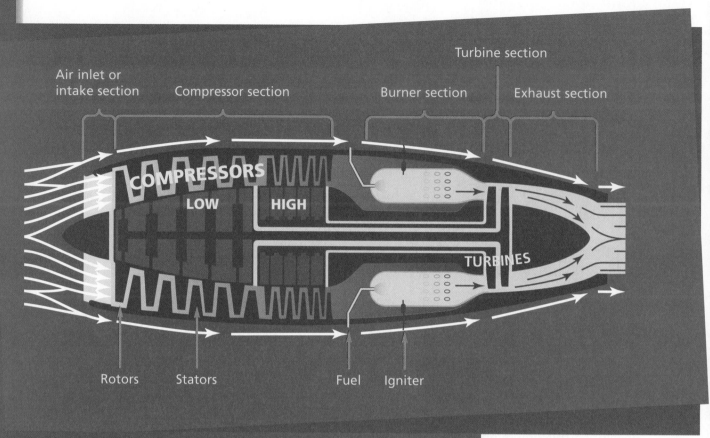

Air inlet or intake section

Compressor section

Burner section

Turbine section

Exhaust section

COMPRESSORS

LOW   HIGH

TURBINES

Rotors   Stators   Fuel   Igniter

FIGURE 2.1 SECTIONS AND PARTS OF A TURBOJET ENGINE SIMPLIFED

How the Jet Engine Works

The word *turbine* means "whirl" or "spinning top." A turbine engine, or jet engine, *is an engine driven by a moving fluid, such as water, steam, or air, that pushes against blades or paddles attached to a central shaft.*

Hot flowing gases power the turbine engines in aircraft. Some turbine engines connect to propellers.

The materials and engineering that go into a jet engine are complex. But the operation of a jet engine is simple.

A jet engine takes in air and accelerates it to extremely high speeds through an exhaust nozzle. The fast-moving air pushes the plane forward. This is the thrust force generated by the engine.

Jet engines have rotating parts. These parts can spin at tens of thousands of revolutions per minute.

A jet's spinning motions make it different from a reciprocating engine—*an engine that goes back and forth.* Most of the aircraft you've read about so far had reciprocating internal-combustion engines.

Propulsion *is a driving or propelling force*. There are two basic types of jet propulsion: turboprop and pure jet. Both use a gas turbine engine. In a turboprop, the gas turbine is connected to a propeller. The jet exhaust provides some thrust, but the propeller provides most of it. In a pure jet, all the thrust comes from the jet exhaust.

All turbine engines have five basic parts: the *inlet*, the *compressor*, the *burner (combustor)*, the *turbine*, and the *exhaust (nozzle)*.

The Significance of the Jet Engine

Turbine engines have many advantages over reciprocating engines. Turbine engines can fly higher and faster. They vibrate less because their parts spin, rather than slide back and forth. Cooling a turbine engine is easier because it takes in so much air.

But the biggest advantage of turbine engines is that they produce more thrust per pound of engine weight than reciprocating engines do. As a result, turbine engines can carry heavier loads.

Aeronautics has a special definition of weight. That definition relates to the basic forces of flight. **Weight** *is the force that directly opposes lift*.

Aviators always have to think about weight. It's possible to load an aircraft with so many passengers and so much baggage that it can't take off. The more weight an engine can lift, the better.

BOEING 707

Pan Am used the 707 to introduce jet service across the Atlantic Ocean.

Courtesy of Bettmann/Corbis

Developments in Jet Aircraft

By the mid-1950s Boeing had been building military jets for years. That experience helped Boeing build the 707. Once again, civil aviation benefited from lessons learned building military aircraft.

The 707—Pan Am's choice for its new transatlantic service in 1958—soon became the standard long-range jet. But airlines had other options: the DC-8 and the Convair 880 and 890.

MCDONNELL DOUGLAS DC-8

NASA uses a DC-8 as a flying science laboratory.

Courtesy of NASA

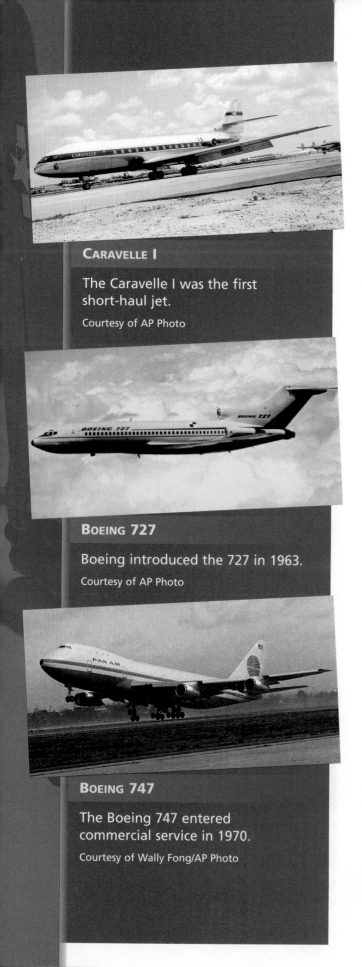

CARAVELLE I

The Caravelle I was the first short-haul jet.

Courtesy of AP Photo

BOEING 727

Boeing introduced the 727 in 1963.

Courtesy of AP Photo

BOEING 747

The Boeing 747 entered commercial service in 1970.

Courtesy of Wally Fong/AP Photo

Jets Get Smaller

Soon manufacturers started building smaller jets. These smaller jets worked well for short hauls. For example, in 1959 Air France put a new jet—the Caravelle I—into service. The French company Sud-Est Aviation built it. The Caravelle had an engine on each side of the rear fuselage. It was the first short-haul jet. It carried up to 90 passengers.

Only one US carrier, United Airlines, flew the Caravelle. But the French aircraft had a big influence on American manufacturers. Soon they, too, started building smaller jets. They wanted to offer the benefits of jet speed, altitude, and comfort on shorter routes.

In February 1963 Boeing introduced the 727. It was versatile, but noisy. Boeing produced more than 1,700 of these tri-jet aircraft. A tri-jet *is an aircraft with three engines*. The 727 was good for smaller airports with shorter runways and fewer passengers. It is the most successful jet ever built.

Douglas introduced its short-haul jet, the DC-9, in 1965. The company merged with McDonnell Aircraft Corp. in 1967, forming McDonnell Douglas.

Jumbo Jets

In April 1966 Boeing announced plans for the wide-body 747. It made its first flight in 1969. Airlines started flying it the next year.

The 747 carried hundreds of passengers. It dwarfed the 707. The aisle of the 747's economy-class section alone was longer than the Wright brothers' historic 1903 flight. The 747 was luxurious. Some models even had an upstairs cocktail lounge.

Airlines still fly 747s. Even people who don't know much about aircraft can spot a 747. It has a distinctive bump on the top of its fuselage.

McDonnell Douglas DC-10
Courtesy of George Hall/Corbis

Lockheed and McDonnell Douglas were not far behind Boeing. They announced plans for jumbo jets in 1966. Both companies rolled out their new planes in 1970. The McDonnell Douglas DC-10 came out in August. The Lockheed L-1011 followed in November. Both aircraft can carry as many as 350 passengers. They can fly nonstop up to 4,000 miles.

Like the Boeing 747, the McDonnell Douglas DC-10 and the Lockheed L-1011 are still in use.

A Global Industry

Until 1978 American manufacturers dominated the global aircraft industry. US manufacturers had 85 percent of the world market at that time.

But other countries soon started to catch up. US manufacturers felt heat from Airbus Industrie, a European consortium working on an aircraft called the A-310 advanced technology transport. A consortium *is an association of companies for some specific purpose.*

American manufacturers responded to this competitive threat. They came up with new products of their own. McDonnell-Douglas brought out its DC-9 Super 80. Boeing developed its 757 and 767.

Boeing and McDonnell Douglas merged in 1997. In 2001, Airbus became a single company. Today Boeing and Airbus are the world's major competitors in aircraft manufacturing.

Key Developments in the Commercial Flight Industry

As you have read, airlines didn't switch to jet engines immediately. But once jets caught on, they caught on big.

The Transition From Propellers to Jets

Early jets had their greatest advantage for long flights. But by the early 1960s, airlines wanted to offer jet service on shorter flights, too.

At first it was difficult. But the newer jets were more reliable and efficient. They were quieter. That helped jets continue to squeeze propeller aircraft out of service. Smaller jets soon competed with prop planes for business.

Taking its cue from the Caravelle, Boeing introduced the 727. With three engines, it was well suited to short- and medium-distance runs. It was available in several configurations—*setups for specific purposes*. This let Boeing serve customers with many different needs.

The "big four" US airlines you read about in Lesson 1—American, Eastern, TWA, and United—introduced the 727 within four months of one another in 1964. Douglas soon followed with its DC-9.

Soon "air travel" became synonymous with "jet travel."

The Impact of the Jet Engine on the Commercial Flight Industry

Jet travel literally brought people around the world closer together. Friends on two continents could now keep in touch much more easily. Services such as Eastern's Air Shuttle, which required no reservations, let business people fly on the spur of the moment. They could make day trips between Boston, New York, and Washington.

Jet travel let American students spend summers in Europe. Middle class families could cross the country over a long weekend to ski or surf or visit grandma.

Jet travel even brought a new term into the language: jet lag. Jet lag *is fatigue and sleep disturbance as a result of crossing time zones on a jet.*

The jet era brought changes to airports as well. They built longer, thicker runways. Chicago's O'Hare Airport introduced parallel runways. These let more than one aircraft land or take off at a time. Passengers boarded their aircraft through enclosed "jet bridges" instead of the old-fashioned passenger stairs.

When airlines switched to jets they had to improve their maintenance standards. That meant better facilities on the ground and better-trained employees.

Major Commercial Airlines Operating During This Period

The "big four" airlines—American, Eastern, TWA, and United—were still on the scene as the jet era began. They competed for passengers with several other domestic carriers.

The Civil Aeronautics Board (CAB) controlled airline routes. It decided who could enter a market; that is, which carriers could offer service between specific points.

When an airline applied to serve a new market, the CAB gave carriers already flying in that area a chance to review the application. Not surprisingly, the established carriers often found a reason to turn down the applicant. They didn't want more competition. That made it hard for newcomers.

The purpose of federal regulation was to ensure that the airlines operated efficiently and with the greatest good for the greatest number. But regulation sometimes had the opposite effect. It controlled airfares. As a result, many people thought it cost more to fly than it should. They thought that regulation worked against free-market principles. A free market *is one that operates on the basis of competition and is not controlled by government.*

When Jimmy Carter became US president in 1977, pressure for deregulation began to build. Congress passed the Airline Deregulation Act of 1978. This let airlines enter or leave markets and set fares as they saw fit.

Several things happened in response. First, airlines stopped serving many smaller cities where they weren't making money. The larger carriers shifted from "point-to-point" routing to a "hub-and-spoke" system. Passengers now flew from their local airports to a "hub" city, perhaps changed planes, and then continued on. Travelers flying from Boston to Chicago, for example, might have to stop in Philadelphia.

Second, new airlines sprang up. Donald Burr founded People Express, for instance. It was a tight, "no frills" operation. His fares were almost as low as those on intercity buses. For a few years, his business boomed.

As a result, fares dropped dramatically. Airlines made a lot of money. More people flew. The number of air passengers peaked at 317 million in 1979.

Then some problems arose. Fuel costs skyrocketed. The US economy went into recession. The airlines expanded faster than they could manage. They began to lose money. The established carriers, with expensive union contracts, couldn't compete against newer carriers that paid their workers less. In 1981 US airlines had a net operating loss of $421 million. The number of passengers fell to 286 million.

A wave of airline bankruptcies followed over the next two decades. Two of the big four, Eastern and TWA, failed. So did Pan Am. Continental, United, and US Airways went bankrupt, too, but were able to reorganize and stay in business.

Analysts are still debating whether deregulation was a good idea. It certainly led to upheaval in the industry. Big airlines were hit worst. Passengers and small carriers benefited the most. Passenger travel more than doubled from the 1979 level, to 656 million people in 2006.

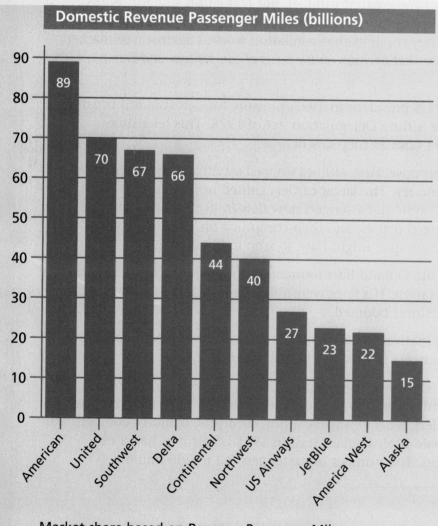

Airline Domestic Market Share November 2005—October 2006

Domestic Revenue Passenger Miles (billions)

American: 89
United: 70
Southwest: 67
Delta: 66
Continental: 44
Northwest: 40
US Airways: 27
JetBlue: 23
America West: 22
Alaska: 15

Airlines	Share
American	15.6%
United	12.1%
Southwest	11.6%
Delta	11.5%
Continental	7.6%
Northwest	7.0%
US Airways	4.6%
JetBlue	3.9%
America West	3.9%
Alaska	2.6%
Other	19.6%

Market share based on Revenue Passenger Miles
November 2005–October 2006

Source: Bureau of Transportation Statistics

Discount carriers, such as Southwest Airlines, made great strides. Founded in 1971 by Herb Kelliher and Rollin King, Southwest's formula for success was simple. It flew to less-expensive secondary airports. It used only one model of aircraft, so maintenance could be standardized. It turned flights around at the gate as fast as possible. By 2007 Southwest flew more than 80 million passengers a year to 62 cities.

How Federal Regulation Has Evolved

Congress enacted a new law covering air safety—the Federal Aviation Act of 1958—after a series of midair collisions. Jet airliners were coming into service around that time, too. That gave Congress another reason to pass a new law for aviation.

The act transferred the duties of the Civil Aeronautics Administration (CAA) to a new body, the Federal Aviation Agency (FAA). The FAA had broader authority on safety matters than the CAA. The FAA also took over responsibility from the Civil Aviation Board (CAB) for making rules covering air safety. The CAB continued to regulate the airlines.

Retired Air Force Lt Gen Elwood "Pete" Quesada was the first chief of the FAA. As FAA chief, he campaigned for better airline safety.

In 1966 Congress set up the Department of Transportation (DOT). The FAA was renamed the Federal Aviation Administration and became part of the DOT.

The CAB's role in investigating accidents went to the new National Transportation Safety Board (NTSB) in 1967. The CAB lost its primary duty when Congress deregulated the airlines in 1978. It was abolished in 1984.

The FAA, on the other hand, kept getting new duties. After a rash of airplane hijackings broke out in the 1960s, Congress gave the FAA a bigger role in security.

Another new area for the FAA was aircraft-noise reduction. In 1968 Congress gave the head of the FAA power to set standards to limit aircraft noise.

A 1970 law put the FAA in charge of a new airport development program. That law also gave the FAA responsibility for certifying airport safety.

Air safety is essential to keeping the public's trust in the air travel system. The National Transportation Safety Board (NTSB) investigates all air and other transportation accidents. It then makes recommendations to the FAA and the airlines on changes to make the system safer.

Take, for example, the crash of an Air Florida jet on a snowy day in Washington, D.C., in 1982. Safety experts and the industry learned lessons from that accident that have made flight safer for everyone.

Seconds after taking off from Washington National Airport on 13 January 1982, Air Florida Flight 90 slammed into the 14th Street Bridge over the Potomac River. The crash killed 78 passengers, crew members, and motorists.

Federal investigators from the NTSB found a big problem afterward: a copilot who couldn't persuade the pilot it wasn't safe to take off. They also found errors in the way the plane was de-iced.

The aircraft was covered with ice. Investigators believe that ice kept the plane's instruments from giving a true reading. The copilot noticed something wrong. He mentioned it to the pilot. But when the pilot ignored him, he didn't speak up again.

The silence was fatal.

One lesson: leaders need to make clear that it's OK to ask questions or point out problems. And followers need to know they have the right to speak up.

"This accident was pivotal because it helped draw attention to the fact that pilots need to communicate better," Robert L. Sumwalt III, vice chairman of the National Transportation Safety Board and a former airline pilot, told *The Washington Post* in 2007. "I don't know of any other accident that has had this amount of impact on aviation but also in other industries," he added.

Maritime and rail industries learned a lot from the Air Florida crash. So have hospital executives concerned about medical errors.

At the Nebraska Medical Center in Omaha, for instance, surgical teams now use checklists similar to the ones pilots use. Medical center staff adapted these lists to cover the steps necessary for a safe surgical procedure. An operating team, like the team controlling a plane, has many members. Each team member has a vital role in safety.

The last item on the Nebraska team's checklist reflects a lesson straight from Flight 90: "If anybody sees any red flags, something they are uncomfortable with, bring it to [the surgeon's] attention."

Pros and Cons of Commercial Flight Travel for Passengers

During less than a century, aviation went from a circus act led by the barnstormers to a mode of transport that held the United States together. Travel by air and by private auto largely replaced travel by rail and sea. Still, some travelers weigh the pros and cons before they fly.

Pros

Jetliners offer passengers one big advantage: speed. And because flying is faster, a transcontinental flight is usually more comfortable than a cross-country bus or train ride. A flight across the ocean is far more comfortable than a week-long voyage by ship.

Many parts of the world are accessible only by air. Jetliners can soar over miles of terrain that have no roads. They can fly over oceans to reach places once accessible only by ship.

Cons

Air travel has disadvantages, too. Some people still can't afford it. Airport security has added to travel times. That sometimes defeats the speed advantage of air travel. Weather delays can play havoc with the system. Especially in the northeastern United States, a train may get travelers to their destinations more quickly than a plane.

Flying has become much safer. But some people are still nervous about being confined in an aircraft. Some find the sensations of flying uncomfortable. Also, in an age of terrorism, planes have become a major target. Some people stay away from planes because they worry about hijackings. Some are put off by the security checks passengers must go through at airports to prevent terrorism.

Finally, travelers who want to see places, rather than just fly over them, prefer trains, buses, or cars.

The Switch to Air Travel

As air travel became cheaper, safer, and more accessible, bus and train service dwindled, except in densely populated areas.

In 1940 airlines of the United States carried around about 3 million passengers. In 1950 they carried 17 million.

In 1958, the year the first commercial jets were introduced, the number of passengers reached 30 million. In that year, for the first time, more transatlantic passengers arrived at their destinations by air than by sea.

By 1966 the scale had tipped in the direction of air travel. An estimated 5,322,000 passengers crossed the North Atlantic that year. Of these, 89 percent traveled by air.

Today, the US economy—indeed, the economy of much of the world—depends greatly on the safety and efficiency of domestic and international air travel. The Wright brothers' short flight in 1903 has changed civilian life as much, if not more, than it did military history.

The Heroes of United 93

Modern aviation is a world of routines, procedures, and checklists.

But sometimes people have to act fast. They have to improvise. They have to find within themselves the ability to cope with situations they could never have imagined. The heroic actions of the passengers of United Flight 93 on 11 September 2001 are an example.

On that day terrorists hijacked four aircraft at almost the same time. They planned to turn the planes into guided missiles.

The terrorists used two jetliners to bring down the twin towers of the World Trade Center in New York. They slammed a third plane into the Pentagon, outside Washington, D.C. Nearly 3,000 people died in these attacks.

No one knows for sure what the hijackers intended to do with the fourth plane. That plane, United 93, was en route from Newark, New Jersey, to San Francisco. It had 37 passengers aboard, including four hijackers.

The hijackers took over the plane at 9:28 a.m. At 9:32 a.m. one of the hijackers announced there was a bomb on the plane. This was a lie. The terrorists made the announcement to explain why the aircraft had changed its course abruptly in the air over northeastern Ohio.

Passengers and crew made phone calls from the plane. They learned about the attacks on the World Trade Center. They decided to rush the terrorists and try to retake the plane.

At 9:57 a.m., 29 minutes after the hijackers took over, the passengers made their move. As they tried to break through to the cockpit, the hijacker pilot rolled the plane from side to side. He pushed its nose up and down, trying to throw the counterattacking passengers and crew off balance.

The passengers continued their brave effort. They were seconds away from breaking through when the pilot pushed the nose of the plane earthward.

At 10:03 a.m., United 93 plowed into a field in Shanksville, Pennsylvania.

It was all over in less than seven minutes.

The hijacker pilot's objective "was to crash his airliner into symbols of the American Republic," the 9/11 Commission report stated. "He was defeated by the unarmed, alerted passengers of United 93."

"We are sure that the nation owes a debt to the passengers of United 93." the report also said. "Their actions saved the lives of countless others, and may have saved either the US Capitol or the White House from destruction."

CHECKPOINTS

Lesson 2 Review

Using complete sentences, answer the following questions on a sheet of paper.

1. Why do jet engines use alloys?

2. What caused the Comet crashes of 1954?

3. What are the advantages of turbine engines over reciprocating engines?

4. What was the particular disadvantage of the Boeing 727?

5. How did American manufacturers respond to the threat posed by the Airbus consortium?

6. How did airports have to change to handle jet aircraft?

7. What happened after Congress deregulated the airlines?

8. What prompted the US Congress to pass the Federal Aviation Act of 1958?

9. What duties has the FAA acquired since the 1960s?

10. What lessons did airlines learn from the Air Florida crash?

Applying Your Learning

11. If you'd been a member of Congress in 1978, would you have voted to deregulate the airlines? Why or why not?

CHAPTER 6

F-16 Fighting Falcon

Courtesy of the US Air Force

The Modern Air Force

Chapter Outline

LESSON 1

Air Force Beginnings Through the Korean War

LESSON 2

The Vietnam War and Other Military Operations

LESSON 3

Global Interventions From 1990

> "Nobody dislikes war more than warriors, but we value the causes of peace so highly that we will not duck a war in an effort to get a lasting peace."

Gen Daniel "Chappie" James, Jr, USAF

Air Force Beginnings Through the Korean War

You've already read about the aces of World War I— brave men such as Eddie Rickenbacker. The Korean War, which began in 1950, introduced a new kind of ace: the jet ace. The name changed for a simple reason: most fighter aircraft flown in Korea had jet engines. Jet aces, like the earlier aces, had to score five kills to earn the title.

Col James Jabara was the first jet ace in history. He earned that record in the Korean War. The Oklahoma-born pilot's parents were from Lebanon. By the time the Korean War began, he was an experienced fighter pilot. He'd flown a P-51 in Europe during World War II. He went on 108 combat missions. He shot down one enemy aircraft and shared credit for a second kill.

In Korea, Jabara piloted an F-86 Sabrejet. These fighters flew about 670 miles per hour (mph). In his first tour of duty, Jabara scored six kills. During his second tour, he shot down nine more enemy aircraft. All 15 kills were MiG-15s, which were very tough and quick Soviet-built planes. Only one pilot shot down more MiGs than Jabara. He earned many medals in Korea and World War II, including a Distinguished Service Cross and two Silver Stars.

Sadly, Jabara died in a car accident in 1966 as he was preparing for his first tour in Vietnam. He was buried in Arlington National Cemetery along with his daughter, who also died as a result of the crash. The Colonel James Jabara Airport outside Wichita, Kansas, is named for him.

COL JAMES JABARA

Courtesy of Bettmann/Corbis

F-86 SABREJET

The F-86 Sabrejet (right) was the best American jet fighter in the Korean War.

Courtesy of Bettmann/Corbis

The Creation of an Independent Air Force in 1947

Learn About...

- the creation of an independent Air Force in 1947
- the Cold War and how it began
- the USAF role in the Berlin Airlift
- the role of air power in the Korean War

As you read in Chapter 5, air power was vital to the Allies' victory in World War II. Between 1941 and 1945, the Army Air Forces developed new strategies and tactics. Engineers built more-powerful bombers and fighters. US planes delivered the atomic bombs on Japan that ended the war in 1945. US air power grew up fast, and the atomic bomb made it mature even faster. By 1947, most people were convinced it was time for the Air Forces to gain independence from the Army.

The National Security Act of 1947

The size of the military shrank after World War II, just as it had after World War I. The Army Air Forces ended the war in 1945 with 2.3 million Airmen and 72,000 aircraft. By 1947 they had only 300,000 Airmen and 10,000 planes. Yet even as the government was reducing the size of all military branches, it was rethinking how to fight wars. The atomic bomb had drastically changed warfare. And Congress wanted to correct the poor coordination between the branches of the military that helped lead to the disaster at Pearl Harbor.

Vocabulary

- nuclear deterrence
- arms
- United Nations
- Marshall Plan
- Strategic Triad
- missiles
- satellite
- Mach
- Western Allies
- airlift
- colony
- 38th parallel
- latitude
- limited war

In July 1947 President Harry S. Truman signed into law the National Security Act of 1947. This act set the stage for military development in the years to come. It authorized the founding of the National Military Establishment (today's Department of Defense). The law created the post of secretary of defense, who would answer to the president of the United States. It created the National Security Council and the Central Intelligence Agency. It established three branches within the National Military Establishment: the Department of the Navy, the Department of the Army, and the Department of the Air Force. This last change marked the creation of an independent United States Air Force. The first secretary of the Air Force, Stuart Symington, was appointed in September 1947. But it would take two years for all responsibility to shift from the Army to the Air Force.

The First Air Force Chief of Staff

GEN CARL SPAATZ

Gen Carl Spaatz was the first chief of staff of the Air Force, serving from 1947 to 1948.

Courtesy of Corbis Images

Gen Carl Spaatz was the first US Air Force chief of staff. He had commanded many World War II operations in the European and Pacific theaters. As chief of staff, Gen Spaatz was in charge of military operations for the Air Force. Secretary Symington was in charge of administrative matters.

Spaatz oversaw three major operating commands created in 1946: the Strategic Air Command (SAC), the Tactical Air Command (TAC), and the Air Defense Command (ADC). SAC was the atomic-weapons command. It was the best-funded command of the three. TAC was in charge of tactical, or smaller, air operations. ADC's role was to defend the country from air strikes.

The Implications of a Separate Air Force

As the creation of SAC showed, the atomic bomb would shape the mission of the Air Force. Today there are many means of delivering atomic bombs, including submarines. But just after World War II, only airplanes could do this job.

Military and civilian leaders thought the atomic bomb would protect the United States from aggression. They called this protection nuclear deterrence, *or prevention of war by convincing an enemy that if he attacks, he will be destroyed by nuclear weapons.* The main duty of the Air Force at that time was to deliver the atomic bomb. SAC was the command within the Air Force that would fulfill the mission. Its bombers would drop the bombs if need be.

The invention and use of the atomic bomb during World War II finally led to the Air Force getting its independence from the Army. The Air Force could now perform a function that no other branch of the military could carry out.

The Cold War and How It Began

Most Americans expected a long period of peace after World War II. But that didn't happen. The country was about to enter a new kind of war. It wouldn't be another world war. It would be fought in smaller theaters. It would include a huge buildup of arms—*weapons*—including atomic weapons.

The United States would wage this war against a powerful country that had been one of its major allies in World War II: the Soviet Union.

What the Cold War Was

The Cold War, as it came to be called, lasted for more than four decades—roughly from 1948 until 1989. The primary players were the United States and the Soviet Union. (The Soviet Union was the country formed from the old Russian empire after the Communists took over in 1917.) The two countries disagreed on how the world should run in the postwar years. The Cold War was their political, economic, and military rivalry. But both also had something in common. They wanted to avoid another worldwide war, a "hot" war.

The Cold War got its name from Bernard Baruch, an American delegate to the United Nations. The United Nations (UN) *is a worldwide organization first formed in 1945 by the victorious Allies to maintain international peace*. In a 1947 speech, Baruch said, "Let us not be deceived—today we are in the midst of a cold war."

The Soviets were putting Communist governments in place in the countries along their borders in Eastern Europe. The Soviet Army had occupied these countries at the end of World War II. The Soviets' greatest fear was another war with Germany. They hoped a Communist Eastern Europe might buffer them from Germany. But they were afraid that America's powerful new atomic bomb would threaten their plan. The Soviets were still trying to develop the bomb.

CAPSULES

The Communists believed that the state should own all means of production. They permitted no private ownership of land, factories, or businesses. They also supported dictatorship by a single party—the Communist Party—and did not permit free elections or respect human rights such as a free press, freedom of religion, freedom of speech, or freedom of association.

Most Communist governments collapsed as the Cold War ended. At the end of 2006, Cambodia, China, Cuba, Laos, North Korea, and Vietnam were the only surviving Communist governments.

The United States had other priorities. It wanted to preserve freedom in Europe. After all, Americans had fought hard for it in World War II. In addition, Europe was in bad shape after the war. The economies of European countries were suffering. American leaders feared that if Western Europe remained weak, it would fall into the Communist camp. The United States wanted to help Europe get back on its feet. So Congress enacted the Marshall Plan, *a strategy for rebuilding the countries of Europe and repelling communism after World War II.* The initiative was named for US Secretary of State George Marshall, who proposed it. The Soviets refused to allow the countries they occupied to participate in the plan.

The United States was confident it could keep the Soviets out of Western Europe because America alone had the atomic bomb. It developed a three-pronged method of delivering nuclear weapons called the Strategic Triad. (A *triad* is a group of three.) The Strategic Triad *consisted of land-based intercontinental ballistic missiles (ICBMs), submarine-launched ballistic missiles (SLBMs), and long-range bombers.* In other words, it consisted of land-, sea-, and air-based nuclear weapons.

The purpose of multiple methods for delivering nuclear weapons is to ensure that the United States can retaliate if it is attacked. If one type of weapon becomes vulnerable to an enemy (for example, because of an enemy's technological breakthrough), the other types would still be protected—and the United States would remain safe.

Then in 1949 the Soviets tested their first atomic weapon. Tensions increased between the two nations. Each side worried that the other might use its atomic bombs, with dreadful results. Yet it was this threat of total destruction that each side hoped would prevent the other from ever striking.

In a way, that fear had a preventive effect. But some serious face-offs did take place. Among them were the Berlin Airlift (1948–1949) and the Korean War (1950–1953), which you'll read about later in this lesson.

The Creation of the North Atlantic Treaty Organization (NATO)

Eleven Western European countries and the United States formed the North Atlantic Treaty Organization (NATO) in 1949. NATO nations promised to defend one another from Communist aggression. They agreed that "an armed attack against one or more of them shall be considered an attack against them all." NATO headquarters was in Paris.

Some people wondered why the United States joined NATO. After all, America tended to be an isolationist nation. So why did it join a military pact in a time of peace? The reason was simple: the United States was intent on keeping communism from spreading around the globe. NATO seemed a good way to bond countries with a similar goal. As another indication of its support, the United States agreed to keep US troops in Western Europe in case any of its allies needed help.

In 1955 the Soviets responded to NATO's creation. They drew up the Warsaw Pact—named for the capital of Poland—with the Communist allies that they dominated. In this pact, or treaty, the Soviet leaders promised to safeguard any of their friends who came under attack.

How the USAF Was Organized to Fight the Cold War

SAC was one of the most crucial commands in the Air Force. To deliver the atomic bomb, SAC had hundreds of B-52 bombers and KC-135 tankers. The tankers refueled the bombers in mid-air.

SAC's role eventually expanded to running aerial reconnaissance. It used planes equipped with the Airborne Warning and Control System (AWACS). In addition, spy planes, like the U-2, allowed SAC to spot Soviet missiles—*rocket-propelled vehicles that carry a weapon or warhead.*

Finally, as technology further improved, each side launched satellites into space. A satellite *is an object that orbits another object in space, such as a planet.* The satellites could check for missiles on the ground of an enemy nation. The US military built underground bunkers from which to keep track of its satellites. But SAC found that enemy atomic bombs could target its bunkers. So it created flying command centers called "Looking Glass." These planes flew 24/7 for more than 29 years.

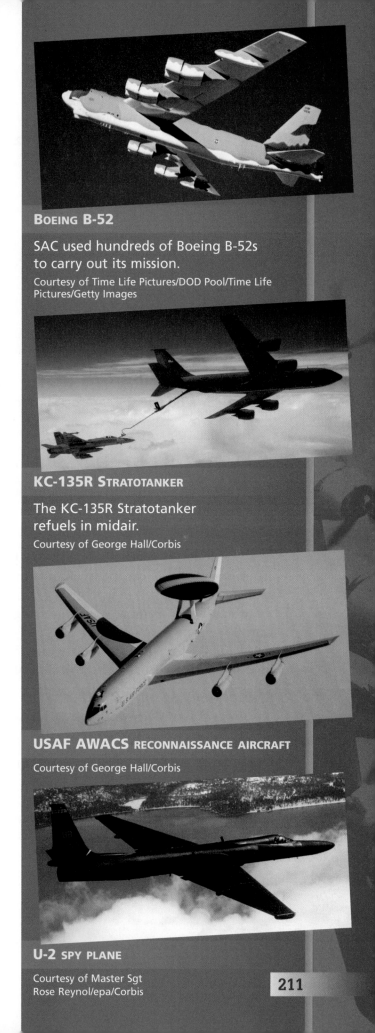

BOEING B-52

SAC used hundreds of Boeing B-52s to carry out its mission.
Courtesy of Time Life Pictures/DOD Pool/Time Life Pictures/Getty Images

KC-135R STRATOTANKER

The KC-135R Stratotanker refuels in midair.
Courtesy of George Hall/Corbis

USAF AWACS RECONNAISSANCE AIRCRAFT
Courtesy of George Hall/Corbis

U-2 SPY PLANE

Courtesy of Master Sgt Rose Reynol/epa/Corbis

211

B-47 BOMBER

The Air Force bought the B-47 bomber for SAC in 1947.

How the Cold War Drove Developments in the USAF

The US-Soviet rivalry and the atomic bomb drove decisions in aviation development. The B-52 bomber, with its 10,000-mile range, became SAC's main bomber. But it wasn't the first or last.

Before the B-52 was the Boeing B-47. It had jet engines and straight wings. To improve it, the company changed to a sweptback wing designed by the Germans during World War II. A sweptback wing—a wing angled rearward from the point of attachment—is more efficient at higher speeds than a straight wing. The wind can flow more easily over it. The Air Force adopted this improved Boeing B-47 in 1947. But this plane could fly only 3,000 miles without refueling. That prompted Boeing to build its longer-range B-52 in 1952.

Decades later, in 1988, another major bomber joined SAC's arsenal—the B-2 stealth bomber. The missile was another breakthrough in bomb delivery. You'll read more about these in the next lessons.

For a while, achieving faster speeds remained a challenge. In the 1950s the government, universities, and private industry all wanted to build faster fighters. But whenever such planes approached what came to be known as the "sound barrier"—the speed of sound—they shook badly. Sometimes they fell apart. Test pilots sometimes died.

The breakthrough occurred on 14 October 1947. Capt Charles "Chuck" Yeager broke the sound barrier with the Bell X-1. He reached 670 mph at 42,000 feet. Supersonic flight was born.

Yeager's feat brought a new word into the aviation dictionary—Mach. Mach (pronounced "mock") *is the speed of sound*. That is about 670 miles per hour.

After this breakthrough, aircraft got faster and faster. In 1956 a test pilot flew the experimental Bell X-2 at 2,094 miles per hour. That is three times the speed of sound, or Mach 3. Today's fighters are built on ideas first applied in these speedy aircraft.

Flight Paths

THEN-COL CHARLES YEAGER

Then-Col Charles Yeager and a model of the X-1, the plane in which he broke the sound barrier for the first time.

Courtesy of Bettmann/Corbis

Brig Gen Charles Yeager, Test Pilot

Brig Gen Charles "Chuck" Yeager is best known for breaking the sound barrier in 1947. But he already had a long record of service by that time.

In 1941, at age 18, Yeager joined the Army Air Forces. He worked as an aircraft mechanic and pilot. Later, he fought during World War II. After the war he trained to be a test pilot. That's how he got to fly the X-1. Yeager beat out 125 other pilots to get the job.

Yeager also served in the Vietnam War. He was a wing commander in 1966 and flew more than 120 combat missions. Yeager retired from the US Air Force in 1973.

FIGURE 1.1

The Soviets controlled East Germany, while the United States, Britain, and France controlled West Germany.

The USAF Role in the Berlin Airlift

Before the end of World War II, the Allies were already talking about what to do with Germany when it surrendered. Based on the lessons they learned after World War I (see Chapter 4, Lesson 2), the United States, Britain, and France wanted Germany to prosper. That way it wouldn't drag Europe into yet another world war. But the Soviet Union had a different view. It wanted to dominate Germany so the Germans would never again invade Soviet borders.

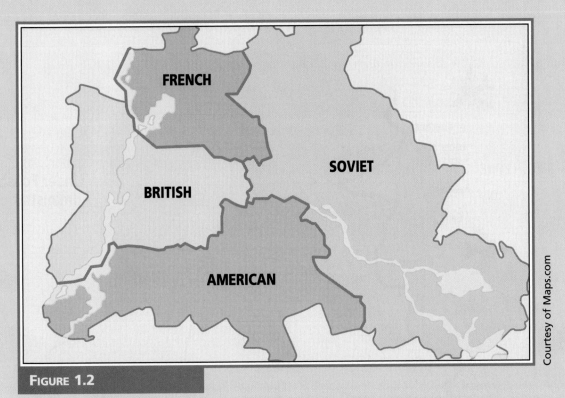

FIGURE 1.2

Courtesy of Maps.com

Berlin, the capital of Germany, was divided between the Soviets, who would run East Berlin, and the Western Allies, who would manage West Berlin.

The Allies' solution was to divide Germany in two parts. Each side could rule its part as it wished. The Soviets controlled East Germany, where they set up a Communist dictatorship. The Western Allies—*the United States, Britain, and France*—controlled West Germany, where they set up a democracy.

Germany's capital, Berlin, posed a problem. It was in East Germany. The four Allies split Berlin into four sectors, too. The Soviets got one sector—East Berlin. The three sectors of West Berlin were controlled by the Western Allies. But by June 1948 the Soviets decided they wanted all of Berlin. After all, it was in the Soviet-run part of Germany. The Soviets decreed that the Western Allies could no longer use roads, railroads, or canals to enter East Germany to deliver goods to Berlin. The first big clash of the Cold War and the first test of the new independent Air Force had begun.

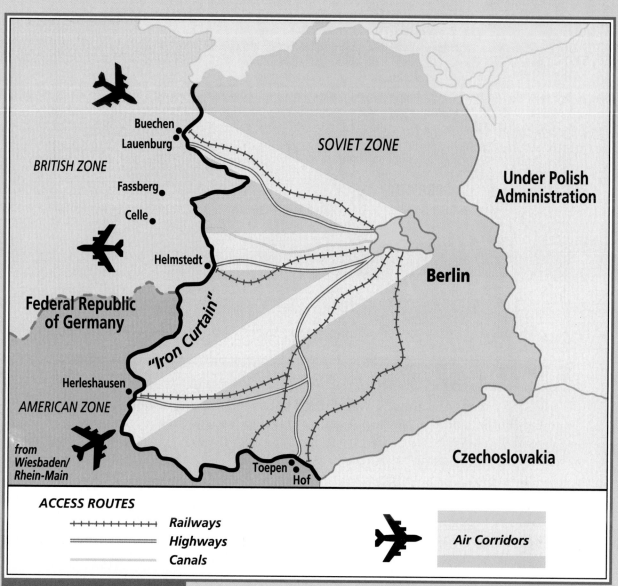

FIGURE 1.3

According to a 1945 agreement, the United States, Britain, and France could use three air routes over Soviet-controlled East Germany to enter Berlin.

Courtesy of Maps.com

How the USAF Broke the Berlin Blockade

The Western Allies had to get goods such as coal and food to their sectors in Berlin. Otherwise, more than 2 million West Berliners could freeze in winter and starve. If the Western Allies couldn't get into Berlin by ground transport, what about the air? A previous agreement between the four former Allies in 1945 gave the United States, Britain, and France the right to three 20-mile-wide air corridors that ended in Berlin.

Gen Lucius Clay, US commander in Europe, took action. The Western Allies would prevent the Soviet takeover of West Berlin through a massive airlift—*the transportation of personnel or material by air*. Thus the Berlin Airlift began. (It was also called "Operation Vittles.")

While war usually calls for bombers and fighters, this was to be a bloodless battle conducted by cargo aircraft. Clay ordered Lt Gen Curtis LeMay, then commander of US Air Forces in Europe, to make available as many cargo planes as possible. Clay asked Maj Gen William Tunner, the transport expert from World War II, to command the airlift into West Berlin. The airlift began in June 1948, the same month in which the Soviets set up the blockade.

The Cargo Plane

Lt Gen LeMay gathered more than 100 C-47 cargo planes for Maj Gen Tunner (see Chapter 3, Lesson 3). The *Gooney Birds*, as they were nicknamed, could each lug two to three tons of goods. But West Berliners needed 4,500 tons of food, coal, oil, and other supplies each day.

So LeMay got an even larger, faster transport plane into service— the C-54. It carried about 10 tons of cargo. By October 1948 200 C-54s were shuttling cargo to the city. Some days, almost one cargo plane a minute landed in Berlin.

By May 1949 the Soviets caved. They realized that the US, Britain, and France would not give up their airlift, no matter the cost. By that time, the Allies had airlifted 1.75 million tons of goods into the blockaded city.

C-54

The C-54 was the primary cargo plane of the Berlin Airlift.

Courtesy of the US Air Force

Lt Gen William Tunner: Cargo Commander

Lt Gen William Tunner (1906–1982) was a West Point graduate. He spent his career with the Army Air Corps and the Air Force.

Tunner's specialty was transport planes. During World War II he was chief of the Air Transport Command Ferrying Division. While in that post, he asked Nancy Love to form the Women's Auxiliary Ferry Squadron. Also during that war, he figured out how to safely transport supplies across the Himalayan Mountains to China. China was one of the Allies at that time.

Because of Tunner's success in China, Gen Lucius Clay tapped him to head the Berlin Airlift. Tunner was a very organized person. He knew that for any transport mission to succeed, it must run in an orderly manner. Tunner demanded schedules for flights, schedules for crews, and weather reports. As a result, the airlift had an excellent safety record. And the amount of cargo ferried to Berlin rocketed between 1948 and 1949.

Tunner recognized the importance of cargo planes to any Air Force operation. He also knew how undervalued they were. With the triumph of the Berlin Airlift, Tunner showed the world how to command transport missions.

Lt Gen William Tunner

Courtesy of Robert Lackenbach/
Time Life Pictures/Getty Images

Lessons the USAF Learned From the Berlin Airlift

The Berlin airlift helped convince American leaders of the need to build a stronger Air Force. The cargo plane came into its own during the airlift. It wasn't as flashy as bombers or fighters, but it saved a city from a Communist takeover. These workhorse transports formed the critical element in the American response to the Soviet blockade of Berlin.

The intensity of the airlift also taught cargo crews a lot about what they could achieve. They had daily chances to perfect air support. One year later, transports, bombers, and fighters would all be called on to fight the next stage of the Cold War: the Korean War.

Flight Paths

1st Lt Gail Halvorsen: The Candy Bomber

1st Lt Gail Halvorsen was one of the US pilots picked to fly C-54s during the Berlin Airlift. These pilots often had little to do while waiting for their cargo aircraft to be unloaded. One day, trying to pass the time, he talked with some German children who were peering through the airport fence. They asked if he had any candy. He told them that the next time he flew in, he'd wiggle the wings of his plane and then drop small packages of candy to them.

Halvorsen kept his promise. Soon many other pilots wanted to help. Many German children who didn't live near the airport wrote Halvorsen asking for candy to be dropped in their neighborhoods. They called him "Uncle Wiggly Wings." He was also known as the "Candy Bomber."

1ST LT GAIL HALVORSEN

1st LT Gail Halvorsen, USAF, became famous for "Operation Little Vittles." He rigged miniature parachutes with American candy bars and gum and then dropped them over Berlin for German children to retrieve.

Courtesy of the US Air Force

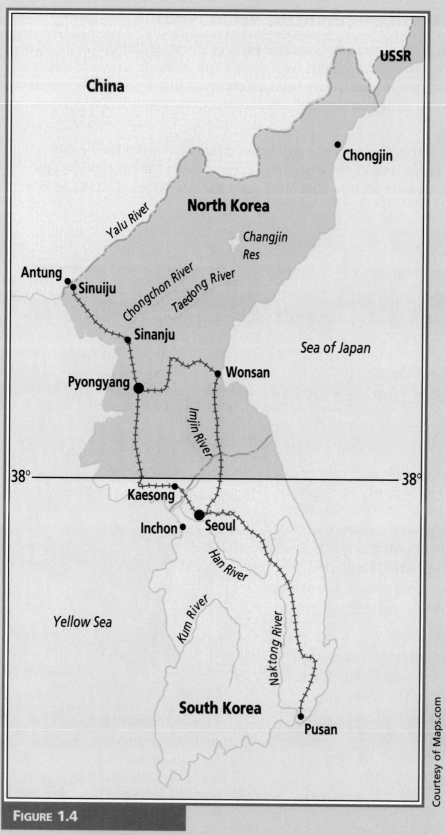

FIGURE 1.4

The 38th parallel divided Korea into North Korea and South Korea.

Courtesy of Maps.com

The Role of Air Power in the Korean War

Korea was a Japanese colony from 1910 until 1945, when Japan surrendered to the Allies. A colony *is a region under the political control of a distant country.* After Japan surrendered, the Soviets and Western Allies needed to decide what to do with the Japanese troops stationed in Korea. They agreed that all troops north of Korea's 38th parallel would give up their arms to the Soviets. The United States would handle all Japanese soldiers south of the 38th parallel. The 38th parallel *is a line marking the original boundary between North and South Korea.* It refers to the boundary's latitude— *a line north or south from Earth's equator and parallel to it.*

But things didn't go according to plan. The Soviets set up Korean Communist Kim Il-Sung as North Korea's new leader. They wanted to spread communism not only throughout Europe but also through their neighboring countries in Asia. China had become a Communist country in 1949. If North Korea became a Communist country, the Soviets could protect their border along Asia much as they were doing along their border with the countries of Eastern Europe.

On 25 June 1950 North Korean military forces crossed the 38th parallel in a move to take over South Korea. Two days later, the United Nations agreed to go to South Korea's aid. Here was a chance for the United Nations to prevent a third worldwide conflict. American Gen Douglas MacArthur was the first commander of UN troops in this effort.

The United States entered the Korean War for much the same reason it conducted the Berlin Airlift. It wanted to stop the spread of communism. The Soviets and Americans weren't fighting with each other directly. Korea was the scene of the action. But they were fighting. They were engaged in a limited war—*a war in which opposing sides try to avoid a worldwide war and the possible use of atomic bombs by fighting with each other outside their own lands and sometimes through troops who aren't their own.* The Korean War was the first military action of the Cold War.

Aircraft Used by the USAF During the Korean War

Rather than using long-range strategic bombing as it had in World War II, the US Air Force often conducted tactical air operations in Korea. The fighter plane was the weapon of choice. It dropped bombs to soften enemy positions and disrupt supply routes. It strafed North Korean troops to support UN forces. The Air Force used some B-29 bombers, however, to destroy roads and bridges.

F-80 Shooting Star

Courtesy of Horace Bristol/Corbis

The Navy's F-9F Pantherjet

Courtesy of the US Navy

HRS-1 Sikorsky helicopter

Helicopters, like this HRS-1 Sikorsky, flew troops and supplies to the front lines. They also evacuated wounded troops.

Courtesy of Corbis Images

At first US Air Force fighters took off from bases in Japan. Later the Air Force set up bases in South Korea. The most widely used US Air Force fighters were the F-80 Shooting Star, F-51, F-84 Thunderjet, and F-86 Sabrejet. The F-51 was formerly known as the P-51 Mustang of World War II fame. (By the time of the Korean War, fighters carried the designation of "F" for "fighter" rather than the old "P" for "pursuit.")

The F-51 saw heavy use at the start of the Korean War because it had a longer range than the F-80 jet. This longer range was especially important when US fighters had to take off from Japan. The F-86 that pilots flew later in the war was the best American fighter jet of the time.

The US Navy also provided fighters. The F-9F Pantherjet, AD/A-1 Skyraiders, and the F-4U Corsair took off from aircraft carriers. Among the F-9F pilots was Maj John H. Glenn of the US Marine Corps. He also flew the Air Force F-86 and scored three kills. Glenn became an astronaut in 1959.

The helicopter saw lots of use in Korea. It flew troops and supplies to the front lines. The Air Force used it to evacuate wounded troops, too.

Ways the United States Used Air Power in the Korean War

Fighting between Soviet-supported Communist forces and UN forces moved back and forth across the 38th parallel throughout the three-year Korean War. Air power played a big part in these frequent swings. In the summer of 1950 the North Koreans drove the UN forces all the way to Pusan, a coastal city in the southeast corner of South Korea. US fighter planes, stationed in Japan and on aircraft carriers, managed to gain time for UN ground forces to dig in. A few months later, in September 1950, the UN landed troops at Inchon, a town on the west coast of South Korea. These new UN forces, along with those still in Pusan, drove the North Koreans almost back to the 38th parallel. UN aircraft supported the ground troops.

Up to this point, the North Koreans hadn't offered much resistance from the air. Their air force was weak: it consisted of about 120 old Russian planes. But on 25 November 1950 things changed. Gen MacArthur led troops across the 38th parallel to the edge of China. The UN wanted to eliminate communism from all of Korea, not just from South Korea.

China didn't want the UN pushing along its borders. It entered the war on North Korea's side with 850,000 soldiers and 1,000 Soviet-made MiG-15 fighter jets. The MiG-15 was better than any plane the Americans had initially. In January 1951, with Chinese help, the North Koreans recrossed the 38th parallel and grabbed the South Korean capital, Seoul, a second time.

The United States and the UN wouldn't give up. Tough air battles took place. Although flying inferior fighters, US pilots received better training. They shot down nine MiG-15s for every one US fighter destroyed. Air power proved once again it was a crucial part of modern war. The UN forces under MacArthur took Seoul yet again in March 1951. They drove the North Koreans back across the 38th parallel.

A SOVIET-BUILT MiG-15 FIGHTER

Courtesy of George Hall/Corbis

At this point both sides realized they couldn't win. They began negotiating and finally signed a cease-fire agreement on 27 July 1953. The two Koreas remained divided.

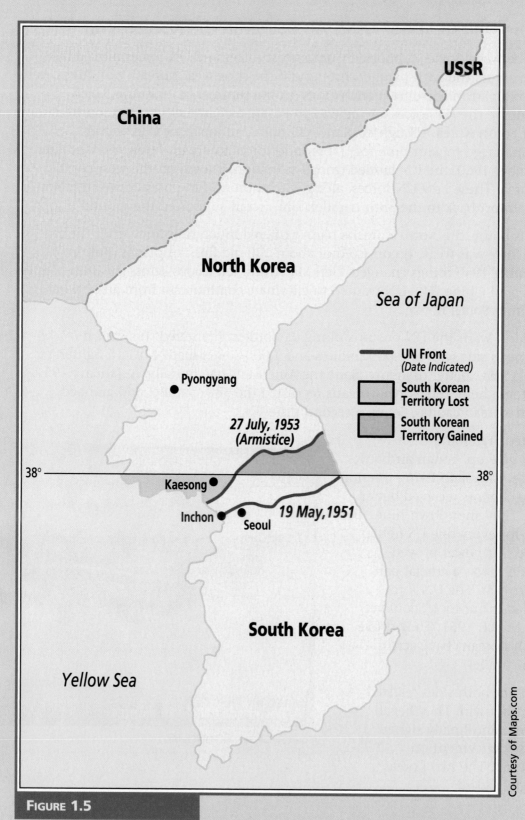

FIGURE 1.5

Korea as it was divided after the Korean War

Lessons the USAF Learned From the Korean War

The US Air Force learned a number of important lessons from the Korean War. First, it realized it had been putting too much emphasis on the atomic bomb. The military had diverted too many funds from fighter development to bombers. The Korean experience made US planners understand that there were now two types of war: total war, like World War II, and limited war, like the Korean War. In a limited war, atomic bombs aren't used. The purpose of a limited war is to prevent an all-out war in which atomic bombs might be used.

Flight Paths

Capt Manuel Fernandez: Jet Ace

Capt Manuel "Pete" Fernandez (1925–1980) was the third jet ace of the Korean War. He took part in 124 combat missions. He shot down 14 MiG-15s and shared credit for a 15th kill. He was an F-86 Sabrejet pilot.

Fernandez didn't stop flying after the war. In 1956 he raced a new jet called the F-100C Super Sabre from California to Oklahoma. He averaged 666 mph. He set a record with this speed and won a Bendix Trophy. He also joined the Mach Riders of Nellis Air Force Base, Nevada. This group performed stunts as the barnstormers had done in the 1920s and 1930s. He retired in 1963.

CAPT MANUEL "PETE" FERNANDEZ

Courtesy of the US Air Force

NORTH AMERICAN F-100 SUPER SABRE

Courtesy of Bettmann/Corbis

A second lesson was simply a reminder of one learned in World War II—the importance of air superiority. UN air power took control of air space over Korea early in the war. This helped UN forces drive the North Koreans back across the 38th parallel. The MiG-15s may have been as good as any US planes, but the better-trained American pilots more than made up for that. US pilots controlled the air.

Third, all branches of the military learned the importance of flexibility. They had to be prepared for all-out war as well as limited war. Each war demands different strategies and tactics. Each war needs different kinds of equipment. Therefore, fighters, bombers, helicopters, and training must be maintained for all options in warfare.

As the Cold War continued, those lessons would be put to severe tests.

Flight Paths

LT COL GEORGE A. DAVIS JR.

Courtesy of the US Air Force

Lt Col George A. Davis Jr.: Medal of Honor Winner

Lt Col George A. Davis Jr. (1920–1952) served in World War II and the Korean War. Because the two wars were so close together, many Airmen fought in both conflicts.

Davis had an extraordinary career. During World War II he flew 266 combat missions. He shot down seven enemy aircraft in the Pacific theater. He earned a Silver Star, a Distinguished Flying Cross, and an Air Medal.

On 10 February 1952, Davis led a group of four F-86 fighters on a mission over North Korea. Two of his planes had to head home because of damage. Davis knew he and the remaining plane must stick with their mission. They had to provide cover for a group of fighters bombing a North Korean railroad. Davis spotted 12 MiG-15s headed their way. He plunged his fighter toward the enemy formation, despite being outnumbered. He managed to shoot down two of the MiGs before his own plane was hit. He died when his plane crashed into nearby mountains. For his brave act of self-sacrifice, Davis was one of only four Airmen who earned the Medal of Honor during the Korean War.

CHECKPOINTS

Lesson 1 Review

Using complete sentences, answer the following questions on a sheet of paper.

1. What is the name of the law that created the independent United States Air Force?

2. Who was the first chief of staff of the USAF?

3. Which command was responsible for delivering the atomic bomb in the post-World War II years?

4. Define "nuclear deterrence."

5. Which were the two main countries involved in the Cold War?

6. The Cold War involved the threatened use of which weapon?

7. What was the name of the organization formed by the United States and 11 European countries with a promise to defend one another from Communist aggression?

8. Name three bombers used by Strategic Air Command.

9. Since the Western Allies weren't allowed to use ground-transportation routes to deliver goods to Berlin, how did they get supplies to that German city?

10. Which were the two main cargo aircraft of the Berlin Airlift, and how many tons could each carry?

11. What did the North Koreans do that set off the Korean War?

12. Define "limited war."

13. Which was the main type of aircraft—fighter or bomber—used during the Korean War?

Applying Your Learning

14. How important do you think it is for the United States to maintain air superiority today?

The Vietnam War and Other Military Operations

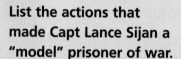
One military historian has called Capt Lance Sijan the "model on how to behave as a POW." A POW *is a prisoner of war*. Sijan was a US Air Force pilot in the Vietnam War. He was only two years out of the Air Force Academy when the North Vietnamese shot him down on his 52nd mission. It was 9 November 1967.

Sijan landed with a broken leg, a damaged hand, and a fractured skull. Yet when radioed by a search-and-rescue team, he refused help. He said he didn't want anyone placed in mortal danger on his account. He tried without success to grab a steel cable the rescue aircraft lowered to pull him out of the jungle. Antiaircraft fire forced the rescue aircraft to leave after 33 minutes. Sijan was stranded in enemy territory.

For more than six weeks, Sijan eluded the North Vietnamese in their jungles. He had to drag himself along the ground because of his broken leg. Finally, the North Vietnamese captured him. But Sijan escaped. When caught again, he was tortured. But he never gave his captors more than his name. They moved him to a POW camp in Hanoi, the North Vietnamese capital. Because of the mistreatment, his health gave out. He died 21 January 1968 as a POW.

The United States took a number of steps to honor Sijan. President Gerald Ford awarded him the Medal of Honor in 1976. The Air Force promoted Sijan to the rank of captain. The Air Force Academy named a cadet dormitory Sijan Hall. And the Air Force grants the Lance P. Sijan Award to those members who show similar bravery and professionalism.

1ST LT LANCE SIJAN

Courtesy of the the US Air Force

The Role of Air Power in the Cuban Missile Crisis

Learn About...

- the role of air power in the Cuban Missile Crisis
- the role of air power in the Vietnam War
- how the USAF gained an increasingly significant role in other US military operations during the Cold War
- key developments in aircraft, missile capability, and nuclear capability during the Cold War

Many conflicts took place during the Cold War. There was the bloodless Berlin Airlift. There was the bloody Korean War. Then came the Cuban Missile Crisis in 1962. This event was the closest the United States and the Soviet Union got to nuclear war—*war involving the atomic bomb or the hydrogen bomb.* The hydrogen bomb, invented in 1953, was even more powerful than the atomic bomb.

Cuba had become a Communist country in 1960. In 1962 the Soviets sent bombers, fighters, and shiploads of equipment and men to build missile sites there. The Soviets wanted to intimidate the United States in its own backyard. Cuba is only 90 miles south of the southernmost point of Florida. Had the United States allowed the Soviet Union to keep these missiles in Cuba, the Soviets could have struck the US mainland with little warning.

How Aircraft Were Used During the Cuban Missile Crisis

The United States carefully watched developments in Cuba. US Air Force pilots went on aerial reconnaissance in the U-2. These pilots were from Strategic Air Command's (SAC) 4080th Strategic Reconnaissance Wing. They took photographs of Soviet missile bases in Cuba.

You read about the U-2 spy plane in the last lesson. It was a single-engine, high-altitude aircraft. Its purpose was to gather information on enemy activities. It could fly at altitudes above 55,000 feet. Its glider-like wings worked well in the thin upper atmosphere. It was first tested in 1955.

Reconnaissance missions can be dangerous. Maj Rudolf Anderson Jr. had already provided the US government with photos of missile sites. He went on another mission over Cuba on 27 October 1962. The Cubans shot him down with a surface-to-air missile (SAM). Anderson was the only American to die in the Cuban Missile Crisis.

Vocabulary

- POW
- nuclear war
- arms race
- international waters
- guerrilla warfare
- solitary confinement
- neutral
- ballistic
- warhead

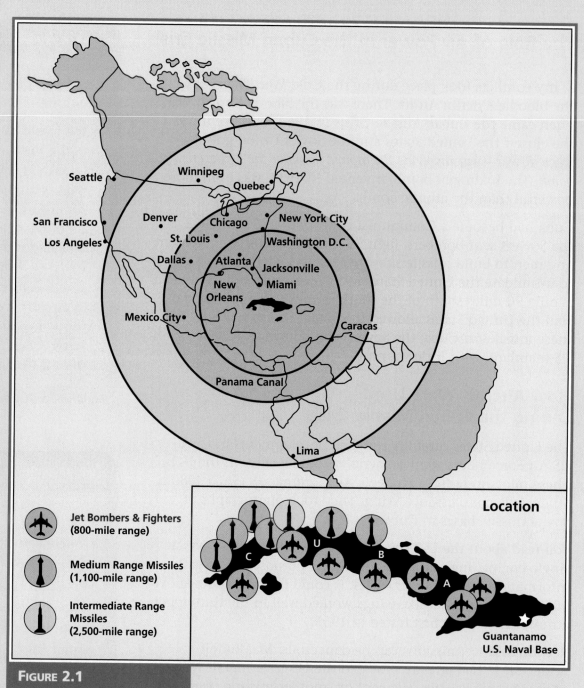

Jet Bombers & Fighters (800-mile range)

Medium Range Missiles (1,100-mile range)

Intermediate Range Missiles (2,500-mile range)

FIGURE 2.1

This map shows the location of Russian aircraft and missiles around Cuba in 1962.

Courtesy of Bettmann/Corbis

A U-2 TOOK THIS PHOTO OF A MISSILE SITE IN CUBA.

President John F. Kennedy ordered a naval blockade of Cuba on 24 October. A *blockade* is isolating a country, city, or harbor with ships or troops so that no traffic can leave or enter. Soviet ships could no longer enter Cuban ports. At the same time, SAC prepared to deliver nuclear bombs. These two moves let the Soviets know how seriously the United States took the Soviet missiles.

Now a big question arose: would the Soviets try to break through the blockade and risk war?

The Outcome of the Cuban Missile Crisis

Twenty Soviet ships were sailing toward Cuba when Kennedy set up the blockade. About 500 miles from the United States, the Soviet ships turned away. One reason the Soviets backed down: they had fewer nuclear weapons than the Americans.

A few days later Soviet Premier Nikita Khrushchev ordered the missile sites dismantled. American U-2s flew over Cuba to make sure the Soviets kept their word.

The crisis had passed. But the standoff started an arms race between the Americans and Soviets. An arms race *is a competition for military supremacy*. Each party in an arms race tries to produce larger numbers of weapons and a better military force than the other.

The Soviets wanted to make sure the United States could not force their hand again. They poured money into building their nuclear stockpile. The United States was equally determined to keep its superiority. The arms race accelerated after the Cuban Missile Crisis. It continued until after the Cold War ended in 1989.

The Role of Air Power in the Vietnam War

America's gradual entry into the Vietnam War marked another phase of the Cold War. After World War II, France tried to regain control of its colonies in Indochina—Vietnam, Laos, and Cambodia. Japan had occupied these colonies during the war. France was fighting Vietnamese forces led by Communist Ho Chi Minh. In July 1950 the United States supplied money to the French effort.

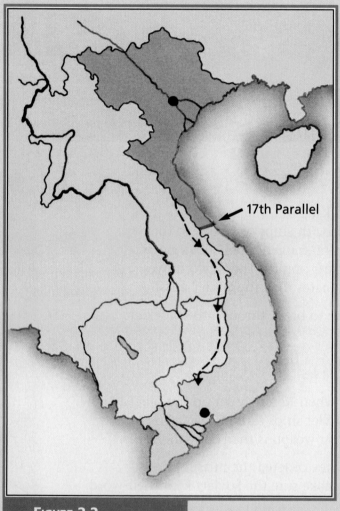

17th Parallel

In 1954 France withdrew from Vietnam after a serious military defeat. The Geneva Accords of 1954, an international agreement, split Vietnam in half along the 17th parallel. Soon the country fell into a civil war as the north tried to occupy the south. To the north were the Communists. Their allies were the Soviets and the Chinese. To the south were Vietnamese who opposed communism. The United States soon began providing military training and supplies to South Vietnam.

Not until 1961, however, did US forces see combat in Vietnam. About 11,000 troops, including Airmen, saw action in the early 1960s. They served mostly as advisers to South Vietnamese forces.

In 1964 things really heated up. North Vietnamese patrol boats attacked the USS *Maddox*. The American destroyer was off the North Vietnamese coast in international waters. International waters *are areas of the seas where ships from any nation have the right to travel*. The North Vietnamese thought the destroyer was involved in secret US raids along their coast.

Congress quickly passed the Tonkin Gulf Resolution. It allowed President Lyndon Johnson to order the military to strike back at North Vietnam. This was not a declaration of war. But it led to a huge land- and air-based campaign that lasted until 1973. At the war's peak, the United States had more than a half-million troops in Vietnam.

THE US AIR FORCE TRAINED MEMBERS OF THE SOUTH VIETNAMESE AIR FORCE.

Ways the USAF Trained the Vietnamese Air Force

Communist ground troops were the main threat to South Vietnam. For much of the war, these troops, called Viet Cong, conducted guerrilla warfare. That's *a type of fighting in which small bands of fighters hit more-powerful forces by surprise.* The Communists didn't have much air power. Even so, the US Air Force trained members of South Vietnam's Vietnamese Air Force (VNAF). Given their experience in World War II and the Korean War, the US Air Force knew how to effectively bomb supply routes and hit enemy troops.

The focus of the US Air Force was threefold. It gave the VNAF practice in tactical air operations. VNAF pilots flew as passengers with American pilots to study needed skills. And the US Air Force developed ways to fight guerrillas from the air. Eventually, it introduced reconnaissance and airlift operations.

The Geneva Accords prohibited the use of fighter jets in Vietnam. So at first the US Air Force trained the VNAF pilots to fly propeller aircraft. These slower-moving aircraft were actually well suited for reconnaissance missions. The VNAF could buzz low over the jungles to spot guerrilla movements. But the North Vietnamese kept crossing the 17th parallel into South Vietnam. This was a violation of the Geneva Accords. So the Air Force taught the VNAF how to fly jets. If one side could break the rules, the United States reasoned, then so could the other.

Ways the US Used Air Power in the Vietnam War

The US Air Force conducted tactical air missions throughout the Vietnam War. The theater was small. The targets were even smaller. In the end, however, it was strategic bombing that forced the North Vietnamese to negotiate an agreement to end the war.

Operation Rolling Thunder

President Johnson ordered the Air Force not to strike sites linked with the Soviets or Chinese. Johnson didn't want any Russian or Chinese advisers killed. He did not want to draw those two powerful countries into a full-scale war. (This had happened with Chinese troops during the Korean War.) The US conducted limited tactical air strikes on railroads, oil depots, and warehouses. Their purpose was to wear down the North Vietnamese without provoking the Soviets and Chinese.

These tactical strikes, called Operation Rolling Thunder, took place from 1965 to 1968. They weren't as successful as the United States hoped. Because they were limited, the strikes gave the north too much opportunity to rebuild and repair. Several hundred US personnel were shot down and became POWs. These men were held for many years and most were severely mistreated. Meanwhile, regular North Vietnamese Army troops entered South Vietnam through Laos and Cambodia.

The Tet Offensive

In January 1968 the North Vietnamese and Viet Cong surprised US and South Vietnamese forces with the Tet Offensive. The offensive got that name because it occurred over the Tet holiday, which is when the Vietnamese celebrate the lunar new year. Communist troops and guerrillas attacked 36 major cities in South Vietnam. The US Air Force airlifted troops to the front lines, attacked enemy soldiers, and bombed supply routes.

When the enemy surrounded 6,000 US Marines at their base in an area called Khe Sanh, air power helped save the day. For two months, US cargo planes airlifted supplies. US aircraft also dropped 110,000 tons of bombs around Khe Sanh and blew up 3,000 enemy supply trucks. The Tet Offensive ended when US and South Vietnamese forces expelled the North Vietnamese from the south's major cities. Many North Vietnamese troops retreated north across the 17th parallel.

Operations Linebacker I and II

When President Richard Nixon took office in 1969, US tactics in Vietnam changed. Nixon wanted to get American troops out of Vietnam. He wanted to turn the effort over to South Vietnamese forces. He began dramatically cutting the number of US ground forces. But in 1972, the North Vietnamese tried another invasion similar to the Tet Offensive. Nixon told his military leaders to do whatever was needed to drive the North Vietnamese out of the south for good. The very short, but devastating strategic-bombing phase of the war began.

Courtesy of George Hall/Corbis

THE UH-1 HUEY

The UH-1 Huey was the most popular helicopter used in the Vietnam War.

In 1972 Air Force B-52s and Navy aircraft pounded North Vietnamese supply routes. The United States called this action Operation Linebacker. During this phase, US aircraft bombed many targets that were off limits during Operation Rolling Thunder. For a while, the North Vietnamese seemed willing to discuss a treaty. But they changed their minds.

In reply, Nixon ordered Operation Linebacker II in mid-December. B-52s flew over North Vietnam with 15,000 tons of bombs. The B-52s relentlessly bombed targets that had been off limits for years. Fifteen bombers were lost during the operation. In January 1973 the North Vietnamese signed a peace treaty with the United States. The final US troops withdrew. Unfortunately, in 1975, the Communist North Vietnamese violated the treaty. They invaded the south, and took over South Vietnam anyway. This time the US did not help. Congress prohibited President Gerald R. Ford from spending money to do so.

Significant Aircraft Used by the USAF During the Vietnam War

A quiet star of the war was the helicopter. Vietnam saw a new use for these aircraft. Units of helicopters transporting ground forces were referred to as "air cavalry." This was a reminder of the fighting units on horseback from previous centuries.

The helicopter is a delicate aircraft compared with fighters and bombers. The military lost 5,000 of them in the war. But it was a very effective aircraft in the jungles of Vietnam. It could drop troops at the front lines so they wouldn't have to make long marches through thick undergrowth. It could hover while delivering supplies. Because it didn't need a runway, it could pick up the wounded in the field.

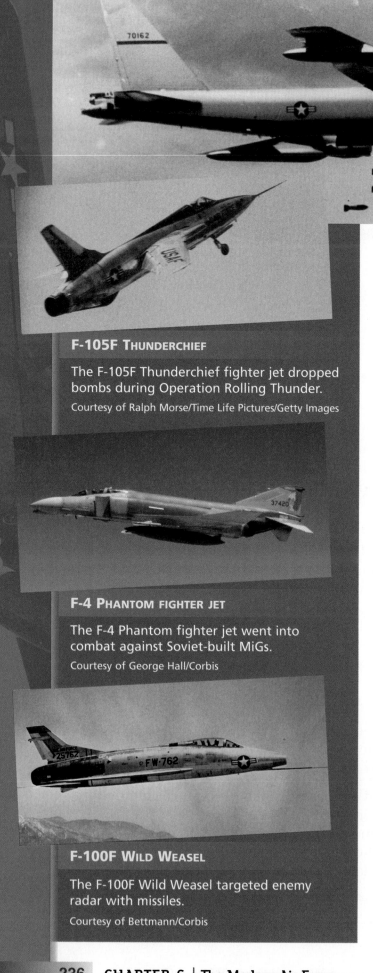

A B-52 BOMBS NORTH VIETNAM
Courtesy of the US Air Force

F-105F THUNDERCHIEF

The F-105F Thunderchief fighter jet dropped bombs during Operation Rolling Thunder.

Courtesy of Ralph Morse/Time Life Pictures/Getty Images

F-4 PHANTOM FIGHTER JET

The F-4 Phantom fighter jet went into combat against Soviet-built MiGs.

Courtesy of George Hall/Corbis

F-100F WILD WEASEL

The F-100F Wild Weasel targeted enemy radar with missiles.

Courtesy of Bettmann/Corbis

Other aircraft also saw action in Vietnam. In the early years of the war US and VNAF pilots flew B-26 bombers. Another combat plane was the T-28, an aircraft originally built to train pilots. The "T" in T-28 stands for "trainer."

But in 1964 and 1965 Communist ground forces began to attack US bases. The US Air Force brought over B-52 bombers and F-105 Thunderchief fighter jets. It sent F-4 Phantoms into aerial combat with Soviet-built North Vietnamese MiGs.

Three other important aircraft were high-tech. These were the EC-121, the EB-66, and the F-100F Wild Weasel. The EC-121 was a radar-equipped cargo plane. The EC-121 searched for enemy MiGs over the skies of Vietnam. EC-121 crews could tell US and VNAF fighters where to find MiGs.

The EB-66 jammed enemy radar by sending out electronic pulses. Radar on the F-100F fighter could spot the location of enemy radar and send a missile right at it.

A1C William Robinson:
From POW to Second Lieutenant

A1C William Robinson was a member of a search-and-rescue team during the Vietnam War. He flew in an HH-43 helicopter.

On 20 September 1965 Robinson's group set out to rescue a downed pilot in North Vietnam. They flew 80 miles to the site with an armed escort. Enemy fire hit both US aircraft. Rules from headquarters forbade the escort to return fire. So it headed back to base. Enemy forces shot down Robinson's helicopter. It crashed into the jungle. The crew was taken prisoner.

Robinson spent eight years as a POW. The captors didn't treat the prisoners' wounds. They tortured the prisoners instead. They denied the POWs adequate food. They exposed them to all kinds of weather. All POWs spent time in solitary confinement. During solitary confinement, *a prisoner is held in a cell alone and not allowed to talk to anyone.*

Robinson described this as "weeks, months, and years of boredom punctuated by moments, hours, and days of stark terror." But he survived. During his incarceration, he received "informal" Officer Candidate School training. When he returned to the United States, he was offered and accepted a direct presidential appointment to the rank of second lieutenant. He received many awards, including the Air Force Cross.

A1C WILLIAM ROBINSON

The North Vietnamese parade A1C William Robinson on his way to the "Hanoi Hilton" POW camp.

Taken from the National Prisoner of War Museum

A1C William Pitsenbarger: A First-Class Hero

A1C William Pitsenbarger (1944–1966) was a crewman aboard an HH-43 helicopter that went on search-and-rescue missions. He was a pararescueman. His job was to care for the wounded and get them out of the jungle.

Pitsenbarger performed this role bravely on 11 April 1966 near Cam My, Republic of Vietnam. On that day, his job was to care for Soldiers who were under fire in South Vietnam. He treated the wounded in the middle of the action on the jungle floor. He placed the casualties in hoists to lift them 100 feet in the air to the chopper. When the enemy launched a major assault, he joined the firefight. Wounded three times, he continued fighting and helping others. He died in action that day.

The Air Force awarded Pitsenbarger the Air Force Cross. But Soldiers who were at the firefight that day asked that he receive a higher honor: the Medal of Honor. The secretary of the Air Force presented the medal to Pitsenbarger's father in 2000.

A1C WILLIAM PITSENBARGER

Courtesy of the US Air Force

Lessons the USAF Learned From the Vietnam War

During the first few years of the war, the United States did not use air power consistently. From time to time it halted the bombing raids. During these pauses, the United States tried to get the Communists to stop fighting. Instead, the North Vietnamese used the time to repair their supply routes and communication lines.

This experience taught the US Air Force that it must thoroughly defeat an enemy. It must not spare locations where Soviet and Chinese advisers might be stationed. During Operations Linebacker I and II, B-52 bombers pounded supply routes and Communist positions until the North Vietnamese were compelled to talk.

The Top-Secret Mission of CMSgt Richard Etchberger

CMSgt Richard Etchberger (1933–1968) started out as a radar operator. He learned fast. During the Vietnam War, his superiors asked if he'd like to join a top-secret mission called Project Heavy Green.

The project was a joint mission of the US Air Force and the Central Intelligence Agency (CIA). The military needed a radar site close to the border of North Vietnam to better direct bombing runs. The site was in Laos, a country that was neutral, *not taking sides*. Because Laos was neutral, no US military member could be stationed there. So anyone wanting to take part in the mission had to resign from the military and secretly join the CIA. Etchberger did just this.

From 1967 to 1968, Etchberger and 18 other Americans worked at the secret radar station in Laos. They directed 25 percent of all bombing missions over North Vietnam. But then the North Vietnamese forces learned of their site. They launched an air attack on 12 January 1968. That didn't succeed. So they launched a ground attack from 10 March to 11 March 1968.

Etchberger and his fellow workers fought as best they could. But many were injured or killed. Etchberger escaped enemy fire. He continued to fight until a helicopter came to pick up the survivors. He loaded his fallen friends one by one until it was his turn. He was fatally shot only after he boarded the copter.

After his death the Air Force awarded Etchberger the Air Force Cross. In a secret Pentagon ceremony in 1969, it was accepted by his wife Katherine.

CMSGT RICHARD ETCHBERGER

CMSgt Richard Etchberger in jungle fatigues

Courtesy of the Air Force Heritage Research Institute

THE RADAR SITE IN LAOS BEFORE THE ATTACK

Courtesy of Ron Haden

A1C John Levitow Earns a Medal of Honor

A1C John Levitow (1945–2000) was a gunship loadmaster in Vietnam. His duties included working with flares. On 24 February 1969 he displayed extraordinary courage on a night mission near Long Binh, South Vietnam.

The AC-47 gunship he was on came under heavy fire. (The crew later found out their ship had 3,500 punctures from enemy fire.) A mortar shell exploded on the ship's right wing. The explosion sent shrapnel through the body of the plane. It wounded many crewmen.

Forty pieces of shrapnel hit Levitow. Even so, he saved the life of one of his comrades who was about to fall through an open cargo door. When Levitow saw a loose flare headed toward the ammunition supply, he threw himself on top of it. He threw the flare out the cargo door barely a second before it exploded.

Levitow spent two months recuperating. Then he went on 20 more missions. For his brave act in 1969, he received the Medal of Honor in 1970. No other Airman of his rank or lower had ever received that award—the nation's highest military medal.

SGT JOHN LEVITOW

Sgt John Levitow receives the Medal of Honor from President Richard Nixon in 1970.

Courtesy of the Air Force Heritage Research Institute

Maj Robert Undorf and the Rescue of the *Mayaguez*

Maj Robert Undorf was another Airman who served with honor during the Vietnam War.

Undorf was an on-scene commander in 1975 for the rescue of the US merchant ship *S.S. Mayaguez* and its crew. Cambodian Communists grabbed the ship in May 1975. It was 60 miles off the Cambodian coast.

The Cambodian Communists took the *Mayaguez* to Koh Tang Island off the Cambodian coast. President Gerald R. Ford dispatched a force of roughly 200 Marines to retake the vessel and rescue the crew. The Marines expected light resistance on Koh Tang. But they soon found themselves in a tough firefight with up to 200 Cambodian troops. Three of their eight helicopters crashed and two others were disabled.

Meanwhile, a Marine boarding party seized the *Mayaguez* but found no crew members aboard. US aircraft carried out a bombing strike on the Cambodian mainland. After that, the Cambodians released the *Mayaguez*'s crew.

Getting the Marines off Koh Tang was another matter. While they fiercely defended their position, Maj Undorf flew above the battle in an OV-10 forward-air-control aircraft. He directed supporting fire from USAF aircraft and helicopters on the scene. He then directed the rescue of the Marines from the island while continuing to bring in supporting fire. This was tricky, because at the end only three helicopters were available to pick up the Marines. More than once, Undorf himself made several strafing passes against Cambodian troops.

For his intelligent and brave execution of duties Undorf earned the Silver Star and the Mackay Trophy. The Air Force gives the trophy for the most outstanding flight by an Airman each year.

US MARINES STORM THE *MAYAGUEZ*

Courtesy of Time Life Pictures/US Navy/Time Life Pictures/ Getty Images

TSgt Wayne Fisk and the Last Firefight in Southeast Asia

TSgt Wayne Fisk earned two Silver Stars in the Vietnam War. He was a pararescueman.

Fisk earned his first Silver Star for taking part in a raid to try to rescue POWs in 1970 from the Son Tay POW camp in North Vietnam, in enemy territory. He earned his second Silver Star helping US Marines fight Cambodian Communist forces. Fisk was a member of the assault force that recovered the *Mayaguez*, its crew, and the entrapped Marines. During this operation, he traded fire with an enemy sniper while trying to recover a Marine's body. This made Fisk the last US serviceman to engage the enemy in Southeast Asia.

CMSgt Wayne Fisk

Courtesy of the US Air Force

Gen Daniel James Jr.: The Military's First African-American Four-Star General

Gen Daniel "Chappie" James Jr. (1920–1978) was the first African-American to attain four-star general rank. He received a bachelor of science degree in 1942 from Tuskegee Institute and completed the Civilian Pilot Training Program.

During World War II James trained pilots, including the famous Tuskegee Airmen. He flew 101 combat missions in Korea. He went on 78 missions in Vietnam. He led one operation in Vietnam in which US Airmen shot down seven MiGs. This was a record during the Vietnam War.

James received his fourth star in 1975. At that time, he was commander in chief of the North American Air Defense Command and the Aerospace Defense Command. He directed all strategic aerospace defense forces in the United States and Canada.

He retired in 1978 as a special assistant to the Air Force chief of staff.

Gen Daniel "Chappie" James Jr.

Gen Daniel "Chappie" James Jr. set a record as a pilot in the Vietnam War.

Courtesy of the US Air Force

How the USAF Gained an Increasingly Significant Role in Other US Military Operations During the Cold War

The mission of the US Air Force expanded during the Cold War. Although its main role was still to deliver the atomic bomb, it took on new missions. These included a lead role in the Berlin Airlift, rescuing US citizens in harm's way, and securing Europe by helping rearm Germany.

The US public's desire to avoid heavy casualties led to more reliance on air power to support US goals. In addition, the Air Force's ability to attack more precisely and with less risk of losing aircraft made air power an attractive option.

US and NATO Military Operations

The United States and NATO nations had two big fears during the Cold War: a Soviet ground attack and Soviet nuclear weapons.

The US and NATO took steps to increase security. They accepted West Germany into NATO in 1955. West Germany bordered Soviet-controlled East Germany. As a member of NATO, West Germany was a geographic barrier to Communist expansion. The US and NATO also rearmed West Germany to a limited extent. Remembering World War II, most people were still wary of Germany.

Starting in 1957 the United States began placing nuclear bombs all over Western Europe. It was the Air Force's job to deliver these weapons if needed. The purpose was to keep Soviet ground forces at bay. Soviet ground forces were far more numerous than NATO forces.

Other Significant Military Operations During the Cold War

Besides coordinating operations with NATO, the United States conducted missions of its own during the Cold War. Four of these involved saving civilian lives or establishing democracies.

Operation Eagle Claw

On 4 November 1979 Islamic "students" raided the US embassy in Iran. They took more than 90 US diplomats hostage. In return for the hostages' release, the Iranians demanded the US government return the Shah of Iran. He was in the United States for surgery. The unpopular Iranian leader had fled his country earlier that year.

Negotiations to gain the hostages' release failed. So President Jimmy Carter ordered a military rescue. Operation Eagle Claw began—and ended—on 24 April 1980. Eight Navy helicopters took off from the aircraft carrier USS *Nimitz* in the Persian Gulf. They headed for a patch of Iranian desert from which they planned to launch the rescue. Three of the helicopters had mechanical problems. The mission was canceled. As the remaining aircraft were leaving Iran, one of the helicopters and a USAF cargo plane collided. Five Airmen and three Marines died.

FIGURE 2.3

Iran and the Middle East

Courtesy of Maps.com

Months later on 20 January 1981—the day President Ronald Reagan assumed office—the US and Iran reached an agreement to free the last 52 hostages. (Iran had released some earlier.)

The US military learned from the experience. It needed to better coordinate joint ventures between different branches of the military. In 1987 Congress passed a law that set up the US Special Operations Command. Its purpose was to conduct special operations, which often involve more than one branch of the military.

FIGURE 2.4

Grenada and the Caribbean Sea

Courtesy of Maps.com

Operation Urgent Fury

On 13 October 1983 Communists in the government of Grenada overthrew the prime minister and took over the island in the Caribbean. Many suspected Cuba and the Soviet Union were behind the plot.

The Communist takeover put at risk some 600 American students attending a medical college in Grenada. It also endangered hundreds of other Americans living on the island. President Ronald Reagan sent US troops into Grenada on 25 October to rid it of communism and to bring home the American citizens. The mission was dubbed Operation Urgent Fury.

AMERICAN STUDENTS BOARD A C-141B STARLIFTER ON THEIR WAY OUT OF GRENADA.

Courtesy of Corbis Images

Many US Air Force aircraft took part in the mission. One was the AC-130, a gunship that gave cover to troops securing an airfield in Grenada. The AC-130 took on enemy foot soldiers and attacked antiaircraft systems. Another aircraft was the EC-130, which can broadcast to enemy radio and TV receivers. In Grenada, the EC-130 crews relayed radio messages to local people so they'd know what was happening. The C-141 Starlifter ferried home the students, plus nearly 11,000 other Americans.

The US and troops from several Caribbean nations ousted the would-be Communist government. By 15 December they restored security. The US troops could go home.

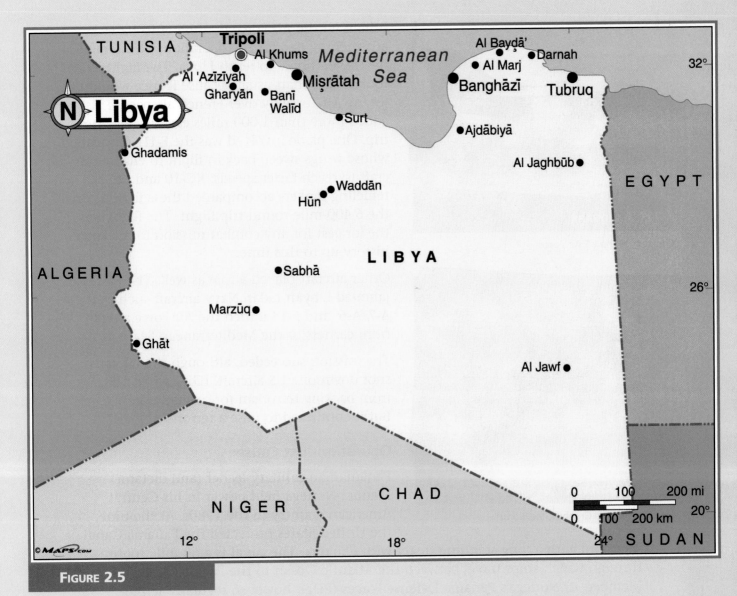

FIGURE 2.5

Libya and the Mediterranean Sea

Courtesy of Maps.com

Operation El Dorado Canyon

Libya, a country in North Africa, was a center of anti-US terrorism in the 1980s. In one Libyan bombing of a club in Germany, for instance, two US servicemen died. On 14 April 1986 Operation El Dorado Canyon targeted five military sites in Libya. President Reagan authorized the mission. The operation was a joint venture of the US Air Force and Navy.

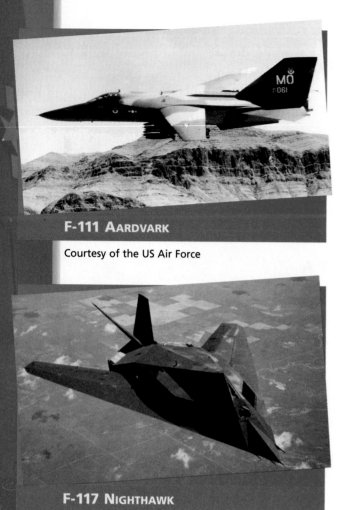

F-111 AARDVARK

Courtesy of the US Air Force

F-117 NIGHTHAWK

Courtesy of Aero Graphics, Inc./Corbis

Britain let the Air Force use one of its bases as a launching pad for the operation. US aircraft flew seven hours to reach Libya. The flight took longer than usual because France wouldn't let the Air Force fly over French airspace. This added more than 1,000 miles each way to the trip. One plane involved was the F-111 Aardvark, whose wings sweep back in flight to enable the craft to reach faster speeds. KC-10 and KC-135 refueling tankers accompanied these fighters on the 6,400-mile round-trip flight. The flight was the longest for any combat mission in Air Force history up to this time.

Other aircraft played a role as well. The EF-111 jammed Libyan radar. Navy aircraft such as the A-7, A-6, and F-14 joined the Air Force aircraft from carriers in the Mediterranean Sea.

The mission succeeded, although the Libyans shot down one US aircraft. Libya eased off from backing terrorism for several years. But it continued to pose a terrorist threat.

Operation Just Cause

Panamanian military leader (and dictator) Manuel Noriega held power in his Central American country in the 1980s. At the time, the United States protected the Panama Canal in accord with a long-standing treaty with Panama. The canal is a 50-mile route through which ships travel between the Atlantic Ocean to the Pacific Ocean. Members of Noriega's Panama Defense Forces (PDF), however, regularly seized, beat, and harassed US military personnel. In 1989 the PDF even detained nine school buses filled with American children from nearby US bases. Noriega was also involved with smuggling illegal drugs.

In response to these threats, the United States undertook Operation Just Cause. President George H. W. Bush said the purpose was to "safeguard the lives of Americans, to defend democracy in Panama, to combat drug trafficking, and to protect the integrity of the Panama Canal treaty."

Just Cause was a joint operation of the Air Force, Army, Navy, and Marines. The Air Force's new F-117 Nighthawk stealth fighter saw its first combat duty. Furthermore, the Air Force delivered 9,500 paratroopers in the largest airdrop since D-Day in 1944. The mission ran from December 1989 until February 1990. US forces arrested Noriega on 3 January 1990. He was convicted in a US court of drug trafficking and money laundering. A Panamanian court convicted him of murder. In February 2007, he was still in a US prison in Miami, with one report saying he might be released in September.

Key Developments in Aircraft, Missile Capability, and Nuclear Capability During the Cold War

Between 1945 and 1989, both the United States and the Soviet Union spent billions on defense. Because of this huge investment, the United States made several advances in aircraft, missiles, and nuclear power during those years.

Aircraft Developments

The Douglas X-3 Stiletto was introduced in 1952. It was different from the X-1 and X-2, which you read about in Chapter 6, Lesson 1. While the X-1 and X-2 were rocket-driven, the X-3 was jet-driven. And while the X-1 and X-2 had to be launched like a glider in mid-air, the X-3 took off from the ground.

Engineers built the X-3 to be the first jet aircraft to break Mach 3. But in 20 tries, it failed to do so. So the designers went back to the drawing board. They came up with three new aircraft: the F-104 Starfighter, the experimental X-15, and the reconnaissance aircraft SR-71 Blackbird.

The F-104 flew 1,404 mph in 1958 and reached an altitude of 103,395 feet in 1959.

The X-15 tested two kinds of limits: speed and altitude. Like the first jets in the X-series, the rocket-propelled X-15 had to be carried into the air for release. But it soon broke records. The X-15 flew at speeds that exceeded 4,000 miles an hour. It soared more than 50 miles into the sky. Pilots tested the X-15s from 1959 until 1968.

F-104 Starfighter

Courtesy of George Hall/Corbis

The X-15 under the wing of a B-52

Courtesy of Dean Conger/Corbis

SR-71 BLACKBIRD

Courtesy of George Hall/Corbis

BELL X-5

Courtesy of Loomis Dean/Time Life Pictures/Getty Images

B-1 LANCER

Courtesy of George Hall/Corbis

The SR-71 was the fastest (2,193 mph) and could reach the highest altitudes (85,068 feet) of all reconnaissance planes.

The Bell X-5 first flew in 1951. It had a jet engine. Its main experimental function was its wing design. The X-5 had wings that could sweep back up to 60 degrees during flight. The sweptback-wing design meant faster flight. The F-111 that dropped bombs over Libya during Operation El Dorado Canyon in 1986 had the same swing-back wing design.

As the B-52 fleet aged, the Air Force modernized its bomber fleet. It upgraded the B-52s to accept air-launched cruise missiles. And in 1984 it accepted the first B-1 Lancer long-range bomber. The B-1 could carry twice the payload of a B-52. The Air Force thought the B-1's range, speed, and ability to attack at low altitude would allow it penetrate Soviet defenses. Its design called for a maximum speed of Mach 2.1 (1,400 mph) and a range of 6,100 miles without refueling.

Missile and Nuclear Developments

At the end of World War II, the Germans invented and used the V-2 ballistic missile. A ballistic missile *is one that free-falls after a self-powered flight.* During the final months of the war Germany fired thousands of these rocket-driven missiles. The missiles flew 100 miles into the sky before plunging to Earth at speeds as high as 3,600 mph. They carried 2,000-pound warheads. A warhead *is the explosive tip of a missile.*

Based on captured V-2 technology, the US developed its own ballistic missiles after the war. Their purpose was to deliver nuclear weapons on the Soviet Union and its allies. *Ballistic missiles* were rocket or jet propelled. They weren't guided by radar. Once they finished their forward, upward motion, they plummeted to Earth much like a bomb dropped from a plane. The Soviets likewise developed a series of increasingly effective missiles aimed at the US and other NATO countries.

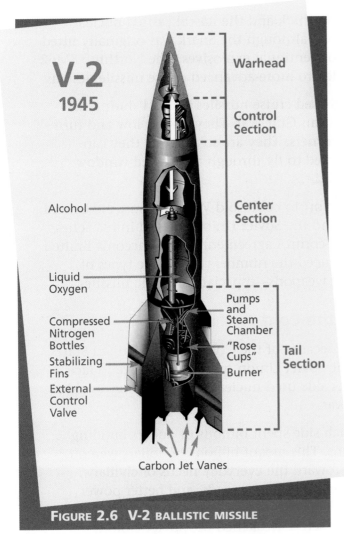

V-2
1945

- Warhead
- Control Section
- Center Section
- Alcohol
- Liquid Oxygen
- Pumps and Steam Chamber
- Compressed Nitrogen Bottles
- "Rose Cups"
- Tail Section
- Stabilizing Fins
- Burner
- External Control Valve
- Carbon Jet Vanes

FIGURE 2.6 V-2 BALLISTIC MISSILE

The Germans dropped thousands of V-2 ballistic missiles on England during World War II.

Other Cold War era inventions were smart bombs and cruise missiles. *Smart bombs* are dropped from an aircraft and guided to their targets by laser or other precision-delivery devices. They have fins to stabilize them in flight. *Cruise missiles* are both guided and propelled. The first cruise missile was the German V-1 from World War II.

In the 1950s US researchers invented a jet-propelled missile. The Northrop SM62 Snark could fly for 6,300 miles at Mach 0.94. This was nearly the speed of sound. The rocket-propelled GAM 63 Rascal was smaller and more controllable than the Snark. SAC bomber crews could guide the Rascal by radar from up to 100 miles away. This distance better protected bombers from antiaircraft fire.

NORTHROP SM62 SNARK

Courtesy of the US Air Force

GAM 63 RASCAL

Courtesy of the US Air Force

Both the Snark and the Rascal carried nuclear warheads, although the Snark was originally fitted with conventional explosives. The Northrop SM62 Snark led to more-advanced cruise missile designs.

The US used cruise missiles in 1991 during the first Persian Gulf War. They can fly low and turn sharp corners. They are so accurate they can be directed to fly through a specified window of a building.

In an effort to cool Cold War tensions, the United States and the Soviet Union entered into a series of arms-control agreements. These accords limited and reduced the numbers of specific types of nuclear weapons—especially ballistic missiles.

How the Cold War Ended

In the decades of the Cold War, the United States and the Soviet Union never fought face to face. Neither side used nuclear weapons. They avoided total war.

But each side spent billions of dollars building up arms. This meant billions of dollars weren't going toward the everyday needs of civilians: better schools, better roads, and better power plants. This failure to pay attention to its people's needs severely weakened the Soviet Union.

The country's economy suffered. People had to wait in line to buy basic foods, such as bread. The people in the Communist countries of Europe also began to demand more respect for human rights. They wanted freedom of speech, freedom of religion, and the freedom to travel to other countries.

The Cold War came to a critical point in 1989. Soviet leader Mikhail Gorbachev had come to power in 1985. He tried to reform the Communist system by freeing the economy and improving human rights. But the effort came too late for Soviet communism. The Soviets' Eastern European allies saw their Communist governments fall one by one. In most cases, democracies took their place. East Germany and West Germany reunited into one democratic country. The Soviet Union broke apart into 15 independent countries, including Russia. Gorbachev was unable stop the disintegration of the Soviet Union.

After four decades of tension, the contest of wills was over. The United States and its democratic allies in NATO had won.

Some people thought the Cold War's end would bring a long period of peace. But instead, the ending of the Cold War ushered in a whole new era of regional conflicts. This would challenge the US and NATO in a much different way than the Cold War did.

CHECKPOINTS

Lesson 2 Review

Using complete sentences, answer the following questions on a sheet of paper.

1. What was an aircraft used during the Cuban Missile Crisis and how was it used?

2. What did President John F. Kennedy set up around Cuba when the Soviets were building missile sites on the island nation?

3. Which country was better equipped with nuclear weapons during the Cuban Missile Crisis—the United States or the Soviet Union?

4. What did Congress pass that gave President Lyndon Johnson the right strike at North Vietnam?

5. Which aircraft was the new quiet "star" of the Vietnam War?

6. What lessons did the USAF learn from the Vietnam War?

7. What important lesson did the US military learn from Operation Eagle Claw?

8. What was special about the X-5 aircraft?

Applying Your Learning

9. Why do you think the US and NATO won the Cold War?

Global Interventions From 1990

_____

_____

_____

Why did TSgt Timothy Wilkinson receive the Air Force Cross?

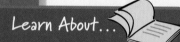
Learn About...

- **the significance of stealth aircraft**
- **the role of air power in the Gulf War (Operation Desert Storm)**
- **the role of air power in Operation Enduring Freedom**
- **the role of air power in Operation Iraqi Freedom**
- **the role of air power in various other US military operations**

In 1993 followers of African warlord Mohammed Farah Aidid shot down two UH-60 Blackhawk helicopters in Mogadishu, Somalia. Nineteen US military personnel and one Malaysian soldier were killed, along with hundreds of Somalis. The US and other troops were in Somalia to support a United Nations peacekeeping mission.

TSgt Timothy Wilkinson was a member of the combat search-and-rescue team sent to the crash site. When his unit arrived, it got caught in a 15-hour firefight with Aidid's followers. It was the longest firefight since the Vietnam War.

Wilkinson's duty was to treat the wounded. Again and again, he darted into the firefight to retrieve wounded crewmen as well as the bodies of Soldiers who had died.

During one dash, a bullet took a piece of skin off Wilkinson's face. "I learned then that life is a matter of millimeters and nanoseconds. If my head was turned a different way, I might be dead," Wilkinson said later. "Fortunately, all the bullets missed me, and my scars healed up nice."

Just as the rescue team's ammunition was starting to run out, help arrived. The crew was evacuated safely. Wilkinson was awarded an Air Force Cross for his courage that day. He was the first enlisted person to get this award since 1975.

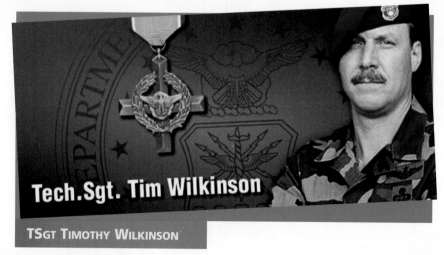

Tech.Sgt. Tim Wilkinson

TSGT TIMOTHY WILKINSON

Courtesy of the US Air Force

The Significance of Stealth Aircraft

In 1988 the B-2 Spirit stealth bomber entered the arsenal of the US Air Force. Stealth aircraft are unique for one important reason: they can evade radar. This means they can fly nearly undetected.

Stealth ability allows aircraft to run reconnaissance without being caught. A stealth aircraft can bomb an enemy with little chance of being spotted, especially at night. Imagine if the Germans had been able to escape radar as they approached the British Isles in 1941. The Battle of Britain, and perhaps World War II, might have ended differently.

An aircraft such as the B-2 is invisible because it's made of special materials. Its paint can absorb and deflect electronic pulses from radar. Its shape cloaks the aircraft as well. Every part of the plane is designed to hide it from radar. Many details about the materials are classified— *they are secret.*

Among the other stealth aircraft the US Air Force flies are the F-117 Nighthawk and the F-22 Raptor fighters. The first home of the F-22, which will replace the F-117, was at Langley AFB, Va. The F-35 stealth fighter will be next to join the Air Force fleet.

Later in this lesson, you'll read about the roles stealth aircraft played in various military operations.

THE **F-22** RAPTOR IS THE NEWEST STEALTH AIRCRAFT DEPLOYED IN THE **US** AIR FORCE FLEET.
Courtesy of the US Air Force

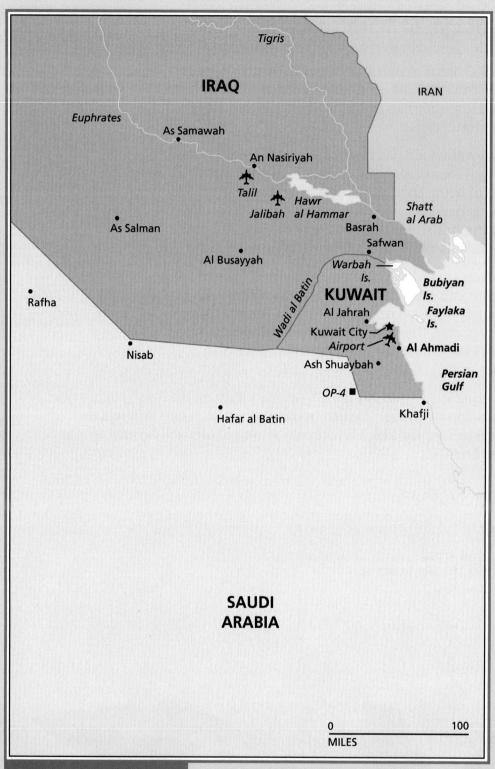

FIGURE 3.1

Kuwait, Iraq, and Saudi Arabia

Taken from *Crusade: The Untold Story of the Persian Gulf War* by Rick Atkinson.
Reprinted by permission of Houghton Mifflin Company.

The Role of Air Power in the Gulf War (Operation Desert Storm)

The end of the Cold War did not bring the hoped-for peace. Instead, it created new tensions. Some alliances crumbled. The Soviet Union no longer had the might to spread communism. Only the United States remained a superpower, *a powerful, dominant country that has nuclear weapons.*

Some saw opportunity in these changes. Saddam Hussein, dictator of Iraq in the Middle East, was one of them. He wanted to grab the oil fields of Kuwait, a tiny country south of Iraq. Hussein assumed no one would interfere with his plan, since the Soviet Union and the United States were no longer engaged in the Cold War. He thought the Soviets and Americans wouldn't take sides in conflicts outside their borders as they had in the past. He was wrong.

On 2 August 1990 Iraqi forces marched into Kuwait. By 4 August, Iraq controlled its neighbor. Iraq had prepared well for the invasion. With 550,000 troops, it had the fourth-largest army in the world. It had 16,000 surface-to-air missiles (SAMs) and 750 aircraft. But Iraq would not get to keep Kuwait.

Why the United States Got Involved in the Gulf War

On 6 August 1990 Saudi Arabia—a US ally and a major oil supplier—asked its allies to protect it from neighboring Iraq. Saudi Arabia saw what had happened in Kuwait. It feared Iraq would try to take over Saudi oil fields next.

The United Nations responded with Resolution 660, which ordered Iraq to leave Kuwait. The UN also passed Resolution 678, which permitted a coalition of UN troops to force Iraq out of Kuwait if it didn't withdraw by 15 January 1991. A coalition *is an alliance among nations.* The Allies, for example, were a coalition during World War II.

On 8 August the United States sent forces to Saudi Arabia to deter an Iraqi invasion. The military dubbed the mission Operation Desert Shield. American and other UN troops "shielded" Saudi Arabia from aggression by placing troops and weapons on Saudi soil. The US Air Force arrived with Airmen, fighter planes, stealth fighters, bombers, gunships, tankers, reconnaissance planes, and transports.

At the same time, US military planners prepared for a second operation in case Iraq didn't meet the deadline to leave Kuwait. The United States called this action Operation Desert Storm. Many UN members, including Britain and France, contributed to it.

Iraq did not exit Kuwait as ordered. The stage was set for battle between Iraqi and UN forces.

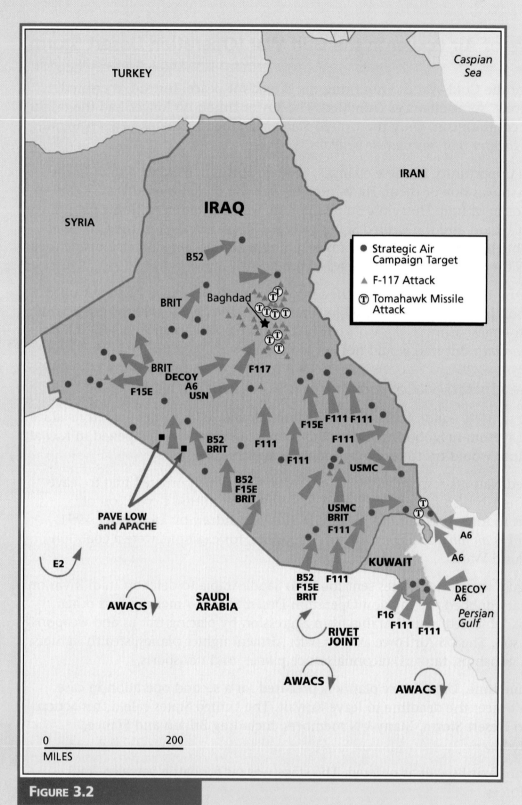

FIGURE 3.2

Initial US air strikes on Iraq

Taken from *Crusade: The Untold Story of the Persian Gulf War* by Rick Atkinson.
Reprinted by permission of Houghton Mifflin Company.

How the United States Used Air Power in the Gulf War

The US Air Force worked out a plan to fight Operation Desert Storm. Both military strategists and President George H. W. Bush wanted to avoid another Vietnam. They settled on three tactics:

1. *Keep the air battle going.* Do not pause. In Vietnam, such pauses gave the North Vietnamese time to rebuild and repair.

2. *Conduct parallel air strikes.* In other words, bomb many targets simultaneously. Don't focus on one target at a time.

3. *Coordinate air-strike efforts of the US Air Force, US Navy, and other coalition air forces* using one overall commander and one unified plan called an Air Tasking Order.

The Targets

The United States and United Nations decided that their air strikes would aim for four kinds of targets. They based their decisions on the theories of a 19th-century European named Carl von Clausewitz. He said that the best targets were at the "center of the enemy's gravity." This meant that US forces ought to begin by taking out the important targets, such as lines of communication. This would prevent Hussein from giving orders to his troops. The targets were Iraqi:

1. communication sites
2. air defenses
3. supply lines and enemy troops
4. threats to UN ground troops.

The Execution

On 17 January 1991 US air strikes on Iraq began. The US Air Force's first targets were communications links, such as TV stations and telephone-relay stations in Baghdad, Iraq's capital. Also, the Air Force made parallel air strikes. It targeted large numbers of these sites, rather than just one at a time.

Second, US aircraft went after Iraq's air-defense systems, such as SAMs. The third target was supply lines and warehouses. With air superiority secured, UN ground troops were ready to move into Iraq.

On 29 January 1991 Iraq launched an attack against UN forces in Saudi Arabia. This attack failed. Then on 22 February 1991 a 100-hour battle began to drive the Iraqis out of Kuwait for good. US air power took the skies over Kuwait. UN ground forces followed. Kuwait was at last free of Iraqi rule.

Lessons the USAF Learned From the Gulf War

The US Air Force had two goals in Operation Desert Shield and Operation Desert Storm: to protect Saudi Arabia and to free Kuwait.

To achieve these aims, the US military drew up clear tactics and targets. The Air Force based many of these tactics and targets on lessons learned in other wars like Vietnam. One important lesson: don't give the enemy a chance to repair and rearm.

Grabbing air superiority early on gave the US and UN forces an edge as well. Once these forces had struck Iraqi air bases and destroyed communication lines, Iraqi pilots couldn't receive directions from commanders or get into the air.

Finally, US technology gave the UN effort the upper hand in the air. The F-117 stealth fighter, for instance, flew 1,271 sorties during Operation Desert Storm. A sortie *is a flight or an attack by a single combat aircraft.* The F-117 was the only aircraft to bomb central Baghdad. In addition, the KC-135 and KC-10 tankers made the long-distance war possible. They refueled more than 14,500 aircraft in mid-air.

F-117 NIGHTHAWK

Courtesy of the US Air Force

The Role of Air Power in Operation Enduring Freedom

On 11 September 2001, 19 Islamic extremists hijacked four American commercial airliners. The hijackers flew two of these planes into the twin towers of the World Trade Center in New York City. They crashed a third aircraft into the Pentagon just outside Washington, D.C. Passengers on a fourth airliner fought the terrorists, who crashed the plane into a field in Pennsylvania. More than 3,000 people died in the attacks.

Less than a month later, the US military unleashed Operation Enduring Freedom (OEF). The goal was to destroy the terrorists' organization and their bases in Afghanistan, a country in southwest Asia. The terrorists were from a group called Al-Qaeda. The Taliban regime, which ruled Afghanistan at that time, let Al-Qaeda forces train in its country. Therefore, OEF targeted members of the Taliban as well as of Al-Qaeda.

US Aircraft in Afghanistan

OEF began on 7 October 2001, when US Air Force bombers struck terrorist training camps and bases. At the same time, US Navy fighters made strikes from aircraft carriers, and US and British submarines launched missiles at targets in Afghanistan.

Within 18 months, coalition air forces flew more than 85,000 sorties. They conducted more than 48,000 airlifts of troops and cargo. They dropped more than 9,650 tons of bombs.

The main US Air Force combat aircraft involved were the B-1, B-2, B-52, F-15E, F-16, A-10, and AC-130. OEF began with eight B-1s. In the first six months of operations, these aircraft accounted for 40 percent of the guided and unguided explosives dropped in Afghanistan.

The B-2 stealth bomber made the longest flight in its history early in OEF, when it flew from Whiteman Air Force Base, Missouri, to Afghanistan.

While the war removed the Taliban regime and led to a new government in Afghanistan, attacks by pro-Taliban fighters and Al-Qaeda terrorists continue. The United States, however, now joined by its NATO allies, has made great strides against the terrorists.

Precision Weapons

Among the weapons the Air Force used in Afghanistan are precision weapons. Precision weapons *are guided missiles and bombs.* They are so accurate that they can be placed within feet of their target.

The Hellfire missile is one of the precision weapons used in Afghanistan. The MQ-1 Predator delivers the Hellfire. The Predator is an unmanned aircraft that a pilot controls remotely. (Think of the remote-control device you use to change channels on your TV. It allows you to channel-surf from across the room, or "remotely.") After the pilot has fired the missile, sensor operators then guide the missiles to their targets.

Precision weapons are the wave of the future because they can keep US forces far from combat. This helps keep casualties down.

MQ-1 PREDATOR

The MQ-1 Predator delivers the Hellfire missile.

Courtesy of the US Air Force

F-16 FIGHTING FALCON

An F-16 Fighting Falcon flies over the Pentagon as part of Operation Noble Eagle.

Courtesy of the US Air Force

Operation Noble Eagle and NORAD

In addition to fighting terrorists overseas, Airmen have duties back home. Members of the Air National Guard, Air Force Reserve, and active Air Force serve in Operation Noble Eagle (ONE). Its goal is to safeguard American soil.

The North American Aerospace Defense Command (NORAD) runs ONE. As its name implies, NORAD has a big job: to defend the skies over the United States and Canada.

ONE began shortly after 11 September 2001. Within 16 months, US aircraft flew more than 27,000 sorties over American cities. They were on the lookout for suspicious aircraft, and they continue this job today. Fighters such as the F-15 Eagle or the F-16 Fighting Falcon shoot flares if they find an airplane flying in space where it is not supposed to be. For example, planes may not fly over the White House unless they have permission. If an airplane enters that airspace, Air Force fighters have the right to shoot it down if it does not respond to warnings and depart.

TSgt John Chapman: An Exceptional Brand of Courage

TSgt John Chapman was a combat controller during Operation Anaconda in Afghanistan. Air Force combat-control teams support special operations in the field.

It was in the early hours of 4 March 2002, in what became a 17-hour ordeal on top of Tukur Ghar mountain in southeastern Afghanistan. Operation Anaconda—a coalition effort to destroy Taliban and Al-Qaeda units—was just starting.

Sergeant Chapman was attached to a Navy sea-air-land (SEAL) team. The team's MH-47 helicopter was hit by Al-Qaeda enemy machine gun fire. A rocket-propelled grenade then hit the helicopter, causing a SEAL team member to fall from the aircraft into enemy-held territory.

The helicopter made an emergency landing more than four miles from the fallen SEAL. Chapman called in an AC-130 gunship to protect the stranded team.

Chapman called in another helicopter to evacuate his stranded team. Then he volunteered to rescue his missing team member from the enemy stronghold. He engaged and killed two of the enemy before advancing and engaging a second enemy position—a dug-in machine gun nest.

From close range with little cover, Chapman exchanged fire with the enemy. Finally he died after receiving multiple wounds. Because of his actions, his team was able to move to cover and break enemy contact.

The Navy SEAL leader credited Chapman with saving the lives of the entire team. In gratitude, the Navy named a cargo ship after him. For his bravery and courage, the Air Force awarded him the Air Force Cross. He became the service's highest-decorated combat controller.

MEMORIAL TO TSGT JOHN CHAPMAN

A memorial at the Air Force Enlisted Heritage Hall at Maxwell AFB, Gunter Annex, in Montgomery, Alabama

Courtesy of the US Air Force

FIGURE 3.3

Operation Anaconda in Afghanistan began in March 2002.

Courtesy of Maps.com

SrA Jason Cunningham:
A Display of Uncommon Valor

SrA Jason Cunningham was in the Navy before he decided to switch to the Air Force. He wanted to be a pararescueman. The pararescuemen's motto is "That others may live."

Airman Cunningham was the primary Air Force Combat Search and Rescue medic assigned to a Quick Reaction Force. His team was sent to recover American servicemen in the battle in which TSgt John Chapman was killed. Shortly before landing, his MH-47E helicopter took rocket-propelled grenade and small-arms fire. This severely disabled the aircraft and caused it to crash land. The assault force formed a hasty defense. Three members were killed immediately; five others were critically wounded.

Despite enemy fire, and at great risk to his own life, Cunningham stayed in the burning fuselage of the aircraft to treat the wounded. As he moved his patients to a more secure location, mortar rounds began to hit within 50 feet of his position. Disregarding this extreme danger, he continued the movement and exposed himself to enemy fire on seven separate occasions.

After a time the second casualty collection point was also endangered. Cunningham braved an intense attack while moving the critically wounded to a third collection point. He was mortally wounded and quickly deteriorating, but he continued to direct his patients' movement and transferred care to another medic.

Cunningham had given medical treatment to the wounded while under fire for seven hours. He was killed saving the lives of 10 service members. The Air Force awarded him the Air Force Cross after his death.

SrA Jason Cunningham

SrA Jason Cunningham gave his life on a rescue mission in Afghanistan.

Courtesy of the US Air Force

MEDAL OF HONOR

Courtesy of the US Air Force

AIR FORCE CROSS

Courtesy of the US Air Force

SILVER STAR

Courtesy of the US Air Force

BRONZE STAR

Courtesy of A.Y. Owen/Time Life Pictures/Getty Images

Medal of Honor

The Medal of Honor is the nation's highest US military decoration for valor or bravery in combat, awarded to members of the armed forces. It is given for conspicuous gallantry and courage at the risk of life, above and beyond the call of duty. The Medal of Honor is sometimes called the "Congressional Medal of Honor" because the president awards it on behalf of the Congress. It is awarded rarely, and then only to the bravest of the brave. The recipients' valor must be well documented.

Air Force Cross

The Air Force Cross is second only to the Medal of Honor as an award for valor. The other military services have a similar award. It is awarded to members of the Air Force for extraordinary heroism while engaged in military operations involving conflict with an opposing foreign force or while serving with friendly forces against an opposing enemy force.

Silver Star

The Silver Star Medal is the nation's third highest award designed solely for valor in combat. It is awarded to members of the military for distinguished gallantry in action against an enemy of the United States or while serving with friendly forces against an opposing enemy force.

Bronze Star

The Bronze Star Medal is awarded to any person in the military who distinguishes himself or herself by heroic or meritorious achievement or service. The service must not involve participation in aerial flight. It must occur while he or she is engaged in an action against an enemy of the United States.

B-2 SPIRIT BOMBER
Courtesy of the US Air Force

The Role of Air Power in Operation Iraqi Freedom

Another front in the war on terror is Operation Iraqi Freedom (OIF). The US military and its coalition partners launched OIF on 19 March 2003. It began with an air and ground campaign that quickly became known as "Shock and Awe." Within 22 days, coalition forces reached Baghdad. The coalition met some resistance. But the coalition forces mostly overwhelmed the Iraqis with air power, tanks, and troops.

The objective of OIF was to remove Iraqi leader Saddam Hussein from power and to rid the country of weapons of mass destruction (WMD). A weapon of mass destruction *is a chemical, biological, or atomic weapon that can kill large numbers of people in one use.*

US forces captured Hussein on 13 December 2003. After a long trial, the new Iraqi government executed him on 30 December 2006. Despite their success in capturing Hussein, however, US and coalition forces found no WMDs in Iraq.

Throughout OIF, insurgents, including members of Al-Qaeda, have poured into the country to fight US and allied forces. An insurgent *is a rebel or guerrilla fighter.*

US air power and ground troops are the main players in this ongoing mission. As of early 2007 British troops were stationed in southern Iraq. US Soldiers, Marines, Airmen, and Sailors were operating in the rest of that country.

US Aircraft in Iraq

Among the aircraft the US Air Force has used in Iraq are stealth aircraft. Twelve F-117 fighters flew into Baghdad to hit command and control targets on 20 March 2003. This attack weakened Hussein's ability to communicate with his military. US F-117 pilots flew 100 sorties.

As of June 2006, the B-2 stealth bomber had flown 49 sorties in OIF. It had dropped more than 1.5 million pounds of bombs. First employed in combat during Operation Allied Force (discussed later in this lesson) the B-2 bomber achieved "full operational capability" in December 2003.

Precision Weapons

Precision weapons have also played a large role in Iraq. About 70 percent of all weapons used in OIF have been of precision type. Two of the newer ones are the GBU-38 and GBU-39. GBU stands for "guided-bomb unit."

The GBU-38 went into action for the first time in 2004, when it was used to bomb a terrorist meeting in central Iraq. F-16 fighters delivered those GBU-38s. Weighing 500 pounds, they are smaller than some other bombs. But the GBU-38's size and accuracy allow the military to target a particular building without seriously damaging surrounding buildings. This precision approach puts civilians at less risk. The US military tries to avoid civilian deaths when fighting in crowded areas such as Baghdad.

The US Air Force used the GBU-39 in combat for the first time on 5 October 2006 in support of ground troops in Iraq. At 250 pounds, it is the smallest guided bomb the Air Force has. F-15Es employ this weapon, which can strike within six feet of a target from 60 miles away.

SSgt Kevin Harvey secures a weapons carriage with GBU-39/B small-diameter bombs to an F-15E Strike Eagle.

CMSgt Kevin Lynn: A Historic Impact on the Future of the Iraqi Army

Meritorious service can involve many types of action. For example, CMSgt Kevin Lynn helped establish the first military police academy in Iraq. He was deployed there from 28 February to 23 July 2004. Chief Lynn and fellow Air Force security forces members renovated a bombed-out former Republican Guard base in Taji, Iraq. They turned it into a new police academy. Lynn served as commandant of the school. Starting from scratch, they developed and taught a course for the academy in just nine days.

At the same time, he was also a battle-tested veteran. He and his team continued to train forces during the "April Offensive." This consisted of 18 days of nonstop mortar and rocket attacks. Overall, Lynn survived 31 mortar and 34 rocket attacks that killed 10 soldiers and injured many others. He continually risked his personal safety to ensure mission success and guarantee his team's safety. He provided security on numerous convoy missions and patrolled East Gate on Taji Military Training Base.

In all, Lynn and his team graduated more than 500 military policemen and 40 military police instructors. For his work, Lynn received the Bronze Star Medal on Dec. 14, 2004.

CMSGT KEVIN LYNN

CMSgt Kevin Lynn and his team transformed a war-torn environment into a successful Military Police academy.

Courtesy of CMSgt Kevin Lynn

A1C Elizabeth Jacobson: An Extraordinary Commitment to Her Country

A1C Elizabeth Jacobson, 21, was providing convoy security 28 September 2005 near Camp Bucca, Iraq, when a roadside bomb struck the vehicle she was riding in.

The Riviera Beach, Fla., native was assigned to the 17th Security Forces Squadron at Goodfellow Air Force Base, Texas. Airman Jacobson had been in the Air Force for two years and had been in Iraq for more than three months. She was the first female Airman killed in the line of duty in support of Operation Iraqi Freedom.

"She was an outstanding Airman who embraced life and took on all the challenges and responsibilities with extraordinary commitment to her country, her comrades, and her family," said Col. Scott Bethel, 17th Training Wing commander at Goodfellow.

"Her dedication to the U.S. Air Force and serving her country was evident in all aspects of who this young lady was," he said.

A1C ELIZABETH JACOBSON

Courtesy of the US Air Force

GEN RICHARD B. MYERS

Gen Richard B. Myers was the 15th chairman of the Joint Chiefs of Staff.

Courtesy of the US Air Force

Gen Richard Myers: Chairman of the Joint Chiefs of Staff

Born in 1942, Gen Richard Myers entered military service as a member of ROTC during his college days. In 2001 he became chairman of the Joint Chiefs of Staff. The Joint Chiefs is the military advisory group to the president of the United States. Besides the chairman, the top-ranking officer from each branch of the military, including the Marine Corps, is in the group.

Myers helped shape the direction of the campaigns in Afghanistan and Iraq. He retired in September 2005. Two months later President George W. Bush awarded him the Presidential Medal of Freedom.

The Role of Air Power in Various Other US Military Operations

The "Air Force has been at war continuously for over 15 years, since the opening rounds of Operation Desert Storm . . . ," said Gen T. Michael Moseley, chief of staff of the Air Force, in a letter to US Airmen in March 2006.

In addition to the major military operations you've just read about, Airmen have flown other missions since 1991. Some were combat missions. Others were humanitarian. Some were both.

US Global Interventions, 1990 Through 2006

Name of Operation	Location	Years	Type
Desert Shield	Saudi Arabia	1990	military
Desert Storm	Iraq, Kuwait	1991	military
Provide Comfort	Iraq, Turkey	1991–1996	humanitarian
Southern Watch	Iraq	1992–2003	military
Provide Hope	Former Soviet Union	1992–1993	humanitarian
Provide Relief	Somalia	1992–1993	humanitarian
Provide Promise	Bosnia	1992–1996	humanitarian
Restore Hope/ Restore Hope II	Somalia	1993–1994	humanitarian/ military
Deny Flight	Bosnia	1993–1995	military
Uphold Democracy	Haiti	1994–1995	military
Deliberate Force	Bosnia	1995	military
Northern Watch	Iraq	1997–2003	military
Allied Force	Serbia	1999	military
Shining Hope	Serbia	1999	humanitarian
Noble Eagle	United States	2001–	military
Enduring Freedom	Afghanistan	2001–	military
Iraqi Freedom	Iraq	2003–	military

Operation Provide Comfort

Following the 1991 Gulf War, the United States launched Operation Provide Comfort. Its purpose was to protect the Kurds, an ethnic minority in northern Iraq, and to provide food for Kurdish refugees fleeing into Turkey. Iraq's Saddam Hussein was fighting a rebellion the Kurds had launched against his government. He was also after Kurdish oil fields. Employing C-130s, the US Air Force delivered thousands of tons of relief supplies, including food, tents, and blankets to Kurdish camps. Operation Provide Comfort ended in 1996 and was replaced by Operation Northern Watch.

Operation Southern Watch

Starting in August 1992, the United States enforced a no-fly zone in Iraq. A no-fly zone *is airspace enemy aircraft aren't allowed to enter.* This zone was in southern Iraq. Its purpose was to protect the Shiite Muslim population and Kuwait. Its name was Operation Southern Watch.

Iraqi pilots regularly shot at US aircraft. Sometimes they entered no-fly airspace. This operation ended just before OIF kicked off.

F-15

A crew chief checks an F-15 as it prepares for flight on 16 March 2003 in Operation Southern Watch.

Courtesy of the US Air Force

Operation Northern Watch

After US and UN troops subdued Iraqi forces operating against the Kurds, they still couldn't go home. They had to make sure Hussein didn't send his troops and aircraft into hostile action again. So the United Nations set up a second no-fly zone in the northern half of Iraq. This was done in part to protect the Kurds. The name of this mission was Operation Northern Watch.

Between 1997 and 2003, 1,400 US, British, and Turkish fliers served in the mission with 50 aircraft. The Iraqis shot at them daily, often using SAMs. The UN aircraft would occasionally strike back. The last US aircraft serving in the mission headed home on 17 March 2003. OIF began two days later.

Operation Provide Hope

When the Soviet Union collapsed in 1991, it split into 15 countries. Food and medical supply shortages followed. Many of the new countries were not stable because for 70 years they had relied on a central Communist government in Moscow. The United States provided supplies through Operation Provide Hope. This humanitarian mission ran from February 1992 to May 1993.

US Airmen flew cargo planes like the C-5 Galaxy, the C-141 Starlifter, and the C-130 Hercules. They delivered 6,000 tons of food and medicines. NATO provided bases in Germany and Turkey. The mission was a success.

C-5 GALAXY

Courtesy of the US Air Force

FIGURE 3.4

Bosnia and Herzegovina, Croatia, Montenegro, Serbia, and Slovenia

Courtesy of Maps.com

Operation Provide Promise

Yugoslavia was formed from the southern Slav territories of Serbia, Bosnia and Herzegovina, Croatia, Montenegro, and Slovenia after World War I. The federation began to fracture in 1992. Ethnic strife and civil war had long been a part of this country's history.

The Bosnian Muslims (Bosniaks) and Bosnian Croats wanted to be independent of Yugoslavia. But the Bosnian Serbs and the Serbs in Serbia, under Yugoslav leader Slobodan Milosevic, didn't want them to secede, or *break away*. The Bosnian Serbs fought the Bosniaks and Bosnian Croats to keep Bosnia and Herzegovina in Yugoslavia. In 1992 the Serbs cut off food and other supplies to Sarajevo, Bosnia's capital.

In July 1992, the United States and 20 other countries launched a massive airlift, Operation Provide Promise. The United States and other nations flew in 160,000 tons of goods in 13,000 sorties. C-130s, C-141s, C-5s, and C-17s took part in this mission. It was risky business. The Serbs shot at the cargo aircraft. They hit 10 US planes and shot down one Italian aircraft. The airlift lasted until January 1996. The Dayton Accords, signed 14 December 1995 at Wright-Patterson AFB in the Wright brothers' hometown, brought an end to the fighting.

CAPSULES

The former Yugoslav republics each contain a mixture of ethnic groups. Serbs were the majority in Serbia, but made up significant minorities in Bosnia and Herzegovina, Croatia, and Montenegro. Likewise, large numbers of Croats live in Serbia and Bosnia and Herzegovina. Serbia's province of Kosovo contained a large majority of ethnic Albanians. This ethnic mixture made the breakup of Yugoslavia more difficult, because the Serb minorities in the breakaway republics and Kosovo wanted to live under Serbian rule, not that of other ethnic groups. The dictator of Yugoslavia, Slobodan Milosevic, maintained his power partly by stirring up Serbs' fears of what would happen if Yugoslavia broke up.

A *Serb* is a member of the Serb ethnic group. A *Serbian* is a resident of Serbia.

C-130

C-130s like this one participated in Operation Provide Promise.

Courtesy of the US Air Force

Operations Deny Flight and Deliberate Force

Combined with the Provide Promise effort, NATO opened Operation Deny Flight over Bosnia. It ran from April 1993 to December 1995. NATO forces created no-fly zones for Serbian aircraft.

US pilots in fighters such as the F-16 shot down Serbian aircraft that violated the no-fly zone. In retaliation, Serbs grabbed UN peacekeepers. So NATO launched a mission called Operation Deliberate Force. NATO forces used precision-guided weapons and aircraft to hit the Serbians hard. UN forces also began protecting the peacekeepers. The Serbians gave in toward the end of 1995.

Operations Allied Force and Shining Hope

Despite the end of the Bosnian war, Yugoslavia continued to be a center of conflict. In 1999 Milosevic directed Serbian forces to attack ethnic Albanians in Kosovo. Kosovo is a province in southern Serbia.

Milosevic didn't heed NATO's warnings to stop his attacks. So NATO launched an air campaign called Operation Allied Force in March 1999. NATO air forces flew more than 38,000 sorties. The air campaign succeeded in forcing Milosevic to withdraw his forces from Kosovo after 78 days. No ground forces were involved.

The US Air Force marked two "firsts" in this effort. The B-2 stealth bomber engaged in combat for the first time. And the United States used its 2,000-pound GBU-31 precision weapon for the first time. In fact, the B-2 bombers dropped the GBU-31s. B-2s flew 30-hour round-trip missions from their base in Missouri. They caused 33 percent of the damage inflicted on the Serbs in the first eight weeks of Operation Allied Force.

Humanitarian airlifts were key to the success of this campaign. US airlifts, as part of Operation Shining Hope, kept Albanian refugees from starving while NATO crushed the Serbian attack on Kosovo.

Milosevic was indicted as a war criminal in 2000 and tried before a United Nations court. He was charged with crimes against humanity in Kosovo, violating the laws of war in Croatia and Bosnia, and genocide in Bosnia. He died in 2006 just before the end of his trial in the Netherlands.

Developing Flight

Operations Provide Relief and Restore Hope

Somalia, an East African country, had a severe food shortage in 1992. Its people risked starvation. Beginning in August, the United States, along with other friendly countries, airlifted food through Operation Provide Relief. C-141s carried the goods to Kenya, another African nation. Smaller C-130s then flew the food into Somalia.

But there was a snag. Somali warlords often stole the food before it could reach the people. These warlords fired at US cargo planes. The United States shut down Operation Provide Relief in 1993. But it soon launched another mission, Operation Restore Hope.

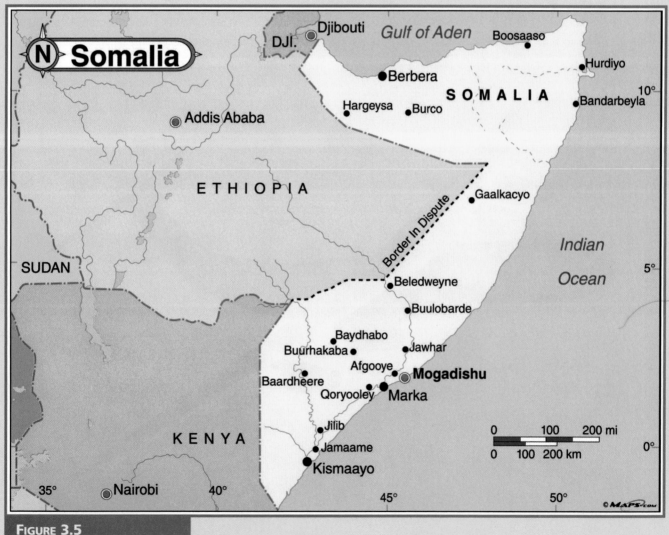

FIGURE 3.5

Somalia and neighboring countries in Africa

LESSON 3 | Global Interventions From 1990   277

Restore Hope had two goals. The first was to distribute food. The second was to go after the warlords and their gangs. Restore Hope ended in May 1993, when the United Nations took over the relief mission.

But in mid-1993 a warlord named Mohammed Farah Aidid directed his supporters to interfere with the aid mission. They ambushed and wiped out a Pakistani convoy. During the US effort to arrest some of his top lieutenants, the firefight in Mogadishu—which you read about at the beginning of this lesson—broke out.

In response, the United States started Operation Restore Hope II. It airlifted combat forces back into Mogadishu, and stationed AC-130s at bases in Kenya. But many Somalis supported Aidid. The United States abandoned the effort to arrest him and sought a political solution instead. US troops left Somalia in March 1994.

C-141 STARLIFTER

Courtesy of the US Air Force

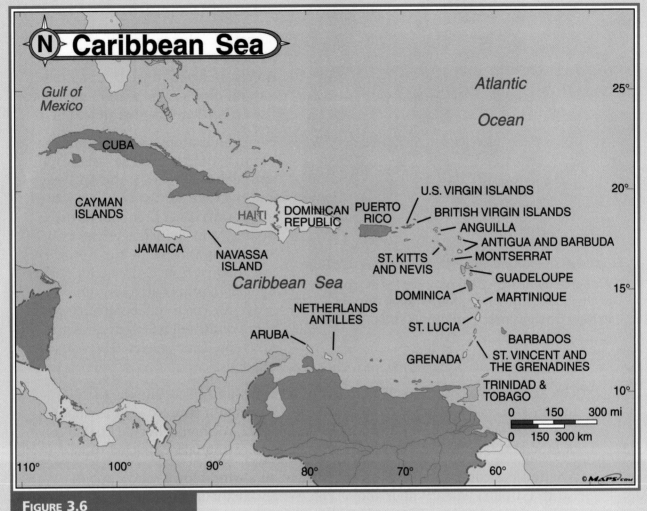

FIGURE 3.6

Haiti and the Caribbean Sea

Operation Uphold Democracy

Haiti is a small country on a Caribbean island. In 1991 a military coup removed its elected president, Jean-Bertrand Aristide, from office. A military coup *is a sudden takeover of power by the military.* The new leaders suppressed the Haitian people's rights. Many Haitians fled to the United States in boats or anything that would float. They tried to enter the country illegally.

Despite diplomatic efforts, by 1994 no solution was in sight. The Haitian economy was weak. More and more Haitians were trying to make the dangerous, 700-mile sea voyage to US shores. The United States drew up a plan to return Aristide to power. It was called Operation Uphold Democracy. In September 60 C-130s packed with US paratroopers headed toward Haiti. When the Haitian military leaders found out that US forces were headed their way, they gave up power. US troops entered Haiti peacefully.

In 1995 the United Nations took over the mission. It put a US commander in charge of UN operations in Haiti.

AIR FORCE MEDICS AFTER HURRICANE KATRINA

Air Force medics prepare patients for evacuation at the Louis Armstrong International Airport in New Orleans after Hurricane Katrina.

Courtesy of the US Air Force

Natural Disasters

Sometimes there's no military coup to overcome; no no-fly zones to enforce; no war refugees to feed. Sometimes natural disasters are reason enough for the US Air Force to step in and help.

Here's an example: when Hurricane Katrina struck Louisiana, Mississippi, and Alabama in 2005, the Air Force and the Civil Air Patrol (CAP) joined forces with other branches of the military and civilian agencies to help Americans affected by the storm. This was the first time CAP, the Air Force's official volunteer auxiliary, and the active Air Force collaborated. Together, they conducted search-and-rescue missions. They delivered 30,000 tons of goods.

The Air Force has been involved in many such missions. For example, in 1991 the Air Force aided Bangladesh in southern Asia when it suffered serious flooding. When Hurricane Andrew hit south Florida in 1992, Airmen delivered 20,000 tons of food and supplies. In 1993 it delivered help to earthquake-damaged India.

Aviation has come a long way from that day on a wind-blown sand dune in North Carolina when Wilbur and Orville Wright first launched their frail flyer. Today it's hard to imagine a world without flight. The US Air Force has grown from a tiny unit of the Army to an independent, equal military service. Rotary or fixed-winged aircraft are essential equipment for all branches of the military. On the civilian front, each day millions of ordinary people board commercial aircraft of all sizes and travel across the country and around the world.

But there's another part of the story of flight—the development of rockets and humans' entry into space. The next few lessons will tell that story, starting with the solar system and people's struggle to understand it.

CAPSULES

"Air superiority is not the God-given right of Americans. It doesn't just happen. It takes a lot of people working hard to produce the capabilities that provide it for US forces."

GEN RONALD R. FOGLEMAN, USAF

CHECKPOINTS

Lesson 3 Review

Using complete sentences, answer the following questions on a sheet of paper.

1. Name three stealth aircraft used by the US Air Force.

2. What did US forces want to target first in Operation Desert Storm? Why?

3. What is a precision weapon? Name one such weapon used in Operation Enduring Freedom. Name one used in Operation Iraqi Freedom.

4. What is the goal of Operation Noble Eagle? What do participants in ONE do?

5. What is a no-fly zone?

6. What are two of the main cargo aircraft used to airlift food in missions like Operation Provide Hope?

7. What first-time event occurred after Hurricane Katrina struck?

Applying Your Learning

8. Reviewing the operations discussed in this lesson, do you think airpower alone can win a conflict? Or are ground troops always necessary as well?

UNIT FOUR

Exten

Space Shuttle *Discovery* lifts off.

ding FLIGHT

Unit Chapters

CHAPTER 7

Astronomy and Space

CHAPTER 8

Exploring Space

The Andromeda galaxy

Astronomy and Space

Chapter Outline

LESSON 1

The Solar System
and Some Early Astronomers

LESSON 2

Rocketry and the Space Race

"The Congress declares that the general welfare
and security of the United States require that adequate
provision be made for aeronautical and space activities.
The Congress further declares that such activities
shall be the responsibility of, and shall be directed by,
a civilian agency exercising control over aeronautical
and space activities sponsored by the United States."

National Space Act creating NASA, 1958

The Solar System and Some Early Astronomers

The Polish astronomer Nicolaus Copernicus (1473–1543) loved to study the night sky. He didn't have a fancy telescope. It hadn't been invented yet.

But when it got dark in Copernicus's city of Fromburk, Poland, it got very dark. It was a world before electric light. So he had a wonderful view of the sky. He studied it from the tower of the city's cathedral.

Copernicus went to the tower night after night. Based on what he'd seen, he came up with a theory that would revolutionize astronomy.

In Copernicus's day, people thought the sun and the planets revolved around Earth. They had a geocentric, or *Earth-centered*, view of the solar system. The solar system *is the sun and all the objects in space that circle around it.* According to this theory, the sun and the planets revolve around Earth in circular paths.

Astronomers had believed for centuries that the Earth was the center of the solar system. Their belief originated with astronomers such as Ptolemy, who worked in Egypt in the second century AD.

Belief in a geocentric solar system was even part of church doctrine. At this time there was only one church in Western Europe, the Roman Catholic Church. It had a great deal of political power. Most universities had a church connection, and so, therefore, did most scientists.

NICOLAUS COPERNICUS

Courtesy of Paul Almasv/Corbis

But some ancient astronomers saw a problem with the geocentric theory. As the planets moved across the sky, they generally seemed to move in one direction. But once in a while they seemed to reverse course and go backward.

These astronomers tried to explain the reversal by suggesting that, in addition to their main cycles around Earth, the planets moved in epicycles—*cycles within cycles*.

This explanation didn't totally challenge people's thinking. It left Earth at the center of things. But the idea of epicycles was complex. And it didn't fully explain the planets' movements.

Copernicus decided to defy tradition. He proposed a heliocentric—*sun-centered*—view of the solar system. Like good scientists of today, he then tried to confirm that hypothesis—*an unconfirmed explanation that can be tested for truthfulness*—based on his observations.

COPERNICUS OBSERVED THE SKIES FROM A WINDOW IN THE TOWER ON THE WALL OF THE CATHEDRAL OF FROMBURK (FRAUENBURG), POLAND.

Courtesy of Erich Lessing/Art Resource, NY

- **geocentric**
- **solar system**
- **epicycle**
- **heliocentric**
- **hypothesis**
- **revolve**
- **orbit**
- **rotate**
- **galaxy**
- **gravity**
- **elliptical**
- **geosynchronous**
- **asteroid**
- **comet**
- **light-year**
- **meteoroid**
- **meteorite**
- **meteor**
- **constellation**
- **observatory**
- **sunspot**

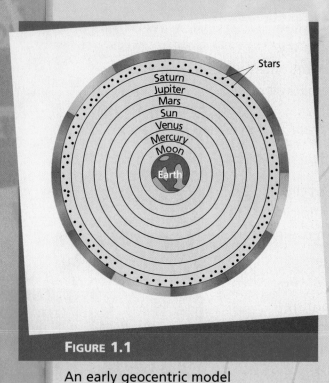

FIGURE 1.1

An early geocentric model

FIGURE 1.2

An early heliocentric model

Although he didn't have a telescope, Copernicus did have other instruments to study the sky. These instruments were better than those that earlier astronomers had. Once he assumed that the solar system was heliocentric, Copernicus found he could easily explain the planets' puzzling motions.

Copernicus had made a great discovery. But it took him a long time to put the word out. He spent years on his great work. He published it in 1593 in Latin, as was the custom of the day. Translated into English, the title is *On the Revolutions of the Celestial Spheres*. He died soon after the book came out.

Why did it take Copernicus so long? Some people say it was because he feared the reactions of church officials. Others say he was just being careful. He wanted to get everything right.

With his new theory, Copernicus set in motion a revolution. He didn't just change the way people thought about the solar system. He changed the way people thought—period.

Today, scientists still respect Copernicus's work. "The Copernican Revolution was a revolution in ideas, a transformation of man's perception of the universe and of his relation to it," wrote historian Thomas S. Kuhn.

The Objects in the Solar System

The solar system includes eight planets, their moons, and many other objects.

Each of the planets revolves, or *circles in an orbit*, around the sun. An orbit *is the path of a celestial body as it revolves around another body*. Mercury, the closest planet to the sun, makes a revolution in 88 days; Neptune, the farthest planet out, takes 165 years.

In addition, each planet rotates, or *spins on its axis*. These times vary, too. One Earth day, 24 hours, is the standard by which astronomers measure the other planets' rotation times.

The Sun

The sun is the largest object in the solar system. It contains more than 99.8 percent of the total mass—the "stuff"—of the solar system. It is one of 100 billion stars in the Milky Way Galaxy. A galaxy *is a huge mass of stars, gas, and dust clouds that exists in one area of space*. Based on mass, the sun is in the top 10 percent of all stars in the Milky Way. Our galaxy is one of billions in the universe.

The Planets and Their Key Satellites

Galaxies and the solar system hold together because of gravity. Gravity *is an invisible force that pulls all objects toward one another*. The gravity of the sun holds the planets in place as they revolve around it. Likewise, the gravity of a planet holds its moons in place.

Mercury

Mercury is the smallest planet. It's also the one closest to the sun. It has a rocky, cratered surface. Mercury revolves around the sun every 88 Earth days. Mercury rotates very slowly. It takes 59 Earth days to make a rotation. Mercury has no atmosphere, except for small amounts of helium and hydrogen.

Temperatures on Mercury are extreme: 750 degrees Fahrenheit (F) during the day and 330 degrees F below zero at night. The Mariner 10 spacecraft made flybys in 1974 and 1975 and found pockets of polar ice in deep craters where solar heat cannot melt it.

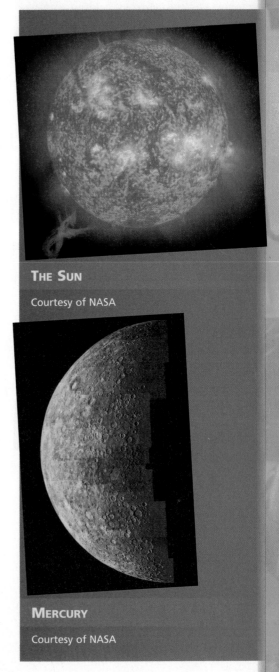

THE SUN

Courtesy of NASA

MERCURY

Courtesy of NASA

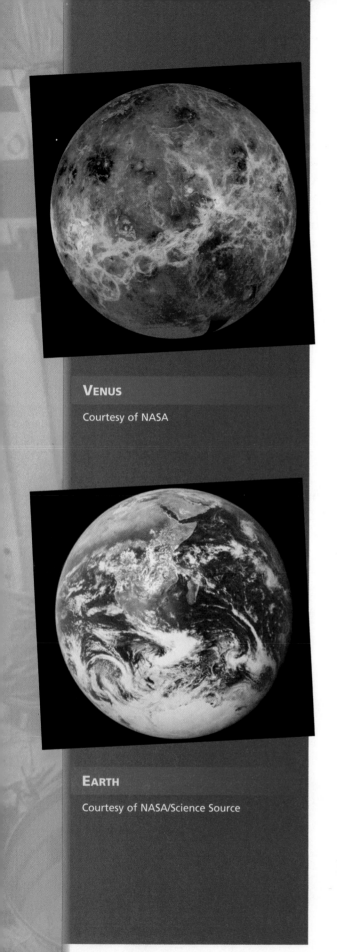

VENUS

Courtesy of NASA

EARTH

Courtesy of NASA/Science Source

Venus

At 67 million miles from the sun, Venus is the planet closest to Earth. It's also closest to Earth in terms of size. Its "year"—the time it takes to orbit around the sun—lasts 225 Earth days. Its "day"—the time it takes to make one rotation—is 243 Earth days. It is the only planet to rotate "backwards"—the opposite direction of all the other planets.

Venus is cloaked in a thick layer of clouds made up of water and sulfuric acid.

Scientists think that the sulfuric acid comes from volcanoes on the planet's surface. The volcanic activity, plus the cloud cover, makes Venus the hottest planet in the solar system. Its surface temperature is almost 900 degrees F.

Earth and Its Moon

Earth is the only planet to sustain life as far as we know. Its atmosphere is 78 percent nitrogen and 21 percent oxygen. The remaining 1 percent is argon, carbon dioxide, neon, helium, ozone, and hydrogen. The clouds of Earth's atmosphere help protect the planet from the sun's radiation. More than 70 percent of Earth's surface is covered with water.

Earth makes a complete rotation every 24 hours. It completes an orbit around the sun every 365 1/4 days.

Earth has one moon. The moon has no atmosphere to protect it. As a result, it has extreme temperatures and a rough surface.

The moon revolves around Earth in an elliptical orbit—*an orbit shaped like an oval, not a circle.* Because of this elliptical orbit, the moon's distance from Earth varies. At its closest, the moon is 221,000 miles from Earth. At its farthest, it is 252,000 miles.

The moon orbits Earth in a little less than 28 days. Both Earth and its moon rotate at about the same rate. That means the moon always has same "face" turned toward Earth. This kind of orbit is known as geosynchronous—*an orbit "in sync" with Earth that takes one day to complete.* From Earth, we can never see the moon's dark side.

The pull of the moon's gravity creates tides on Earth.

Mars

Mars, the Red Planet, is visible to the naked eye as a reddish dot in the sky. The color comes from the iron that makes up much of the planet's core. The Martian atmosphere is very thin, mostly carbon dioxide. Mars is covered with deserts, mountains, craters, and volcanoes. One mountain on Mars is 17 miles high. That's the highest known mountain in our solar system.

A day on Mars is a little longer than an Earth day: 24 hours, 37 minutes. Mars takes 687 Earth days to orbit the sun.

Mars has two tiny moons, Demos and Phobos. These are Greek words meaning "terror" and "fear." These are fitting companions for this planet, which is named for the ancient god of war.

Jupiter

Jupiter is by far the largest planet. It rotates quickly—about once every 10 hours. This speed flattens it at the top and makes it bulge in the middle. Jupiter has windy, stormy weather.

Scientists call the four planets that are closest to the sun "rocky planets" because they are made up mostly of rock. Jupiter is different. It's made up mostly of gases and has no solid surface. For that reason, and because of its size, astronomers call Jupiter a "gas giant."

The liquids of Jupiter's outer core mix with the gases in its atmosphere to form swift-moving belts of colorful clouds. One colorful feature of Jupiter is the Great Red Spot. It is a kind of never-ending hurricane 30,000 miles long and 10,000 miles wide.

Jupiter has 16 known moons. The famous astronomer Galileo discovered the four largest—Io, Europa, Ganymede, and Callisto—in 1610.

MARS

Courtesy of NASA

JUPITER

Jupiter, with the Great Red Spot in the lower left quarter

Courtesy of the US Geological Survey/ the US Department of the Interior

Saturn

The second-largest planet in the solar system, Saturn is called the "ringed planet." Its seven rings are made of icy chunks of rocks. The rings extend about 250,000 miles out from the planet.

The rings have fascinated people for centuries. Galileo discovered five of them in 1610. The Pioneer spacecraft discovered the other two in the 1970s.

Like Jupiter, Saturn is a gas giant. It rotates quickly. It has stormy weather and 18 known moons. One of these, Titan, is the only moon in the solar system known to have its own atmosphere.

Uranus

Uranus, the third-largest planet, is another gas giant. Its main claim to fame is that it spins on its side. Scientists think that a long time ago, it may have collided with some other body that tilted it. Space probes of the 1970s discovered rings around Uranus. But they aren't as impressive as Saturn's. Uranus has 15 known moons.

SATURN

Courtesy of NASA

URANUS

Courtesy of California Association for Research in Astronomy/Photo Researchers, Inc.

THE ICY RINGS OF SATURN

Courtesy of NASA

Neptune

Neptune is Uranus's smaller twin. Astronomers discovered it in 1846, after noticing that some body was exerting a gravitational tug on Uranus. Neptune is the windiest planet in the solar system. Its winds blow up to 1,500 miles an hour. Like Jupiter, it has several dark storms, the largest of which is the Great Dark Spot.

Neptune has eight moons. The largest is Triton. About three-fourths the size of Earth's moon, Triton zips around Neptune in just 5.9 days.

Pluto and the Dwarf Planets

Pluto is unique for many reasons. It's very small and very far away. It's also unique because its career as a planet had a clearly marked beginning—and end.

Clyde W. Tombaugh discovered Pluto on 18 February 1930. He was a 24-year-old astronomer at the Lowell Observatory in Arizona. For seven months he searched for something he knew had to be there: a heavenly body that tugged on Neptune, just as Neptune tugged on Uranus.

Finally he found it. It was named Pluto and declared the ninth planet.

But on 24 August 2006 the International Astronomical Union voted to reclassify Pluto as a "dwarf planet." In making this decision, astronomers defined for the first time what it takes to qualify as a planet. Pluto didn't make the cut. It doesn't dominate its moon, Charon, as a planet should. Besides, Pluto's orbit is not fixed. Sometimes it loops inside Neptune's.

As a dwarf planet, Pluto has lots of company. Scientists have identified more than 40 dwarfs and they expect to find more. Beyond Pluto lies the Edgeworth-Kuiper Belt of "ice dwarfs" or minor planets.

NEPTUNE

Courtesy of NASA

PLUTO AND CHARON

Courtesy of NASA

The Asteroids

An asteroid *is a rocky and metallic object orbiting the sun.* Most asteroids are in a belt that lies between Mars and Jupiter. Astronomers have found and catalogued more than 15,000 asteroids.

Some asteroids are no bigger than pebbles. The largest asteroid is Ceres. It has a diameter of 623 miles.

Key Comets, the Edgeworth-Kuiper Belt, and the Oort Cloud

Comets

A comet *is a small, odd-shaped body with a center of ice, rock, and frozen gas.* Comets have elliptical orbits. They draw close to the sun and then fly far out into space.

A comet has a head made up of dust and gas wrapped around a nucleus, or center, of ice and rock. As a comet nears the sun, it forms a tail. Some of these tails are 100 million miles long.

Some people call comets "dirty snowballs," because they are made up largely of ice. After enough trips to the sun, the ice melts, and a comet becomes just another rocky object in space. By the standards of outer space, comets have short lives.

Halley's is one of the best-known comets. It makes a complete revolution of the sun every 76 years. It last swung by the inner solar system in 1986. Hale-Bopp, another well-known comet, was last visible from Earth in 1997. Swift-Tuttle and Hyakutake are two other well-known comets.

The Edgeworth-Kuiper Belt

The Edgeworth-Kuiper Belt is a vast region extending beyond Neptune. Scientists think there are millions of small, rocky or icy objects orbiting there. Pluto and Charon may be part of the belt. NASA hopes to visit this region around 2010 with its Pluto-Kuiper Express. The goal of this mission is to learn more about Pluto, Charon, and the outer reaches of our solar system.

The Oort Cloud

The Oort Cloud is an immense spherical cloud. It surrounds the solar system and reaches about three light-years from the sun. A light-year *is the distance light travels in a year.* Astronomers think this distance is the outer limit of the sun's gravitational influence.

About a trillion icy objects are in the outer region of the Oort Cloud. Another five trillion are thought to be in the core. The estimated mass of the cloud is 40 times that of Earth.

Meteoroids, Meteorites, and Meteors

A meteoroid *is a piece of rock or metal that travels in space.* Meteoroids are the smallest objects in the solar system. The smallest bits, dust particles, are called micrometeorites.

No one is sure where meteoroids come from. They may be chunks of rock melting away from comets as they approach the sun.

Some meteoroids orbit the sun, and some enter Earth's atmosphere. When they enter Earth's atmosphere, they usually burn up right away. But some land on Earth. A meteorite *is a meteoroid that lands on Earth's surface.* A meteor *is a meteoroid passing through Earth's atmosphere, leaving a visible trail.* Other terms for meteors are shooting stars or falling stars.

The Significant Contributions of Key Early Astronomers

The history of astronomy is the story of humanity's attempts to make sense of the heavens. All peoples have looked up to the skies and wondered about the movements of the sun, moon, and stars. People of many cultures have thought their gods live in the skies. For some, the skies were places where humans could never go.

But as time passed, people began to see the stars and planets as ordinary physical objects. People learned that heavenly bodies obey the same laws that objects on Earth do. This idea began in the Middle East and spread to other cultures.

The Contributions of Ptolemy

The names of many of the first astronomers are no longer known. These astronomers lived in Egypt, Mexico, and what is now Iraq.

The earliest widely known astronomer is Claudius Ptolemy, often known as Ptolemy of Alexandria. He was a Roman citizen of Greek background. Alexandria was a center of learning in Egypt. Ptolemy lived from around AD 85 until AD 165.

Ptolemy is known not for his own work but for the way he combined other astronomers' ideas. The system he came up with, called the Ptolemaic system, put Earth at the center of the universe. Copernicus, as you read earlier, would later show that system to be wrong. But it made sense to the best minds of Ptolemy's day.

Ptolemy was the first astronomer to make scientific maps of the heavens. He also developed a catalog listing 48 constellations. A constellation *is a group of stars people think of as forming a picture in the sky.* Scientists still use this catalog.

PTOLEMY OF ALEXANDRIA

Courtesy of Dr. Jeremy Burgess/
Photo Researchers, Inc.

Ulug Bek: Astronomer of the East

Ulug Bek (1393–1449) was born in what is now Iran. His grandfather was Timur, or Tamerlane, one of the great Mongol conquerors. Timur ruled a territory that included the modern countries of Iran, Iraq, and eastern Turkey. His warriors, riding on horseback and armed with bows and arrows, thundered across much of Asia.

Ulug Bek's father, Shah Rukh, was the youngest of Timur's four sons. He succeeded his father as emperor. His capital was Herat, in today's Afghanistan. Shah Rukh turned over the city of Samarkand, in Uzbekistan, to Ulug Bek when the boy was only 16.

Ulug Bek's greatest desire was to make Samarkand a center of culture and learning. He was an astronomer and a mathematician. He also wrote poetry and history. He studied the Koran, the book of sacred writings of people of the Muslim faith.

To promote the study of astronomy, Ulug Bek built a madrassah, a center for higher education. He recruited the best scientists he could find to teach there.

Ulug Bek was most famous for the observatory he built in Samarkand in 1428. There he could study the skies and observe the stars and planets.

His observatory was the best in the world at that time. It helped make Samarkand an influential scientific center.

Architect, artist, scholar, scientist, and astronomer, Ulug Bek was a man of many talents. Some Americans compare him to Thomas Jefferson.

THE CENTRAL SQUARE OF SAMARKAND
Courtesy of Orban Thierry/Corbis Sygma

The Contributions of Ulug Bek

ULUG BEK

Courtesy of K.M. Westermann/Corbis

Ulug Bek was a mathematician and an astronomer. He had an observatory, or *a building designed to observe the stars*, in what is today Uzbekistan. He made detailed observations and calculations. He set a new standard for scientific work.

In 1437 Ulug Bek published a catalog of the stars (*Zij-i Sultani*). It gave the positions of 992 stars. It was the first major catalog of stars since Ptolemy's.

Ulug Bek also discovered several errors in Ptolemy's calculations. No one had ever before questioned Ptolemy's work. Using data he'd recorded in his observatory, Ulug Bek calculated the length of the year as 365 days, 5 hours, 49 minutes, and 15 seconds. He also produced data for the movements of the sun, the moon, and the planets.

These numbers were very accurate, even by today's standards. Some of his estimates were off by less than five seconds.

The Contributions of Copernicus

Copernicus wasn't the first astronomer to think Earth might revolve around the sun.

A Greek astronomer named Aristarchus (320–250 BC) gets that honor. He thought the sun was bigger than Earth, and that a smaller body would revolve around a larger one. He was right, but had no instruments to help him gather the data to prove it.

And although Copernicus didn't have a telescope, he did have access to records of the observations made over centuries, beginning with the ancient Greeks. He combined his study of those records with his own observations to come up with his own ideas.

Although he never explained what inspired him to propose a heliocentric solar system, one thing is sure: he wasn't trying to stir up a revolution.

But the Ptolemaic system, with its cycles and epicycles, was complicated. To a true scientist, it also seemed messy. The motions of each planet were independent. In his book Copernicus compared the Ptolemaic system to a monster made up of spare parts, with a head from here, feet from there, and the arms from somewhere else.

The Copernican system had fewer circles. It also had a unity and a logic that the Ptolemaic system lacked.

Nicolaus Copernicus:
The Monk Who Reordered the Heavens

Nicolaus Copernicus (1473–1543) was born in Torun, Poland. He was a Renaissance man. That means he was interested in both science and art, and was able to do many things well.

His parents died when Nicolaus was young. But his mother's brother was a church official. Through this uncle, Nicolaus won a position in the church.

For many years he served at the cathedral in Fromburk, Poland. This city, also called Frauenburg, is on the Baltic Sea, not far from Russia.

But before coming to the cathedral, Copernicus traveled widely. He studied mathematics and optics in Krakow. He studied church law and medicine in Italy, where learned about astronomy.

He moved in privileged circles. But he always remained a student.

Johannes Kepler:
Pioneer of the Scientific Method

Johannes Kepler (1571–1630) was born in southern Germany. He was a sickly child of a poor family. But he was also bright. He won a scholarship to the University of Tübingen. He was supposed to study for the ministry. Instead he learned about Copernicus's new theory of the solar system. It fascinated him. He became a champion of the new thinking.

It was a time of religious upheaval between the Protestants (Lutherans) and the Catholics. Kepler got caught up in the debate. He had to move from place to place because he was Lutheran. He finally moved to Czechoslovakia.

There, in the city of Prague, he worked with Tycho Brahe. Tycho was a well-known Danish astronomer who was mathematician to Emperor Rudolf II. When Tycho died in 1601, Kepler took over his job.

Using Tycho's data, Kepler discovered that Mars had an elliptical orbit. That led him to other discoveries about the planets. In 1609 he shared his findings in a book called *Astronomia Nova*, which means "New Astronomy" in Latin.

Kepler's discoveries were important on two levels. First, it was important to astronomy to understand how Mars orbits the sun. But Kepler was also one of the first to use the modern scientific method. He made observations, collected and analyzed data, and then drew accurate conclusions, so his work was also important to the overall advancement of science.

The Contributions of Kepler

Copernicus put the sun at the center of the solar system. But he still thought that the planets' orbits were perfect circles. Even in the Renaissance, people had an idea of celestial, or heavenly, perfection.

Johannes Kepler studied the work of Copernicus in Germany late in the 16th century. As a young professor, he wrote the first outspoken defense of the Copernican system in 1596.

But Kepler also improved on the Copernican theory. He showed that orbits of the planets weren't perfect circles, but ellipses, or ovals. He also formulated three laws of planetary motion that astronomers still use today.

JOHANNES KEPLER

Courtesy of The Granger Collection, New York

The Contributions of Galileo

Galileo didn't invent the telescope. It was probably invented in the Netherlands in the early 1600s. But Galileo was among the first to appreciate the importance of this device. He read about the Dutch telescopes and soon started building his own.

Galileo was also the first to use the telescope to methodically observe the sky. He was the first to see the moon's craters. He risked blindness by looking straight into the sun to observe sunspots, or *the relatively cool dark spots that sometimes appear on the surface of the sun.*

Galileo also turned his telescope on Venus. He saw that it goes through phases, just as Earth's moon does. He spotted four "stars" near Jupiter and decided they were moons that circled that planet.

For Galileo, this was further confirmation that Copernicus's view of the solar system was correct. Galileo became an advocate of the Copernican view.

In a famous trial in 1633 the Catholic Church condemned Galileo for taking this position. In 1992, however, Pope John Paul II determined the church had acted "imprudently" in opposing Galileo.

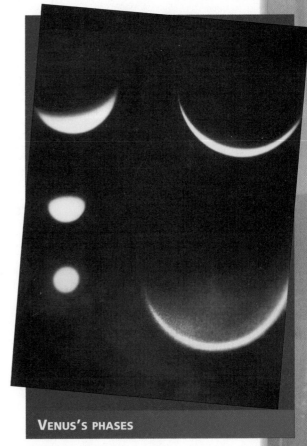

VENUS'S PHASES

Through his telescope, Galileo saw that Venus has phases.

Courtesy of the Lowell Observatory

Galileo Galilei:
The Father of Science Was Wrong About Tides

Galileo Galilei (1564–1642) made enormous contributions to mathematics, physics, and astronomy. People have called him the "father of the telescope," the "father of modern astronomy," and even the "father of modern science."

But he was wrong about what causes the tides in the ocean.

Galileo had a theory about tides that he pushed for years. During boat rides around Venice, he noticed that water inside the boat sloshed around as the boat changed direction. If the boat hit a sandbar and stopped, the water inside would slosh forward and then move back. Sometimes this happened several times before the water came to a stop. This action was the result of the water's momentum.

GALILEO GALILEI

Courtesy of Bettmann/Corbis

Galileo thought something similar happened to the water in the oceans as Earth rotated. He thought Earth's rotation created tides.

Now we know that the pull of the moon's gravity causes the tides. Kepler understood this. But until Sir Isaac Newton explained gravity in 1687, the moon theory of tides didn't win wide acceptance. That was years after Galileo's death.

Galileo's "big mistake" is instructive. It shows that even someone known as "the father of modern science" can make a mistake.

CHECKPOINTS

Lesson 1 Review

Using complete sentences, answer the following questions on a sheet of paper.

1. What part of planetary movement in the sky did Ptolemy's theory fail to explain well?

2. Where does the sun rank among stars in the Milky Way galaxy?

3. What causes Jupiter's colorful clouds?

4. Explain the start and finish of Pluto's career as a planet.

5. How did Ulug Bek improve on Ptolemy's work?

6. How is Kepler's work a good example of the scientific method?

7. How did Kepler improve on Copernicus's findings?

8. What did Galileo discover about Venus?

9. What did Galileo see about Jupiter that confirmed Copernicus's findings?

Applying Your Learning

10. How was Galileo wrong about tides, and what lessons can you draw from this?

Rocketry and the Space Race

On 19 October 1899 Robert H. Goddard, 17 years old, climbed into a cherry tree in the backyard of his home in Worcester, Mass. He'd been asked to prune off its dead limbs.

Using a saw and hatchet, he started to work. But not for long. Perched in the tree, he began to daydream—and not for the first time.

Here's what he later wrote about the experience:

> It was one of the quiet, colorful afternoons of sheer beauty which we have in October in New England, and as I looked toward the fields at the east, I imagined how wonderful it would be to make some device which had even the possibility of ascending to Mars, and how it would look on a small scale, if sent up from the meadow at my feet.

At that moment, young Goddard conceived the idea of pursuing spaceflight. "I was a different boy when I descended the tree from when I ascended, for existence at last seemed very purposive," he wrote.

In 1899 spaceflight was a very bold dream. Even airplanes lay in the future. It would be four years before the Wright brothers' historic flight at Kitty Hawk.

Goddard studied hard. He earned an advanced degree. He became a university professor. But even so, once he began experimenting with rockets in earnest, his efforts drew ridicule.

In 1920 Goddard built an 11-foot rocket. It caused such excitement in Worcester that people called the police. The local paper ran a story about the event. The headline read "Moon Rocket Misses Target by 238,799 1/2 Miles!"

But the boy in the tree would go on to become known as the "father of modern rocketry." He would become a pioneer of the space age.

How Developments in Rocketry Made Space Exploration Possible

Before people could explore space, they needed a way to get there. The rocket proved to be the vehicle that broke Earth's bounds.

People have built rockets for centuries. And armies have long used them in battle.

Rockets were always hard to control, however. Military engineers found other kinds of weapons, such as cannons, more reliable. But when big thinkers like Robert Goddard began to dream of spaceflight, they turned again to rockets.

Rocketry Before the 20th Century

The first rockets had nothing to do with space exploration.

The Chinese had rockets by around 1000. They used them in the battle of Kai-feng Fu in 1232. They called them "fire arrows." In 1405 a German engineer, Konrad Kyeser von Eichstadt, made a rocket propelled by gunpowder.

The French used rockets against the British in 1429 and 1449, during the Hundred Years' War (1337–1453). During the Thirty Years' War (1618–1648) armies fired rockets weighing up to 100 pounds. They sent small pieces of metal flying everywhere.

In India, rockets were fired on the British during the battles of Seringapatam (1792 and 1799). That action caught the attention of Col William Congreve, a British artillery expert. He started experimenting with rockets. He standardized the kinds of gunpowder used in them. He added guide sticks to hold them steady in flight. He built the first launching pad. With these improvements, Congreve extended the range of British rockets from 300 yards to several thousand yards.

Soon the British had a rocket brigade. It fought in the Napoleonic Wars in Europe and in the United States during the War of 1812. You may recall that our national anthem mentions "the rockets' red glare." That's a reference to those British rockets, which were named after Congreve.

But even with these improvements, rockets weren't used much in war. They were too hard to aim well.

The Contributions of Robert Goddard

During the early years of the 20th century, scientists began to think of another use for rockets: spaceflight.

In 1903 a Russian scientist made the first computations for rocket flights into space. He was Konstantin Eduardovich Tsiolkovsky. He never built a rocket, but he designed several. He also calculated how a rocket engine could escape from and reenter Earth's atmosphere.

DR. ROBERT H. GODDARD

The work of two men—Robert H. Goddard in the United States and Hermann Oberth in Germany—sparked new interest in rocketry. Both men had studied science at an advanced level.

For the next 20 years Goddard continued to do pioneering research on liquid-fuel rockets. He also developed ways to steer rockets.

Goddard was a hands-on scientist. He didn't just crunch the numbers. He built the hardware. He worked systematically, step by step. And he created the foundation on which the space age was built.

Dr. Robert H. Goddard with the first successful liquid-fuel chemical rocket, launched 16 March 1926

Courtesy of NASA Marshall Space Flight Center

Flight Paths

Robert H. Goddard:
The Father of Modern Rocketry

Robert H. Goddard (1882–1945) was born in Worcester, Mass. He did his undergraduate studies at Worcester Polytechnic Institute. He did graduate studies and earned his doctoral degree from what's now Clark University, also in Worcester. He became a professor.

Goddard had an ambitious goal: to build a rocket that could travel to the moon.

In 1919 the Smithsonian Institution published his paper, "A Method of Reaching Extreme Altitudes." In this report he described a solid-propellant rocket that would go the moon.

During the 1920s Goddard began experimenting with liquid instead of solid propellants. He also developed a theory of multistage rockets. Perhaps that's what was needed, he thought, to get all the way to the moon.

DR. ROBERT H. GODDARD

Courtesy of the Library of Congress/ Photo Researchers, Inc.

During World War II Goddard helped the US Navy develop rocket motors. He also worked on jet-assisted takeoff devices for aircraft.

Goddard died in 1945. He didn't live long enough to see some of his biggest dreams realized. NASA's spaceflight center in Greenville, Md., is named in his honor.

Herman Oberth

Hermann Oberth (1894–1989) was another rocket pioneer of the 20th century. He was a German born in Romania.

As an 11-year-old, he read the Jules Verne novel, *From the Earth to the Moon*. In this science fiction book, a capsule containing three men and two dogs is blasted out of a huge cannon to the moon.

The book fascinated Oberth. It sparked a lifelong interest in spaceflight and travel to other planets.

As a student at the University of Heidelberg, Oberth wrote a dissertation on rocket-powered flight. If his professors didn't accept his paper, he would not get his degree. The professors rejected the paper in 1922. They called his work "too speculative," or *not practical or based on facts.*

But Oberth didn't give up. The following year he published the paper under the title "By Rocket to Space." It became a popular classic. It explained the math behind rocket science. It even discussed space stations and human travel to other planets.

The German V-1 and V-2 Rockets

As you read in Chapter 6, Lesson 2, the German V-1 rocket was the first guided missile used in war. The Germans introduced it near the end of World War II. It was a small, pilotless craft similar to today's cruise missiles. It didn't have much of a guidance system, but it carried a large warhead.

The V-1s first hit London 13 June 1944. The Germans launched them across the English Channel from France and the Netherlands. Later they launched them from the air. The Germans also used V-1s against Antwerp, in Belgium.

The Germans were already on the defensive when they introduced the V-1s. The "V" stood for "vengeance" (*Vergeltung*, in German). But the British called them "flying bombs," "buzz bombs," or "doodlebugs."

V-1s weren't very accurate, and they didn't turn the tide of the war. But they were effective terror weapons. They killed thousands of people. And they forced the Allies to devote large amounts of time and resources against them.

Allied pilots eventually learned to shoot down V-1s. But then came the V-2. And there was no defense against it.

The V-2 was the world's first ballistic missile. Recall that a *ballistic missile is one that free-falls after a self-powered flight.*

The V-2 was the largest, most complex missile in the German arsenal. It could deliver a ton of explosives 150 miles down range in five minutes. It traveled like a modern rocket ship. It moved faster than the speed of sound.

The V-2 was guided by radio signals from the ground or by onboard gyroscopes and a device that measured the rocket's acceleration. Germany fired almost 3,000 V-2s on England, France, and Belgium.

Wernher von Braun

Wernher von Braun (1912–1977) was one of the most important champions of space exploration of the 20th century. He had a lead role in developing missiles for Nazi Germany, the US enemy in World War II. After the war he came to the United States and worked in missile programs. Later he helped the United States in the space race with the Soviet Union, another of Germany's former foes.

As a youth Von Braun read the science fiction novels of Jules Verne and H. G. Wells. He also read Hermann Oberth's 1923 study "By Rocket to Space." Von Braun wanted to understand the physics of rockets. And so he mastered calculus and trigonometry. He earned a doctoral degree in physics at age 22.

Von Braun led the team that developed the V-2 ballistic missile for the German Army during World War II. The rockets were made at a forced-labor factory in Germany.

DR. WERNHER VON BRAUN

Courtesy of NASA

Historians are still assessing Von Braun's relationship with the Nazi regime. It is certain, however, that he ultimately made a major contribution to the US missile and space programs. He worked with the US Army to adapt the V-2 for an American missile program.

Later, for the US Army, Von Braun helped get *Explorer 1*, the first successful US satellite, into orbit. This landmark event occurred just months after the Soviet Union stunned the world with the launch of *Sputnik 1* in October 1957.

In 1960 Von Braun's rocket-development center moved to NASA. His new job was to build the giant Saturn rockets. He became director of NASA's Marshall Space Flight Center. He was also the chief architect of the Saturn V launch vehicle. This device propelled Americans to the moon.

Von Braun retired from NASA in 1972.

The V-2 had a longer range and greater payload than the V-1. A payload *is what a rocket carries that is necessary to its mission.* The payload may include astronauts or a satellite. With the V-2, the payload was explosives. The Allies had no way to stop a V-2, or even to see this deadly missile coming.

The V-2 rocket was the model for rockets that the United States and the Soviet Union would later use in their space-exploration programs.

Wernher von Braun

The V-2 was the brainchild of Dr. Wernher von Braun. He was an engineer the German Army recruited to work on its missile program. He became the program's technical director. He headed the team that developed the V-2.

The team did not have to start from scratch. The German Army had been working on long-range rockets since the 1930s. The Germans first flew the liquid-propellant V-2 successfully in October 1942.

At the end of the war, before the Allies could capture his lab, Von Braun made a deal with them. He engineered the surrender of 500 of his top scientists, along with their plans and test vehicles.

The Allies brought V-2s, whole or in pieces, home for study. For 15 years Von Braun worked with the US Army to develop ballistic missiles.

At first Von Braun's group was based at Fort Bliss, Texas. The US Army had brought V-2 parts to the White Sands Proving Ground in nearby New Mexico. There General Electric was managing a missile-development program called Project Hermes. Von Braun and his team advised GE on how to reassemble the missiles. As the design improved, American components, or *parts*, replaced the German ones.

The Principles of Rocketry

Certain laws of physics govern rocket propulsion, flight, and control. Galileo (1564–1642) and Sir Isaac Newton (1643–1727) discovered these laws.

Rocketry is based on the propelling of a vehicle by a reactive force. The action of the rocket's exhaust gases produces a reaction. This forces the rocket to move in the opposite direction.

A rocket engine, or motor, is a reaction engine. So are jet engines, which power most airliners.

A rocket engine differs from a jet engine in one important way. A jet engine burns a mix of air and fuel. A rocket engine needs no air. It carries within itself all it needs to create a reactive force. This is why rockets work in space, where there is no air, as well as in Earth's atmosphere.

Newton's Laws of Motion

1. A body in a state of rest and a body in motion tend to remain at rest or in uniform motion unless acted upon by some outside force.

2. The rate of change in the momentum of a body is proportional to the force acting upon the body and is in the direction of the force.

3. For every action, there is an equal and opposite reaction.

Rockets and Newton's Laws

Sir Isaac Newton is well known for his three laws of motion. Each of these laws applies to an aspect of rocketry.

The first law concerns overcoming inertia—*the tendency for a body at rest to stay at rest until some force acts on it.* To get a rocket off a launch pad, the force (thrust) in pounds must be greater than the weight of the rocket.

The Saturn V rockets that launched the Apollo spacecraft that took US astronauts to the moon weighed 6 million pounds apiece. That's a lot of inertia to overcome. So the Saturn engines needed to produce more than 6 million pounds of thrust. In fact, they produced 7.5 million pounds.

Newton's second law of motion says that the amount of force needed to make an object move depends on its mass. The more mass a body has, the more force is needed to make it move.

You've probably seen an illustration of this if you've ever watched a film of a rocket launch. At the moment of liftoff, the rocket barely moves. That's because it's so heavy. But second by second, propellant burns off. So second by second, the mass of the rocket is less. Thrust, though, remains constant. The engines keep burning. As the load lightens, the rocket picks up speed. Eventually it disappears from view.

Newton's third law is essential to making rockets go. This law states that for every action there is an equal and opposite reaction.

If you've ever blown up a balloon, then released it and watched it zip across the room, you've experienced this law in action. The force of the air escaping from one end of the balloon pushes it in the opposite direction.

A rocket engine is more complex than a balloon. But the physics of motion are the same. The combustion, or burning, of fuel within a chamber generates exhaust gases. These gases are like the air you blow into a balloon that you then hold pinched shut.

But the rocket engine includes a nozzle and throat that are made of sturdier material than a balloon is. So the escape of exhaust from a rocket can be engineered with greater precision.

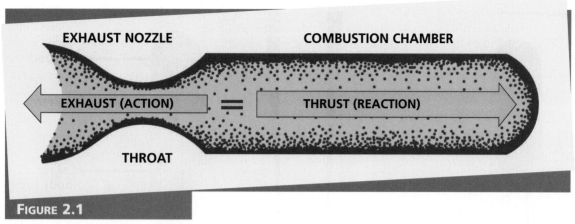

EXHAUST NOZZLE

COMBUSTION CHAMBER

EXHAUST (ACTION) = THRUST (REACTION)

THROAT

FIGURE 2.1

A basic rocket engine

In designing a rocket engine, an aerospace engineer wants two things:

1. pressure as high as possible in the combustion chamber
2. as much acceleration as possible of exhaust particles through the throat and nozzle.

Both contribute to acceleration of a rocket.

Today's military space rockets are made up of four major systems:

1. airframe
2. propulsion
3. guidance
4. control.

These systems are there to deliver the rocket's payload.

Airframe

The airframe contains the other three systems and provides the streamlined shape. An airframe has to stand up to heat, stress, and vibration. But it also has to be as light as possible.

The Atlas rocket is a good example of airframe design. Its skin serves as the wall of the propellant tank. There's no need for separate internal tanks. This saves weight. The skin of the Atlas is thinner than a dime. In fact, when Atlas has no fuel aboard, it has to be pressurized to keep it from collapsing.

ATLAS ROCKET
Courtesy of Lockheed Martin/
Duffin McGee/AP Photo

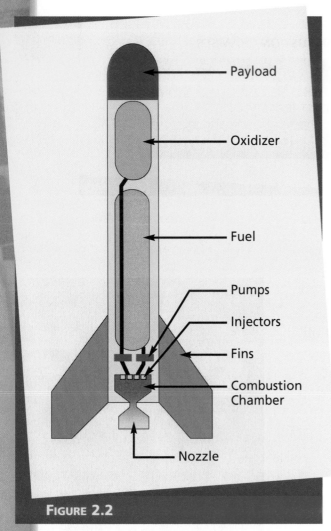

FIGURE 2.2

Liquid fuel–propulsion system

Labels (top to bottom): Payload, Oxidizer, Fuel, Pumps, Injectors, Fins, Combustion Chamber, Nozzle

FIGURE 2.3

Solid fuel–propulsion system

Labels (top to bottom): Payload, Igniter, Casing (Body tube), Core, Propellant (Grain), Combustion Chamber, Fins, Throat, Nozzle

Propulsion

The propulsion system includes propellant, containers for the propellant, the plumbing needed to get the propellant from the containers to the engine, and the rocket engine itself. *Propellant* is the fuel that gives the rocket its thrust.

A rocket may have a liquid or solid propellant. A liquid propellant is carried in a separate compartment. A solid propellant is carried in the combustion chamber. Each type of propellant requires a different engine structure.

Guidance

A large rocket's guidance system is its "brain." It includes a computer and an inertial platform—a collection of sensing devices. It may also include a star-tracking system for space navigation.

The computer holds instructions for the rocket's course. The rocket also has a radio link in case the onboard systems fail and ground controllers have to take over.

The guidance systems in today's rockets are quite small. Like cell phones and computers, they have benefited from miniaturization.

Control

The control system's job is to carry out the orders of the guidance system.

Some elements of a rocket's control system are like those of an airplane. They function while the rocket is within Earth's atmosphere. But once a rocket gets up into space, where the air is thin, it needs other ways of steering.

One way to change a rocket's flight path is to redirect its exhaust stream. Another way is to fire up small rockets attached to the airframe. These methods can be used in combination. They work inside Earth's atmosphere as well as in space.

How the Cold War Led to a Race in Space

The United States and the Soviet Union fought together against the Axis Powers during World War II. But after the war, differences between these two former allies became clear.

As you read in Chapter 6, the two countries entered a long period known as the Cold War. It wasn't a shooting war, like World War II. But each side knew who the enemy was.

The two countries faced off in a global power struggle—American democracy versus Soviet totalitarianism. Totalitarianism *is a form of government under which the people are completely under the control of a state authority that oppresses all opposition.*

President Eisenhower said in 1958, "What makes the Soviet threat unique in history is its all-inclusiveness. Every human activity is pressed into service as a weapon of expansion. Trade, economic development, military power, arts, science, education, the whole world of ideas. . . . The Soviets are, in short, waging total cold war."

In the Cold War, space was a crucial arena of competition.

How the Space Race Started

Many people think the space race began on Friday, 4 October 1957, when the Soviets launched *Sputnik 1*. But the Soviets were off and running in this race before the Americans had even heard the starting gun.

The period 1957–1958 had been set as the International Geophysical Year. The United States and the Soviet Union pledged to work together to send satellites into space.

A US effort to launch a tiny satellite called *Vanguard* was in the works. But work was behind schedule. Meanwhile, the Soviets were working on a satellite of their own. Americans hoped they were behind, too.

That Friday evening, the Soviet Embassy in Washington, D.C., gave a reception for space scientists from many countries. The party came at the end of a six-day scientific conference.

At the conference, the Soviets hinted that their satellite wasn't just on schedule— it was ahead of schedule. American scientists wondered: how close to a launch might the Soviets be?

They soon found out.

During the party, a *New York Times* reporter got a phone call from his boss. Big news: TASS, the Soviet news agency, had just announced the launch of *Sputnik 1*. It was the first Earth-orbiting artificial satellite. ("Sputnik" is the Russian word for satellite.)

Word spread around the gathering: "It's up!"

The chief American delegate to the conference was known for his diplomacy. He announced the news and congratulated his Soviet hosts. But the American scientific team was crushed.

And many ordinary Americans, caught in the tensions of the time, felt as if their country were reliving the 1941 attack on Pearl Harbor. *Sputnik* was a wake-up call.

The Significance of *Sputnik* and *Explorer*

Sputnik 1 was a small satellite. It weighed less than 200 pounds. It spent only three months in orbit.

But it greatly worried Americans. They remembered how Soviet leader Nikita Khrushchev had threatened that his country would "bury" the Americans. Was *Sputnik 1* a sign that he was right?

Then on 3 November 1957, the Soviets launched *Sputnik 2*. It had a dog named Laika aboard. This satellite weighed 1,120 pounds.

Americans swung into action. Congress held hearings to find out why the United States had fallen so far behind the Soviets.

Meanwhile American scientists scrambled to get a *Vanguard* satellite into space. They sent the first one up on 5 February 1958. But four miles up, the launch vehicle exploded.

Then Wernher von Braun entered the picture. He'd been working with the US Army. He had a plan for something called Project Explorer. He dusted off the plan, got it approved, and put things in motion.

His team had to abort a couple of launches. But on 31 January 1958 a Juno 1 booster carrying *Explorer 1* lifted off from Cape Canaveral, Florida.

It took a while to be sure the satellite had made it into orbit. Early the following day confirmation came from the Jet Propulsion Laboratory at the California Institute of Technology in Pasadena. A day later, US newspapers showed Von Braun and two associates beaming in triumph after announcing the news.

The United States hadn't been first off the mark. But it was still in the space race.

How NASA Was Established

The success of *Explorer 1* relieved many Americans. But soul-searching continued. How should the United States respond to the Soviet challenge in space?

The White House and the US Congress wanted a permanent federal space agency. Some suggested creating a Cabinet-level department of science and technology.

But other players were in the picture. The Department of Defense claimed a role in space. The Army and the Air Force were working on a plan to send robotic probes to the moon. In March 1958 the secretary of defense announced plans to send robotic probes elsewhere in the solar system.

But President Dwight Eisenhower didn't want the military to take the lead in the space race. He preferred a civilian space agency. A peaceful approach to space would win more friends at home and abroad, he reasoned.

Congress supported his idea. It passed a law creating the National Aeronautics and Space Administration, which quickly became known as NASA. NASA began operations on 1 October 1958.

The Space Act of 1958, which created NASA, commits the United States to peaceful purposes in space. But the United States reserves the right to use space systems for military deterrence. It wants to do what it can to keep away potential enemies, as long as it can do so without putting another country's security at risk.

The military continued to play an important role in space, even after the creation of NASA. In 1982 the Air Force created Space Command. The command is responsible for strategic surveillance—for warning of missile attacks. The space systems included under Space Command also help the military with communications, navigation, and weather information.

For many Americans, winning the space race was a matter of national security. The decade of the 1960s would determine whether the agency Congress created was up to the task.

NASA and the Air Force

NASA is a civilian agency, but many of its astronauts have come from the Air Force. Three of the original seven Mercury astronauts named in the early 1960s were active-duty Air Force officers: Capt Virgil I. (Gus) Grissom, Capt Donald K. (Deke) Slayton, and Maj L. Gordon Cooper Jr.

These men were the first of more than 80 Air Force astronauts in NASA programs, from Mercury on through the space shuttle and the International Space Station. Eight Air Force astronauts became general officers. Most notable is Gen Kevin P. Chilton, who became the head of Air Force Space Command in 2006. He reached four-star rank after flying on three space shuttle missions, becoming the first astronaut to earn a fourth star.

Sadly, Air Force officers have also borne the cost of space travel. Of the 27 NASA astronauts who have died while on a space mission, eight were from the Air Force.

GEN KEVIN P. CHILTON

Courtesy of the US Air Force

CHECKPOINTS

Lesson 2 Review

Using complete sentences, answer the following questions
on a sheet of paper.

1. How did Col William Congreve improve rockets?

2. How did Konstantin Eduardovich Tsiolkovsky advance
    rocket science?

3. What influence did Jules Verne have on Hermann Oberth?

4. Why did the Allies fear the V-2 rocket?

5. What did the Allies do with pieces of the V-2 they captured
    during World War II?

6. How are rocket engines like jet engines? How are they different?

7. What are the four systems of a rocket?

8. What effect did *Sputnik 1* have on Americans?

9. What effect did *Explorer 1* have on Americans?

Applying Your Learning

10. Do you think it was a good idea for President Eisenhower
    and Congress to establish NASA as a civilian agency instead
    of a military agency? Why or why not?

CHAPTER 8

Buzz Aldrin and the American flag
on the moon

Exploring Space

Chapter Outline

LESSON 1

The Space Program

LESSON 2

The Future of Air and Space Power

"America will return to the Moon as early as 2015 and no later than 2020 and use it as a steppingstone for more ambitious missions. A series of robotic missions to the Moon, similar to the Spirit Rover that is sending remarkable images back to Earth from Mars, will explore the lunar surface beginning no later than 2008 to research and prepare for future human exploration."

President George Bush, 14 January 2004

The Space Program

Quick Write

_____
_____
_____

List some of Col Guion Bluford's accomplishments.

Learn About...

- the key steps in the US and Soviet space programs
- the key steps in the development of spacecraft
- the significance of the phrase "One small step for [a] man, one giant leap for mankind"
- the key space shuttle missions
- the purpose of the international space station

Col Guion S. Bluford Jr. was the first black astronaut, or _person who flies aboard a spacecraft_. In college, he was an Air Force ROTC cadet. After graduation in 1964, he trained with the Air Force to be a pilot. By 1966 he was serving in Vietnam. He flew 144 combat missions in an F-4C Phantom.

Born in Philadelphia in 1942, Bluford continued his education after his tour of duty in Vietnam. He has a stack of academic degrees to prove it. Among them is a doctoral degree (called a Ph.D.) in aerospace engineering from the Air Force Institute of Technology. He received that degree in 1978. In 1979 he joined NASA's astronaut program. He went into space four times as a mission specialist—_someone who helps with experiments or the technical aspects of running a spacecraft._

In 1983 Bluford was a crew member on the space shuttle _Challenger_. The crew performed scientific tests, such as studying the effects of living in space.

In 1985 Bluford flew his second mission aboard _Challenger_. The crew was the largest ever. It had eight members. Also on board was a German-built _Spacelab_ that contained equipment for scientific experiments.

In 1991 Bluford climbed aboard the space shuttle _Discovery_ for another science-oriented mission. A year later he flew his fourth and final operation, also on _Discovery_. During that 1992 mission the crew performed many tests for the US Department of Defense.

Bluford spent 688 hours in space over the course of his four missions. He left NASA in 1993.

COL GUION BLUFORD

Col Guion Bluford was the first black astronaut.

Courtesy of NASA

The Key Steps in the US and Soviet Space Programs

Vocabulary

- **astronaut**
- **mission specialist**
- **suborbital flight**
- **orbital flight**
- **lunar**
- **apogee**
- **perigee**
- **aquanaut**
- **cosmonaut**
- **module**
- **probe**
- **European Space Agency**

You read in the previous lesson that in 1957 the Soviets sent a dog named Laika into space on board *Sputnik 2*. Although Laika did not survive her trip, she paved the way for humans to enter space. At that time the Soviet Union and the United States were engaged in a space race as well as a Cold War arms race. Each country wanted to be the first to put a man into space.

The US Mercury, Gemini, and Apollo Programs

In 1958, in response to the Soviets' *Sputnik* series, the United States created the National Aeronautics and Space Administration (NASA). Also in 1958 the United States launched its first unmanned spacecraft, *Explorer I*.

After that, action picked up quickly. Between 1961 and 1972 the United States worked on three projects. All aimed to get a man into space and, ultimately, to the moon.

ON 3 NOVEMBER 1957 THE SOVIETS LAUNCHED *SPUTNIK 2*. ON BOARD WAS A DOG NAMED LAIKA.

Courtesy of AP Photo/HO

NASA PICKED SEVEN ASTRONAUTS FOR PROJECT MERCURY.

Project Mercury

The first of the US manned programs was Project Mercury. Each mission included a single astronaut. NASA picked seven astronauts for the job: Scott Carpenter, Gordon Cooper, John Glenn, Virgil Grissom, Walter Schirra, Alan Shepard, and Donald Slayton. Shepard piloted the first voyage of the Mercury project on 5 May 1961. He spent 15 minutes in suborbital flight. A suborbital flight *is one that makes less than one revolution around Earth.* On 20 February 1962 Glenn made the first orbital flight—*a full revolution around Earth.* On 15 May 1963 Cooper made Project Mercury's sixth and final flight. He orbited Earth 22 times in 34 hours.

Project Mercury proved that a man could be sent into space and that he could orbit Earth.

NASA began selecting the Mercury crews in January 1959. There were 508 candidates. All were test pilots. NASA thought the rigors of being a test pilot mirrored the challenges astronauts would face.

The candidates went through physical, psychological, and intelligence exams. The further into the process the candidates got, the tougher the tests became. By 1 April 1959 the NASA selection committee had made its choices. On 9 April 1959 NASA introduced the "Mercury Seven" to the public.

THE ORIGINAL SEVEN MERCURY ASTRONAUTS

Here are some glimpses into the backgrounds of the original seven Mercury astronauts.

Rear Adm Alan Shepard

Rear Adm Alan Shepard (1923–1998) graduated from the US Naval Academy in 1944 and from the Naval Test Pilot School in 1951. In between, he served in World War II in the Pacific theater.

In 1961 Shepard became the first American in space. Each pilot in the Mercury program named his own spacecraft. Shepard named his *Freedom VII*. (The "VII" was in honor of the seven Mercury astronauts.) In 1971 Shepard flew to the moon on *Apollo 14*. He and another astronaut gathered 100 pounds of lunar materials to be studied by scientists on Earth. Lunar means *relating to the moon*.

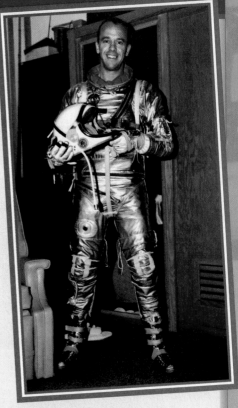

ALAN SHEPARD PREPARES FOR HIS 1961 MERCURY FLIGHT.
Courtesy of NASA

Lt Col Virgil Grissom

Air Force Lt Col Virgil Grissom (1926–1967) flew 100 combat missions in an F-86 during the Korean War. In 1957 he became a test pilot.

On 21 July 1961 Grissom piloted the second Mercury spacecraft, the *Liberty Bell VII*. This was a suborbital flight. On 23 March 1965 he was command pilot on the first of the manned Gemini flights. Sadly, on 27 January 1967 he and his two fellow crew members died during a preflight test of *Apollo 1*.

LT COL VIRGIL GRISSOM FLEW THE *LIBERTY BELL VII* DURING PROJECT MERCURY.
Courtesy of AP Photo

JOHN GLENN CLIMBS ABROAD FRIENDSHIP VII.

Courtesy of NASA/
John F. Kennedy Space Center

Col John Glenn

Col John Glenn (born in 1921) was a US Marine Corps pilot. He flew combat missions in World War II and Korea. After the Korean War, he went to test-pilot school at the Naval Air Test Center in Maryland.

Glenn flew the third of the Mercury missions on *Friendship VII*. On that 20 February 1962 flight, he became the first American to orbit Earth. He soared to an apogee, or *maximum altitude*, of 162 miles. (The opposite of apogee is perigee, *the lowest point of an orbit*.) He orbited Earth at 17,500 miles per hour (mph). In 1998 Glenn entered space a second time at the age of 77 on the space shuttle *Discovery*. This made him the oldest human to enter space.

After leaving NASA Glenn became a US senator. He represented Ohio from 1974 until 1999.

CMDR SCOTT CARPENTER WAS THE FIRST PERSON IN THE WORLD TO HOLD THE TITLES OF ASTRONAUT AND AQUANAUT.

Courtesy of NASA

Cmdr Scott Carpenter

Cmdr Scott Carpenter (born in 1925) of the US Navy flew antisubmarine missions in Korea. After Korea, he received test pilot training.

On 24 May 1962 Carpenter piloted the second orbital Mercury flight, *Aurora VII*. He reached an apogee of 164 miles.

Besides being an astronaut, Carpenter was an aquanaut. An aquanaut *is a person who conducts work or research under water*. Carpenter worked on the Navy's Man-in-the-Sea Program in 1965. He lived in an underwater lab for 45 days. He was the first American to hold the titles of both astronaut and aquanaut.

Capt Walter Schirra

Capt Walter Schirra (born in 1923) graduated from the US Naval Academy in 1945 and from the US Navy Test Pilot School in 1958. He flew in all three early spacecraft programs.

Schirra took *Sigma VII* on six orbits of Earth on 3 October 1962 for Project Mercury. From 15 to 16 December 1965, on *Gemini VI*, he docked in space with *Gemini VII*. And on 11 October 1968 he launched with a three-man crew on *Apollo 7*, one of several prep flights for the *Apollo 11* moon-landing mission.

CAPT WALTER SCHIRRA FLEW IN PROJECTS MERCURY, GEMINI, AND APOLLO.
Courtesy of NASA

Col L. Gordon Cooper

Air Force Col L. Gordon Cooper (1927–2004) piloted the last of the Project Mercury missions. His 15 to 16 May 1963 flight on the *Faith VII* was the longest of the Mercury flights. He remained in space more than 34 hours, and his spacecraft orbited Earth 22 times.

Cooper was command pilot on *Gemini V*. On 21 August 1965 he and copilot Charles Conrad began an eight-day trip. They orbited Earth 120 times—more than 3 million miles.

Cooper graduated from the Air Force Institute of Technology in 1956 and from the Air Force Experimental Test Flight School in 1957. He retired in 1970.

COL L. GORDON COOPER TRAVELED MORE THAN 3 MILLION MILES ON *GEMINI V*.
Courtesy of Bettmann/Corbis

Maj Donald Slayton

Maj Donald Slayton (1924–1993) flew B-25s during World War II. He flew 56 combat missions in the European theater. Later the Air Force sent him on seven missions over Japan. After the war, he tested fighters.

Because of health problems, Slayton didn't get to fly into space for Mercury. However, in 1972 NASA doctors proclaimed him well enough to travel in space. Slayton took part in the 1975 *Apollo-Soyuz* mission. This was a joint project of the United States and Soviet Union, which you'll read about later in this lesson. He remained with NASA until 1982.

CAPT DONALD SLAYTON FLEW WITH THE 1975 *APOLLO-SOYUZ* MISSION.
Courtesy of Bettmann/Corbis

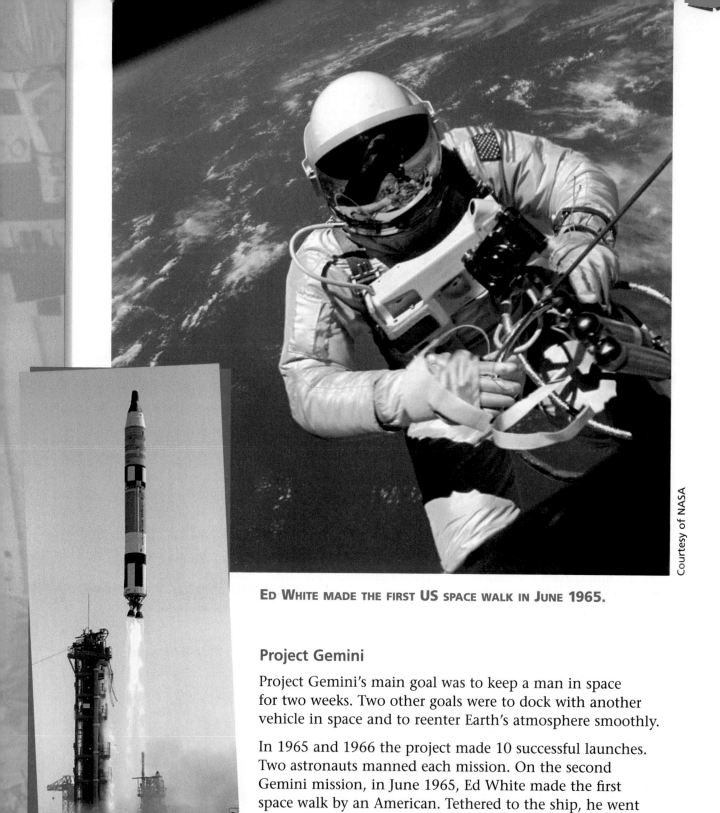

Courtesy of NASA

ED WHITE MADE THE FIRST US SPACE WALK IN JUNE 1965.

GEMINI IV LAUNCH

Gemini IV launched into space on 3 June 1965.

Courtesy of NASA

Project Gemini

Project Gemini's main goal was to keep a man in space for two weeks. Two other goals were to dock with another vehicle in space and to reenter Earth's atmosphere smoothly.

In 1965 and 1966 the project made 10 successful launches. Two astronauts manned each mission. On the second Gemini mission, in June 1965, Ed White made the first space walk by an American. Tethered to the ship, he went outside the spacecraft. His walk lasted 22 minutes.

Project Apollo

Project Apollo's purpose was to land a man on the moon. That memorable event occurred on 20 July 1969. The flight was *Apollo 11*. Five other Apollo flights reached the moon—*Apollo 12*, *14*, *15*, *16*, and *17*.

Two other Apollo missions were notable for different reasons. On 27 January 1967 *Apollo 1* ended in tragedy during a preflight test. The launch pad caught fire, and all three astronauts on board died. In April 1970 the mission of *Apollo 13* was cut short because of an explosion on board. The spacecraft made it safely home because of quick thinking by the astronauts and NASA scientists at mission-control headquarters.

BUZZ ALDRIN ON THE MOON

As part of the *Apollo 11* team in 1969, Buzz Aldrin was the second man to walk on the moon.

Courtesy of NASA

The Apollo 1 Disaster and the Lessons Learned From It

The *Apollo 1* astronauts were Virgil Grissom, Ed White, and Roger Chaffee. On 27 January 1967 the men were aboard the command module to conduct a test for a planned February launch. A fire broke out on the launch pad, and all three men perished.

NASA delayed Apollo flights for nearly two years. Its engineers reworked the module and the space suits to make them safer in a fire. As a result of this work, *Apollo 7* soared into space with astronauts Walter Schirra, Walt Cunningham, and Donn Eisele on 11 October 1968.

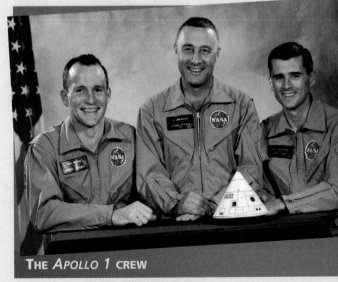

THE APOLLO 1 CREW

Members of the *Apollo 1* crew were (from left) Ed White, Virgil Grissom, and Roger Chaffee.

Courtesy of NASA

In April 1961 cosmonaut Yuri Gagarin became the first man in space.
Courtesy of Bettmann/Corbis

A Soviet Soyuz launches into space.
Courtesy of NASA/Corbis

The Soviet Vostok, Voskhod, and Soyuz Programs

The satellites in the Sputnik program were unmanned. In 1961 the Soviet Union introduced the first of its manned space programs: Vostok. Two others followed: Voskhod and Soyuz. All three programs marked milestones in space travel.

Vostok

During the early years the Soviet space program was slightly ahead of the US program. Just as the Soviet Union launched its unmanned *Sputnik 1* before the United States got into space, the Soviets sent a man into space before the Americans did. On 12 April 1961 Yuri Gagarin, flying solo, became the first man in space. He was a cosmonaut, *a Soviet, or Russian, astronaut.* He flew on *Vostok 1.*

The Soviet Union was also the first country to send a woman into space. In June 1963 Valentina Tereshkova made 48 orbits around Earth in *Vostok 6.*

Voskhod

The Soviet Voskhod missions carried three cosmonauts each. *Voskhod 1* launched in 1964. *Voskhod 2* rocketed into space in March 1965. On 18 March 1965 cosmonaut Alexei Leonov became the first man to take a space walk.

Soyuz

Like the astronauts on the Gemini missions, the Soviet Soyuz mission crews practiced docking in space. Docking required spacecraft with more than one module. A module *is a unit of a spacecraft.*

The Soviet Union built a spacecraft with three modules. One module was for takeoff. The second was for performing scientific tests in space. The third was for returning to Earth. The cosmonauts dumped the first two modules into space when they were ready to head home.

In April 1967 *Soyuz 1* crashed and cosmonaut Vladimir Komarov died. But in January 1969 *Soyuz 4* and *Soyuz 5* docked in space. The crews practiced moving from one spacecraft to the other.

The Soviet Union next turned its attention to building a space station.

The Key Steps in the Development of Spacecraft

To understand the space missions, you need to know some basic terms. Three of the most important are *rocket*, *missile*, and *launch vehicle*.

Put most simply, a *rocket* shoots into the air when fuel burns and releases gases that propel it. A rocket tipped with a bomb is called a *missile*. A rocket tipped with a Project Gemini or other mission capsule is called a *launch vehicle*.

Expendable and Reusable Launch Vehicles

There are two types of launch vehicles: expendable and reusable. An *expendable* launch vehicle is used just once. Examples are the Atlas, Delta, and Titan booster rockets. A *reusable* launch vehicle can be used again and again. The space shuttle, which you'll read about later in this lesson, is the sole example of a reusable launch vehicle.

Key US and Soviet Launch Vehicles

The US and the Soviet space programs used the same models of rockets as their military programs did.

US Launch Vehicles

The US Air Force used Atlas rockets as ballistic missiles until 1965. Atlas rockets under NASA control shot the early Mercury spacecraft into orbit. The Air Force tipped its Titan II rockets with nuclear warheads beginning in 1964. NASA later tipped its Titan II rockets with Gemini capsules for manned orbital flight.

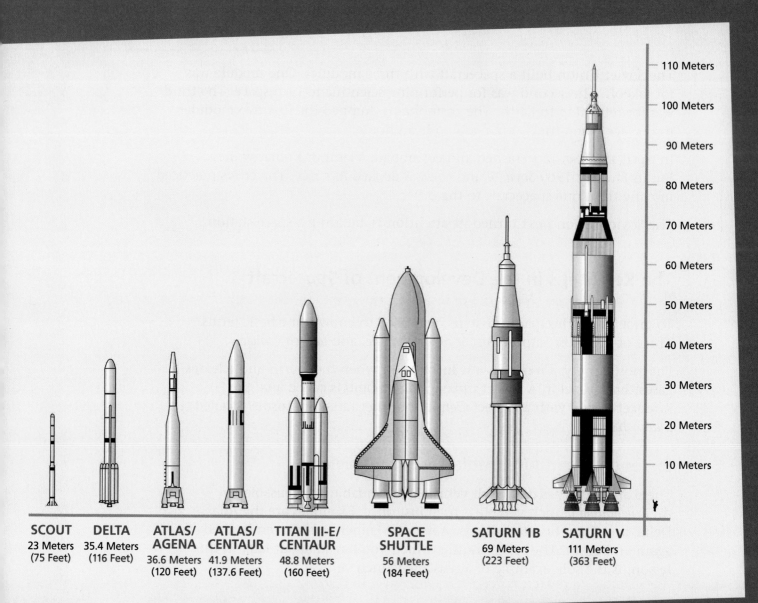

SCOUT	DELTA	ATLAS/ AGENA	ATLAS/ CENTAUR	TITAN III-E/ CENTAUR	SPACE SHUTTLE	SATURN 1B	SATURN V
23 Meters (75 Feet)	35.4 Meters (116 Feet)	36.6 Meters (120 Feet)	41.9 Meters (137.6 Feet)	48.8 Meters (160 Feet)	56 Meters (184 Feet)	69 Meters (223 Feet)	111 Meters (363 Feet)

FIGURE 1.1

An assortment of US launch vehicles

The United States had developed another type of rocket booster, Thor, in the 1950s. The first Thor boosters were designed as medium-range ballistic missiles to be fired from bases in Europe. But this program served peaceful purposes as well. Thor rockets, renamed Thor-Delta or Delta rockets, launched unmanned spacecraft.

The reusable US space shuttles launch with two solid rocket boosters and an external fuel tank. The rocket boosters can be reused, but the fuel tanks cannot. Some 32 miles up, the boosters separate and deploy parachutes. They land in the ocean, and ships pick them up. The fuel tank continues pushing the spacecraft into orbit. When the fuel is used up, the tank releases and disintegrates. Engines on the shuttle steer the ship in space and upon reentry into the Earth's atmosphere.

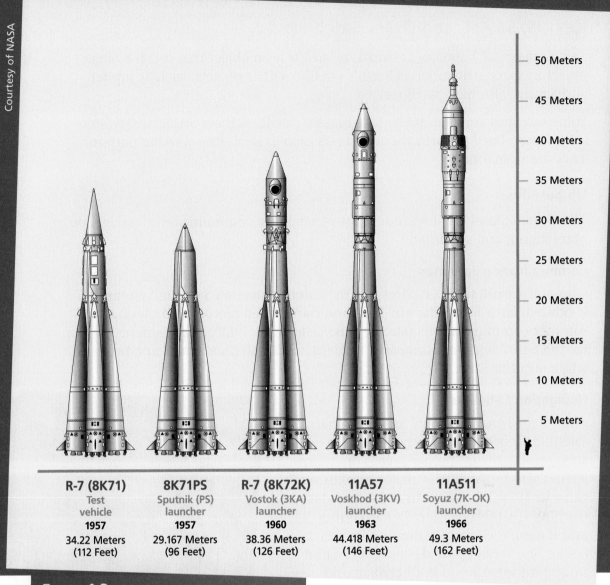

R-7 (8K71)	8K71PS	R-7 (8K72K)	11A57	11A511
Test vehicle	Sputnik (PS) launcher	Vostok (3KA) launcher	Voskhod (3KV) launcher	Soyuz (7K-OK) launcher
1957	**1957**	**1960**	**1963**	**1966**
34.22 Meters (112 Feet)	29.167 Meters (96 Feet)	38.36 Meters (126 Feet)	44.418 Meters (146 Feet)	49.3 Meters (162 Feet)

FIGURE 1.2

These illustrations show the evolution of Soviet launch vehicles. Included are (from left) the rockets for *Sputnik*, *Vostok*, *Voskhod*, and *Soyuz* space vehicles.

Soviet Launch Vehicles

The Soviet space program borrowed the R-7 intercontinental ballistic missile (ICBM) from its military. The Soviets tipped their R-7s with their Vostok, Voskhod, and Soyuz manned capsules, called *upper stages*.

Engineers have improved the R-7 over the years, but its basic design is the same. It has four rocket boosters, referred to as the *first stage*. The four boosters attach to a large, central rocket dubbed the *second stage*. Minutes after launch, the four boosters drop away. The second-stage rocket powers the spacecraft until the upper stage ignites. The engines of the upper stage then maneuver the spacecraft. An updated version of the R-7 launches manned Soyuz flights into space to this day.

Key US, Soviet, and Other Satellites

As you read in Chapter 6, Lesson 1, a *satellite* is an object that orbits a larger object in space. The moon is Earth's satellite. Other planets, such as Jupiter and Saturn, also have satellites.

Some satellites are man-made. Like natural satellites, these artificial satellites orbit Earth. They perform scientific tasks such as analyzing weather patterns. They are unmanned.

US Satellites

The United States employs four kinds of satellites: communication, navigation, observation, and scientific.

Communication Satellites

One of the earliest US satellites was the Communication Satellite System. It orbited Earth for 13 days in 1958 and transmitted prerecorded messages. Another communications satellite was *Telstar 1*. In 1962 NASA launched *Telstar* for the Bell Telephone Company. It could handle 60 phone calls at a time while orbiting Earth.

Navigation Satellites

The US Air Force and Navy use navigation satellites to help guide aircraft and submarines. The US military relies on radio signals sent by satellite. A major breakthrough came in 1978, when the Air Force introduced the NAVSTAR (**Nav**igation **S**ignal **T**iming **a**nd **R**anging) Global Positioning System (GPS). The system provides navigation and timing information to both civilian and military users worldwide. Twenty-four GPS satellites orbit the Earth every 12 hours. The satellites act as precise reference points and continuously broadcast position and date information. Five monitoring stations and three antennas located throughout the world track the satellites and send the data to a master control station. Each satellite broadcasts its time and the time that it sent the signal. A receiver then measures how long it took to receive the signal, thus determining relative distance. Users with hand-held receivers can precisely determine position, speed, and time.

GPS DEVICE

A Soldier uses a GPS device that receives signals from NAVSTAR.

Courtesy of Michael Ainsworth/
Dallas Morning News/Corbis

Observation Satellites

Observation satellites come in three varieties. Weather satellites study temperature, humidity, and clouds. In 1960 the United States launched its first weather satellite, *Tiros 1*. The military has its own weather-satellite system. It is called the Defense Meteorological Satellite Program.

The second kind of observation satellite measures the heat and light that bounce off Earth's surface. LANDSAT (**land sat**ellite) is the best known of these satellites. They help farmers with their crops, for instance.

The third type of observation satellite is the reconnaissance satellite. Its defense purposes include spotting enemy missile launches or military preparation. The operational details of most of these satellites are military secrets. But the Defense Support Program (DSP) satellite system is an exception. Publicizing the existence of this early warning system lets possible enemies know that the United States can detect their missile launches and nuclear tests.

Scientific Satellites

Some scientific satellites study outer space. Included in this group is the groundbreaking *Explorer I*, launched in 1958. It gathered data on radiation.

More famous today is the Hubble Space Telescope, which takes clear, detailed photos of objects in space. Other scientific satellites study Earth. An example is the Earth Radiation Budget Satellite, launched in 1984 to explore radiation on Earth.

A probe *is a scientific satellite that studies a planet or another object in space other than Earth.* The earliest probes, called Rangers, studied the moon. Other probes included the *Pioneer*, which took pictures of Jupiter in the 1970s, and the Vikings, launched in 1975 to study Mars. *Voyagers 1* and *2*, launched in 1977, studied Jupiter and Saturn. Another famous probe was *Galileo*, which explored Jupiter. It launched in 1989. *Cassini* flew into space in 1997 to study Saturn.

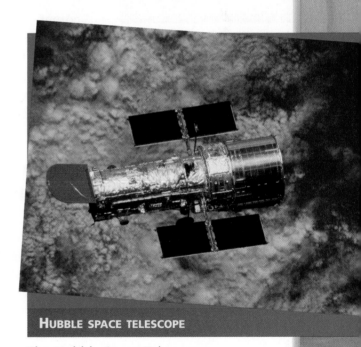

HUBBLE SPACE TELESCOPE

The Hubble Space Telescope takes photos as it orbits Earth.

Courtesy of NASA

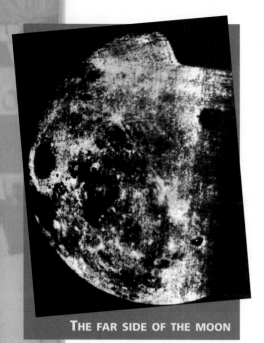

THE FAR SIDE OF THE MOON

In 1959 *Luna 3* took the first photos of the far side of the moon.

Courtesy of NASA

Soviet and Other Satellites

With the launch of *Sputnik 1* and *2* in 1957, the Soviets achieved the distinction of sending the first artificial satellites into space. In 1959 the Soviets sent the first of the Luna probes to explore the moon. That year *Luna 2* crashed into the moon as planned after making scientific observations and *Luna 3* took the first photographs of the far side of the moon.

In 1960 the Soviet Union sent the first of its *Marsnik* probes to study Mars. Only one of 15 missions was a complete success. In 1961 the Soviet *Venera* probe flew by Venus.

The US and the Soviets were not the only countries involved in space exploration. The European Space Agency (ESA) sent up its first satellite in 1985 to study Halley's comet. The ESA *is a group of 17 countries in Europe that pool their funds and knowledge to explore space.* The satellite came within a few hundred miles of the comet. Japan also participated in the probe of that comet with the launches of *Sakigake* and *Suisei.* The Soviet Union's *Vega 1* and *Vega 2* also flew by Halley's comet in 1985.

The Significance of the Phrase "One Small Step for [a] Man, One Giant Leap for Mankind"

Projects Mercury and Gemini showed the world that NASA could send men into space. NASA now knew how to design spacecraft that could orbit Earth and dock in space. Under NASA's guidance, astronauts had walked in space and come home safely. Next stop: the moon.

The First Moon Mission and the Astronauts Who Conducted It

Apollo 11 was the first spacecraft to land on the moon. The earlier Apollo flights were tests. Some went all the way to the moon, but they didn't land there.

On 16 July 1969 astronauts Neil Armstrong, Edwin (Buzz) Aldrin, and Michael Collins climbed into *Apollo 11* and took off for the moon. The launch site was Kennedy Space Center in Florida. On 20 July Armstrong and Aldrin landed on the moon in the lunar module *Eagle.* Collins stayed in orbit around the moon in the command module. Later, when the crew was ready to return to Earth, the two modules docked in space.

APOLLO 11 ASTRONAUTS

The astronauts on *Apollo 11* were
(from left) Neil Armstrong, Michael Collins,
and Edwin "Buzz" Aldrin.

Courtesy of NASA

SATURN 5 ROCKETS LAUNCHED
APOLLO 11 TO THE MOON.

Courtesy of NASA

Armstrong was the first man to step
on the moon. As he did so, he said,
"That's one small step for [a] man, one
giant leap for mankind." Aldrin then
stepped out of the *Eagle*. The men spent
a few hours photographing the lunar
surface, gathering rocks, and running
scientific tests.

Hundreds of millions of people back
on Earth watched on television as
Armstrong made that first step. When
Armstrong and Aldrin returned to space
they left behind a plaque that said,
"Here men from the planet Earth first
set foot on the moon. July 1969, A.D.
We came in peace for all mankind."

With the *Apollo 11* mission, the United
States won the space race. No other
country has landed men on the moon.

EDWIN ALDRIN IN *EAGLE*

Neil Armstrong took this picture
of fellow astronaut Edwin Aldrin
in the lunar module *Eagle*.

Courtesy of NASA

Neil Armstrong: First Man on the Moon

Neil Armstrong (born in 1930) earned his student pilot's license before he got a license to drive a car. He was 16, and he loved to fly.

He was a Navy pilot during the Korean War. He flew 78 combat missions, taking off from the deck of an aircraft carrier. After the war, Armstrong earned his bachelor's degree in 1955 and a master's degree in aerospace engineering in 1970. He also filled a number of roles with a group that was the precursor to NASA. Among those roles was test pilot. He tested more than 200 types of aircraft, from fighters to helicopters.

Armstrong became an astronaut in 1962. He spent four years in training. Unlike many of the other astronauts, Armstrong was a civilian, even though he'd served with the Navy in Korea. His first space mission was with Project Gemini in 1966. Three years later he took his famous "leap for mankind" onto the moon.

Col Edwin Aldrin: Astronaut and Scholar

Col Edwin "Buzz" Aldrin (born in 1930) graduated from West Point in 1951. He became a pilot with the US Air Force. He flew 66 combat missions in Korea. He later got his doctoral degree in astronautics from the Massachusetts Institute of Technology (MIT).

The first time Aldrin applied to be an astronaut, NASA turned him down. He tried again and joined NASA's astronaut program in 1963. Because of his advanced degree, he was well qualified to work on the technical aspects of docking in space and walking on the moon. He was part of the *Gemini XII* mission in 1966, where the crew practiced docking. As a crew member of *Apollo 11* he was the second man to walk on the moon. He later was commander of the test-pilot school at Edwards AFB in California, where the space shuttle was being tested.

Lt Col Michael Collins: Alone in Lunar Orbit

Air Force Lt Col Michael Collins (born in 1930) graduated from West Point in 1952. He was a fighter pilot and a test pilot before he became an astronaut. He joined NASA in 1963.

Collins had duties in both the Gemini and Apollo missions. On *Gemini X* in 1966, he was the third man in history to walk in space. For *Apollo 11*, he was lead pilot of the command module. He stayed in orbit around the moon while Neil Armstrong and Edwin Aldrin walked on the moon. The command module and the *Eagle* lunar module docked in space before the crew's return to Earth. He attained the rank of major general before retiring from the Air Force in 1978.

Subsequent Moon Missions and What Each Contributed

Six Apollo missions followed *Apollo 11*. Five of them reached the moon: *Apollo 12, 14, 15, 16*, and *17*.

Apollo 12 was aloft from 12 to 24 November 1969. The crew conducted experiments and gathered samples. They also collected pieces of an unmanned US satellite called *Surveyor 3* that landed on the moon in 1967.

Astronauts with *Apollo 14* (31 January to 9 February 1971) were the first to use a cart to carry rocks on the moon's surface. The crew collected 94 pounds of samples.

Apollo 15 (26 July to 7 August 1971) had several firsts. The astronauts had better space suits so they were able to stay on the moon nearly 67 hours. They also drove 17 miles on the moon's surface in a lunar roving vehicle (LRV). They even released a small satellite into lunar orbit.

During the *Apollo 16* mission (16 to 27 April 1972), the astronauts explored a hilly area on the moon's surface. They stayed on the moon for 71 hours.

In the final moon mission, *Apollo 17* (7 to 19 December 1972), one of the team members was the first scientist to land on the moon. All the other astronauts who'd landed on the moon were pilots.

The *Apollo 13* Mission and the Effort to Rescue It

On 11 April 1970 *Apollo 13* took off for the moon. On board were James Lovell, John Swigert, and Fred Haise. About two days after the launch, one of the people in charge of mission control in Florida said, "The spacecraft is in real good shape as far as we are concerned. We're bored to tears down here."

He spoke too soon.

About 55 hours into the mission, one of *Apollo 13*'s oxygen tanks blew up. The explosion ruptured the ship's second oxygen tank as well. It quickly became clear that the mission would no longer be to get to the moon. The goal now was to get the crew back to Earth as soon as possible—and alive.

The lack of oxygen affected the ship's fuel cells, which were needed to get the spacecraft back to Earth. Engineers at mission control had to think on their feet. They realized the lunar module was a ready source of supplies. It had oxygen for the crew and for the fuel cells. And it had power that could be transferred to the command module to get the crew home.

Meanwhile, the crew faced other problems. Carbon dioxide (the gas people exhale) built up in the ship. Mission control had to find a way to purify the air. The controllers advised the astronauts how to build an air purifier from the limited materials they had on board.

Amazingly, despite all these obstacles, *Apollo 13* landed safely on 17 April. The expertise of the crew and mission-control staff, combined with steady nerves, pulled them through.

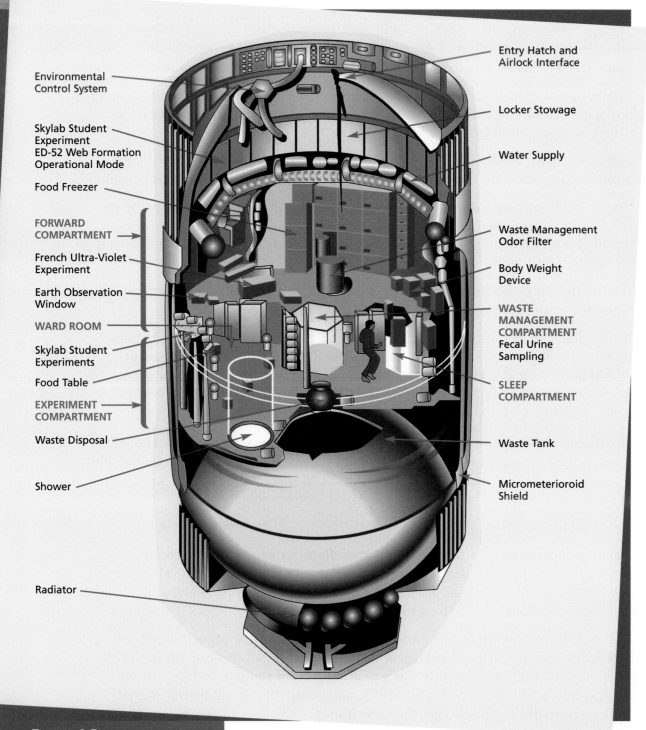

Environmental Control System

Skylab Student Experiment ED-52 Web Formation Operational Mode

Food Freezer

FORWARD COMPARTMENT

French Ultra-Violet Experiment

Earth Observation Window

WARD ROOM

Skylab Student Experiments

Food Table

EXPERIMENT COMPARTMENT

Waste Disposal

Shower

Radiator

Entry Hatch and Airlock Interface

Locker Stowage

Water Supply

Waste Management Odor Filter

Body Weight Device

WASTE MANAGEMENT COMPARTMENT Fecal Urine Sampling

SLEEP COMPARTMENT

Waste Tank

Micrometerioroid Shield

FIGURE 1.3

NASA's *Skylab* was about the size of a three-bedroom house. It launched in 1973.

Courtesy of NASA

Skylab, Salyut, Apollo-Soyuz, Spacelab, and Mir

NASA, the Soviet Union, and the ESA each put laboratories into space. Astronauts conducted experiments in these orbiting labs. But the astronauts themselves were the main targets of the tests. All the space agencies wanted to learn about the impact that being in space for long periods would have on the health of human beings.

A VIEW OF *SKYLAB* FROM SPACE
Courtesy of MPI/Getty Images

In 1973 NASA launched its first lab, *Skylab*. It was the size of a three-bedroom house. *Skylab* was mostly made up of parts used during the Apollo project. In addition, astronauts reached the lab in an Apollo spacecraft. Crews visited the lab three times. The first stay was 28 days. The second was 58 days. The third visit lasted 84 days. NASA concluded that three months in space didn't seem to adversely affect human health.

The Soviets had two space station programs: Salyut and Mir. They tried sending up *Salyut 1* to space as early as 1971. Salyut met with success and failure. The crew aboard *Salyut 1* died on their journey home because of a problem with the spacecraft. But in 1984 a crew broke a record when they remained in *Salyut 7* for 234 days.

In 1975 the United States and Soviet Union teamed up for a space lab mission called Apollo-Soyuz. This cooperation was remarkable because the Cold War was still in full swing. Both countries sent men into orbit in capsules, which then docked in space. US astronauts and Soviet cosmonauts jointly conducted science tests for two days.

MIR

The Soviets called their second space lab *Mir.*

Courtesy of NASA/Getty Images

APOLLO-SOYUZ DOCKING MISSION

The United States and Soviet Union met in space through the *Apollo-Soyuz* docking mission in 1975.

Courtesy of NASA

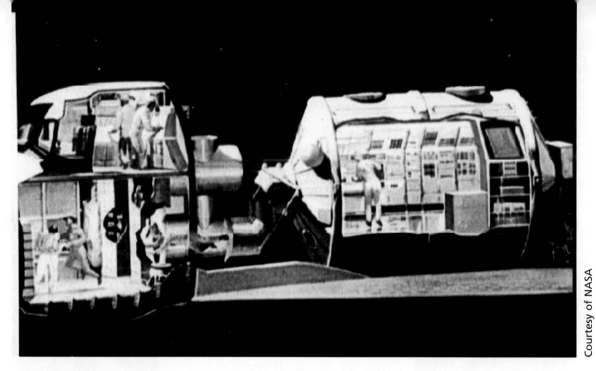

TEN EUROPEAN NATIONS BUILT *SPACELAB*,
WHICH FLEW ABOARD US SPACE SHUTTLE FLIGHTS FROM **1983** UNTIL **1997**.
This illustration shows the *Spacelab* pallet aboard the space shuttle *Columbia*.

Europe also got in on the space lab business. Ten European countries built and financed *Spacelab*. The United States built and financed the means of launching *Spacelab*. The first mission launched in 1983; the last in 1997. *Spacelab* travels in the cargo hold of US space shuttles. It contains tools for tests in space.

Mir entered space in 1986. The Soviets modified this lab by lightening the load of scientific equipment, which left more living room for the cosmonauts. *Mir* had six docking stations. The United States sent astronauts on missions to *Mir*.

Key Space Shuttle Missions

The US space shuttle program began in 1981. As of 2007, it was still in operation and had logged more than 100 missions. A mission lasts up to 30 days. The shuttles are shaped like airplanes. Astronauts fly aboard these reusable spacecraft.

There have been six shuttles: *Enterprise, Columbia, Challenger, Discovery, Atlantis,* and *Endeavour*. Each shuttle consists of an orbiter, solid rocket boosters, and an external tank. Astronauts and cargo ride in the orbiter. The boosters and tank launch the spacecraft into orbit.

Mae Jemison: First African-American Woman in Space

MAE JEMISON

Mae Jemison was the first African-American woman to enter space.

Courtesy of NASA

Mae Jemison (born in 1956) was the first African-American woman to enter space. NASA admitted her to the astronaut program in 1987. She was a civilian. She holds a Ph.D. degree in medicine. Jemison is fluent in four languages: English, Japanese, Russian, and Swahili.

Jemison launched aboard the space shuttle *Endeavour* in 1992. She worked on *Spacelab* while in orbit, conducting life sciences and materials experiments for a joint US–Japanese project. In 1993 Jemison left NASA to begin her own company.

Taylor Wang: Breaking Scientific Ground

Taylor Wang was born in China in 1940. He later became a US citizen. He was a payload specialist aboard *Challenger* in 1985.

Wang had a Ph.D. degree in physics. His job was to conduct scientific experiments that required the weightlessness of space. He performed these tests in *Spacelab 3*, carried in the cargo hold of *Challenger*. The 1985 voyage was the first time tests were made in a *Spacelab* container.

Wang worked for Jet Propulsion Laboratory in California, rather than NASA. Because of his expertise in science, he was allowed to fly on the NASA mission.

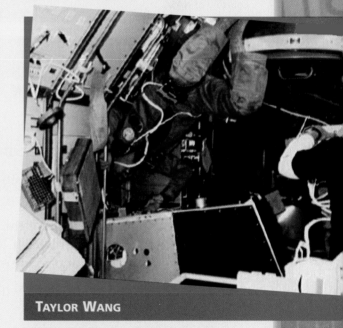

TAYLOR WANG

Payload specialist Taylor Wang (floating upside down) repairs *Spacelab* science equipment during a 1985 *Challenger* mission.

Courtesy of NASA

Col Eileen Collins: First Woman Space Shuttle Pilot and Commander

COL EILEEN COLLINS

Col Eileen Collins was the first woman commander of a space shuttle.

Courtesy of NASA

Col Eileen Collins (born in 1956) flew more than 30 types of aircraft for the Air Force. She became the first woman pilot, and later commander, on space shuttle flights.

Collins went on four space shuttle missions after joining NASA in 1990. In 1995 she served as pilot on a *Discovery* mission. During this flight *Discovery* docked with the Russian space station *Mir*. In 1997 she flew as pilot aboard *Atlantis*. This flight also met up with *Mir* and transferred four tons of supplies to the station.

Collins commanded two flights. During a 1999 *Columbia* voyage, the crew deployed a special telescope. On a 2005 *Discovery* trip, the spacecraft docked with the International Space Station, which you'll read about later in this lesson.

Crew Positions on Space Shuttles

A space shuttle crew has four positions: commander, pilot, mission specialist, and payload specialist.

The commander is in charge of the mission. The commander oversees everything, from the crew to the shuttle itself. The commander's job is to make sure the mission meets its goals and to ensure safety. The commander is always a pilot.

The pilot helps the commander with flying the shuttle as well as with launching or retrieving satellites.

Mission specialists aid the commander and pilot with technical aspects of running the shuttle.

Payload specialists conduct scientific research. The equipment to run scientific trials is often referred to as the "payload."

Maj Gen Ronald Sega: From Mission Specialist to Under Secretary of the Air Force

MAJ GEN RONALD SEGA

Maj Gen Ronald Sega flew two space shuttle missions with NASA and went on to become under secretary of the Air Force.
Courtesy of the US Air Force

It would take more than the fingers on two hands to count the roles Air Force Academy graduate Maj Gen Ronald Sega has filled in his career.

Born in 1952, Sega started as an Air Force pilot, a flight instructor, and a physics professor at the Air Force Academy. With a Ph.D. degree in electrical engineering, he taught physics for eight years. Then he joined NASA. He went on two shuttle missions. In 1994 he flew aboard *Discovery* as a mission specialist. That mission was the first shuttle trip to include both US and Russian astronauts. In 1996, during Sega's second mission, *Atlantis* docked with the Russian space station *Mir*. The commander for that missions was Col Kevin Chilton.

In 2005 Sega became under secretary of the Air Force. In this position, he oversees the recruiting, training, and equipping of approximately 700,000 Air Force personnel.

Maj William Pailes: Payload Specialist

Maj William Pailes (born in 1952) was a payload specialist aboard the space shuttle *Atlantis* in 1985. It was *Atlantis's* first flight.

The payload was from the Department of Defense (DoD). Pailes's task was to conduct experiments in space for DoD. The shuttle orbited Earth 98 times.

Before joining NASA, Pailes attended the US Air Force Academy. After graduation, he trained as a rescue pilot. He retired as a colonel and became a senior aerospace science instructor for the Air Force Junior Reserve Officer Training Corps at TX-952, Corsicana High School in Corsicana, Texas.

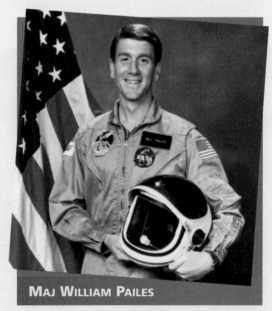

MAJ WILLIAM PAILES

Maj William Pailes was a payload specialist who worked on US DoD experiments aboard the space shuttle *Atlantis* in 1985.
Courtesy of NASA

Key Space Shuttle Missions and What They Accomplished

NASA began its shuttle missions cautiously. The *Enterprise* flew only test flights. It never entered space.

Columbia was the first vehicle to launch into space. Even so, its first four missions were also test flights. NASA scientists studied the impact of reentry on the vehicle and its shields. The missions were dubbed STS-1 through STS-4. STS stands for "Space Transportation System."

When STS-5 was ready in November 1982, *Columbia* was set for a full-fledged mission. The crew released two satellites into orbit.

The space shuttle *Challenger* carried the first American woman astronaut— Sally Ride—into space during STS-7 in 1983. The first European *Spacelab* payload was aboard mission STS-9 in the *Columbia* in 1983.

On STS-31 in 1990 *Discovery* launched the Hubble Space Telescope. The telescope takes much clearer photos of space than telescopes on Earth do because Hubble doesn't need to "see" through Earth's atmosphere. *Atlantis* had its day in the spotlight when it deployed a space probe called *Galileo* to study Jupiter.

Endeavour broke ground during its first voyage in May 1992. For the first time in space shuttle history, three astronauts walked in space at the same time. The longest space walk in history—eight hours—also took place during this mission. That record hadn't been broken as of early 2007.

Because *Endeavour* is the newest of the shuttles, it's equipped with the latest features. For instance, *Endeavour* is the first shuttle outfitted with a drag chute for landings.

THE SPACE SHUTTLE *ENDEAVOUR* TOOK OFF IN MARCH 1995.

Courtesy of NASA

SALLY RIDE

Sally Ride was the first American woman astronaut to go on a space mission.
Courtesy of Bettmann/Corbis

Sally Ride: First American Woman in Space

In 1983 Sally Ride (born in 1951) became the first American woman astronaut in space. She was a mission specialist.

NASA accepted Ride into the astronaut program in 1978. Unlike many of the other astronauts, Ride didn't have a military background. But she did have a Ph.D. degree in physics. As part of her training, she served on the support crews for two *Columbia* shuttle missions.

Ride first flew into space in 1983 aboard the *Challenger*. Her second trip was in 1984, again on the *Challenger*.

Col Sidney Gutierrez: First Hispanic Pilot and Commander

Col Sidney Gutierrez (born in 1951) was the first Hispanic to pilot and command space shuttle missions. He graduated from the US Air Force Academy in 1973 and from the Air Force Test Pilot School in 1981.

NASA picked Gutierrez for its astronaut program in 1984. He spent several years as a ground-support crew member for shuttle missions.

In 1991 it was Gutierrez's turn to soar into space. He was pilot for the *Columbia*. During this mission, the crew ran tests to determine the effects of weightlessness on people, animals, and plants. *Columbia* was in space for nine days.

Gutierrez commanded his second mission in 1994 aboard *Endeavour*. During this mission, payload specialists studied Earth's atmosphere. Col Kevin Chilton was the pilot on this flight. Later that year Gutierrez retired from NASA and from the Air Force.

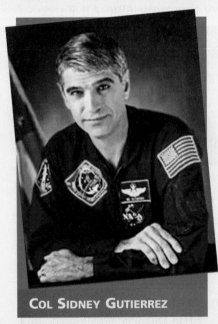

COL SIDNEY GUTIERREZ

Col Sidney Gutierrez was the first Hispanic to command a space shuttle mission.
Courtesy of NASA

Col Ellison Onizuka: First Asian-American in Space

COL ELLISON ONIZUKA

Col Ellison Onizuka was the first Asian-American to fly a space shuttle mission.

Courtesy of NASA

Col Ellison Onizuka (1946–1986) began his career in space as an Air Force ROTC cadet. After graduating from the University of Colorado with a master's degree in aerospace engineering, he entered the Air Force. He became a test pilot. In 1978 he began astronaut training with NASA.

Like many other astronauts, Onizuka spent his early years with NASA on the ground at mission control. In 1985 he got his first chance to fly into space as a mission specialist. *Discovery* flight STS-51C was the first to conduct tests for the Department of Defense. STS-51C held another first. Onizuka was the first Asian-American to enter space.

In 1986 Onizuka flew as part of a seven-member crew on the *Challenger*. Less than two minutes after takeoff, the shuttle exploded because of a leak in one of the rocket boosters. Onizuka was killed with the rest of the crew. The Air Force promoted him to colonel after his death.

The Challenger and Columbia Accidents

While there have been more than 100 successful space shuttle missions, two ended tragically. On 28 January 1986 *Challenger* blew up 73 seconds after launch. The seven-member crew died. The problem, investigators found, was a leaky booster rocket. NASA delayed future shuttle missions until 1988 as engineers made changes to prevent similar accidents.

Then on 1 February 2003 *Columbia* fell apart while reentering Earth's atmosphere. All seven crew members perished. After studying a videotape of the launch, investigators learned that foam from the external tank had struck protective panels on the left wing during liftoff. This allowed superheated gases to break down the wing structure, causing the shuttle to disintegrate. NASA delayed future shuttle flights until 2005 to correct the causes of the failure.

Selected NASA Manned Space Flights

Date	Project	Spacecraft	Astronaut(s)	Notes
1961	Mercury	*Freedom VII*	Alan Shepard	First American in space
1961	Mercury	*Liberty Bell VII*	Virgil Grissom	Second Mercury flight
1962	Mercury	*Friendship VII*	John Glenn	First American to orbit Earth
1962	Mercury	*Aurora VII*	Scott Carpenter	First American to hold titles of *astronaut* and *aquanaut*
1962	Mercury	*Sigma VII*	Walter Schirra	Six orbits
1963	Mercury	*Faith VII*	L. Gordon Cooper	Longest Mercury flight
1965	Gemini	*Gemini IV*	Ed White, James McDivitt	First American space walk
1969	Apollo	*Apollo 11*	Neil Armstrong, Edwin Aldrin, Michael Collins	First man on the moon
1969	Apollo	*Apollo 12*	Charles Conrad, Richard Gordon, Alan Bean	Conducted experiments and gathered samples
1970	Apollo	*Apollo 13*	James Lovell, John Swigert, Fred Haise	Oxygen tanks blew up; extraordinary efforts brought astronauts back safely
1971	Apollo	*Apollo 14*	Alan Shepard, Stuart Roosa, Edgar Mitchell	First to use a cart to carry rocks on moon's surface
1971	Apollo	*Apollo 15*	David Scott, James Irwin, Alfred Worden	First use of lunar roving vehicle
1972	Apollo	*Apollo 16*	John Young, Thomas Mattingly, Charles Duke	First study of lunar hills
1972	Apollo	*Apollo 17*	Eugene Cernan, Ronald Evans, Harrison Schmitt	First non-pilot scientist to land on the moon
1975	Apollo-	*Apollo 18*	Thomas Stafford, Vance Brand, Donald Slayton	First US–Soviet docking in space
1981	STS	*Columbia*	John Young, Robert Crippen	First space shuttle test flight

continued on next page

Selected NASA Manned Space Flights, *continued*

Date	Project	Spacecraft	Astronaut(s)	Notes
1981	STS	*Columbia*	Joseph Engle, Richard Truly	First full-fledged shuttle flight; two satellites released
1983	STS	*Challenger*	Robert Crippen, Frederick Hauck, John Fabian, Sally Ride, Norman Thagard	First American woman in space
1983	STS	*Challenger*	Richard Truly, Daniel Branstein, Dale Gardner, Guion Bluford, William Thornton	First African-American in space
1983	STS	*Columbia*	John Young, Brewster Shaw, Owen Garriott, Robert Parker, Byron Lichtenberg, Ulf Merbold	First *Spacelab* payload; first European Space Agency astronaut
1985	STS	*Discovery*	Thomas Mattingly, Loren Shriver, Ellison Onizuka, James Buchli, Gary Payton	First Asian-American in space
1985	STS	*Challenger*	Robert Overmyer, Frederick Gregory, Don Lind, Norman Thagard, William Thornton, Lodewijk van den Berg, Taylor Wang	First non-NASA scientist to fly in the space shuttle
1985	STS	*Atlantis*	Karol Bobko, Ronald Grabe, David Hilmers, Robert Stewart, William Pailes	Maiden flight of *Atlantis*
1986	STS	*Challenger*	Francis Scobee, Michael Smith, Judith Resnick, Ellison Onizuka, Ronald McNair, Gregory Jarvis, Christa McAuliffe	Shuttle explodes 73 seconds after launch; all crew members died
1990	STS	*Discovery*	Loren Shriver, Charles Bolden, Steven Hawley, Bruce McCandless, Kathryn Sullivan	Hubble Space Telescope launched

Selected NASA Manned Space Flights, continued

Date	Project	Spacecraft	Astronaut(s)	Notes
1991	STS	*Columbia*	Bryan O'Connor, Sidney Gutierrez, James Bagian, Tamara Jernigan, M. Rhea Seddon, F. Drew Gaffney, Mille Hughes-Fulford	First Hispanic shuttle pilot
1992	STS	*Endeavour*	Daniel Brandenstein, Kevin Chilton, Pierre Thuot, Kathryn Thornton, Richard Heib, Thomas Akers, Bruce Melnick	First flight of *Endeavour*; first three-person spacewalk
1992	STS	*Endeavour*	Robert Gibson, Curtis Brown, Mark Lee, N. Jan Davis, Jay Apt, Mae Jemison, Mamoru Mohri	First African-American woman in space
1993	STS	*Endeavour*	John Casper, Donald McMonagle, Mario Runco, Gregory Harbaugh, Susan Helms	First military woman to enter space
1994	STS	*Discovery*	Charles Bolden, Kenneth Reightler, N. Jan Davis, Ronald Sega, Franklin Chang-Diaz, Sergei Krikalev	First shuttle to include both US and Russian astronauts
1995	STS	*Discovery*	James D. Wetherbee, Eileen Collins, Michael Foale, Janice Voss, Bernard Harris, Vladimir Titov	First woman space-shuttle pilot
2003	STS	*Columbia*	Rick Husband, Laurel Clark, Kalpana Chawla, Ilan Ramon, Willie McCool, Michael Anderson, David Brown	Shuttle breaks up during reentry; all crew members perished

BRIG GEN SUSAN HELMS

Brig Gen Susan Helms was the first military woman to fly in space.

Courtesy of AP Photo/NASA

Brig Gen Susan Helms: First Military Woman in Space

Brig Gen Susan Helms (born in 1958) was an Air Force major when she became the first military woman to enter space. She flew aboard the *Endeavour* in 1993.

Helms graduated in 1980 from the Air Force Academy, where she majored in aeronautical engineering. After getting her master's degree in 1985, she taught at the academy before going for test-pilot training. In 1990 NASA picked her for the astronaut program.

Helms went on five missions. Besides her mission on *Endeavour*, Helms's other most notable voyage was to the International Space Station, where she spent 163 days in 2001. She returned to the Air Force in 2002.

The Purpose of the International Space Station

THE INTERNATIONAL SPACE STATION

The ISS orbits 240 miles above Earth at 17,500 mph.

Courtesy of Getty Images, Inc.

The International Space Station (ISS) is the product of 16 countries: the United States, Russia, Canada, Brazil, Belgium, Denmark, France, Germany, Italy, Japan, the Netherlands, Norway, Spain, Sweden, Switzerland, and the United Kingdom.

The ISS is the world's first permanent space lab. It orbits 240 miles above Earth at 17,500 mph. Crews are an international mix. Most crews stay for six months. The first crew, named *Expedition 1*, arrived in 2000 aboard a Russian *Soyuz* spacecraft.

The ISS provides a means of studying the effects of living in space on human bodies and minds. It's also a platform for conducting science tests in a weightless setting. These tests research medicines, technologies, and industrial materials. According to NASA this "ability to control the variable of gravity in experiments opens up unimaginable research possibilities."

Equally important, the ISS offers scientists a chance to work out the difficulties of living and traveling in space within a reasonable distance from Earth. It is paving the way for flights to Mars and beyond.

The International Parts That Make Up the ISS

The ISS is a work in progress. It grows as new pieces become ready. The construction began in space in 1998 with the arrival of the Russian-built *Zarya* module.

Zarya and the Russian *Zvezda* service module provide astronauts' and cosmonauts' living quarters and life support. Russia also supplied *Pirs*, another docking station. The US components are the *Destiny Laboratory* for conducting science tests; the *Quest Airlock*, a portal to and from the ISS for space walks; and the *Unity* connecting module. Canada assembled *Canadarm2*, a robotic crane. Japan and Europe are working on more labs for space experiments.

As of 2006 the ISS weighed 471,000 pounds and had 15,000 cubic feet of living and working space. Solar panels generate power.

The history of humans' exploration of space to date is one of experimentation, discovery, and heroism. The future of air and space power promises an equal amount of each.

CHECKPOINTS

Lesson 1 Review

Using complete sentences, answer the following questions on a sheet of paper.

1. What organization did the United States form after the launch of the Soviet satellites *Sputnik 1* and *2*?

2. What are the names of the first three US manned space projects?

3. Who was the first astronaut that Project Mercury sent into space?

4. What was the goal of Project Apollo?

5. Name three expendable launch vehicles and one reusable launch vehicle.

6. What are the four kinds of satellites the United States employs?

7. What was the name of the first manned spacecraft that landed on the moon?

8. What are the four positions astronauts fill on the space shuttle?

9. Why did the space shuttle *Challenger* explode in 1986?

Applying Your Learning

10. What advantages are there to having many countries participate in the International Space Station?

The Future of Air and Space Power

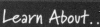

Imagine that you're an astronaut.

You're peering out a porthole in your spacecraft. You've been soaring through space for months. At last you see your destination—Mars.

You and your crew know there's lots of work ahead. But for a few minutes everyone is silent. You realize that you will be the first people in the world to walk on a planet other than Earth.

You wonder whether the surface of Mars at your landing point will be firm or give way under your feet like sand. How hard will it be to move around in your spacesuit? What will Martian gravity really feel like? You practiced many times back on Earth, but this is the real thing.

You suddenly realize how far away from Earth you are. At this moment, it's about 50 million miles. You and your fellow space travelers are truly on your own as you've never been before. It will be more than a year before you can make the return flight home.

But as you take another glance out the window, your fear dissolves. The excitement of this historic moment takes over. You are a space traveler. You are an explorer. It's time to guide the landing module down to the Martian surface. You've reached a new frontier.

Current and Anticipated Developments in Manned Air Vehicles

Vocabulary

- **hypersonic**
- **surveillance**
- **autonomous**
- **micro-UAV**
- **nanotechnology**
- **nano-UAV**
- **virtual**
- **cyberspace**
- **hacker**
- **deep space**

Today's advanced manned aircraft would seem like the stuff of science fiction to early inventors such as the Wright brothers. In little more than a century, aircraft have progressed from clumsy gliders to jets that fly many times the speed of sound. The modern US arsenal features even more futuristic technology.

The F-35 Lightning II Joint Strike Fighter

The F-35 Lightning II Joint Strike Fighter is a perfect example of a modern military aircraft. It's a stealth fighter with a single engine. A single pilot flies it.

As of early 2007 the F-35 was still in the testing phase. Manufacturer Lockheed-Martin is designing three models, each for a different branch of the US military. The Air Force will get the conventional takeoff/landing model (CTOL). The Navy will receive the carrier variant (CV), which will make takeoffs and landings from carriers. And the Marines will fly the short takeoff/vertical landing aircraft (STOVL) version.

Many countries are taking part in the development of the F-35. The United States and Britain are the main sponsors of the new fighter. Other countries invested in the project are Italy, the Netherlands, Turkey, Canada, Denmark, Australia, and Norway.

What's attracting so many nations to invest in the F-35?

First, the parts of all three F-35 models are interchangeable. Between 70 percent and 90 percent of the parts can be used on any of the models. Second, it's a stealth fighter. It has radar that helps it avoid detection. Third, it can engage in dogfights as well as fight forces on the ground. It's not easy for an aircraft to take on both air and ground combat, but the F-35 can do it. It can carry missiles on its wingtips. It can also hold about 15,000 pounds of other kinds of ordnance.

Finally, the F-35 boasts sci-fi-style features. For example, it has a pilot's helmet that displays warnings about approaching missiles on the visor.

THE STEALTH F-35 LIGHTNING II

Courtesy of the US Air Force

THE AIRBORNE LASER IS DESIGNED TO SHOOT DOWN ENEMY MISSILES. IT IS STILL IN THE TESTING PHASE.

The Airborne Laser

The Airborne Laser is another aircraft under development as of 2007. Its purpose is to find and blow up airborne ballistic missiles.

The Airborne Laser is an outfitted 747. Six modules with lasers and sensors make up the defense weaponry on board. Each module is the size of a sport utility vehicle. Each weighs 6,500 pounds and has 3,600 parts. Working together, these modules can destroy missiles from hundreds of miles away.

The modules begin by tracking a missile's exhaust trail. Once they've pinpointed a missile's position, the lasers focus through a telescope in the nose of the plane. Then they fire at the missile until it breaks apart.

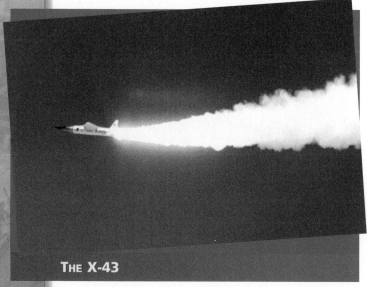

THE X-43

Hypersonic Air Vehicles

Some new types of speedy aircraft are also in the works. They're called hypersonic aircraft. Hypersonic means *able to fly at or beyond Mach 5*, which is five times the speed of sound. One is the X-43, or Hyper-X. During a 2004 test flight, it flew at Mach 10, or about 7,000 miles per hour. Another model of the X-43 that's intended to fly at Mach 15 is under development.

Some of these aircraft use an engine called a *ramjet*. A ramjet is like a rocket. It gets its thrust by forcing gases from burned fuel through an exhaust pipe. The ramjet totes its own oxygen to help the fuel burn.

The X-43 goes a step beyond this. It relies on a *scramjet*. A scramjet propels a plane in much the same way as a ramjet does, but it sucks its needed oxygen from the surrounding air. For this reason, some people describe the class of aircraft to which the X-43 belongs as "air breathing."

Another hypersonic aircraft is the HyperSoar. This aircraft is still only a concept. Flying at speeds up to Mach 10, it would skip along Earth's atmosphere, coasting in space for hundreds of miles at a time. It would burn liquid hydrogen, which gives off water vapors. Therefore, it would run on clean fuel.

The HyperSoar could carry heavier loads than other aircraft of its size because of the way it bounces between Earth's atmosphere and space. It could launch satellites and other payloads into space. It could strike military targets. One day, it might even carry passengers in record time. A flight from Los Angeles to New York City might take only 35 minutes.

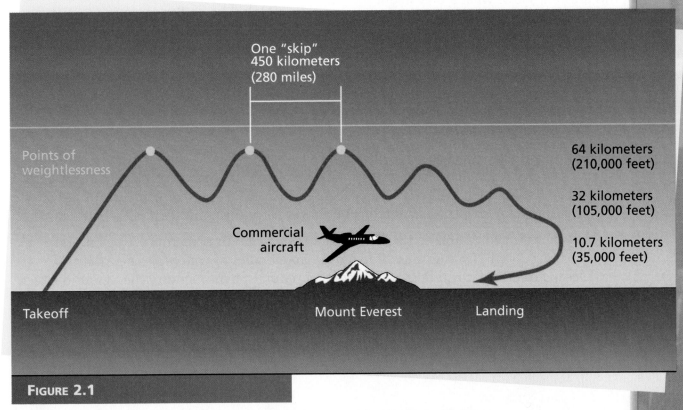

FIGURE 2.1

The HyperSoar aircraft is still only a concept. It would gain fuel efficiency by skipping along the Earth's s atmosphere.

Courtesy of the Lawrence Livermore National Laboratory

Current and Anticipated Developments in Unmanned Systems

A UAV

This drawing shows what a UAV might look like while refueling in midair.

Courtesy of Northrop Grumman. Illustration by Peter A. Barnett, Anne Beamon, and Christine D. Smith.

New developments are also in the works for unmanned air vehicles (UAVs). UAVs have traditionally flown reconnaissance. But they are now taking roles in combat. As technology improves, engineers will find many more uses for UAVs.

The current generation of UAVs includes the Predator. It conducts surveillance— or *reconnaissance*—and strikes enemy targets. It has been successful, but it is a small aircraft. Its small fuel tank limits its range.

To achieve longer-range missions, among other goals, the Air Force is developing the Joint Unmanned Combat Air System. The UAV for this project is the X-45. As of 2007 UAVs could not refuel during flight. But one day the X-45 should be able to refuel in midair. The ability for autonomous refueling—*independent of human control*— would enable UAVs to conduct much longer missions.

The X-45 should also be able to carry bombs such as the 2,000-pound Joint Direct Attack Munition. And it will be a stealth aircraft. Ground crews will remotely direct the X-45's operations.

But the military also needs an efficient way to transport UAVs to faraway missions such as Operation Enduring Freedom in Afghanistan. The manned Pelican aircraft, now under development, will carry heavy loads such as smaller unmanned aircraft. It will be as long as a football field and will be able to carry the equivalent of 17 battle tanks.

The Pelican will be able to fly as high as 20,000 feet. But sometimes, to gain fuel efficiency, it will fly as low as 20 feet over large bodies of water like the Atlantic Ocean. To do so, it will take advantage of a natural phenomenon called ground effect, which decreases drag.

THE PELICAN CARGO PLANE

Courtesy of Boeing

Anticipated Developments in UAV Technology

In addition to autonomous refueling, military planners hope to make other important advances with UAVs. These advances involve three things: sight, size, and tactics.

First is sight. At the controls of a plane, the pilot can see if the aircraft is about to collide with another aircraft or a tall building. But having no pilot, a UAV has no human eyes. Sight is a problem. As of early 2007, for instance, there had been three midair collisions between UAVs and helicopters in Afghanistan during Operation Enduring Freedom.

Engineers are trying to give UAVs sight using electronic sensors. They are using a micro-UAV—*an aircraft that weighs as little as a few ounces or a few pounds*—to research the possibility of sight.

UAV sight probably won't become a reality until around 2015. But when it does, micro-UAVs may take on important roles in reconnaissance. Because of their small size, they could enter enemy territory unobserved. They could zoom around inside buildings to check for enemy positions. This means they could save lives, because people now must do this risky work.

Another avenue of research into size is nanotechnology. Nanotechnology *is the science and technology of building electronic circuits and devices from single atoms and molecules.* A nano-UAV, still to be invented, *is a UAV so small that it is invisible to the naked eye.* Nano-UAVs might one day take on the task of building a fighter jet. One futurist even predicts that billions of programmed nanos, equipped with microscopic robotic arms, could converge on a vat of supplies in liquid form and put together a fighter in only a minute. Sounds like the stuff of science fiction now, but researchers think it may one day be possible.

As designers make it possible for UAVs to see, a new application of warfare will become possible—combining UAVs and piloted aircraft on a mission. To do this, more effective command and control will be needed—leaders will need to coordinate the efforts of both types of aircraft. They will also have to train pilots to be comfortable flying alongside UAVs.

How the Use of Smart Systems and Other Developments Will Change the Traditional Concept of the "Pilot"

Sending pilots into battle means putting their lives at risk. By contrast, UAVs spare Airmen's lives. Pilots remotely control UAVs from a base on the ground. They can direct missiles and run reconnaissance while remaining hundreds of miles away from the action.

As progress in UAV technology continues, remote flight will become more common. This will change the definition of the word *pilot*. No longer will the pilot be a daring aviator flying Mach 2 over enemy territory. More and more, combat will involve skilled pilots, navigators, and missile-sensor operators who work with computers. UAVs will have major roles in the US military of the 21st century.

Current and Anticipated Developments in Cyber Warfare

Computers, chips, hardware, monitors, and plugs—these are the physical tools of the Internet. But the information we retrieve from the Internet is not physical. The data are stored in a place that is virtual, or *existing in ideas and outside the physical world.* Cyberspace *is a virtual place where information is stored.*

The US Air Force is expanding its responsibilities into the cyber world.

Why the US Air Force Established Air Force Cyberspace Command

In 2005 the US Air Force released a new mission statement. It says that the mission is "the defense of the United States of America and its global interests—to fly and fight in air, space, and cyberspace."

In 2006 Secretary of the Air Force Michael Wynne announced the formation of the Air Force Cyberspace Command. He cited many reasons for founding this organization. A key reason is that hackers, terrorists, and criminals often use the Internet to further their plans.

A hacker *is someone who uses programming skills to gain illegal access to a computer network or file.* If they apply these skills to military actions, hackers can disrupt communication lines between commanders and their troops. "Our ability to fight in ground, sea, air, and space depends on communications that could be attacked through cyberspace," Secretary Wynne said. He added that the "cost of entry into the cyberspace domain is low." This means that anyone wishing to do the United States harm has an easy means to do so.

Islamist terrorists who use the World Wide Web to recruit suicide bombers are an example of those who abuse cyberspace. Criminals who use the Global Positioning System (GPS) to arrange drug drops are another. Many new kinds of threats can hit the United States through the Web. That's why the Air Force has stepped in to defend cyberspace.

The Current Operations of Air Force Cyberspace Command

The 8th Air Force became the new Air Force Cyberspace Command in November 2006. Although the command continues to conduct bombing missions, it also focuses on guarding America's cyberspace.

The Air Force is mapping out career paths for Airmen who wish to enter the Cyberspace Command. It is also deciding how to train personnel to work in this field.

The goals of the Cyberspace Command are to:

- Protect cyberspace
- Make sure commanders have full access to all battlefield information available through cyberspace
- Carry out offensive missions in cyberspace
- Support reconnaissance missions.

The Air Force's Plan to Exploit Cyberspace by Offensive Means

What would an offensive cyberspace mission look like? It might involve an effort to destroy an enemy's power grid. Without power, enemy field commanders couldn't get orders to their troops. Radar couldn't spot approaching US fighters and bombers. And the enemy couldn't interfere with US lines of communications.

Computer viruses are another weapon in the US cyberspace arsenal. Airmen could infect an enemy's computer systems and cripple its ability to wage war with the United States.

Cyberspace can also be used for training. Pilots can practice combat scenarios in a modern simulator, a piece of computerized equipment offering virtual experiences. Using a simulator, a pilot can "fly" through a severe thunderstorm or enemy fire without having to go through the real experience. This virtual experience prepares pilots for actual combat. It also saves fuel and wear on aircraft.

The Possibility of Battles in Cyberspace

In his speeches, Secretary Wynne has discussed the possibility of cyber warfare. "One rough-and-ready demonstration that cyberspace is a true domain on a par with land, air, space, and sea is to apply the basic questions of the principles of war," he said in a 2006 address.

"For example, can one mass forces in cyber? Yes. Does surprise give an advantage in cyber? Of course. Simplicity? Economy of force? Clarity of objective? Yes, yes, and yes."

The Air Force is preparing for this very real possibility.

Anticipated Air Force Plans
for Integrating Air and Space Operations

In addition to air and cyberspace, the Air Force exploits space to guard the United States.

For instance, satellites monitor the weather. They transmit communications. They pinpoint targets. These functions support military actions in the air and on the ground.

The Air Force uses the GPS satellite system for precision strikes. GPS satellites can see through bad weather to their targets. With GPS satellites, sandstorms don't present a problem during a desert mission such as Operation Iraqi Freedom (OIF). Operation Noble Eagle, which protects the US skies, relies on satellites to detect planes entering restricted airspace.

The US Space-Based Infrared System can detect missiles shot toward the United States and give warning. The Air Force's Counter Communications System can jam enemy satellites.

But other countries' technologies are challenging those of the United States. During OIF, the Iraqis jammed the US GPS to prevent precision strikes. The Air Force has devised ways to block the jamming attempts. It is working on even more-powerful defenses for its satellites through its Rapid Attack Identification Detection and Reporting System.

While still in the early stages, space operations are already taking a role in warfare. It's the military's job to figure out how to integrate these missions with its land, air, and sea resources.

Space-Based Missile Defense

The United States also protects its territory and its interests through a missile-defense system. This effort has three parts. All are space based. They are supported by GPS, by other satellites, and by radar.

You read about the first part earlier in this lesson. It's the Airborne Laser. The Airborne Laser targets hostile missiles in the early stage, or "boost phase," of flight.

Courtesy of the Missile Defense Agency

AEGIS DESTROYERS AND CRUISERS WORK WITH SATELLITES AS PART OF THE US MISSILE-DEFENSE SYSTEM.

The second part is US Navy Aegis cruisers and destroyers. Aided by communications satellites, they monitor missiles in midcourse. Navy ships will then try to shoot down these missiles. The task also sometimes falls to ground-based missile-command centers in Alaska or California.

The final part is the PAC-3, which is the latest version of the Patriot missile. The PAC-3 can destroy hostile missiles shortly before impact.

Evolved Expendable Launch Vehicles and Air Platforms

The Air Force launches its satellites into orbit aboard the Evolved Expendable Launch Vehicle (EELV). There are two varieties: the Boeing Delta IV and the Lockheed-Martin Atlas V. But expendable launch vehicles may have reached the limits of their effectiveness.

AN EELV FIRES UP FOR LAUNCH

Courtesy of the US Air Force

So the Air Force is increasing its use of *air platforms*, which are command-and-control centers carried aloft by aircraft. The command-and-control packages are usually fitted into a trailer. The trailer is then placed in the hold of a cargo plane. Command-and-control centers, also known as C2s, run combat missions from the air. C2s rely on satellites launched by EELV to gather information. An example of a C2 is the Ground Mobile-3 (GM-3), which fits into a C-17 Globemaster III cargo plane.

GM-3 LOADING

An Air Force crew loads a GM-3 onto a C-17 Globemaster III.

Courtesy of the US Air Force

Reusable Launch Platforms and Space Maneuver Vehicles

But the future may lie with reusable launch platforms. These platforms carry payloads into space and bring them back to Earth.

One such platform now under development for the Air Force is the unmanned Orbital Test Vehicle (OTV). It's about one-quarter the size of a space shuttle. It will get into space atop an Atlas V launch vehicle.

The Air Force will use the OTV for testing new satellites. The Air Force can send the new satellite aloft in the OTV. When the testing is done, the OTV returns to Earth with the satellite still on board. Engineers then study the results. Construction of the first OTV was nearly complete at the end of 2006.

Another platform in the works is the Space Maneuver Vehicle. This spacecraft will stay in orbit up to a year. It will carry payloads of less than 20,000 pounds. Its purpose will be to pinpoint hostile targets from space.

NASA's Vision for the Future

While the Air Force works on its futuristic aircraft and spacecraft, NASA is busy planning for future space exploration, too. Some people think space travel isn't practical. NASA doesn't agree. It's working now on concepts and inventions that will help get humans into deep space. Deep space *is any region beyond the solar system.*

Why NASA Plans to Explore Beyond Earth's Orbit

NASA flew men to the moon in the 1960s. Today it routinely sends astronauts to the International Space Station (ISS). But some people still ask: why explore space?

NASA Administrator Michael Griffin explains NASA's view:

> Throughout history, the great nations have been the ones at the forefront of the frontiers of their time. Britain became great in the 17th century through its exploration and mastery of the seas. America's greatness in the 20th century stemmed largely from its mastery of the air. For the next generations, the frontier will be space.

Pushing the boundaries of space keeps the United States ahead technologically. It keeps the country dominant militarily. Scientists can conduct studies in space that are not possible on Earth. Since the 1970s hundreds of NASA inventions have benefited US industry and improved Americans' lives. NASA research has led to many breakthroughs in medical technology, for example. And Apollo research even helped improve athletic shoe design! Other important discoveries continue to be made.

Plus, many find the very idea of space travel exciting. Just as the Wright brothers had the thrill of being the first to achieve heavier-than-air flight, some brave astronaut may one day make history as the first person to step onto Mars.

NASA's New Orion Spacecraft and Ares Launch Vehicle

But you can't get to space without a spacecraft. The Orion spacecraft is NASA's newest vehicle for exploring space. Engineers hope to have it ready for its first mission by 2014. At that point, Orion will replace the space shuttles and begin ferrying people to the ISS. After Orion passes the needed tests, NASA will send it to the moon—and one day to Mars. It will also serve as the reentry vehicle into Earth's atmosphere.

AN ARTIST'S CONCEPTION OF THE ORION SPACECRAFT ORBITING THE MOON.

Orion will be similar in shape to the Apollo spacecraft that first carried men to the moon. Engineers are sticking with the Apollo model because it successfully completed the tricky reentry. NASA is aiming for a lunar mission in 2020.

When the day comes for a lunar launch, a cargo launch vehicle called the Ares V will shoot into space to deliver a lunar module and a departing stage into low-Earth orbit. Orion will launch separately atop the Ares I launch vehicle. Orion will then dock with the lunar module. The departing stage will propel Orion and the lunar module to the moon.

Plans for Future Manned Exploration of the Moon, Mars, and Beyond

After successful Orion missions to the moon and Mars, what next? Try this on for size: establishing a space colony on Mars. NASA is already moving in this direction.

In the 1990s, for instance, NASA worked on the X-34. It was to be a reusable spacecraft that provided its own launch ability. Congress cut funding for this project in 2001, but the X-34 is still part of NASA's overall plan to explore deep space.

Additional trips to the moon are many years away. Voyages to Mars are likely decades away. But NASA keeps its options open. It's always pushing the envelope. It's always thinking ahead.

After Mars, what? NASA itself doesn't know yet. But one thing is sure: exploration of space will continue.

In this book, you've read about the history of aviation, airpower, and the exploration of space. You read how the imaginative thinking of Leonardo da Vinci led people in following centuries to experiment with parachutes and gliders. You read about the Wright brothers' careful and logical experiments that led to the first controlled, manned, heavier-than-air flight. You studied how aviation developed rapidly during World War I, how Charles Lindbergh captured imaginations with his trans-Atlantic solo flight, and how brave Allied flyers helped liberate Europe and the Pacific region in World War II. You read about the birth of the independent Air Force and the role air power has played in US global interventions since then. Finally, you read about the beginnings of the space program, the first men to reach the moon, and the accomplishments and tragedies of the space shuttles.

An X-34

Courtesy of NASA

Before you, as before no other generation in the history of mankind, the future of air and space power lies bright with promise and possibilities. Will you be part of it?

Lesson 2 Review

Using complete sentences, answer the following questions on a sheet of paper.

1. What's attracting so many nations to invest in the F-35?

2. What is the purpose of the Airborne Laser?

3. How fast is a plane flying if it's going at hypersonic speed?

4. What improvement is the Air Force making to the X-45 UAV that will give it a longer range than the Predator?

5. How small is a nano-UAV?

6. Define cyberspace.

7. What are the three parts of space-based missile defense?

8. When does NASA expect to launch the next moon mission?

Applying Your Learning

9. What are some of the reasons behind the exploration of space?

Unit One: Imagining Flight

Correlated to McREL Standards for:

History, **Geography**, **Science**, and **Language Arts**

McREL Standards	Unit 1: Imagining Flight
History	
Historical Understanding (HU)	
HU 1. Understands and knows how to analyze chronological relationships and patterns	Timeline of Aviation History, 12
HU 2. Understands the historical perspective	Checkpoints, 13, 25 Flight Paths, 9, 17, 22 Quick Write Story, 6, 14
US History (US)	
Era 5—Civil War and Reconstruction (1850–1877)	
US 14. Understands the course and character of the Civil War and its effects on the American people	Ways Balloons Were Used During the US Civil War, 20–21
Era 6—The Development of the Industrial United States (1870–1900)	Developments in Lighter-than-Air Flight From Da Vinci to the Wright Brothers, 16–20 Developments in Heavier-than-Air Flight From Da Vinci to the Wright Brothers, 21–24
Era 7—The Emergence of Modern America (1890–1930)	
US 21. Understands the changing role of the United States in world affairs through World War I	Quick Write Story, 14–15 Capsules: Teddy Roosevelt's Rough Riders, 16 Ways the Balloon Contributed to US Victory in the Battle of San Juan Hill, 21
US 22. Understands how the United States changed between the post–World War I years and the eve of the Great Depression	Quick Write Story, 6

World History (WH)

Era 3—Classical Traditions, Major Religions, and Giant Empires, 1000 BCE–300 CE	
WH 7. Understands technological and cultural innovation and change from 1000 to 600 BCE	How Humans Tried to Fly in Ancient Times, 7 Skynotes: Using Kites to Spot the enemy, 8
Era 5—Intensified Hemispheric Interactions 1000–1500 CE	
WH 19. Understands the maturation of an interregional system of communication, trade, and cultural exchange during a period of Chinese economic power and Islamic expansion	Key Aviation Devices Created During Ancient Times, 7–10
Era 6—Global Expansion and Encounter, 1450–1770	

WH 27. Understands how European society experienced political, economic, and cultural transformations in an age of global intercommunication between 1450 and 1750	Key Aviation Devices Created During
	    Ancient Times, 7–10
	Developments in Lighter-than-Air Flight
	    From Da Vinci to the Wright Brothers, 16–20
	Developments in Heavier-than-Air Flight
	    From Da Vinci to the Wright Brothers, 21–24

Era 7—An Age of Revolutions, 1750–1914	

WH 33. Understands the causes and consequences of the agricultural and industrial revolutions from 1700 to 1850	Developments in Lighter-than-Air Flight
	    From Da Vinci to the Wright Brothers, 16–20
	Capsules: Steam Engines, 18
	Developments in Heavier-than-Air Flight
	    From Da Vinci to the Wright Brothers, 21–24

Geography (G)

The World in Spatial Terms	
G 1. Understands the characteristics and uses of maps, globes, and other geographic tools and technologies	Map, 15
G 2. Knows the location of places, geographic features, and patterns of the environment	Map, 15

Science (SC)

Physical Sciences	
SC 10. Understands forces and motion	Why Machines Do Not Fly the Way Birds Do, 11–13 Newton's Three Laws of Motion, 12 Bernoullian Lift (Induced Lift), 12 Newtonian Lift (Dynamic Lift), 12 Capsules: Steam Engines, 18 Concept of Lift, 18 Concept of Drag, 22 Concept of Thrust, 22 Flight Paths, 9, 22

Language Arts (LA)

Writing

LA 1. Uses the general skills and strategies of the writing process	Quick Write, 6, 14 Checkpoints, 13, 25
LA 2. Uses the stylistic and rhetorical aspects of writing	Quick Write, 6, 14 Checkpoints, 13, 25
LA 3. Uses grammatical and mechanical conventions in written compositions	Quick Write, 6, 14 Checkpoints, 13, 25
LA 4. Gathers and uses information for research purposes	Applying Your Learning, 13, 25

Reading

LA 5. Uses the general skills and strategies of the reading process	Learn About, 6, 14 Checkpoints, 13, 25
LA 6. Uses reading skills and strategies to understand and interpret a variety of literary texts	Quick Write Story, 6, 14
LA 7. Uses reading skills and strategies to understand and interpret a variety of informational texts	Learn About, 6, 14 Checkpoints, 13, 25

Viewing

LA 9. Uses viewing skills and strategies to understand and interpret visual media	Map, 15 Photos, 17, 19, 23, 24 Drawings, 9, 10, 11, 22

Unit Two: Exploring Flight

Correlated to McREL Standards for:

History, Geography, Civics, Science, Language Arts, Life Skills, and Technology

McREL Standards	Unit 2: Exploring Flight
History	
Historical Understanding (HU)	
HU 2. Understands the historical perspective	Checkpoints, 43, 61, 79, 91, 105, 115 Flight Paths, 38, 53, 89, 95, 96, 98, 100, 101, 102, 114 Quick Write Story, 30, 44, 62, 82, 92, 106

US History (US)

Era 7—The Emergence of Modern America (1890–1930)	How the Wright Brothers Succeeded in the First Flight, 31–37 The Anatomy of the *Wright Flyer*, 38–39 The History of the Wright Brothers' Involvement With the US Army, 40–42 Key Individuals Involved in Early Aircraft Development, 45–47 The Names and Anatomy of Period Aircraft, 48–50 Other American Pioneers in Aviation Following the Wright Brothers, 51–60
US 21. Understands the changing role of the United States in world affairs through World War I	Quick Write Story, 62 The Contributions of US Pilots During World War I, 63–71 The Role of Air Power During World War I, 72–76 How Air Power Expanded During World War I, 76–78
US 22. Understands how the United States changed between the post–World War I years and the eve of the Great Depression	The Barnstormers, 84–88 The Barnstormers' Major Contributions, 88–89 How the Barnstormers Contributed to Public Awareness of Aviation, 90 Charles Lindbergh's Famous Contribution to Aviation, 94 The Significance of the First Transatlantic Solo Flight, 94–98 Other Significant Contributions That Helped Flight Become Mainstream, 99–104 Early Developments in Commercial Flight, 108–110 The Use of the Airplane in Delivering Mail, 111–112 The Development and Use of Helicopters, 112–114

World History (WH)

Era 8—A Half-Century of Crisis and Achievement, 1900–1945	How the Wright Brothers Succeeded in the First Flight, 31–37 The Anatomy of the *Wright Flyer*, 38–39 The History of the Wright Brothers' Involvement With the US Army, 40–42 Key Individuals Involved in Early Aircraft Development, 45–47 The Names and Anatomy of Period Aircraft, 48–50 Other American Pioneers in Aviation Following the Wright Brothers, 51–60

WH 39. Understands the causes and global consequences of World War I	Quick Write Story, 62 The Contributions of US Pilots During World War I, 63–71 The Role of Air Power During World War I, 72–76 How Air Power Expanded During World War I, 76–78
WH 40. Understands the search for peace and stability throughout the world in the 1920s and 1930s	The Significance of the First Transatlantic Solo Flight, 94–98 Other Significant Contributions That Helped Flight Become Mainstream, 99–104 Early Developments in Commercial Flight, 108–110 The Use of the Airplane in Delivering Mail, 111–112

Geography (G)

The World in Spatial Terms

G 1. Understands the characteristics and uses of maps, globes, and other geographic tools and technologies	Maps, 64, 93

Human Systems

G 13. Understands the forces of cooperation and conflict that shape the divisions of Earth's surface	The Outbreak of World War I, 63

Civics (C)

What Is Government and What Should It Do?

C 1. Understands ideas about civic life, politics, and government	The History of the Wright Brothers' Involvement With the US Army, 40–42 US Contributions to the Air War, 71 Capsules, 72 How War Sped Up Aviation Development in the United States, 78 Air Commerce Act, 104 Applying Your Learning, 105 The Use of the Airplane in Delivering Mail, 111–112

What Are the Basic Values and Principles of American Democracy?

C 10. Understands the roles of voluntarism and organized groups in American social and political life	The Aero Club of America, 41 The Aerial Experiment Association, 46 The Lafayette Escadrille, 65 The Barnstormers' Major Contributions, 88–89 How the Barnstormers Contributed to Public Awareness of Aviation, 90

How Does the Government Established
by the Constitution Embody the Purposes, Values,
and Principles of American Democracy?

C 14. Understands issues concerning the disparities between ideals and reality in American political and social life	Bessie Coleman, 54, 82–83 Opportunities for Women in Aviation, 54–60 Eugene Bullard, 69 Phoebe Fairgrave Omilie, 87 Anne Morrow Lindbergh, 96 Amelia Earhart's Record Flights, 97–98 Katherine Sui Fun Cheung, 101

What Is the Relationship of the United States
to Other Nations and to World Affairs?

C 22. Understands how the world is organized politically into nation-states, how nation-states interact with one another, and issues surrounding US foreign policy	The Contributions of US Pilots During World War I, 63–71 The Role of Air Power During World War I, 72–76 How Air Power Expanded During World War I, 76–78

Science (SC)

Physical Sciences

SC 10. Understands forces and motion	How the Wright Brothers Succeeded
	    in the First Flight, 31–37
	Center of Pressure, 34
	Angle of Attack, 36
	Relative Wind, 36
	The Principles of Airplane Flight, 40
	Lateral Balance, 46
	Torque, 50
	Altitude, 88
	Aerodynamic, 88
	Other Significant Contributions That Helped
	    Flight Become Mainstream, 99–104
	The Problem of Control, 113

Language Arts (LA)

Writing

LA 1. Uses the general skills and strategies of the writing process	Quick Write, 30, 44, 62, 82, 92, 106 Checkpoints, 43, 61, 79, 91, 105, 115
LA 2. Uses the stylistic and rhetorical aspects of writing	Quick Write, 30, 44, 62, 82, 92, 106 Checkpoints, 43, 61, 79, 91, 105, 115
LA 3. Uses grammatical and mechanical conventions in written compositions	Quick Write, 30, 44, 62, 82, 92, 106 Checkpoints, 43, 61, 79, 91, 105, 115
LA 4. Gathers and uses information for research purposes	Applying Your Learning, 43, 61, 79, 91, 105, 115

Reading

LA 5. Uses the general skills and strategies of the reading process	Learn About, 30, 44, 62, 82, 92, 106 Checkpoints, 43, 61, 79, 91, 105, 115
LA 6. Uses reading skills and strategies to understand and interpret a variety of literary texts	Quick Write Story, 30, 44, 62, 82, 92, 106
LA 7. Uses reading skills and strategies to understand and interpret a variety of informational texts	Learn About, 30, 44, 62, 82, 92, 106 Checkpoints, 43, 61, 79, 91, 105, 115

Viewing

LA 9. Uses viewing skills and strategies to understand and interpret visual media	Photos, 33, 35, 36, 37, 42, 45, 46, 47, 48, 50, 51, 52, 53, 54, 55, 56, 57, 58, 59, 60, 62, 65, 66, 67, 68, 69, 70, 74, 75, 77, 78, 83, 84, 85, 86, 87, 90, 103, 108, 109, 110, 111, 113 Diagram, 34, 49, 99 Maps, 64, 93

Life Skills

Self-Regulation (SR)

SR 1. Sets and manages goals	How the Wright Brothers Succeeded in the First Flight, 31–37 The Anatomy of the *Wright Flyer*, 38–39 The History of the Wright Brothers' Involvement With the US Army, 40–42 Other American Pioneers in Aviation Following the Wright Brothers, 51–60 Quick Write Story, 82–83 Flight Paths, 102 Flight Paths, 114
SR 4. Demonstrates perseverance	How the Wright Brothers Succeeded in the First Flight, 31–37 The Anatomy of the *Wright Flyer*, 38–39 The History of the Wright Brothers' Involvement With the US Army, 40–42 Key Individuals Involved in Early Aircraft Development, 45–47 The Names and Anatomy of Period Aircraft, 48–50 Other American Pioneers in Aviation Following the Wright Brothers, 51–60 The Contributions of US Pilots During World War I, 63–71 Quick Write Story, 82–83 Quick Write Story, 92–93 The Significance of the First Transatlantic Solo Flight, 94–98 Quick Write Story, 106–107 Flight Paths, 114

Thinking and Reasoning (TR)

TR 5. Applies basic trouble-shooting and problem-solving techniques	How the Wright Brothers Succeeded in the First Flight, 31–37 The Anatomy of the *Wright Flyer*, 38–39 The History of the Wright Brothers' Involvement With the US Army, 40–42 Checkpoints, 43 Key Individuals Involved in Early Aircraft Development, 45–47 The Names and Anatomy of Period Aircraft, 48–50 Other American Pioneers in Aviation Following the Wright Brothers, 51–60 How Air Power Expanded During World War I, 76–78
TR 6. Applies decision-making techniques	Checkpoints, 43 Louis Biériot, 47

Working With Others (WO)

WO 1. Contributes to the overall effort of a group	Flight Paths, 38, 53, 89, 95, 96, 98, 100, 101, 102, 114
WO 5. Demonstrates leadership skills	Flight Paths, 38, 53, 89, 95, 96, 98, 100, 101, 102, 114

Technology (T)

T 3. Understands the relationships among science, technology, society, and the individual	How the Wright Brothers Succeeded in the First Flight, 31–37 The Anatomy of the *Wright Flyer*, 38–39 The Principles of Airplane Flight, 40 The History of the Wright Brothers' Involvement With the US Army, 40–42 Key Individuals Involved in Early Aircraft Development, 45–47 The Names and Anatomy of Period Aircraft, 48–50 How the Airplane Revolutionized War, 75 How Air Power Expanded During World War I, 76–78 Other Significant Contributions That Helped Flight Become Mainstream, 99–104 Early Developments in Commercial Flight, 108–110 The Use of the Airplane in Delivering Mail, 111–112 The Development and Use of Helicopters, 112–114

T 4. Understands the nature of technological design	How the Wright Brothers Succeeded in the First Flight, 31–37
	The Anatomy of the *Wright Flyer*, 38–39
	The Principles of Airplane Flight, 40
	Key Individuals Involved in Early Aircraft Development, 45–47
	The Names and Anatomy of Period Aircraft, 48–50
	The Role of Air Power During World War I, 72–76
	How Air Power Expanded During World War I, 76–78
	The Barnstormers' Major Contributions, 88–89
	Other Significant Contributions That Helped Flight Become Mainstream, 99–104
	Early Developments in Commercial Flight, 108–110
	The Development and Use of Helicopters, 112–114
T 6. Understands the nature and uses of different forms of technology	The History of the Wright Brothers' Involvement With the US Army, 40–42
	Key Individuals Involved in Early Aircraft Development, 45–47
	The Names and Anatomy of Period Aircraft, 48–50
	The Role of Air Power During World War I, 72–76
	How Air Power Expanded During World War I, 76–78
	The Barnstormers' Major Contributions, 88–89
	Other Significant Contributions That Helped Flight Become Mainstream, 99–104
	The Development and Use of Helicopters, 112–114

Unit Three: Developing Flight

Correlated to McREL Standards for:

History, Geography, Civics, Economics, Science, Language Arts, Life Skills, and **Technology**

McREL Standards	Unit 3: Developing Flight
History	
Historical Understanding (HU)	
HU 1. Understands and knows how to analyze chronological relationships and patterns	Chronological Order, 122
	Developments in General Aviation, 186
	US Global Interventions, 1990 Through 2006, 271

HU 2. Understands the historical perspective

Checkpoints, 135, 169, 187, 203, 227, 253, 281
Flight Paths, 126, 128, 133, 140, 142, 146, 148,
   150, 157, 160, 162, 163, 166, 174, 179, 190,
   213, 218, 219, 225, 226, 237, 238
Quick Write Story, 120, 136, 172, 188, 206,
   228, 254
Capsules, 139, 154, 209

US History (US)

Era 7—The Emergence of Modern America
(1890–1930)

US 22. Understands how the United States
changed between the post-World War I years
and the eve of the Great Depression

Quick Write Story, 120–121
The Predecessors of the US Air Force, 122–128
How the Army Air Corps Developed, 129–132
The Air Force's Path Toward Independence, 132–134

Era 8—The Great Depression and World War II
(1929–1945)

US 25. Understands the causes and course
of World War II, the character of the war at home
and abroad, and its reshaping of the US role
in world affairs

The Role Air Power Played in World War II
   and Its Significance, 137–142
How Air Power Was Developed During
   World War II, 143–154
The Significance of the Allied Air Campaign,
   155–168

Era 9—Postwar United States (1945 to early 1970s)

US 26. Understands the economic boom and social
transformation of post–World War II United States

Key Developments in Commercial Aircraft, 174–180
Key Developments in Commercial Flight Use, 181
Key Contributions to the Expansion of Commercial
   Flight, 182–186

US 27. Understands how the Cold War and
conflicts in Korea and Vietnam influenced
domestic and international politics

The Creation of an Independent Air Force
   in 1947, 207–208
The Cold War and How It Began, 209–213
The USAF Role in the Berlin Airlift, 214–220
The Role of Air Power in the Korean War, 221–226
The Role of Air Power in the Cuban Missile
   Crisis, 229–231
The Role of Air Power in the Vietnam War,
   232–242
How the USAF Gained an Increasingly
   Significant Role in Other US Military
   Operations During the Cold War, 243–248
Key Developments in Aircraft, Missile Capability,
   and Nuclear Capability During the Cold War,
   249–252

US 29. Understands the struggle for racial and gender equality and for the extension of civil liberties	The Tuskegee Airmen and President Harry Truman, 147
Era 10—Contemporary United States (1968 to the present)	
US 30. Understands developments in foreign policy and domestic politics between the Nixon and Clinton presidencies	The Role of Air Power in the Vietnam War, 232–242 The Role of Air Power in the Gulf War (Operation Desert Storm), 257–260
US 31. Understands economic, social, and cultural developments in the contemporary United States	The Role of Air Power in Operation Enduring Freedom, 261–266 The Role of Air Power in Operation Iraqi Freedom, 267–270 The Role of Air Power in Various Other US Military Operations, 271–280

World History (WH)

Era 3—Classical Traditions, Major Religions, and Giant Empires, 1000 BCE–300 CE	
WH 9. Understand how major religious and large-scale empires arose in the Mediterranean Basin, China, and India from 500 BCE to 300 CE	Hero of Alexandria, 191
Era 8—A Half-Century of Crisis and Achievement, 1900–1945	
WH 40. Understands the search for peace and stability Throughout the world in the 1920s and 1930s	The Predecessors of the US Air Force, 122–128 How the Army Air Corps Developed, 129–132 The Air Force's Path Toward Independence, 132–134
WH 41. Understands the causes and global consequences of World War II	The Role Air Power Played in World War II and Its Significance, 137–142 How Air Power Was Developed During World War II, 143–154 The Significance of the Allied Air Campaign, 155–168
WH 42. Understands major global trends from 1900 to the end of World War II	The Predecessors of the US Air Force, 122–128 How the Army Air Corps Developed, 129–132 The Air Force's Path Toward Independence, 132–134 The Role Air Power Played in World War II and Its Significance, 137–142 How Air Power Was Developed During World War II, 143–154 The Significance of the Allied Air Campaign, 155–168

WH 43. Understands how post–World War II reconstruction occurred, new international power relations took shape, and colonial empires broke up

National Security Act of 1947, 134

The Creation of an Independent Air Force in 1947, 207–208

The Cold War and How It Began, 209–213

The USAF Role in the Berlin Airlift, 214–220

The Role of Air Power in the Korean War, 221–226

The Role of Air Power in the Cuban Missile Crisis, 229–231

The Role of Air Power in the Vietnam War, 232–242

How the USAF Gained an Increasingly Significant Role in Other US Military Operations During the Cold War, 243–248

Key Developments in Aircraft, Missile Capability, and Nuclear Capability During the Cold War, 249–252

WH 44. Understands the search for community, stability, and peace in an interdependent world

The Creation of an Independent Air Force in 1947, 207–208

The Cold War and How It Began, 209–213

The USAF Role in the Berlin Airlift, 214–220

The Role of Air Power in the Korean War, 221–226

The Role of Air Power in the Cuban Missile Crisis, 229–231

The Role of Air Power in the Vietnam War, 232–242

How the USAF Gained an Increasingly Significant Role in Other US Military Operations During the Cold War, 243–248

Key Developments in Aircraft, Missile Capability, and Nuclear Capability During the Cold War, 249–252

The Role of Air Power in the Gulf War (Operation Desert Storm), 257–260

The Role of Air Power in Operation Enduring Freedom, 261–266

The Role of Air Power in Operation Iraqi Freedom, 267–270

The Role of Air Power in Various Other US Military Operations, 271–280

WH 45. Understands major global trends
since World War II

Air Power in World War II, 136–169

The Propeller Era in Commercial Flight, 172–187

The Creation of an Independent Air Force
in 1947, 207–208

The Cold War and How It Began, 209–213

The USAF Role in the Berlin Airlift, 214–220

The Role of Air Power in the Korean War, 221–226

The Jet Era in Commercial Flight, 188–203

Air Force Beginnings Through the Korean War,
206–227

The Vietnam War and Other Military Operations,
228–253

Global Interventions from 1990, 254–281

US Global Interventions, 1990 Through 2006, 271

Geography (G)

The World in Spatial Terms

G 1. Understands the characteristics and uses
of maps, globes, and other geographic tools
and technologies

Maps, 144, 158, 214, 215, 216, 220, 224,
230, 232, 244, 245, 247, 256, 258, 164,
274, 277, 279

Human Systems

G 13. Understands the forces of cooperation and
conflict that shape the divisions of Earth's surface

Mitchell and Pearl Harbor, 127

The Role Air Power Played in World War II
and Its Significance, 137–142

How Air Power Was Developed During
World War II, 143–154

The Significance of the Allied Air Campaign, 155–168

The Cold War and How It Began, 209–213

The USAF Role in the Berlin Airlift, 214–220

The Role of Air Power in the Korean War, 221–226

The Role of Air Power in the Cuban Missile Crisis,
229–231

The Role of Air Power in the Vietnam War, 232–242

How the USAF Gained an Increasingly Significant
Role in Other US Military Operations During
the Cold War, 243–248

Key Developments in Aircraft, Missile Capability, and
Nuclear Capability During the Cold War, 249–252

The Role of Air Power in the Gulf War
(Operation Desert Storm), 257–260

The Role of Air Power in Operation
Enduring Freedom, 261–266

The Role of Air Power in Operation
Iraqi Freedom, 267–270

The Role of Air Power in Various Other
US Military Operations, 271–280

Uses of Geography

G 17. Understands how geography is used to interpret the past	The Role Air Power Played in World War II and Its Significance, 137–142
	How Air Power Was Developed During World War II, 143–154
	The Significance of the Allied Air Campaign, 155–168
	Maps, 144, 158, 214, 215, 216, 220, 224, 230, 232, 244, 245, 247, 256, 258, 164, 274, 277, 279
	The USAF Role in the Berlin Airlift, 214–220
	Naval Blockade, 231
	International Waters, 232

Civics (C)

What Is Government and What Should It Do?

C 1. Understands ideas about civic life, politics, and government	The National Defense Act, 123
	Civilian Reserve Pilots, 130
	The Tuskegee Airmen and President Harry Truman, 147
	Development of Federal Regulation of Commercial Flight, 181
	How Federal Regulation Has Evolved, 199
	The National Security Act of 1947, 207
C 2. Understands the essential characteristics of limited and unlimited governments	The War's Causes, 138–139
	Communism, 209
	Capsules, 275

What Are the Basic Values and Principles of American Democracy?

C 10. Understands the roles of voluntarism and organized groups in American social and political life	Civilian Reserve Pilots, 130
	Maj Glenn Miller, 157
	The Women's Airforce Service Pilots, 161
	The United Nations, 209
C 14. Understands issues concerning the disparities between ideals and reality in American political and social life	Black Pilots, 130
	Lt Gen Pete Quesada, 146
	The Tuskegee Airmen and President Harry Truman, 147
	Gen Benjamin O. Davis Jr., 148
	1st Lt Charles Hall, 148
	The Women's Air Force Service Pilots, 161
	Jacqueline Cochran, 162
	Nancy Harkness Love, 163
	The Ninety-Nines, 164
	Maj Arthur T. Chin, 166
	Capt Manual Fernandez, 225
	Gen Daniel James Jr., 242
	A1C Elizabeth Jacobson, 270

How Does the Government Established
by the Constitution Embody the Purposes,
Values, and Principles of American Democracy?

C 22. Understands how the world is organized
politically into nation-states, how nation-states
interact with one another, and issues surrounding
US foreign policy

The Predecessors of the US Air Force, 122–128
The Role Air Power Played in World War II
   and Its Significance, 137–142
How Air Power Was Developed
   During World War II, 143–154
The Significance of the Allied Air Campaign,
   155–168
A Global Industry, 195
The Cold War and How It Began, 209–213
The USAF Role in the Berlin Airlift, 214–220
The Role of Air Power in the Korean War, 221–226
The Role of Air Power in the Cuban Missile Crisis,
   229–231
The Role of Air Power in the Vietnam War, 232–242
How the USAF Gained an Increasingly Significant
   Role in Other US Military Operations During
   the Cold War, 243–248
Key Developments in Aircraft, Missile Capability, and
   Nuclear Capability During the Cold War, 249–252
The Role of Air Power in the Gulf War
   (Operation Desert Storm), 257–260
The Role of Air Power in Operation
   Enduring Freedom, 261–266
The Role of Air Power in Operation
   Iraqi Freedom, 267–270
The Role of Air Power in Various Other
   US Military Operations, 271–280

Economics (E)

E 4. Understands basic features of market
structures and exchanges

Free Market, 197
Airline Domestic Market Share, 198

Science (SC)

Physical Sciences

SC 10. Understands forces and motion

Pressurized Cabin, 176
How the Jet Engine Works, 192–193
Concept of Weight, 193
Mach, 213

Language Arts (LA)

Writing

LA 1. Uses the general skills and strategies
of the writing process

Quick Write, 120, 136, 172, 188, 206, 228, 254
Checkpoints, 135, 169, 187, 203, 227, 253, 281

LA 2. Uses the stylistic and rhetorical aspects
of writing

Quick Write, 120, 136, 172, 188, 206, 228, 254
Checkpoints, 135, 169, 187, 203, 227, 253, 281

LA 3. Uses grammatical and mechanical
conventions in written compositions

Quick Write, 120, 136, 172, 188, 206, 228, 254
Checkpoints, 135, 169, 187, 203, 227, 253, 281

LA 4. Gathers and uses information
for research purposes

Applying Your Learning, 135, 169, 187, 203, 227,
253, 281

Reading

LA 5. Uses the general skills and strategies
of the reading process

Learn About, 120, 136, 172, 188, 206, 228, 254
Checkpoints, 135, 169, 187, 203, 227, 253, 281

LA 6. Uses reading skills and strategies to
understand and interpret a variety of literary texts

Quick Write Story, 120, 136, 172, 188, 206,
228, 254

LA 7. Uses reading skills and strategies
to understand and interpret a variety
of informational texts

Learn About, 120, 136, 172, 188, 206, 228, 254
Checkpoints, 135, 169, 187, 203, 227, 253, 281

Viewing

LA 9. Uses viewing skills and strategies
to understand and interpret visual media

Maps, 144, 158, 214, 215, 216, 220, 224, 230,
232, 244, 245, 247, 256, 258, 164, 274, 277,
279
Photos, 120, 121, 123, 124, 125, 126, 128, 130,
131, 132, 136, 137, 140, 142, 146, 147, 148,
149, 150, 151, 152, 153, 154, 159, 160, 161,
162, 163, 166, 167, 168, 173, 175, 176, 177,
178, 179, 180, 182, 183, 184, 186, 189, 190,
193, 194, 195, 206, 207, 208, 211, 212, 213,
217, 218, 219, 222, 223, 225, 226, 228, 231,
233, 235, 236, 237, 238, 239, 240, 241, 242,
246, 248, 249, 250, 252, 254, 255, 260, 262,
263, 265, 266, 267, 268, 269, 270, 272, 273,
275, 278, 280
Drawings, 191
Diagram, 192, 251
Graph, 198
Chart, 122, 139, 271

Life Skills

Self-Regulation (SR)

SR 1. Sets and manages goals	Flight Paths, 126–127, 128, 160
SR 3. Considers risks	Flight Paths, 126-127, 128, 166, 225, 226, 238 Quick Write Story, 136, 206, 228 Heroes of United 93, 202 CMSgt Richard Etchberger, 239 A1C John Levitow, 240 Maj Robert Undorf, 241 TSgt Wayne Fisk, 242 TSgt John Chapman, 263 SrA Jason Cunningham, 265 CMSgt Kevin Lynn, 269
SR 4. Demonstrates perseverance	Quick Write Story, 120–121, 136, 173–174, 206, 228 The Predecessors of the US Air Force, 122–128 Flight Paths, 126–127, 128, 133, 160, 162, 163, 166, 174, 179, 190, 225, 226, 237, 238 The Tuskegee Airmen and President Harry Truman, 147 The Battle of Britain, 155 CMSgt Richard Etchberger, 239 A1C John Levitow, 240 Maj Robert Undorf, 241 TSgt Wayne Fisk, 242 Gen Daniel James Jr., 242 TSgt John Chapman, 263 SrA Jason Cunningham, 265 CMSgt Kevin Lynn, 269
SR 5. Maintains a healthy self-concept	Flight Paths, 126, 128, 133, 140, 142, 146, 150, 157, 160, 162, 163, 166, 174, 179, 190, 213, 218, 219, 225, 226, 237, 238

Thinking and Reasoning (TR)

TR 5. Applies basic trouble-shooting and problem-solving techniques

Quick Write Story, 120–121, 206, 228
The Predecessors of the US Air Force, 122–128
Flight Paths, 126–127, 128, 166, 225, 226, 238
The Air Force's Path Toward Independence, 132–134
Quick Write Story, 136, 206, 228
Tactical Operations: The Three-Point Plan, 145
The Combat Box Formation and Formation
  Pattern Bombing, 149
The Battle of Britain and Radar, 155
Heroes of United 93, 202
CMSgt Richard Etchberger, 239
A1C John Levitow, 240
Maj Robert Undorf, 241
TSgt Wayne Fisk, 242
TSgt John Chapman, 263
SrA Jason Cunningham, 265
CMSgt Kevin Lynn, 269

TR 6. Applies decision-making techniques

The Predecessors of the US Air Force, 122–128
Flight Paths, 126–127, 128, 166, 168, 225, 226, 238
The Air Force's Path Toward Independence, 132–134
Quick Write Story, 136, 206, 228
Tactical Operations: The Three-Point Plan, 145
Heroes of United 93, 202
CMSgt Richard Etchberger, 239
A1C John Levitow, 240
Maj Robert Undorf, 241
TSgt Wayne Fisk, 242
TSgt John Chapman, 263
SrA Jason Cunningham, 265
CMSgt Kevin Lynn, 269

Working With Others (WO)

WO 1. Contributes to the overall effort of a group

Flight Paths, 126, 128, 133, 140, 142, 146, 150,
  157, 160, 162, 163, 166, 174, 179, 190, 213,
  218, 219, 225, 226, 237, 238
Quick Write Story, 120–121, 136
The Tuskegee Airmen and President
  Harry Truman, 147
The Women's Airforce Service Pilots, 161
Heroes of United 93, 202
CMSgt Richard Etchberger, 239
A1C John Levitow, 240
Maj Robert Undorf, 241
TSgt Wayne Fisk, 242
TSgt John Chapman, 263
SrA Jason Cunningham, 265
CMSgt Kevin Lynn, 269

WO 5. Demonstrates leadership skills

Flight Paths, 126, 128, 133, 140, 142, 146, 150, 157, 160, 162, 163, 166, 174, 179, 190, 213, 218, 219, 225, 226, 237, 238

Quick Write Story, 120–121, 136, 228

The Tuskegee Airmen and President Harry Truman, 147

The Women's Airforce Service Pilots, 161

CMSgt Richard Etchberger, 239

A1C John Levitow, 240

Maj Robert Undorf, 241

TSgt Wayne Fisk, 242

TSgt John Chapman, 263

SrA Jason Cunningham, 265

CMSgt Kevin Lynn, 269

Technology (T)

T 3. Understands the relationships among science, technology, society, and the individual

Quick Write Story, 120–121, 188-189

The Predecessors of the US Air Force, 122–128

Significant Missions Conducted by the Army Air Corps, 131–132

How Air Power Was Developed During World War II, 143–154

The Significance of the Allied Air Campaign, 155–168

Key Developments in Commercial Aircraft, 174–180

Key Developments in Commercial Flight Use, 181

Key Contributions to the Expansion of Commercial Flight, 182–186

Development in General Aviation, 186

The Significance of the Development of the Jet Engine, 191–195

Key Developments in the Commercial Flight Industry, 196–200

The Cold War and How It Began, 209–213

The USAF Role in the Berlin Airlift, 214–220

The Role of Air Power in the Korean War, 221–226

Key Developments in Aircraft, Missile Capability, and Nuclear Capability During the Cold War, 249–252

The Significance of Stealth Aircraft, 255

T 4. Understands the nature
of technological design

Significant Missions Conducted by the
Army Air Corps, 131–132
How Air Power Was Developed During
World War II, 143–154
The Significance of the Allied Air Campaign, 155–168
Rigid Airships, 180
Development in General Aviation, 186
How the Jet Engine Works, 192
Hydrogen Bomb, 229
Key Developments in Aircraft, Missile Capability,
and Nuclear Capability During the Cold War,
249–252
The Significance of Stealth Aircraft, 255
Precision Weapons, 262
Precision Weapons, 268

T 6. Understands the nature and uses
of different forms of technology

Quick Write Story, 120–121, 188-189
The Predecessors of the US Air Force, 122–128
Flight Paths: Wireless Communication
and Bombsight, 128
Significant Missions Conducted by the
Army Air Corps, 131–132
How Air Power Was Developed During
World War II, 143–154
The Significance of the Allied Air Campaign, 155–168
Key Developments in Commercial Aircraft, 174–180
Key Developments in Commercial Flight Use, 181
Key Contributions to the Expansion
of Commercial Flight, 182–186
Developments in General Aviation, 186
The Significance of the Development
of the Jet Engine, 191–195
Key Developments in the Commercial
Flight Industry, 196–200
The USAF Role in the Berlin Airlift, 214–220
The Role of Air Power in the Korean War, 221–226
Significant Aircraft Used by the USAF During
the Vietnam War, 235–236
Key Developments in Aircraft, Missile Capability,
and Nuclear Capability During the Cold War,
249–252
The Significance of Stealth Aircraft, 255

Unit Four: Extending Flight

Correlated to McREL Standards for:

History, Geography, Civics, Science, Language Arts, Life Skills, and Technology

McREL Standards	Unit 4: Extending Flight
History	
Historical Understanding (HU)	
HU 1. Understands and knows how to analyze chronological relationships and patterns	Selected NASA Manned Space Flights, 345–347
HU 2. Understands the historical perspective	Checkpoints, 301, 315, 349, 364 Flight Paths, 304, 306, 314 Quick Write Story, 286, 302, 318, 350
US History (US)	
Era 8—The Great Depression and World War II (1929–1945)	
US 25. Understands the causes and course of World War II, the character of the war at home and abroad, and its reshaping of the US role in world affairs	Robert H. Goddard, 304
Era 9—Postwar United States (1945 to early 1970s)	
US 26. Understands the economic boom and social transformation of post–World War II United States	How the Cold War Led to a Race in Space, 311–314 The Key Steps in the US and Soviet Space Programs, 319–327
US 27. Understands how the Cold War and conflicts in Korea and Vietnam influenced domestic and international politics	Wernher von Braun, 306, 307 How the Cold War Led to a Race in Space, 311–314 The Key Steps in the US and Soviet Space Programs, 319–327
US 29. Understands the struggle for racial and gender equality and for the extension of civil liberties	Col Guion S. Bluford Jr. 318
Era 10—Contemporary United States (1968 to the present)	
US 30. Understands developments in foreign policy and domestic politics between the Nixon and Clinton presidencies	How the Cold War Led to a Race in Space, 311–314 The Significance of the Phrase "One Small Step for [a] Man, One Giant Leap for Mankind," 332–338

US 31. Understands economic, social, and cultural developments in the contemporary United States

The Significance of the Phrase "One Small Step for [a] Man, One Giant Leap for Mankind," 332–338

Key Space Shuttle Missions, 338–348

The Purpose of the International Space Station, 348–349

Current and Anticipated Developments in Manned Air Vehicles, 351–353

Current and Anticipated Developments in Unmanned Systems, 354–355

Current and Anticipated Developments in Cyber Warfare, 356–357

Anticipated Air Force Plans for Integrating Air and Space Operations, 358–360

NASA's Vision for the Future, 361–363

World History (WH)

Era 3—Classical Traditions, Major Religions, and Giant Empires, 1000 BCE–300 CE

WH 11. Understands major global trends from 1000 BCE to 300 CE

The Contributions of Ptolemy, 295

Era 5—Intensified Hemispheric Interactions 1000–1500 CE

WH 19. Understands the maturation of an interregional system of communication, trade, and cultural exchange during a period of Chinese economic power and Islamic expansion

Battle of Kai-fen Fu, 303

WH 25. Understands major global trends from 1000 to 1500 CE

Ulug Bek: Astronomer of the East, 296

The Contributions of Uleg Bek, 297

Hundred Years' War, 303

Era 6—Global Expansion and Encounter, 1450–1770

WH 27. Understands how European society experienced political, economic, and cultural transformations in an age of global intercommunication between 1450 and 1750

Nicolaus Copernicus, 286–288, 298

The Contributions of Copernicus, 297

Johannes Kepler, 298

The Contributions of Kepler, 299

The Contributions of Galileo, 299

Galileo Galilei, 300

Thirty Years' War, 303

Era 7—An Age of Revolutions, 1750–1914

WH 33. Understands the causes and consequences of political revolutions in the late 18th and early 19th centuries

Battles of Seringpatam, 303

Col William Congrave, 303

Era 8—A Half-Century of Crisis and Achievement,
1900–1945

WH 41. Understands the causes and global consequences of World War II	The German V-1 and V-2 Rockets, 305

Era 9—The 20th Century Since 1945:
Promises and Paradoxes

WH 43. Understands how post–World War II reconstruction occurred, new international power relations took shape, and colonial empires broke up	How the Cold War Led to a Race in Space, 311–314 The Key Steps in the US and Soviet Space Programs, 319–327 The Key Steps in the Development of Spacecraft, 327–332 The Significance of the Phrase "One Small Step for [a] Man, One Giant Leap for Mankind," 332–338 Key Space Shuttle Missions, 338–348 The Purpose of the International Space Station, 348–349 Current and Anticipated Developments in Manned Air Vehicles, 351–353 Current and Anticipated Developments in Unmanned Systems, 354–355 Current and Anticipated Developments in Cyber Warfare, 356–357 Anticipated Air Force Plans for Integrating Air and Space Operations, 358–360 NASA's Vision for the Future, 361–363
WH 44. Understands the search for community, stability, and peace in an interdependent world	Wernher von Braun, 306, 307 How the Cold War Led to a Race in Space, 311–314 The Key Steps in the US and Soviet Space Programs, 319–327 The Key Steps in the Development of Spacecraft, 327–332 The Significance of the Phrase "One Small Step for [a] Man, One Giant Leap for Mankind," 332–338 Key Space Shuttle Missions, 338–348 The Purpose of the International Space Station, 348–349 Current and Anticipated Developments in Manned Air Vehicles, 351–353 Current and Anticipated Developments in Unmanned Systems, 354–355 Current and Anticipated Developments in Cyber Warfare, 356–357 Anticipated Air Force Plans for Integrating Air and Space Operations, 358–360 NASA's Vision for the Future, 361–363

WH 45. Understands major global trends since World War II	How the Cold War Led to a Race in Space, 311–314
	The Space Program, 318–349
	The Future of Air and Space Power, 350–364

Geography (G)

The World in Spatial Terms

| G 1. Understands the characteristics and uses of maps, globes, and other geographic tools and technologies | Observation Satellites, 331 |

Human Systems

| G 13. Understands the forces of cooperation and conflict that shape the divisions of Earth's surface | The Key Steps in the US and Soviet Space Programs, 319–327 |

Civics (C)

What Is Government and What Should It Do?

| C 1. Understands ideas about civic life, politics, and government | How NASA was Established, 313–314 |

What Are the Basic Values and Principles of American Democracy?

C 14. Understands issues concerning the disparities between ideals and reality in American political and social life	Col Guion S. Bluford Jr. 318
	Mae Jemison, 339
	Taylor Wang, 339
	Col Eileen Collins, 340
	Sally Ride, 343
	Col Sidney Gutierrez, 343
	Col Ellison Onizuka, 344
	Brig Gen Susan Helms, 348

What Is the Relationship of the United States to Other nations and to World Affairs?

| C 22. Understands how the world is organized politically into nation-states, how nation-states interact with one another, and issues surrounding US foreign policy | The Key Steps in the US and Soviet Space Programs, 319–327 |

Science (SC)

Earth and Space Sciences

SC 3. Understands the composition and structure of the universe and the Earth's place in it	Nicolaus Copernicus, 286–288
	The Objects in the Solar System, 289–295
	The Significant Contributions of Key Early Astronomers, 295–300

Physical Sciences

SC 10. Understands forces and motion	Rockets and Newton's Laws, 308–309 Airframe, 309 Propulsion, 310 Guidance, 311 The Key Steps in the Development of Spacecraft, 327–332 HyperSoar, 353

Language Arts (LA)

Writing

LA 1. Uses the general skills and strategies of the writing process	Quick Write, 286, 302, 318, 350 Checkpoints, 301, 315, 349, 364
LA 2. Uses the stylistic and rhetorical aspects of writing	Quick Write, 286, 302, 318, 350 Checkpoints, 301, 315, 349, 364
LA 3. Uses grammatical and mechanical conventions in written compositions	Quick Write, 286, 302, 318, 350 Checkpoints, 301, 315, 349, 364
LA 4. Gathers and uses information for research purposes	Applying Your Learning, 301, 315, 349, 364

Reading

LA 5. Uses the general skills and strategies of the reading process	Learn About, 286, 302, 318, 350 Checkpoints, 301, 315, 349, 364
LA 6. Uses reading skills and strategies to understand and interpret a variety of literary texts	Quick Write Story, 286, 302, 318, 350
LA 7. Uses reading skills and strategies to understand and interpret a variety of informational texts	Learn About, 286, 302, 318, 350 Checkpoints, 301, 315, 349, 364

Viewing

LA 9. Uses viewing skills and strategies to understand and interpret visual media	Photos, 287, 289, 290, 291, 292, 293, 296, 297, 299, 300, 304, 306, 309, 314, 318, 319, 320, 321, 322, 323, 324, 325, 326, 330, 331, 332, 333, 337, 338, 339, 340, 341, 342, 343, 344, 348, 351, 352, 354, 359, 360, 362, 363 Drawings, 286, 295 Diagram, 288, 309, 310, 328, 329, 336, 353 Chart, 345, 346, 347, 349, 364

Life Skills

Life Work (LW)

LW 2. Uses various information sources, including those of a technical nature, to accomplish specific tasks	The *Apollo 13* Mission and the Effort to Rescue It, 335

Self-Regulation (SR)

SR 1. Sets and manages goals

Robert H. Goddard, 302
The Original Seven Mercury Astronauts, 321–323
The Significance of the Phrase "One Small Step for [a] Man, One Giant Leap for Mankind," 332–338
Key Space Shuttle Missions, 338–348

SR 3. Considers risks

The Contributions of Galileo, 299
The Original Seven Mercury Astronauts, 321–323
The Apollo 1 Disaster and the Lessons Learned From It, 325
The Significance of the Phrase "One Small Step for [a] Man, One Giant Leap for Mankind," 332–338
Key Space Shuttle Missions, 338–348

SR 4. Demonstrates perseverance

The Significant Contributions of Key Early Astronomers, 295–300
Herman Oberth, 305
Col Guion S. Bluford Jr. 318
The Original Seven Mercury Astronauts, 321–323
The Significance of the Phrase "One Small Step for [a] Man, One Giant Leap for Mankind," 332–338
Key Space Shuttle Missions, 338–348

SR 5. Maintains a healthy self-concept

Flight Paths, 304, 306, 314
The Original Seven Mercury Astronauts, 321–323
The Significance of the Phrase "One Small Step for [a] Man, One Giant Leap for Mankind," 332–338
Key Space Shuttle Missions, 338–348

Thinking and Reasoning (TR)

TR 5. Applies basic trouble-shooting and problem-solving techniques

The Significant Contributions of Key Early Astronomers, 295–300
Robert H. Goddard, 302, 304
The Original Seven Mercury Astronauts, 321–323
The Significance of the Phrase "One Small Step for [a] Man, One Giant Leap for Mankind," 332–338
Key Space Shuttle Missions, 338-348

TR 6. Applies decision-making techniques

The Significant Contributions of Key Early Astronomers, 295–300
The Original Seven Mercury Astronauts, 321–323
The Significance of the Phrase "One Small Step for [a] Man, One Giant Leap for Mankind," 332–338
Key Space Shuttle Missions, 338–348

Working With Others (WO)

WO 1. Contributes to the overall effort of a group	Flight Paths, 304, 306, 314 Col Guion S. Bluford Jr. 318 The Original Seven Mercury Astronauts, 321–323 The Significance of the Phrase "One Small Step for [a] Man, One Giant Leap for Mankind," 332–338 Key Space Shuttle Missions, 338–348
WO 5. Demonstrates leadership skills	Flight Paths, 304, 306, 314 Col Guion S. Bluford Jr. 318 The Original Seven Mercury Astronauts, 321–323 The Significance of the Phrase "One Small Step for [a] Man, One Giant Leap for Mankind," 332–338 Key Space Shuttle Missions, 338–348

Technology (T)

T 3. Understands the relationships among science, technology, society, and the individual	The Significant Contributions of Key Early Astronomers, 295-300 How Developments in Rocketry Made Space Exploration Possible, 303-311 How the Cold War Led to a Race in Space, 311-314 The Key Steps in the US and Soviet Space Programs, 319-327 The Key Steps in the Development of Spacecraft, 327-332 The Significance of the Phrase "One Small Step for [a] Man, One Giant Leap for Mankind," 332-338 Key Space Shuttle Missions, 338-348 The Purpose of the International Space Station, 348-349 Current and Anticipated Developments in Manned Air Vehicles, 351-353 Current and Anticipated Developments in Unmanned Systems, 354-355 Current and Anticipated Developments in Cyber Warfare, 356-357 Anticipated Air Force Plans for Integrating Air and Space Operations, 358-360 NASA's Vision for the Future, 361-363

T 4. Understands the nature of technological design

Telescope, 299

How Developments in Rocketry Made Space Exploration Possible, 303–311

How the Cold War Led to a Race in Space, 311–314

The Key Steps in the Development of Spacecraft, 327–332

The Significance of the Phrase "One Small Step for [a] Man, One Giant Leap for Mankind," 332–338

Key Space Shuttle Missions, 338–348

The Purpose of the International Space Station, 348–349

Current and Anticipated Developments in Manned Air Vehicles, 351–353

Current and Anticipated Developments in Unmanned Systems, 354–355

Current and Anticipated Developments in Cyber Warfare, 356–357

Anticipated Air Force Plans for Integrating Air and Space Operations, 358–360

T 6. Understands the nature and uses of different forms of technology

The Contributions of Galileo, 299

How Developments in Rocketry Made Space Exploration Possible, 303–311

How the Cold War Led to a Race in Space, 311–314

The Key Steps in the US and Soviet Space Programs, 319–327

The Key Steps in the Development of Spacecraft, 327–332

The Significance of the Phrase "One Small Step for [a] Man, One Giant Leap for Mankind," 332–338

Key Space Shuttle Missions, 338–348

The Purpose of the International Space Station, 348–349

Current and Anticipated Developments in Manned Air Vehicles, 351–353

Current and Anticipated Developments in Unmanned Systems, 354–355

Current and Anticipated Developments in Cyber Warfare, 356–357

Anticipated Air Force Plans for Integrating Air and Space Operations, 358–360

NASA's Vision for the Future, 361–363

Unit 1

CHAPTER 1

LESSON 1—Discovering Flight

Chisolm, DeShana E., Mitchell, Naomi L., & Roberson, Patricia Q. (Eds). (2002). *Aerospace Science: Frontiers of Aviation History* (Second ed.). Maxwell Air Force Base, AL: Air Force Officer Accessions and Training Schools.

Leonardo da Vinci. (n.d.). American Institute of Aeronautics and Astronautics. Retrieved 14 November 2006 from http://www.aiaa.org/content.cfm?pageid=425

Millspaugh, Ben. (2000). *Aerospace Dimensions: Module 1, Introduction to Flight.* Maxwell Air Force Base, AL: Civil Air Patrol National Headquarters.

Montgomery, Jeff (Ed.). (2000). *Aerospace: The Journey of Flight.* Maxwell Air Force Base, AL: Civil Air Patrol National Headquarters.

LESSON 2—The Early Days of Flight

Chisolm, DeShana E., Mitchell, Naomi L., & Roberson, Patricia Q. (Eds.). (2002). *Aerospace Science: Frontiers of Aviation History* (Second ed.). Maxwell Air Force Base, AL: Air Force Officer Accessions and Training Schools.

Chivalette, William I. & Hayes, W. Parker, Jr. (n.d.). *Airmen Heritage Series: Balloons on High.* Suitland, MD: Airmen Memorial Museum.

Millspaugh, Ben. (2000). *Aerospace Dimensions: Module 1, Introduction to Flight.* Maxwell Air Force Base, AL: Civil Air Patrol National Headquarters.

Montgomery, Jeff (Ed.). (2000). *Aerospace: The Journey of Flight.* Maxwell Air Force Base, AL: Civil Air Patrol National Headquarters.

Unit 2

CHAPTER 2

LESSON 1—The Wright Brothers

Bartlett, John. (2002). *Bartlett's Familiar Quotations* (17th ed.). Boston: Little, Brown & Company.

Chisolm, DeShana E., Mitchell, Naomi L., & Roberson, Patricia Q. (Eds.). (2002). *Aerospace Science: Frontiers of Aviation History* (Second ed.). Maxwell Air Force Base, AL: Air Force Officer Accessions and Training Schools.

Fact Sheets: Maj Gen Benjamin D. Foulois. National Museum of the USAF. Retrieved 27 November 2006 fromhttp://www.nationalmuseum.af.mil/factsheets/factsheet.asp?id=934

Haulman, Daniel L. (2003). *One Hundred Years of Flight: USAF Chronology of Significant Air and Space Events 1903–2002.* Retrieved 28 November 2006 from http://afhra.maxwell.af.mil/chronologyofflight.pdf

McNulty, Bernard C. (Ed.) (1997). *Winged Shield, Winged Sword: A History of the U.S. Air Force, Vol. I, 1907–1950.* Washington, DC: United States Air Force.

Millspaugh, Ben. (2000). Aerospace Dimensions, Introduction to Flight, Module 1. Maxwell AFB, AL: National Headquarters, Civil Air Patrol.

Montgomery, Jeff (Ed.). (2000). *Aerospace: The Journey of Flight.* Maxwell Air Force Base, AL: Civil Air Patrol National Headquarters.

The Wright Brothers: The Invention of the Aerial Age. (2006). National Air and Space Museum. Retrieved 28 November 2006 from http://www.nasm.si.edu/wrightbrothers/index.cfm

LESSON 2—Developing Aircraft

Baker, Richard F. (2003). *Glenn H. Curtiss.* US Centennial of Flight Commission. Retrieved 2 December 2006 from http://www.centennialofflight.gov/essay/Explorers_Record_Setters_and_Daredevils/Curtiss/EX3.htm

Black Wings: African American Pioneer Aviators. (2002). National Air and Space Museum Retrieved 4 December 2006 from http://www.nasm.si.edu/blackwings/

Chisolm, DeShana E., Mitchell, Naomi L., & Roberson, Patricia Q. (Eds.). (2002). *Aerospace Science: Frontiers of Aviation History* (Second ed.). Maxwell Air Force Base, AL: Air Force Officer Accessions and Training Schools.

Chivalette, William I. (1 July 2005). Enlisted History. In AFPAM36-2241V1, *Promotion Fitness Examination.* US Air Force.

Chivalette, William I. (n.d.). *Vernon L. Burge: First Enlisted Pilot.* The Airmen Heritage Series. Suitland, MD: Airmen Memorial Museum.

Haulman, Daniel L. (2003). *One Hundred Years of Flight: USAF Chronology of Significant Air and Space Events 1903–2002.* Retrieved 12 December 2006 from http://afhra.maxwell.af.mil/chronologyofflight.pdf

Montgomery, Jeff. (Ed.). (2000). *Aerospace: The Journey of Flight.* Maxwell Air Force Base, AL: Civil Air Patrol National Headquarters.

Women in Aviation and Space History. (n.d.). National Air and Space Museum. Retrieved 4 December 2006 from http://www.nasm.si.edu/research/aero/women_aviators/womenavsp.htm

LESSON 3—Air Power in World War I

Centennial of Flight. (2003). US Centennial of Flight Commission. Retrieved 6 December 2006 from www.centennialofflight.gov/essay/Air_Power/rickenbacker/AP9.htm

Chisolm, DeShana E., Mitchell, Naomi L., & Roberson, Patricia Q. (Eds.). (2002). *Aerospace Science: Frontiers of Aviation History* (Second ed.). Maxwell Air Force Base, AL: Air Force Officer Accessions and Training Schools.

Chivalette, William I. (2005). Corporal Eugene Jacques Bullard: First Black American Fighter Pilot. Retrieved 12 December 2006 from http://www.airpower.maxwell.af.mil/apjinternational/apj-s/2005/3tri05/chivaletteeng.html

Chivalette, William I. (1 July 2005). Enlisted History. In AFPAM36-2241V1, *Promotion Fitness Examination*. US Air Force.

The Great War and the Shaping of the 20th Century. (1996–2004). PBS and KCET. Retrieved 7 December 2006 from www.pbs.org/greatwar

Lauderbaugh, Lt Col George M. (n.d.). The Air Battle of St. Mihiel: Air Campaign Planning Process Background Paper. Retrieved 8 December 2006 from http://www.au.af.mil/au/awc/awcgate/ww1/stmihiel/stmihiel.htm

Manfred Richthofen. (1998). In *The New Encyclopedia Britannica* (Vol. 10, Macropaedia). Chicago: Encyclopaedia Britannica Inc.

Montgomery, Jeff. (Ed.). (2000). *Aerospace: The Journey of Flight*. Maxwell Air Force Base, AL: Civil Air Patrol National Headquarters.

Royal Air Force. (2003). Royal Air Force History. Retrieved 8 December 2006 from http://www.raf.mod.uk/rafhome.html

World War I: Western Front: 1915–1917—Stalemate and Western Front: 1918—The Year of Decision. (1963). In *The Encyclopedia Americana* (Vol. 29). New York: Encyclopedia Americana Corporation.

CHAPTER 3

LESSON 1—The Barnstormers

Air Markers. *Time*, Aug. 24, 1936. Retrieved 18 December 2006 from http://www.time.com/time/magazine/article/0,9171,756537,00.html

Bessie Coleman. (n.d.). Women in History. Lakewood, OH: Lakewood Public Library. Retrieved 16 December 2006 from http://www.lkwdpl.org/wihohio/cole-bes.htm

Chant, Christopher. (2002). *A Century of Triumph: The History of Aviation*. New York: The Free Press, a division of Simon and Schuster.

Chisolm, DeShana E., Mitchell, Naomi L., & Roberson, Patricia Q. (Eds.). (2002). *Aerospace Science: Frontiers of Aviation History* (2nd. ed.). Maxwell Air Force Base, AL: Air Force Officer Accessions and Training Schools.

Floyd Bennett, Warrant Officer, United States Navy. (n.d.). Arlington National Cemetery. Retrieved 17 December 2006 from http://www.arlingtoncemetery.net/bennettf.htm

Goerler, Raimund, and Cullather, Richard. (n.d.). Admiral Richard E. Byrd, 1888–1957. The Byrd Polar Research Center at The Ohio State University. Retrieved 14 December 2006 from http://www-bprc.mps.ohio-state.edu/gpl/AboutByrd/AboutByrd.html

Johnson, Janis. (2003). Heroes of the Sky. *Humanities*, September–October 2003, (Vol 24, No. 5). Retrieved 14 December 2006 from http://www.neh.gov/news/humanities/2003-09/heroes.html

Montgomery, Jeff. (Ed.). (2000). *Aerospace: The Journey of Flight*. Maxwell Air Force Base, AL: Civil Air Patrol National Headquarters.

Onkst, David H. (n.d.). Barnstormers. U.S. Centennial of Flight Commission. Retrieved 27 December 2006 from http://www.centennialofflight.gov/essay/ Explorers_Record_Setters_and_Daredevils/barnstormers/EX12.htm

Rummerman, Judy. (n.d.). The Curtiss JN-4 "Jenny." U.S. Centennial of Flight Commission. Retrieved 27 December 2006 from http://www.centennialofflight. gov/essay/Aerospace/Jenny/Aero3.htm

LESSON 2—Flight Goes Mainstream

Charnov, Bruce H. (2003). Amelia Earhart, John M. Miller and the First Transcontinental Autogiro Flight in 1931. Retrieved 15 January 2007 from http://www.aviation-history.com/airmen/earhart-Autogiro.htm

Chisolm, DeShana E., Mitchell, Naomi L., & Roberson, Patricia Q. (Eds.). (2002). *Aerospace Science: Frontiers of Aviation History* (2nd ed.). Maxwell Air Force Base, AL: Air Force Officer Accessions and Training Schools.

Chivalette, William J. (2005). *Sergeant William Charles Ocker: the Army's Third Enlisted Pilot.* Maxwell AFB, AL: Airmen Memorial Museum.

Haulman, Daniel L. (2003.). *One Hundred Years of Flight; USAF Chronology of Significant Air and Space Events, 1903–2002.* Maxwell Air Force Base, AL: Air University Press.

Milestones of Flight: Ryan NYP "Spirit of St. Louis." (n.d.). National Air and Space Museum. Retrieved 26 December 2006 from http://www.nasm.si.edu/exhibitions/ gal100/stlouis.html

Montgomery, Jeff. (Ed.). (2000). *Aerospace: The Journey of Flight.* Maxwell Air Force Base, AL: Civil Air Patrol National Headquarters.

Nye, Carol A. A. (2005). *Katherine Cheung, Aviatrix.* Retrieved 20 December 2006 from http://www.publicartinla.com/Downtown/Chinatown/cheung.html.

Rummerman, Keri. (n.d.). Amelia Earhart. U.S. Centennial of Flight Commission. Retrieved 15 January 2007 from http://www.centennialofflight.gov/essay/ Explorers_Record_Setters_and_Daredevils/earhart/EX29.htm

Yellowbridge.com. (n.d.). Famous Chinese-Americans in Aviation and Aerospace. Retrieved 20 December 2006 from http://www.yellowbridge.com/people/ aviation.html#cheung and http://www.yellowbridge.com/people/firsts.html

LESSON 3—Commercial Flight, Airmail, and Helicopters

Boeing History: Chronology. (n.d.). The Boeing Company. Retrieved 27 December 2006 from http://www.boeing.com/history/chronology/chron03.html

Boeing History: Model 40 Commercial Transport. (n.d.). The Boeing Company. Retrieved 27 December 2006 from http://www.boeing.com/history/boeing/ 40a.html

Chasing the Sun. (2005). Public Broadcasting Service: KCET. Retrieved 20 April 2006 from http://www.pbs.org/kcet/chasingthesun/innovators/wboeing.html

Chisolm, DeShana E., Mitchell, Naomi L., & Roberson, Patricia Q. (Eds.). (2002). *Aerospace Science: Frontiers of Aviation History.* (2nd ed.). Maxwell Air Force Base, AL: Air Force Officer Accessions and Training Schools.

Douglas C-32. (n.d.). National Museum of the USAF. Retrieved 9 January 9, 2007 from http://www.nationalmuseum.af.mil/factsheets/factsheet.asp?id=3292

Haulman, Daniel L. (2003). *One Hundred Years of Flight; USAF Chronology of Significant Air and Space Events, 1903–2002.* Maxwell Air Force Base, AL: Air University Press.

Igor I. Sikorsky. (n.d.). Igor I. Sikorsky Historical Archives. Retrieved 28 December 2006 from http://www.sikorskyarchives.com/siksky2.htm.

Igor Sikorsky, Industrialist/Inventor. (n.d.). National Aviation Hall of Fame. Retrieved 28 December 2006 from http://nationalaviation.blade6.donet.com/components/content_manager_v02/view_nahf/htdocs/menu_ps.asp?NodeID=666 001144&group_ID=1134656385&Parent_ID=-1

Lombardi, Mike. (n.d.). Century of Flight, 1911–1920: WWI and the Birth of Boeing. Retrieved 27 December 2006 from http://www.boeing.com/news/frontiers/archive/2003/march/i_history.html

Montgomery, Jeff. (Ed.). (2000). *Aerospace: The Journey of Flight.* Maxwell Air Force Base, AL: Civil Air Patrol National Headquarters.

U.S. Centennial of Flight Commission. (2005). *Igor Sikorsky: VS-300.* Retrieved 26 December 2006 from http://www.centennialofflight.gov/essay/Rotary/Sikorsky_VS300/HE8.htm

U.S. Centennial of Flight Commission. (n.d.). *Civil and Commercial Helicopters.* Retrieved 27 December 2006 from http://www.centennialofflight.gov/essay/Rotary/commercial/HE10.htm

When the Going Was Good: The Golden Age of Commercial Air Travel. (n.d.). National Air and Space Museum. Retrieved 22 December 2006 from http://www.nasm.si.edu/exhibition/archives/clipper/clipper.htm

William Boeing, 1881–1956, American Inventor. (n.d.). HistoryCentral.com. Retrieved 27 December 2006 from http://www.historycentral.com/Bio/people/boeing.html

Unit 3

CHAPTER 4

LESSON 1—The Army Air Corps

Air Force History. (1 July 2001.). In AFPAM 36-2241V1, *Promotion Fitness Examination.* US Air Force.

Brigadier General William "Billy" Mitchell. (n.d.). Air Force Link. Retrieved 30 December 2006 from http://www.af.mil/history/person.asp?dec=&pid=123006464

Boyne, Walter J. (February 2003). Foulois. *Air Force Magazine.* Retrieved 2 January 2007 from http://www.afa.org/magazine/feb2003/02foulois03.pdf

Chisolm, DeShana E., Mitchell, Naomi L., & Roberson, Patricia Q. (Eds.). (2002). *Aerospace Science: Frontiers of Aviation History.* (2nd ed.). Maxwell Air Force Base, AL: Air Force Officer Accessions and Training Schools.

Chivalette, William I. (1 July 2005). Enlisted History. In AFPAM 36-2241V1, *Promotion Fitness Examination.* US Air Force.

Chivalette, William I. (n.d.). *Nero the Pioneer.* Suitland, MD: Airmen Memorial Museum.

Court Martial. *Time*, Nov. 2 1925. Retrieved 1 January 2007 from
http://www.time.com/time/magazine/article/0,9171,728580-2,00.html

Gen. Billy Mitchell. (n.d.). National Museum of the USAF. Retrieved 30 December
2006 from http://www.nationalmuseum.af.mil/factsheets/factsheet.asp?id=739

Haulman, Daniel L. (2003). *One Hundred Years of Flight: USAF Chronology of Significant
Air and Space Events, 1903–2002.* Maxwell Air Force Base, AL: Air University Press.

Montgomery, Jeff. (Ed.). (2000). *Aerospace: The Journey of Flight.* Maxwell Air Force
Base, AL: Civil Air Patrol National Headquarters.

Thomas, Maj William C. (30 January 2004). The Cultural Identity of the
United States Air Force. *Air Force Magazine.* Retrieved 2 January 2007 from
http://www.airpower.au.af.mil/airchronicles/cc/thomas.html

LESSON 2—World War II

The Afrocentric Experience. (n.d.). Blacks in Aviation. Retrieved 11 January 2007
from http://www.swagga.com/index.shtml

American Experience: Fly Girls. (1998). PBS Online. Retrieved 5 January 2007
from http://www.pbs.org/wgbh/amex/flygirls/index.html

American Experience: Race for the Superbomb. (1999). PBS Online. Retrieved
11 January 2007 from http://www.pbs.org/wgbh/amex/bomb/index.html

Assets and Liabilities. (1944). National Museum of the USAF. Retrieved 9 January
2007 from http://www.nationalmuseum.af.mil/factsheets/factsheet.asp?id=1688

B-29 Superfortress. (n.d.). Retrieved 16 January 2007 from http://www.boeing.com/
history/boeing/b29.html

Bednarek, Janet (Ed.). (2004). *Generations of Cheverons.* Washington, DC: Air Force
History and Museums Program, USAF.

Bell P-39Q Airacobra. (n.d.). National Museum of the USAF. Retrieved 9 January
2007 from http://www.nationalmuseum.af.mil/factsheets/factsheet.asp?id=477

Black Wings: African American Pioneer Aviators. (2002). National Air & Space
Museum. Retrieved 11 January 2007 from http://www.nasm.si.edu/blackwings/
index.html

Boeing B-29 "Enola Gay." (n.d.). National Museum of the USAF. Retrieved
11 January 2007 from http://www.nationalmuseum.af.mil/factsheets/
factsheet.asp?id=2549

Chief Master Sergeant of the Air Force Paul W. Airey. (n.d.). *Air Force Link.*
Retrieved 11 January 2007 from http://www.af.mil/history/person_print.asp?
storyID=123006506

Chisolm, DeShana E., Mitchell, Naomi L., & Roberson, Patricia Q. (Eds.). (2002).
Aerospace Science: Frontiers of Aviation History (2nd ed.). Maxwell Air Force Base,
AL: Air Force Officer Accessions and Training Schools.

Chivalette, William I. Enlisted History. In AFPAM36-2241V1, *Promotion Fitness
Examination.* 1 July 2005. US Air Force.

Cole, Hugh M. (1965). *The Ardennes: The Battle of the Bulge.* Washington, DC: Office
of the Chief of Military History, Department of the Army. Retrieved 23 January
2007 from http://www.army.mil/cmh-pg/books/wwii/7-8/7-8_25.htm#p660

Consolidated B-24D Liberator. (n.d.). National Museum of the USAF. Retrieved 9 January 2007 from http://www.nationalmuseum.af.mil/factsheets/factsheet.asp?id=494

Curtiss P-40E Warhawk. (n.d.). National Museum of the USAF. Retrieved 9 January 2007 from http://www.nationalmuseum.af.mil/factsheets/factsheet.asp?id=478

Desegregation of the Armed Forces. (n.d.). Truman Presidential Museum & Library. Retrieved 11 January 2007 from http://www.trumanlibrary.org/whistlestop/study_collections/desegregation/large/index.php?action=chronology

Doolittle Tokyo Raiders. (n.d.). National Museum of the USAF. Retrieved 9 January 2007 from http://www.nationalmuseum.af.mil/factsheets/factsheet.asp?id=1514

Douglas C-47D Skytrain. (n.d.). National Museum of the USAF. Retrieved 9 January 2007 from http://www.nationalmuseum.af.mil/factsheets/factsheet.asp?id=502

Feltus, Pamela. (n.d.). The Ninety-Nines. Retrieved 12 January 2007 from http://www.centennialofflight.gov/essay/Explorers_Record_Setters_and_Daredevils/99s/EX21.htm

Gen Carl Spaatz. (n.d.). National Museum of the USAF. Retrieved 11 January 2007 from http://www.nationalmuseum.af.mil/factsheets/factsheet.asp?id=1131

Gen Curtis E. LeMay. (n.d.). National Museum of the USAF. Retrieved 11 January 2007 from http://www.nationalmuseum.af.mil/factsheets/factsheet.asp?id=1115

General Henry H. "Hap" Arnold. (2006). Retrieved 4 April 2007 from http://www.af.mil/history/person.asp?dec=&pid=123006476

Lieutenant General Pete Quesada. (n.d.). *Air Force Link*. Retrieved 11 January 2007 from http://www.af.mil/history/person.asp?dec=&pid=123006493

Lockheed P-38L Lightning. (n.d.). National Museum of the USAF. Retrieved 9 January 2007 from http://www.nationalmuseum.af.mil/factsheets/factsheet.asp?id=495

Maj Glenn Miller. (n.d.). Retrieved 12 January 2007 from http://www.arlingtoncemetery.org/historical_information/glenn_miller.html

Major Arthur T. Chin, Chinese Air Force. (n.d.). Airpower Heritage Museum. Retrieved 11 January 2007 from http://www.airpowermuseum.org/exhibits/acahof/assets/pdf/1997/chin.pdf.

Martin B-26G Marauder. (n.d.). National Museum of the USAF. Retrieved 9 January 2007 from http://www.nationalmuseum.af.mil/factsheets/factsheet.asp?id=500

Master Sergeant Henry E. "Red" Erwin. (n.d.). *Air Force Link*. Retrieved 11 January 2007 from http://www.af.mil/history/person.asp?dec=&pid=123006484

Montgomery, Jeff. (Ed.). (2000). *Aerospace: The Journey of Flight*. Maxwell Air Force Base, AL: Civil Air Patrol National Headquarters.

North American B-25B Mitchell. (n.d.). National Museum of the USAF. Retrieved 9 January 2007 from http://www.nationalmuseum.af.mil/factsheets/factsheet.asp?id=476

North American P-51D Mustang. (n.d.). National Museum of the USAF. Retrieved 9 January 2007 from http://www.nationalmuseum.af.mil/factsheets/factsheet.asp?id=513

The Ninety-Nines: Who Are the Ninety Nines? (2005). The Ninety-Nines Inc. Retrieved 15 January 2007 from http://www.ninety-nines.org/

O'Brien, Joseph V. (n.d.). World War II: Combatants and Casualties (1937–45). Retrieved 16 January 2007 from http://web.jjay.cuny.edu/~jobrien/index.html

Proctor, Annie. (n.d.). Enlisted Pilots: Soaring High From the Lower Ranks. Retrieved 12 January 2007 from http://www.af.mil/news/airman/1296/fly.htm

Tuskegee Airmen. (n.d.). National Museum of the USAF. Retrieved 11 January 2007 from http://www.nationalmuseum.af.mil/factsheets/factsheet.asp?id=1356

USS Arizona Memorial. (n.d.). National Park Service, Department of the Interior. Retrieved 12 January 2007 from http://www.nps.gov/archive/usar/ExtendWeb1.html

Wells, Mark K. (1988). The Human Element and Air Combat: Some Napoleonic Comparisons. *Airpower Journal*, Spring 1988. Retrieved 9 January 2007 from http://www.airpower.maxwell.af.mil/airchronicles/apj/apj88/wells.html

CHAPTER 5

LESSON 1—The Propeller Era in Commercial Flight

The Beginnings of Commercial Transatlantic Services. (n.d.). U.S. Centennial of Flight Commission. Retrieved 17 January 2007 from http://www.centennialofflight.gov/essay/Commercial_Aviation/atlantic_route/Tran4.htm

A Brief History of Aviation. (n.d.). Air Transport Association. Retrieved 18 January 2007 from http://members.airlines.org/about/d.aspx?nid=7946

A Brief History of the Federal Aviation Administration. (n.d.). Federal Aviation Administration. Retrieved 17 January 2007 from http://www.faa.gov/about/history/brief_history/#3

American Airlines. (n.d.). U.S. Centennial of Flight Commission. Retrieved 17 January 2007 from http://www.centennialofflight.gov/essay/Commercial_Aviation/American/Tran15.htm

Chasing the Sun: Constellation. (n.d.). PBS and KCET. Retrieved 18 January 2007 from http://www.pbs.org/kcet/chasingthesun/planes/constellation.html

Chasing the Sun: Howard Hughes. (n.d.). Public Broadcasting Service: KCET. Retrieved 18 January 2007 from http://www.pbs.org/kcet/chasingthesun/innovators/hhughes.html

Chisolm, DeShana E., Mitchell, Naomi L., & Roberson, Patricia Q. (Eds). (2002). *Aerospace Science: Frontiers of Aviation History* (2nd. ed.). Maxwell Air Force Base, AL: Air Force Officer Accessions and Training Schools.

Commercial Flight in the 1930s. (n.d.). U.S. Centennial of Flight Commission. Retrieved 21 January 2007 from http://www.centennialofflight.gov/essay/Commercial_Aviation/passenger_xperience/Tran2.htm

Donald Wills Douglas Sr. (n.d.). Boeing Company. Retrieved 18 January 2007 from http://www.boeing.com/history/mdc/douglas.htm

Eastern Airlines. (n.d.). U.S. Centennial of Flight Commission. Retrieved 17 January 2007 from http://www.centennialofflight.gov/essay/Commercial_Aviation/EasternAirlines/Tran13.htm

Haulman, Daniel L. (2003). *One Hundred Years of Flight: USAF Chronology of Significant Air and Space Events, 1903–2002.* Maxwell Air Force Base, AL: Air University Press.

A History of Commercial Air Freight. (n.d.). U.S. Centennial of Flight Commission. Retrieved 17 January 2007 from http://www.centennialofflight.gov/essay/Commercial_Aviation/AirFreight/Tran10.htm

Montgomery, Jeff (Ed.). (2000). *Aerospace: The Journey of Flight.* Maxwell Air Force Base, AL: Civil Air Patrol National Headquarters.

Simonsen, Eric. (n. d.). Howard Hughes, Aviation Legend. Retrieved 18 January 2007 from http://www.boeing.com/news/frontiers/archive/2005/february/i_history.html.

Trans World Airlines (TWA). (n.d.). U.S. Centennial of Flight Commission. Retrieved 17 January 2007 from http://www.centennialofflight.gov/essay/Commercial_Aviation/TWA/Tran14.htm

United Airlines. (n.d.). U.S. Centennial of Flight Commission. Retrieved 17 January 2007 2006 from http://www.centennialofflight.gov/essay/Commercial_Aviation/UnitedAirlines/Tran16.htm

William "Jack" Frye: Entrepreneur/Record Setter. (n. d.). National Aviation Hall of Fame. Retrieved 21 January 2007 from http://nationalaviation.blade6.donet.com/components/content_manager_v02/view_nahf/htdocs/menu_ps.asp?NodeID=-1915794956&group_ID=1134656385&Parent_ID=-1

LESSON 2—The Jet Era in Commercial Flight

A Brief History of the Federal Aviation Administration. (n.d.). Federal Aviation Administration. Retrieved 23 January 2007 from http://www.faa.gov/about/history/brief_history/

Deregulation and Its Consequences. (n.d.). U.S. Centennial of Flight Commission. Retrieved 23 January 2007 from http://www.centennialofflight.gov/essay/Commercial_Aviation/Dereg/Tran8.htm

The Era of Commercial Jets. (n.d.). U.S. Centennial of Flight Commission. Retrieved 23 January 2007 from http://www.centennialofflight.gov/essay/Commercial_Aviation/Jet_Era/Tran7.htm

Juan Trippe. (n.d.). U.S. Centennial of Flight Commission. Retrieved 23 January 2007 from http://www.centennialofflight.gov/essay/Dictionary/Trippe/DI128.htm

Montgomery, Jeff. (Ed.). (2000). *Aerospace: The Journey of Flight.* Maxwell Air Force Base, AL: Civil Air Patrol National Headquarters.

The 9/11 Commission Report. (2004). National Commission on Terrorist Attacks Upon the United States. Retrieved 23 January 2007 from http://www.9-11commission.gov/report/911Report.pdf

The Opening of the Jet Era. (n.d.). U.S. Centennial of Flight Commission. Retrieved 23 January 2007 from http://www.centennialofflight

TransStats: The Intermodal Transportation Database. (n.d.). Bureau of Transportation Statistics. Retrieved 27 January 2007 from http://www.transtats.bts.gov/

We Weren't Just Airborne Yesterday. (2006). Southwest Airlines. Retrieved 27 January 2007 from http://www.southwest.com/about_swa/airborne.html

Wilber, Del Quentin. (2007). A Crash's Improbable Impact: '82 Air Florida Tragedy Led to Broad Safety Reforms. *The Washington Post* (12 January 2007), p A1.

CHAPTER 6

LESSON 1—Air Force Beginnings Through the Korean War

B-2 Spirit. (June 2006). Air Combat Command: Office of Public Affairs. Retrieved 25 January 2007 from the Air Force Link at http://www.af.mil/factsheets/factsheet.asp?fsID=82

Arlington National Cemetery. (11 December 2006). James Jabara: Colonel, United States Air Force. Retrieved 29 January 2007 from http://www.arlingtoncemetery.net/jabara.htm

Berlin "Candy Bomber." (n.d.). Hill Aerospace Museum, Hill AFB, Utah. Retrieved 29 January 2007 from http://www.hill.af.mil/museum/history/candy.htm

Capt Manuel "Pete" Fernandez Jr. (n.d.). National Museum of the USAF. Retrieved 29 January 2007 from http://www.nationalmuseum.af.mil/factsheets/factsheet.asp?fsID=1082.

Chisolm, DeShana E., Mitchell, Naomi L., & Roberson, Patricia Q. (Eds.). (2002). *Aerospace Science: Frontiers of Aviation History* (2nd ed.). Maxwell Air Force Base, AL: Air Force Officer Accessions and Training Schools.

Chivalette, William I. Enlisted History. In AFPAM36-2241V1, *Promotion Fitness Examination*. 1 July 2005. US Air Force.

Col John H. Glenn Jr. (n.d.). National Museum of the USAF. Retrieved 29 January 2007 from http://www.nationalmuseum.af.mil/factsheets/factsheet_print.asp?fsID=1099&page=1

Fast Attacks and Boomers: Submarines in the Cold War. (2000). The National Museum of American History. Retrieved 24 January 2007 from http://americanhistory.si.edu/subs/intro/index.html

Garber, Steve. (18 September 1997). Charles E. (Chuck) Yeager. National Air and Space Administration History Office. Retrieved 25 January 2007 from http://www.hq.nasa.gov/office/pao/History/x1/chuck.html

Leuchtenburg, William E., and the Editors of Time-Life Books. (1977). *The Life History of the United States: The Age of Change* (Vol. 12: From 1945). Alexandria, VA: Time-Life Books Inc.

Lt Col George A. Davis Jr. (n.d.). National Museum of the USAF. Retrieved 29 January 2007 from http://www.nationalmuseum.af.mil/factsheets/factsheet.asp?id=1073

Montgomery, Jeff. (Ed.). (2000). *Aerospace: The Journey of Flight*. Maxwell Air Force Base, AL: Civil Air Patrol National Headquarters.

North American P-51D Mustang. (n.d.). National Museum of the USAF. Retrieved 29 January 2007 from http://www.nationalmuseum.af.mil/factsheets/factsheet.asp?id=513

William T. Tunner. (n.d.). *Air and Space Power Journal of Air University*. Retrieved 26 January 2007 from http://www.airpower.maxwell.af.mil/airchronicles/cc/tunn.html

LESSON 2—The Vietnam War and Other Military Operations

AC-130H/U Gunship. (October 2005). Air Force Special Operations Command, Public Affairs Office. Retrieved 4 February 2007 from http://www.af.mil/factsheets/factsheet_print.asp?fsID=71&page=1

Andradé, Dale J. & Conboy, Kenneth. (1999). The Secret Side of the Tonkin Gulf Incident. Naval History, August 1999. Retrieved 7 February 2007 from http://www.usni.org/navalhistory/Articles99/NHandrade.htm

Bell X-5. (n.d.). National Museum of the USAF. Retrieved 4 February 2007 from http://www.nationalmuseum.af.mil/factsheets/factsheet.asp?id=630

Bell XGAM-63 Rascal. (n.d.). National Museum of the USAF. Retrieved 4 February 2007 from http://www.nationalmuseum.af.mil/factsheets/factsheet.asp?id=601

Boyne, Walter J. (March 1999). El Dorado Canyon. Retrieved 4 February 2007 from http://www.afa.org/magazine/March1999/0399canyon.asp

Camps, Charles Tustin. (21 December 2006). Operation Eagle Claw: The Iran Hostage Rescue Mission. Retrieved 4 February 2007 from http://www.airpower.maxwell.af.mil/apjinternational/apj-s/2006/3tri06/kampseng.html

Capt Lance P. Sijan. (n.d.). *Air Force Print News Today*. Retrieved 5 February 2007 from http://www.af.mil/mediacenter/transcripts/story_print.asp?storyID=123009132

Chisolm, DeShana E., Mitchell, Naomi L., & Roberson, Patricia Q. (Eds.). (2002). *Aerospace Science: Frontiers of Aviation History* (2nd ed.). Maxwell Air Force Base, AL: Air Force Officer Accessions and Training Schools.

Chivalette, William I. (1 July 2005). Enlisted History. In AFPAM36-2241V1, *Promotion Fitness Examination.*

College of Aerospace Doctrine, Research, and Education. (n.d.). Operation Eagle Claw. Retrieved 3 February 2007 from http://www.apc.maxwell.af.mil/text/excur/eagle.htm

Creen, Tech Sgt Mike J. (n.d.). A Sign of the Times: Operation Urgent Fury: Grenada. Retrieved 4 February 2007 from http://www.af.mil/news/airman/0197/grenada.htm

Des Brisay, Thomas D. (1985). *Fourteen Hours at Koh Tang*. Washington, D.C.: Office of Air Force History, United States Air Force. Retrieved 15 February 2007 from http://books.google.com/books?id=tE7C9PgPAO8C&pg=PA140&lpg=PA140&dq=robert+undorf&source=web&ots=t-97OJwFet&sig=Dl7RODV8UFo9ZK6RYAZQ3LnDkcc#PPP1,M1

Douglas X-3 Stiletto. (n.d.). National Museum of the USAF. Retrieved 4 February 2007 from http://www.nationalmuseum.af.mil/factsheets/factsheet.asp?id=625

EC-130J Commando Solo. (November 2006). US Air Force Special Operations Command, Public Affairs Office. Retrieved 4 February 2007 from http://www.af.mil/factsheets/factsheet_print.asp?fsID=182&page=1

F-111 Aardvark. (n.d.). *Air Force Link*. Retrieved 4 February 2007 from http://www.af.mil/news/story.asp?storyID=123006568

Ferdinando, Lisa. (24 January 2007). Panama's Noriega to be Released from US Prison in September. *Voice of America News*. Retrieved 13 February 2007 from http://www.voanews.com/english/2007-01-24-voa45.cfm

Garamone, Jim. (26 April 2005). America Remembers Desert One Heroes. *American Forces Press Service*. Retrieved 4 February 2007 from http://www.af.mil/news/story.asp?storyID=123010370

General Daniel "Chappie" James Jr. (n.d.). *Air Force Link*. Retrieved 5 February 2007 from http://www.af.mil/history/person.asp?dec=&pid=123006480

Haulman, Daniel L. (2003). *One Hundred Years of Flight: USAF Chronology of Significant Air and Space Events 1903–2002*. Retrieved 5 February 2007 from http://afhra. maxwell.af.mil/chronologyofflight.pdf

Hess, Michael. (27 April 2006). High Alert in 1986. *Air Force Link*. Retrieved 4 February 2007 from http://www.af.mil/news/story.asp?storyID=123018986

Lockheed F-104C Starfighter. (n.d.). National Museum of the USAF. Retrieved 4 February 2007 from http://www.nationalmuseum.af.mil/factsheets/ factsheet.asp?id=377

Lockheed SR-71A. (n.d.). National Museum of the USAF. Retrieved 4 February 2007 from http://www.nationalmuseum.af.mil/factsheets/factsheet.asp?id=395

Lockheed U2-A. (n.d.). National Museum of the USAF. Retrieved 4 February 2007 from http://www.nationalmuseum.af.mil/factsheets/factsheet.asp?id=387

Maj Rudolf Anderson Jr. (n.d.). *Air Force Link*. Retrieved 3 February 2007 from http://www.af.mil/history/spotlight.asp?storyID=123009509

Miskimins, Sean M., & Chivalette, William I. (n.d.). CM Sgt Richard L. Etchberger: Top Secret Enlisted Air Force Cross Recipient. Suitland, Maryland: Airmen Memorial Museum.

Montgomery, Jeff. (Ed.). (2000). *Aerospace: The Journey of Flight*. Maxwell Air Force Base, AL: Civil Air Patrol National Headquarters.

North American X-15A-2. (n.d.). National Museum of the USAF. Retrieved 4 February from http://www.nationalmuseum.af.mil/factsheets/factsheet.asp?id=556

Northrop SM62 Snark. (n.d.). National Museum of the USAF. Retrieved 4 February 2007 from http://www.nationalmuseum.af.mil/factsheets/factsheet.asp?id=4289

Operation Just Cause. (n.d.). *Air Force Link*. Retrieved 4 February 2007 from http://www.af.mil/history/spotlight.asp?storyID=123013656

Phillips, R. Cody. (1 September 2006). Operation Just Cause: The Incursion into Panama. U.S. Army Center of Military History. Retrieved 4 February 2007 from http://www.army.mil/cmh/brochures/Just%20Cause/JustCause.htm#Intro

Robinson, Sue. (May 1988). The 'Nth Degree of OJT.' *Sergeants*, 10–12.

Sgt John L. Levitow. (n.d.). Air Force Link. Retrieved 5 February 2007 from http://www.af.mil/history/person_print.asp?storyID=123006519

Vietnam War: 1961. (n.d.). National Museum of the USAF. Retrieved 4 February 2007 from http://www.nationalmuseum.af.mil/factsheets/factsheet.asp?fsID=1256

Wayne L. Fisk. (n.d.). Air University. Retrieved 5 February 2007 from http://www.au.af.mil/au/goe/eaglebios/05bios/fisk05.htm

LESSON 3—Global Interventions From 1990

Allison, Mae-Li. (4 October 2004). *Airmen Use GBU-38 in Combat*. Retrieved 8 February 2007 from http://www.af.mil/news/story.asp?storyID=123008840

B1-B Lancer. (October 2005). *Air Force Link*. Retrieved 8 February 2007 from http://www.af.mil/factsheets/factsheet.asp?id=81

B-2 Spirit. (n.d.). *Air Force Link*. Retrieved 7 February 2007 from http://www.af.mil/ factsheets/factsheet.asp?fsID=82

Bates, Matthew. (28 October 2006). F-117: A Long, Storied History That Is About to End. *Air Force Link*. Retrieved 7 February 2007 from http://www.af.mil/news/story.asp?storyID=123030185

Brubaker, Tammy. (June 2003). Operation Northern Watch Fighters Say Final Goodbye to Incirlik. *Air Force Link*. Retrieved 9 February 2007 from http://www.af.mil/news/airman/0603/world3.html

Chisolm, DeShana E., Mitchell, Naomi L., & Roberson, Patricia Q. (Eds.). (2002). *Aerospace Science: Frontiers of Aviation History* (2nd ed.). Maxwell Air Force Base, AL: Air Force Officer Accessions and Training Schools.

Duff, Phyllis. (31 August 2006). CAP Proves Worth during Katrina Relief. *Air Force Link*. Retrieved 9 February 2007 from http://www.af.mil/news/story.asp?id=123026197

Elliott, Scott. (9 January 2004). Roche Unveils AF Hero Memorial. *Air Force Print News*. Cited on Arlington National Cemetery website. Retrieved 9 February 2007 from http://arlingtoncemetery.net/jachapman-memorial-at-anc.htm

Everdeen, Bob. (22 August 2006). Small-Diameter Bomb Ready for War on Terror. *Air Force Link*. Retrieved 9 February 2007 from http://www.af.mil/news/story_print.asp?storyID=123025585

F-117A Nighthawk. (n.d.). *Air Force Link*. Retrieved 8 February 2007 from http://www.af.mil/history/aircraft.asp?dec=1970-1980&pid=123006550

F-117A Nighthawk. (October 2005). *Air Force Link*. Retrieved 7 February 2007 from http://www.af.mil/factsheets/factsheet.asp?fsID=104

F-22 Begins First Overseas Deployment. (n.d.). *Air Force Link*. Retrieved 8 February 2007 from http://www.af.mil/news/story.asp?storyID=123040309

F-35 to Deliver Stealth Strike. (December 2001). *Airman*. Retrieved 7 February 2007 from http://www.af.mil/news/airman/1201/world6.html

50 Heroes From 50 States. (15 February 2007). Alabama: Chief Master Sgt. Kevin Lynn. Department of Defense. Retrieved 19 February 2007 from http://www.defenselink.mil/home/dodupdate/heroes/50heroes/AL.html

Frontline: The Gulf War. (2007). WGBH Education Foundation. Retrieved 11 February 2007 from http://www.pbs.org/wgbh/pages/frontline/gulf/maps/2.html

Garamone, Jim. (10 November 2005). General Myers Receives Presidential Medal of Freedom. *American Forces Press Service*. Retrieved 9 February 2007 from http://www.af.mil/news/story.asp?storyID=123012866

General Richard B. Myers. (September 2005). *Air Force Link*. Retrieved 9 February 2007 from http://www.af.mil/bios/bio.asp?bioID=6123

Global War on Terrorism. (9 April 2003). *Air Force Link*. Retrieved 8 February 2007 from http://www.af.mil/airforceoperationscenter/operationenduringfreedom.asp

Jason Dean Cunningham. (29 May 2006). Arlington National Cemetery. Retrieved 9 February 2007 from http://www.arlingtoncemetery.net/jdcunningham.htm

Keeping Watch. (July 2002). *Airman*. Retrieved 9 February 2007 from http://www.af.mil/news/airman/0702/osw.html

Kurle, David. (7 June 2006). Predators Provide Eyes in the Sky Over Afghanistan. *Air Force Link*. Retrieved February 2007 from http://www.af.mil/news/story.asp?storyID=123021334

Miles, Donna. (6 October 2006). Operation Enduring Freedom Marks Five Years. *American Forces Press Service*. Retrieved 8 February from http://www.af.mil/news/story_print.asp?storyID=123028591

Montgomery, Jeff. (Ed.). (2000). *Aerospace: The Journey of Flight*. Maxwell Air Force Base, AL: Civil Air Patrol National Headquarters.

Moseley, T. Michael. (20 March 2006). CSAF's Vector: Operation Iraqi Freedom Anniversary. Retrieved 9 February 2007 from http://www.af.mil/library/viewpoints/csaf.asp?id=223

MQ-1 Predator Unmanned Aerial Vehicle. (January 2007). *Air Force Link*. Retrieved 8 February 2007 from http://www.af.mil/factsheets/factsheet.asp?fsID=122

Noble Eagle Overview. (n.d.). *Air Force Link*. Retrieved 8 February 2007 from http://www.af.mil/airforceoperationscenter/operationnobleeagle.asp

Operation Anaconda: A Day-by-Day Guide to the First Week of Fighting. (10 March 2002). *Time*, March 10, 2002. Retrieved 11 February 2007 from http://www.time.com/time/covers/1101020318/popup/index.html

Operation Iraqi Freedom. (9 April 2003). *Air Force Link*. Retrieved 8 February 2007 from http://www.af.mil/airforceoperationscenter/operationiraqifreedom.asp

Stealth Features. (n.d.). *Airman*. Retrieved 7 February 2007 from http://www.af.mil/news/airman/1005/airsb1_txt.shtml

Technical Sgt Tim Wilkinson. (n.d.). *Air Force Link*. Retrieved 9 February 2007 from http://www.af.mil/history/person.asp?dec=&pid=123006509

USAFE Unit Debuts Small Diameter Bomb in Combat. (5 October 2006). *Air Force Print News*. Retrieved 9 February 2007 from http://www.af.mil/pressreleases/release.asp?storyID=123028471

Wade, Shantece. (13 March 2006). Holloman Airmen Support Operation Noble Eagle. North American Aerospace Defense Command. Retrieved 8 February 2007 from http://www.norad.mil/newsroom/news_releases/2006/031306.htm

Unit 4

CHAPTER 7

LESSON 1—The Solar System and Some Early Astronomers

Arnett, Bill. (2006). A Multimedia Tour of the Solar System: One Star, Eight Planets, and More. Retrieved 15 February 2007 from http://www.nineplanets.org/sol.html

Ask an Astrophysicist. (1998). Goddard Space Flight Center. Retrieved 15 February 2007 from http://imagine.gsfc.nasa.gov/docs/ask_astro/answers/980215e.html

The Astronomer-Prince of Afghanistan. (2001). Space Today Online. Retrieved 15 February 2007 from http://www.spacetoday.org/DeepSpace/Telescopes/Observatories/Afghanistan/AfghanAstronomerPrince.html.

Dawn Community: Flashbacks—Thinking Outside the Box. (n.d.). *Jet Propulsion Laboratory, California Institute of Technology*. Retrieved 15 February 2007 from http://dawn.jpl.nasa.gov/DawnCommunity/flashbacks/fb_01.asp

Exploring the Planets: Discovery. (2002). National Air and Space Museum. Retrieved 15 February 2007 from http://www.nasm.si.edu/research/ceps/etp/discovery/disc_galileo.html

Gingerich, Owen. (n.d.). Truth in Science: Proof, Persuasion, and the Galileo Affair Lecture delivered at St. Edmunds College, Cambridge University. Retrieved 15 February 2007 from http://www.st-edmunds.cam.ac.uk/cis/gingerich/lecture1.html

Inman, Mason. (24 August 1006). Pluto Not a Planet, Astronomers Rule. National Geographic News. Retrieved 15 February 2007 from http://news.nationalgeographic.com/news/2006/08/060824-pluto-planet.html

Johannes Kepler: His Life, His Laws and Times. (n.d.). National Aeronautics and Space Administration. Retrieved 15 February 2007 from http://kepler.nasa.gov/johannes/

Kuhn, Thomas S. (1971). *The Copernican Revolution: Planetary Astronomy in the Development of Western Thought.* Cambridge, MA: Harvard University Press.

Montgomery, Jeff. (Ed.). (2000). *Aerospace: The Journey of Flight.* Maxwell Air Force Base, AL: Civil Air Patrol National Headquarters.

Space and Its Exploration: Brief Biographies. (n.d.). Goddard Space Flight Center. Retrieved 15 February 2007 from http://adc.gsfc.nasa.gov/adc/education/space_ex/biographies.html

Tyson, Peter. (2002). His Big Mistake. Retrieved 15 February 2007 from http://www.pbs.org/wgbh/nova/galileo/mistake.html

Ulugh Beg. (1999). School of Mathematics and Statistics, University of St Andrews, Scotland. Retrieved 15 February 2007 from http://www-history.mcs.st-andrews.ac.uk/Biographies/Ulugh_Beg.html

LESSON 2—Rocketry and the Space Race

Boyne, Walter J. (2006). Air Force Astronauts. *Air Force Magazine Online*, Vol. 89, No. 10. Retrieved 19 February 2007 from http://www.afa.org/magazine/Oct2006/1006astronauts.asp

The Buzz on V1 and V2 Rockets. (2007). Institute of Electrical and Electronics Engineers Virtual Museum. Retrieved 19 February 2007 from http://ieee-virtual-museum.org/collection/tech.php?taid=&id=2345918&lid=1

Chisolm, DeShana E., Mitchell, Naomi L., & Roberson, Patricia Q. (Eds). (2002). *Aerospace Science: Frontiers of Aviation History* (2nd ed.). Maxwell Air Force Base, AL: Air Force Officer Accessions and Training Schools.

Dr. Wernher von Braun: First Center Director, July 1, 1960–Jan. 27, 1970. (n.d.). Marshall Space Flight Center. Retrieved 19 February 2007 from http://history.msfc.nasa.gov/vonbraun/bio.html

Goddard Space Flight Center. (n.d.). Space and Its Exploration: Brief Biographies. Retrieved 19 February 2007 from http://adc.gsfc.nasa.gov/adc/education/space_ex/biographies.html

Hermann Oberth. (n.d.). U.S. Centennial of Flight Commission. Retrieved 19 February 2007 from http://www.centennialofflight.gov/essay/SPACEFLIGHT/oberth/SP2.htm

Launius, Roger D. (2005). *Sputnik* and the Origins of the Space Age. Retrieved 19 February 2007 from http://history.nasa.gov/sputnik/sputorig.html

Montgomery, Jeff. (Ed.). (2000). *Aerospace: The Journey of Flight.* Maxwell Air Force Base, AL: Civil Air Patrol National Headquarters.

Snyder, Amy Paige. (2001). NASA and Planetary Exploration. In *Exploring the Cosmos.* Washington, D.C.: NASA History Office. Retrieved 22 February 2007 from http://science.hq.nasa.gov/missions/docs/Chap2-essay.PDF

Space Race. (2002). National Air and Space Museum. Retrieved 19 February 2007 from http://www.nasm.si.edu/exhibitions/gal114/gal114.htm

Stern, David P. (2006). From Stargazers to Starships: Robert Goddard and His Rockets. National Aeronautics and Space Administration. Retrieved 19 February 2007 from http://www-istp.gsfc.nasa.gov/stargaze/Sgoddard.htm

CHAPTER 8

LESSON 1—The Space Program

Alan B. Shepard Jr. (September 1998). NASA. Retrieved 14 February 2007 from http://www.jsc.nasa.gov/Bios/htmlbios/shepard-alan.html

Apollo. (4 January 2005). NASA. Retrieved 13 February 2007 from http://www-pao.ksc.nasa.gov/kscpao/history/apollo/apollo.htm

Apollo: Mission to the Moon. (6 September 2006). NASA. Retrieved 13 February 2007 from http://www.nasa.gov/mission_pages/apollo/index.html

Apollo 30th Anniversary: Biographies of Apollo 11 Astronauts. (20 September 2002). NASA. Retrieved 14 February 2007 from http://www.hq.nasa.gov/office/pao/History/ap11ann/astrobios.htm#Armstrong

Brigadier General Susan J. Helms. (June 2006). *Air Force Link.* Retrieved 20 February 2007 from http://www.af.mil/bios/bio.asp?bioID=8588

Colonel Susan Helms. (n.d.). *Air Force Link.* Retrieved 20 February 2007 from http://www.af.mil/history/person.asp?dec=&pid=123006503

Countdown! NASA Launch Vehicles and Facilities. (October 1991). NASA. Retrieved 21 February 2007 from http://www-pao.ksc.nasa.gov/nasafact/count1.htm#shuttle

Deke Slayton. (June 1993). NASA. Retrieved 15 February 2007 from http://www.jsc.nasa.gov/Bios/htmlbios/slayton.html

Dick, Steven J. (28 January 2004). Remembering Columbia STS-107. Retrieved 16 February 2007 from http://history.nasa.gov/columbia/index.html

Dr. Mae Jemison. (n.d.). NASA. Retrieved 19 February 2007 from http://starchild.gsfc.nasa.gov/docs/StarChild/whos_who_level2/jemison.html

Dr. Ronald M. Sega. (November 2006). *Air Force Link.* Retrieved 20 February 2007 from http://www.af.mil/bios/bio.asp?bioID=7901

Dumoulin, Jim. (29 June 2001). Apollo 13. NASA. Retrieved 16 February 2007 from http://science.ksc.nasa.gov/history/apollo/apollo-13/apollo-13.html

Dumoulin, Jim. (29 June 2001). STS-7. NASA. Retrieved 16 February 2007 from http://science.ksc.nasa.gov/shuttle/missions/sts-7/mission-sts-7.html

Dumoulin, Jim. (29 June 2001). STS-9. NASA. Retrieved 16 February 2007 from http://science.ksc.nasa.gov/shuttle/missions/sts-9/mission-sts-9.html

Eileen Marie Collins. (May 2006). NASA. Retrieved 19 February 2007 from http://www.jsc.nasa.gov/Bios/htmlbios/collins.html

Ellison S. Onizuka. (January 2007). NASA. Retrieved 20 February 2007 from http://www.jsc.nasa.gov/Bios/htmlbios/onizuka.html

40th Anniversary of the Mercury 7. (n.d.). NASA. Retrieved 14 February 2007 from http://history.nasa.gov/40thmerc7/intro.htm

Froehlich, Walter. (6 August 2004). Spacelab: An International Short-Stay Orbiting Laboratory. NASA. Retrieved 16 February 2007 from http://history.nasa.gov/EP-165/ep165.htm

Gemini. (10 March 2004). NASA. Retrieved 13 February 2007 from http://www-pao.ksc.nasa.gov/kscpao/history/gemini/gemini.htm

Guion S. Bluford Jr. (January 2007). NASA. Retrieved 20 February 2007 from http://www.jsc.nasa.gov/Bios/htmlbios/bluford-gs.html

Hubble Space Telescope. (16 November 2006). NASA. Retrieved 20 February 2007 from http://hubble.nasa.gov/overview/timeline.php

Human Space Flight. (27 June 2003). NASA. Retrieved 16 February 2007 from http://spaceflight.nasa.gov/shuttle/reference/factsheets/asseltrn.html

International Space Station. (April 2006). NASA. Retrieved 19 February 2007 from http://spaceflight.nasa.gov/spacenews/factsheets/pdfs/iss_fact_sheet.pdf

John Herschel Glenn Jr. (January 1999). NASA. Retrieved 15 February 2007 from http://www.jsc.nasa.gov/Bios/htmlbios/glenn-j.html

John W. Young. (May 2005). NASA. Retrieved 20 February 2007 from http://science.ksc.nasa.gov/shuttle/missions/sts-7/mission-sts-7.html

Jones, Eric M. (1995). Apollo 11 Crew Information. NASA. Retrieved 24 February 2007 from http://www.hq.nasa.gov/alsj/a11/a11.crew.html.

Leroy Gordon Cooper Jr. (October 2004). NASA. Retrieved 15 February 2007 from http://www.jsc.nasa.gov/Bios/htmlbios/cooper-lg.html

Mae C. Jemison. (March 1993). NASA. Retrieved 19 February 2007 from http://www.jsc.nasa.gov/Bios/htmlbios/jemison-mc.html

Meet: Sally Ride, First American Woman in Space. (n.d.). NASA Quest. Retrieved 14 February 2007 from http://quest.nasa.gov/space/frontiers/ride.html

Mercury. (24 April 2003). NASA. Retrieved 13 February 2007 from http://www-pao.ksc.nasa.gov/kscpao/history/mercury/mercury.htm

Montgomery, Jeff. (Ed.). (2000). *Aerospace: The Journey of Flight.* Maxwell Air Force Base, AL: Civil Air Patrol National Headquarters

NASA's Orbiter Fleet: Space Shuttle Overview: Challenger (OV-099). (5 January 2007). NASA. Retrieved 16 February 2007 from http://www.nasa.gov/centers/kennedy/shuttleoperations/orbiters/challenger-info.html

NASA's Orbiter Fleet: Space Shuttle Overview: Endeavour (OV-105). (24 January 2007). NASA. Retrieved 16 February 2007 from http://www.nasa.gov/centers/kennedy/shuttleoperations/orbiters/endeavour-info.html

Robert L. Crippen. (September 1997). NASA. Retrieved 20 February 2007 from http://www.jsc.nasa.gov/Bios/htmlbios/crippen-rl.html

Ronald M. Sega. (May 1999). NASA. Retrieved 20 February 2007 from http://www.jsc.nasa.gov/Bios/htmlbios/sega.html

Sally K. Ride. (July 2006). NASA. Retrieved 20 February 2007 from http://www.jsc.
    nasa.gov/Bios/htmlbios/ride-sk.html

Scott Carpenter. (January 2004). NASA. Retrieved 15 February 2007 from
    http://www.jsc.nasa.gov/Bios/htmlbios/carpenter-ms.html

Seelhorst, Mary. (2003). PM People: Buzz Aldrin. *Popular Mechanics*, December 2003.

Sidney M. Gutierrez. (July 1996). NASA. Retrieved 20 February 2007 from
    http://www.jsc.nasa.gov/Bios/htmlbios/gutierrez-sm.html

Solar System Exploration. (21 February 2007). NASA. Retrieved 21 February 2007
    from http://solarsystem.nasa.gov/missions/

Soviet/Russian Launch Vehicles. (n.d.). US Centennial of Flight Commission.
    Retrieved 21 February 2007 from http://www.centennialofflight.gov/essay/
    SPACEFLIGHT/Soviet_launch_vehicles/SP14.htm

Space Shuttle. (2007). NASA. Retrieved 20 February 2007 from
    http://www.nasa.gov/mission_pages/shuttle/main/index.html

Space Station. (2007). NASA. Retrieved 19 February 2007 from
    http://www.nasa.gov/mission_pages/station/main/

Taylor G. Wang. (May 1985). NASA. Retrieved 19 February 2007 from
    http://www.jsc.nasa.gov/Bios/htmlbios/wang-t.html

Virgil I. Grissom. (December 1997). NASA. Retrieved 14 February 2007
    from http://www.jsc.nasa.gov/Bios/htmlbios/grissom-vi.html

Walter M. Schirra. (December 1993). NASA. Retrieved 15 February 2007
    from http://www.jsc.nasa.gov/Bios/htmlbios/schirra-wm.html

Whitehouse, David. (28 October 2002). First Dog in Space Died Within Hours.
    BBC News. Retrieved 13 February 2007 from http://news.bbc.co.uk/1/hi/sci/
    tech/2367681.stm

William A. Pailes. (October 1985). NASA. Retrieved 20 February 2007 from
    http://www.jsc.nasa.gov/Bios/htmlbios/pailes-wa.html

Williams, David R. (27 September 2005). Soviet Lunar Missions. Retrieved 21
    February 2007 from http://nssdc.gsfc.nasa.gov/planetary/lunar/lunarussr.html

LESSON 2—The Future of Air and Space Power

Aegis Ballistic Missile Defense. (July 2006). Missile Defense Agency. Retrieved
    7 March 2007 from http://www.mda.mil/mdalink/pdf/aegis.pdf

The Airborne Laser. (May 2006). Missile Defense Agency. Retrieved 5 March 2007
    from http://www.mda.mil/mdalink/pdf/laser.pdf

Airborne Laser to Test-Fire in Flight. (29 January 2007). *Air Force Times*.
    Retrieved 5 March 2007 from http://www.airforcetimes.com/news/2007/01/
    AFairbornelaser070129/

Branum, Don. (12 September 2006). Tight Fit for GM-3 Will Save AF $360K
    Per Flight. Air Force Space Command. Retrieved 7 March 2007 from
    http://www.afspc.af.mil/news/story.asp?storyID=123026932

Carter, Preston. (January/February 2000). Bringing Hypersonic Flight Down to Earth.
    Lawrence Livermore National Laboratory. Retrieved 5 March 2007 from
    http://www.llnl.gov/str/Carter.html

Cole, William. (September 2002). The Pelican: A Big Bird for the Long Haul. Boeing. Retrieved 6 March 2007 from http://www.boeing.com/news/frontiers/archive/2002/september/i_pw.html

Constellation Program: Orion Crew Vehicle. (2007). NASA. Retrieved 7 March 2007 from http://www.nasa.gov/mission_pages/constellation/orion/index.html

Dolman, Everett Carl. (2006). What is Cyberspace? Air University. Retrieved 8 March 2006 from http://www.maxwell.af.mil/au/aunews/archive/0203/articles/whatiscyberspace.html

Evolved Expendable Launch Vehicle. (December 2006). Air Force Space Command. Retrieved 7 March 2007 from http://www.afspc.af.mil/library/factsheets/factsheet.asp?id=3643

F-35 Lightning II-Joint Strike Fighter (JSF), International. (2007). Airforce-technology.com. Retrieved 5 March 2007 from http://www.airforce-technology.com/projects/jsf/

F-35 Joint Strike Fighter (JSF) Lightning II. (n.d.). GlobalSecurity.org. Retrieved 8 March 2006 from http://www.globalsecurity.org/military/systems/aircraft/f-35.htm

Gettle, Mitch. (8 December 2005). Air Force Releases New Mission Statement. *Air Force Link*. Retrieved 7 March 2007 from http://www.af.mil/news/story.asp?id=123013440

Griffin, Michael. (18 January 2007). Why Explore Space? NASA. Retrieved 7 March 2007 from http://www.nasa.gov/mission_pages/exploration/main/griffin_why_explore.html

Hockmuth, Catherine MacRae. (February 2007). UAVs—the Next Generation. *Air Force Magazine Online*. Retrieved 6 March 2007 from http://www.afa.org/magazine/feb2007/0207UAV.asp

Kinkade, Mark. (December 2003). Future Flight. *Airman*, December 2003. Retrieved 6 March 2007 from http://www.af.mil/news/airman/1203/flight.html

Lopez, C. Todd. (3 November 2006). Eighth Air Force to Become New Cyber Command. *Air Force Link*. Retrieved 7 March 2007 from http://www.af.mil/news/story.asp?storyID=123030505

Lopez, C. Todd. (28 February 2007). Fighting in Cyberspace Means Cyber Domain Dominance. *Air Force Link*. Retrieved 7 March 2007 from http://www.af.mil/news/story.asp?id=123042670

Lopez, C. Todd. (17 November 2006). Unmanned Vehicle Provides Reusable Test Capabilities in Space. *Air Force Link*. Retrieved 7 March 2007 from http://www.af.mil/news/story.asp?storyID=123032226

Montgomery, Jeff. (Ed.). (2000). *Aerospace: The Journey of Flight*. Maxwell Air Force Base, AL: Civil Air Patrol National Headquarters

NASA X-43 (Hyper-X) Hypersonic Aircraft, USA. (2007). Aerospace-technology.com. Retrieved 5 March 2007 from http://www.aerospace-technology.com/projects/x43/

Nielsen, Paul D., Noor, Ahmed K., & Venneri, Samuel L. (2003). The Next Century of Air Power. *Mechanical Engineering*. Retrieved 5 March 2007 from http://www.memagazine.org/backissues/membersonly/nov03/features/airpow/airpow.html

Scramjet Propulsion. (2006). NASA. Retrieved 5 March 2007 from http://www.grc. nasa.gov/WWW/BGH/scramjet.html

Wynne, Michael. (2 November 2006). Cyberspace as a Domain in Which the Air Force Flies and Fights. *Air Force Link*. Retrieved 7 March 2007 from http://www.af.mil/library/speeches/speech.asp?id=283

Wynne, Michael W., & Moseley, T. Michael. (2006). The U.S. Air Force Posture Statement 2006. Washington, DC: US Air Force.

X-34. (2006). NASA. Retrieved 7 March 2007 from http://www.nasa.gov/centers/ dryden/news/FactSheets/FS-060-DFRC.html

Zeihan, Peter. (6 March 2007). The New Logic for Ballistic Missile Defense. *Stratfor: Geopolitical Intelligence Report*. Retrieved 5 April 2007 from http://www.stratfor.com/products/premium/read_article.php?id=285309

ability—the knowledge, experience, and skill a team member or a team brings to a task. (p. 286)

aerial reconnaissance—looking over battlefields from the sky. (p. 18)

aerial refueling—taking on more fuel in flight. (p. 103)

aerodynamic—designed with rounded edges to reduce wind drag. (p. 88)

aeronauts—people who travel in airships or balloons. (p. 20)

aileron—a small flap on the wing for controlling turns. (p. 46)

airfoil—a wing's profile. (p. 34)

airlift—the transportation of personnel or material by air. (p. 217)

air traffic control—the ground-based system for keeping aircraft safely separated from one another. (p. 181)

airways—the routes that planes must follow through the sky. (p. 181)

all-cargo airlines—airlines that carry freight, not passengers. (p. 178)

alloy—a combination of different metals—or of metal and nonmetal—fused for strength, resistance to corrosion, or other desired qualities. (p. 188)

Allies—in World War I, Russia, France, Serbia, and Britain (later joined by the United States and Italy) (p. 63); in World War II, Britain, France, the United States, the Soviet Union, and China. (p. 138)

altitude—the height above Earth's surface. (p. 88)

amendment—a revision or change. (p. 111)

amphibian—designed to take off and land on either water or land. (p. 88)

angle of attack—the angle between the relative wind (the flow of air) and the airfoil. (p. 36)

annex—to incorporate territory into an existing political unit such as a country. (p. 129)

antitrust—intended to prevent concentrations of power in business. (p. 173)

apogee—maximum altitude. (p. 322)

apprentice—a person who works with a skilled master to learn by practical experience. (p. 97)

appropriate—to set aside for a specific use. (p. 71)

aquanaut—a person who conducts work or research under water. (p. 322)

arms—weapons. (p. 209)

arms race—a competition for military supremacy. (p. 231)

asteroid—a rocky and metallic object orbiting the sun. (p. 294)

astronaut—person who flies aboard a spacecraft. (p. 318)

autogiro—an early, helicopter-like vehicle. (p. 97)

autonomous—independent of human control. (p. 354)

autonomy—independence. (p. 134)

auxiliary—functioning as a branch of another military organization. (p. 120)

Axis Powers—in World War II, Germany, Italy, and Japan. (p. 138)

ballistic missile—one that free-falls after a self-powered flight. (p. 251)

barnstormer—a pilot who travels around the country giving exhibits of stunt flying and parachuting. (p. 84)

bid—an offer or a proposal, with a price attached. (p. 41)

biplane—an aircraft with two main supporting surfaces, usually placed one above the other. (p. 23)

blind flight—the act of taking off and landing relying solely on instruments inside the cockpit for guidance. (p. 99)

blitzkrieg—a war conducted with great speed and force. (p. 143)

bombsight—a device that helps determine when to drop a bomb. (p. 128)

boom—the section of a helicopter that connects the tail with the main body. (p. 50)

bracing—support strung diagonally between struts. (p. 32)

canard configuration—another name for an elevator that sits in front of the wings. (p. 33)

casualties—military persons lost through death, wounds, injury, imprisonment, or missing in action. (p. 137)

center of pressure—the focal point of lift. (p. 34)

Central Powers—in World War I, Germany, Austria-Hungary, and Turkey. (p. 63)

circuit—a route that passes through one or more points and then returns to the starting point. (p. 98)

classified—secret. (p. 255)

coalition—an alliance among nations. (p. 257)

cockpit—a space inside the fuselage where the crew sits. (p. 48)

colony—a region under the political control of a distant country. (p. 221)

combined arms—the coordinated efforts of different military branches, such as air and ground. (p. 143)

comet—a small, odd-shaped body with a center of ice, rock, and frozen gas. (p. 294)

components—parts. (p.307)

configurations—setups for specific purposes. (p. 196)

consortium—an association of companies for some specific purpose. (p. 195)

constellation—a group of stars people think of as forming a picture in the sky. (p. 295)

corps—a branch or department of the armed forces having a specialized function. (p. 129)

cosmonaut—a Soviet or Russian astronaut. (p. 326)

cowling—a covering to protect and streamline the engine. (p. 108)

crankshaft—a shaft that turns or is turned by a crank. (p. 49)

cyberspace—a virtual place where information is stored. (p. 356)

deep space—any region beyond the solar system. (p. 361)

dogfight—a battle between fighter planes. (p. 74)

drag—the pull, or slowing effect, of air on an aircraft. (p. 22)

dirigible—a steerable airship. (p. 18)

elevator—a movable, horizontal surface that controls motion up and down. (p. 33)

elliptical—shaped like an oval, not a circle. (p. 290)

embargo—a legal ban on commerce. (p. 165)

enthusiasts—strong supporters or fans. (p 88)

epicycles—cycles within cycles. (p. 287)

equator—the imaginary circle that divides Earth into northern and southern halves. (p. 98)

escadrille—a small squadron of planes. (p. 65)

escort—accompany. (p. 159)

European Space Agency—a group of 17 countries in Europe that pool their funds and knowledge to explore space. (p. 332)

flight—the act of passing through the air on wings (p. 7); an air force unit that has two or more elements. (p. 143)

flight simulator—a training device that simulates, or imitates, the experience and sensation of flight. (p. 102)

free market—one that operates on the basis of competition and is not controlled by government. (p. 197)

fuselage—the body of an airplane containing the crew and passengers (or cargo). (p. 48)

galaxy—a huge mass of stars, gas, and dust clouds that exists in one area of space. (p. 289)

general aviation—all civil aviation other than flights by scheduled airlines and government agencies. (p. 186)

geocentric—Earth-centered. (p. 286)

geosynchronous—an orbit "in sync" with Earth that takes one day to complete. (p. 290)

glider—a light aircraft without an engine, designed to glide after being towed aloft or launched from a catapult. (p. 10)

grades—ranks. (p. 123)

gravity—an invisible force that pulls all objects toward one another. (p. 289)

guerrilla warfare—a type of fighting in which small bands of fighters hit more-powerful forces by surprise. (p. 233)

gunpowder—an explosive powder made of potassium nitrate, charcoal, and sulfur, used to shoot projectiles from guns. (p. 8)

hacker—someone who uses programming skills to gain illegal access to a computer network or file. (p. 356)

helicopter—an aircraft that gets its lift from spinning blades. (p. 9)

heliocentric—sun-centered. (p. 287)

Holocaust—the mass murder of some six million Jews, mostly in death camps, during World War II. (p. 138)

hypersonic—able to fly at or beyond Mach 5, which is five times the speed of sound. (p. 352)

hypothesis—an unconfirmed explanation that can be tested for truthfulness. (p. 287)

incendiary bombs—bombs designed to start fires. (p. 167)

incentive—a motivating reward. (p. 108)

incompetent—lacking the qualities needed for effective action. (p. 127)

inertia—the tendency for a body at rest to stay at rest until some force acts on it. (p. 308)

infantry—soldiers armed and trained to fight on foot. (p. 141)

insubordination—a refusal to submit to authority. (p. 127)

insurgent—a rebel or guerrilla fighter. (p. 267)

interdiction—the act of cutting or destroying an enemy's advance through firepower. (p. 145)

internal-combustion engine—engine in which the fuel is burned inside, rather than in an external furnace. (p. 19)

international waters—areas of the seas where ships from any nation have the right to travel. (p. 232)

isolationist—term used to describe a nation that does not enter alliances with other countries. (p. 141)

jet lag—fatigue and sleep disturbance as result of crossing time zones on a jet. (p. 196)

jumpsuit—a one-piece outfit. (p. 57)

keel—a structure that extends along the center of a craft from the front to the back. (p. 19)

kite—a light framework covered with paper or cloth, provided with a balancing tail, designed to be flown in the air. (p. 7)

lateral—sideways. (p. 33)

latitude—a line north or south from Earth's equator and parallel to it. (p. 221)

legend—an unverified story handed down from earlier times. (p. 8)

lift—the upward force on an aircraft against gravity. (p. 18)

light-year—the distance light travels in a year. (p. 294)

limited war—a war in which opposing sides try to avoid a worldwide war and the possible use of atomic bombs by fighting with each other outside their own lands and sometimes through troops who aren't their own. (p. 221)

logistics—the aspect of military operations that deals with the procurement, distribution, maintenance, and replacement of materiel and personnel. (p. 134)

Luftwaffe—the German air force. (p. 141)

lunar—relating to the moon. (p. 321)

Mach—the speed of sound. (p. 213)

machine gun—an automatic rifle that uses belt-fed ammunition. (p. 67)

mainstream—the current of most people's life and activities. (p. 100)

Marshall Plan—a strategy for rebuilding the countries of Europe and repelling communism after World War II. (p. 210)

materiel—the equipment and supplies of a military force. (p. 156)

mentor—a trusted coach or guide. (p. 83)

metal fatigue—a slow weakening of strength in metal caused by repeated deformation, vibration, or other stress. (p. 191)

meteor—a meteoroid passing through Earth's atmosphere, leaving a visible trail. (p. 295)

meteorite—a meteoroid that lands on Earth's surface. (p. 295)

meteoroid—a piece of rock or metal that travels in space. (p. 295)

micro-UAV—an aircraft that weighs as little as a few ounces or a few pounds. (p. 355)

milestone—an important event, such as a breakthrough in the advancement of knowledge in a field. (p. 94)

military coup—a sudden takeover of power by the military. (p. 279)

missiles—rocket-propelled vehicles that carry a weapon or warhead. (p. 211)

mission specialist—someone who helps with experiments or the technical aspects of running a spacecraft. (p. 318)

multiengine plane—a plane with more than one engine. (p. 48)

module—a unit of a spacecraft. (p. 326)

monoplane—an airplane with one set of wings. (p. 23)

nanotechnology—the science and technology of building electronic circuits and devices from single atoms and molecules. (p. 355)

nano-UAV—a UAV (unmanned air vehicle) so small that it is invisible to the naked eye. (p. 355)

neutral—not taking sides. (p. 239)

no-fly zone—airspace enemy aircraft aren't allowed to enter. (p. 272)

nuclear deterrence—prevention of war by convincing an enemy that if he attacks, he will be destroyed by nuclear weapons. (p. 208)

nuclear war—war involving the atomic bomb or the hydrogen bomb. (p. 229)

observatory—a building designed to observe the stars. (p. 297)

occupation—invasion, conquest, and control of a nation or territory by foreign armed forces. (p. 141)

orbit—the path of a celestial body as it revolves around another body. (p. 289)

orbital flight—a full revolution around Earth. (p. 320)

ordnance—military supply such as weapons, ammunition, combat vehicles, and equipment. (p. 125)

ornithopter—an aircraft designed to get its support and forward motion from flapping wings. (p. 10)

outrigger—a frame extending laterally beyond the main structure of an aircraft. (p. 113)

overhaul—to go over carefully and make needed repairs. (p. 128)

parachute—a device intended to slow free fall from an aircraft or another high point. (p. 7)

paratrooper—an infantry Soldier who is trained to parachute, often behind enemy lines. (p. 159)

payload—what a rocket carries that is necessary to its mission. (p. 307)

patent—a legal document protecting the rights of an inventor. (p. 23)

perigee—the lowest point of an orbit. (p. 322)

pitch—a movement up or down. (p. 33)

porthole—a small, circular window. (p. 48)

POW—a prisoner of war (p. 228)

precision weapons—guided missiles and bombs. (p. 262)

pressurized cabins—cabins with normal air pressure even at high altitudes. (p. 175)

probe—a scientific satellite that studies a planet or another object in space other than Earth. (p. 331)

propulsion—a driving or propelling force. (p. 193)

pursuit aircraft—fighter plane. (p. 129)

pylons—tall, thin towers. (p. 56)

radial—round. (p. 49)

reciprocating engine—an engine that goes back and forth. (p. 192)

relative wind—the flow of air. (p. 36)

revolve—to circle in an orbit. (p. 289)

retractable—the description of landing gear that folds into the aircraft. (p. 108)

ribs—pieces that give shape to the wings. (p. 38)

rocket—a large, cylindrical object that moves very fast by forcing burning gases out one end of the tube. (p. 8)

rotate—to spin on an axis. (p. 289)

rotors—another name for propellers. (p. 50)

rudder—a movable flap or blade attached to the rear of a craft. (p. 18)

sabotage—the destruction of property by enemy agents in time of war. (p. 137)

satellite—an object that orbits another object in space, such as a planet. (p. 211)

scheduled airlines—airlines that have flights that depart and arrive at set times. (p. 109)

secede—break away. (p. 275)

skids—long, thin runners, like a pair of skis. (p. 39)

solar system—the sun and all the objects in space that circle around it. (p. 286)

solitary confinement—a status in which a prisoner is held in a cell alone and not allowed to talk to anyone. (p. 237)

solo—to fly with no one else on board. (p. 55)

sortie—a flight or an attack by a single combat aircraft. (p. 260)

spars—the main, lengthwise pieces of the wing. (p. 38)

spatial disorientation—a condition in which a person's sense of direction does not agree with reality. (p. 99)

spectators—people who come to see an event or show. (p. 84)

speculative—not practical or based on facts. (p. 305)

squadron—an air force unit consisting of two or more flights. (p. 143)

stalemate—a situation in which further action is blocked. (p. 71)

stockholder—a person who owns shares of a public company. (p. 172)

strafe—to attack with a machine gun from a low-flying aircraft. (p. 75)

strategic—designed to strike at the sources of an enemy's military, economic, or political power. (p. 72)

Strategic Triad—the United States's three-pronged method of delivering nuclear weapons, consisting of land-based intercontinental ballistic missiles (ICBMs), submarine-launched ballistic missiles (SLBMs), and long-range bombers. (p. 210)

streamlining—designing an aircraft to reduce resistance to motion through the air. (p. 9)

stressed skin—an outer covering that can stand up to the push-and-pull forces of flight. (p. 108)

strut—a vertical post. (p. 32)

suborbital flight—one that makes less than one revolution around Earth. (p. 320)

subsidy—government money paid to a person or company that serves the public. (p. 108)

sunspots—the relatively cool dark spots that sometimes appear on the surface of the sun. (p. 299)

superpower—a powerful, dominant country that has nuclear weapons. (p. 257)

surveillance—reconnaissance. (p. 354)

tactical—involving military operations that are smaller, closer to base, and of less long-term significance than strategic operations. (p. 145)

tail rotor—a small propeller at the end of a long tail boom. (p. 113)

tandem—two objects with one placed directly behind the other. (p. 48)

tethered flight—flights in which the aircraft is tied to the ground by cables. (p. 113)

theater—a large geographic area in which military operations are coordinated. (p. 140)

38th parallel—a line marking the original boundary between North and South Korea. (p. 221)

thrust—the forward force driving an aircraft. (p. 22)

torque—a twisting force. (p. 50)

totalitarianism—a form of government under which the people are completely under the control of a state authority that oppresses all opposition. (p. 311)

transcontinental—coast-to-coast. (p. 97)

transport—a vehicle—aircraft, ship, or other—that carries people, supplies, tanks, and artillery. (p 154)

treasonable—involving a violation of allegiance towards one's country. (p. 127)

tri-jet—an aircraft with three engines. (p. 194)

turbine engine—an engine driven by a moving fluid, such as water, steam, or air, that pushes against blades or paddles attached to a central shaft. (p. 192)

twin-float—an airplane with floats for landing on or taking off from a body of water. (p. 106)

U-boats—German submarines. (p. 63)

United Nations—a worldwide organization first formed in 1945 by the victorious Allies to maintain international peace. (p. 209)

virtual—existing in ideas and outside the physical world. (p. 356)

warhead—the explosive tip of a missile. (p. 251)

warp—twist. (p. 32)

weapon of mass destruction—a chemical, biological, or atomic weapon that can kill large numbers of people in one use. (p. 267)

weight—the force that directly opposes lift. (p. 193)

Western Allies—the United States, Britain, and France. (p. 215)

yaw—a sidewise movement. (p. 39)

zeppelin—a German dirigible with a rigid frame used for observation and bombing raids. (p. 73)

1st Aero Squadron, 71
8K71PS launcher, 329
9th Fighter Command, 146
11 September 2001, 202, 261
11A511 launcher, 329
11A57 launcher, 329
12th Air Force, 140
12th Fighter Command, 146
15th Air Force, 140
19th Amendment to the
        US Constitution, 88
38th parallel, 221
94th Squadron, 67
96th Article of War, 127
99th Pursuit Squadron (Tuskegee Airmen),
        130, 147–148
305th Bombardment Group, 150
332nd Fighter Group, 147
4080th Strategic Reconnaissance
        Wing, 229
418th Army Air Forces Band, 157

A

Abbott, Robert S., 82–83
Aberdeen Proving Grounds, 128
aces, 62
    Chin, Maj Arthur T., 166
    Fernandez, Capt Manuel "Pete", 225
    Jabara, Col James, 206
    Rickenbacker, Edward, 67
    von Richthofen, Baron Manfred,
        62, 70
Aegis, 359
aeolipile, 191
Aerial Experiment Association, 46
aerial reconnaissance, 18, 14–15, 20
    Cold War, 211
    Cuban Missile Crisis, 229
    satellites, 331
    stealth aircraft, 255, 267
    unmanned air vehicles, 354–355
    Vietnam War, 233
    World War I, 122

aerial refueling, 103
aerodynamic, 88
Aeronautical Division, Army Signal Corps,
        52, 122
aeronauts, 20
African-American pilots
    Bluford Jr., Col Guion S., 318, 346
    Buffalo Soldiers, 15
    Bullard, Eugene, 65, 69–70
    Coleman, Bessie, 51, 54
    Davis Jr., Gen Benjamin O., 148
    Hall, 1st Lt Charles, 148
    James Jr., Gen Daniel "Chappie", 242
    Jemison, Mae, 339, 347
    99th Pursuit Squadron (Tuskegee Airmen),
        130, 147–148
Aidid, Mohammed Farah, 254
aileron, 46, 48
air cavalry, 235
Air Commerce Act, 104
Air Corps Act, 125
Air Defense Command (ADC), 208
Air Florida, 200
Air Force Combat Command, 134
Air Force Cross, 266
    Chapman, TSgt John, 263
    Cunningham, SrA Jason, 265
    Etchberger, CMSgt Richard, 239
    Robinson, A1C William, 237
    Wilkinson, TSgt Timothy, 254
Air Force Cyberspace Command, 356–357
Air Force Reserve, 262
Air Force Space Command, 314
Air National Guard, 262
air platforms, 360
Air Tasking Order, 259
air traffic control, 181
    controllers, 181
Air Transport Command Ferrying
        Division, 218
airborne laser, 352
Airborne Warning and Control System
        (AWACS), 211
Airbus Industrie, 195

Aircraft
  A-6, 248
  A-7, 248
  AC-47, 240
  AC-130, 246
  AD/A-1 Skyraider, 222
  Aerodrome, 24
  Akron, 180
  Albatros, 68, 74
  Ariel, 23
  B-1 Lancer, 250
  B-2 stealth bomber, 212, 255
    first combat, 276
  B-17 "Flying Fortress", 127, 131–132, 151
    D-Day, 159
  B-24 Liberator, 151
  B-25 Mitchell, 151, 167
  B-26 Marauder, 151
  B-29 Superfortress, 150–151
  B-52 bombers, 167, 211, 236, 259
  Beechcraft 35 Bonanza, 186
  Bell P-39 Airacobra, 132, 152
  Bell X-1, 213
  Bell X-2, 213
  Bell X-5, 250
  Bell XP 59-A Airacomet, 191
  Blériot XI monoplane, 47
  Boeing 1 (B-1) biplane, 107
  Boeing 40-A, 107
  Boeing 247, 108
  Boeing 299 (B-17), 131
  Boeing 307B Stratoliner, 176
  Boeing 314, 110
  Boeing 707 jet, 185, 189, 193
  Boeing 727 tri-jet, 194
  Boeing 747, 194
  Boeing 757, 195
  Boeing 767, 195
  Boeing B-47 bomber, 212
  British Comet IV, 185
  C-5 Galaxy, 273
  C-47 *Skytrain "Gooney Bird"*, 109, 154
    Photos of, 118, 154
    Berlin Airlift, 217
  C-54, 217
  C-120 Cessna, 186
  C-130 Hercules, 273, 275, 279
  C-140 Cessna, 186
  C-141 Starlifter, 246, 273, 277
  Caravelle I, 194
  Cessna 140, 186
  Cessna 150/152, 186
  Cessna 182, 186

  Chance-Vought F-4U Corsair, 152
  Chicago, 124
  China Clipper seaplane, 110
  Clippers, 110
  Cloudster, 179
  Convair 240, 178
  Curtiss P-36, 132
  Curtiss P-40 Warhawk, 132, 149, 152, 166
  Curtiss PW-8, 124
  DC-1, 103
  DC-2, 109, 131
  DC-3, 109, 131, 182
  DC-4, 177
  DC-6, 173, 177
    DC-6B, 177
  DC-7, 173, 177
    DC-7B, 177
    DC-7C "Seven Seas", 177
  DC-8, 189, 193
  De Havilland Comet, 185, 188–189, 191
  De Havilland Mosquito, 153
  Douglas X-3, Stiletto, 249
  DT-1, 179
  EB-66, 236
  EC-121, 236
  EC-130, 246
  EF-111, 248
  Enola Gay, 168
  F-4 Phantoms, 236
  F-4F Wildcat, 152
  F-4U Corsair, 152, 222
  F-9F Pantherjet, 222
  F-14, 248
  F-15 Eagle, 272
  F-22 Raptor, 255
  F-35 stealth fighter, 255, 351
  F-51 Mustang, 222
  F-80 Shooting Star, 222
  F-84 Thunderjet, 222
  F-86 Sabrejet, 206, 222
  F-100C Super Sabre, 225
  F-100F Wild Weasel, 236
  F-104 Starfighter, 249
  F-105 Thunderchief, 236
  F-111 Aardvark, 248
  F-117 Nighthawk, 248, 255, 260
  FF-29 Seaplane, 73
  Focke-Achgelis (FA-61), 113
  Focke-Wulf 190, 153
  Fokker C-2, 97, 103
  Fokker Dr-I, 77
  Fokker D-VII, 62, 77
  Fokker monoplane, 88

German FF-29 seaplane, 23
Gloster Gladiator, 166
Golden Flyer, 46
Gotha IV, 73
Grumman F-4F Wildcat, 152
Grumman F-6F Hellcat, 152
Gyroplane-Laboratoire, 112
H-4 Hercules "Spruce Goose", 175
Halberstadt CL-II, 62
Hawker Hurricane, 153, 156
Heinkel 162 Voksjaeger, 153
HH-43 helicopters, 237–238
HRS-1 Sikorsky helicopter, 222
HyperSoar, 353
Hyper-X, 352
JN-4 *Jenny*, 45, 84-85
June Bug, 46
Junkers D1, 77
KC-10, 248, 260
KC-135, 211, 248, 260
L-049 Constellation, 172–173
   Super Constellation, 178
Le Grand, 48, 77, 114
Lockheed C-69 Constellation, 173, 177
   Super Constellation, 178
Lockheed Constellation, 172–173, 177
Lockheed L-1011, 195
Lockheed P-38 Lightning 132, 152, 159
Lockheed Vega, 97
Loening amphibian planes, 88
Looking Glass, 211
Martin 130, 110
Martin 2-0-2, 178
McDonnell Douglas DC-9, 194
      Super 80, 195
McDonnell Douglas DC-10, 195
Messerschmitt 109, 153
Messerschmitt 110, 153
Messerschmitt 262 Schwalbe, 153
MH-47 helicopter, 263
MiG-15 fighter jets, 206, 223
Mitsubishi Zero, 153
Model C seaplanes, 106
New Orleans, 124
Nieuport 28, 77
OV-10, 241
P-51 Mustang, 149, 152
PA-28 Super Cub, 186
Pelican, 354
Piper Cub, 186
Piper J-3 Cubs, 131
Predator, 354
Question Mark, 103

Republic P-47 Thunderbolt, 152
S-6A, 114
S-40 "flying boat", 110
S-42, 110
SC-1, 45
SE-5A, 77
Seversky P-35, 132
Skytrain "Gooney Bird", 109, 118, 154
Sopwith Camel triplane, 77
Spad VII, 77
Spirit of St. Louis, 92, 94
Spruce Goose (H-4 Hercules), 175
SR-71 Blackbird, 249–250
Starliner, Lockheed, 178
Super Constellation, 178
Super-Handley Page bomber, 77
Supermarine Spitfire, 153
T-28, 236
Taylor E-2 Cub, 186
Triple Twin, 48
twin-float seaplane, 106
U-2 spy planes, 211, 229
UH-1 Huey, 235
VS-300 helicopter, 113
Vin Fiz Flyer, 51–52
Wright B, 53
Wright Flyer, 6, 30, 37–42
X-15, 249
X-43, 352
X-45, 354
XF-89 Scorpion, 174
aircraft carriers, 121
Airey, Paul W., 160
airfoil, 34
airframe, 309
airlift, 217
Airline Deregulation Act of 1978, 197
Airmail Acts
   of 1925, 104
   of 1934, 112
   of 1938, 112
airmail service, 104
Airnews, 185
airplanes, early, 16, 20, 23
   first attempts, 23–24
   Wright brothers and, 30–42
airscrew, 9, 22
Airships
   Graf Zeppelin, 180
   Hindenburg, 180
   Macon airship, 180
   Montgolfier hot-air balloon, 17
   Zeppelins, 19, 73, 180

airways, 181
Akers, Thomas, 347
Alaska, 198
Aldrin, Col Edwin (Buzz), 332–334, 345
all-cargo airlines, 178, 185
Allies (WWI), 63
Allies (WWII), 138
alloy, 188
Al-Qaeda, 261, 263
altitude, 88
America First Committee, 95
America West, 198
American Airlines, 67, 182
    DC-3, 109
American Airways, 182, 198. *See also*
        American Airlines
American Export, 185
amphibian planes, Loening, 88
Anderson Jr., Maj Rudolf, 229
Anderson, Michael, 347
angle of attack, 36
annex, 129
Antartica, 89
Antionette, Marie, Queen of France, 17
antitrust, 173
apogee, 322
Apollo 11, 325
    moon walk, 316, 332–334
Apollo 12, 325, 335
Apollo 13, 325, 335
Apollo 14, 325, 335
Apollo 15, 325, 335
Apollo 16, 325, 335
Apollo 17, 325, 335
Apollo, Project, 8, 308, 321
Apollo-Soyuz, 337
apprentice, 97
appropriate, 71
Apt, Jay, 347
aquanaut, 322
Ardennes Forest, 164
Ares I, 362
Aristarchus, 297
Aristide, Jean-Bertrand, 279
Arlandes, François d', 17
arms race, 231
arms, 209
Armstrong, Neil, 332–334, 345
Army Air Corps, 125, 129
    aircraft development, 131
Army Air Force, 95, 122, 132
Army Air Service, 122
Army General Staff, 125–126, 133

Army Reserve, 92
Army Signal Corps' Aeronautical
        Division, 52, 122
Arnold, Gen Henry "Hap", 72, 129, 132
    as Army Air Forces general, 134, 142
asteroids, 294
astronaut, 318
Astronomia Nova, 298
Atlantis, 338, 342
Atlas rocket, 309, 327
Atlas/Agena, 328
Atlas/Centaur, 328
atomic bombs, 168, 208
Aurora VII, 322
Australia, 139
Austria, 129
Austria-Hungary, 63
autogiro, 112
autonomous, 354
autonomy, 134
auxiliary, 120
Aviation Corporation (AVCO), 182
Aviation Section, Army Signal Corps,
        53, 122
Axis Powers (WWII), 138

B

Baghdad, 259
Bagian, James, 347
Baker, Newton, 134
Balchen, Bernt, 89
Baldwin, Thomas, 45
ballistic, 251
Balloon Corps, 20
ballooning, 18
balloons, 14–18, 20–21
    Balloon Corps (Civil War), 20
    first manned flight, 17
    invention of, 16
    reconnaissance with, 14–15, 18, 20
    Spanish-American War and, 14–15
Bangladesh, 280
barnstormers, 84–88
    polar exploration, 88–89
    significance of, 84–85, 90
Baruch, Bernard, 209
Battle of Britain (WWII), 140–141,
        155–156
Battle of Kai-feng Fu, 303
Battle of Midway (WWII), 166–167
Battle of Saint Mihiel (WWI), 71, 74–75
Battle of San Juan Hill, 14–15, 21

Battle of the Bulge (WWII), 164
Battle of the Coral Sea (WWII), 166
Battles of Seringapatam, 303
Beachey, Lincoln, 85
Bean, Alan, 345
Beech, 186
Bek, Ulug, 296–297
Belgium, 129
Bell, Alexander Graham, 46
Bendix race, 162, 225
Bennett, Warrant Officer Floyd, 89
Berlin Airlift, 150, 210, 214–219
  aircraft used, 217
  candy bomber, 219
  cause, 214–215
  Tunner, Lt Gen William, 218
Berlin Blockade. *See* Berlin Airlift
Berliner, Emile and Henry, 50
Bernoulli, Daniel, 11–12
  Bernouillian lift, 12
bid, 41
biplane, 23, 47
  Wright brothers, 38–40
Blériot, Louis, 47
blind flight, 99
blitzkrieg, 143, 145
Bluford Jr., Col Guion S., 318, 346
Bobko, Karol, 346
Boeing Air Transport, 106
Boeing Airplane Company, 106. *See also*
      Boeing Air Transport
Boeing Delta IV, 359
Boeing, William E., 106–107
Bolden, Charles, 346–347
bombers, 76, 151
bombing. *See also* missiles
  atomic, 168, 208
  formation pattern, 149
  long-range, 146
  precision daylight, 132, 149
  smart bombs, 251
  Super-Handley Page, 77
  WWI, 72–73, 75
bombsights, 128, 156
boom, 50
Borelli, Giovanni Alfonso, 10
Bosnia, 275
Boston Air Meet, 57
bracing, 32
Brahe, Tycho, 298
Brand, Vance, 345
Brandenstein, Daniel, 347
Branstein, Daniel, 346

Bréguet, Louis, 50, 112
Brett, Maj Gen George, 134
Britain in WWII, 139
British Air Transport Auxiliary, 162
British Imperial Airways, 185
British Overseas Airways Corporation, 191
British Royal Flying Corps (RFC), 73
Bronze Star, 266
  Lynn, CMSgt Kevin, 269
Brown, Curtis, 347
Brown, David, 347
Brown, Margery, 88
Buchli, James, 346
Buffalo Soldiers, 15
Bulgaria, 139
Bullard, Eugene, 65, 69–70
buoyancy, 16
Bureau of Air Commerce, 112
Bureau of Air Mail, 112
Burge, Private 1st Class Vernon, 52–53
Burr, Donald, 197
Bush, George H.W., 248
Byrd, Rear Adm Richard E., 88–89

C

C2s, 360
Callisto, 291
Canadarm2, 349
canard configuration, 33
cargo airlines, 178
Carpenter, Cmdr Scott, 320, 322, 345
Carter, Jimmy, 197, 243
Casper, John, 347
Cassini, 331
casualties, 137
catapults, 10
Cayley, Sir George, 22
center of pressure, 34
Central Intelligence Agency (CIA), 208
  Project Heavy Green, 239
Central Powers (WWI), 63
Ceres, 294
Cernan, Eugene, 345
Cessna Aircraft, 186
Chaffee, Roger, 325
Challenger, 318, 338, 342
  accident, 344
Chang-Diaz, Franklin, 347
Chanute, Octave, 32
Chapman, TSgt John, 263
Charles, J.A.C., 18

Charon, 293–294
Chawla, Kalpana, 347
Cherokee, 82
Cheung, Katherine Sui Fun, 101
Chicago Weekly Defender, 82
Chief Master Sergeant of the Air Force
    (CMSAF), 160
Chilton, Gen Kevin P., 314, 343, 347
Chin, Maj Arthur T., 166
China, 139
Chinese kites, 7–8
Choctaw, 82
Cierva, Juan de la, 112
circuit, 98
Civil Aeronautics Administration
    (CAA), 181
  as Federal Aviation Agency (FAA), 199
Civil Aeronautics Authority War Training
    Service, 130
Civil Aeronautics Authority, 112, 181
Civil Aeronautics Board (CAB), 181
  as Federal Aviation Agency (FAA), 199
  deregulation, 197
Civil Air Patrol (CAP), 186, 280
civil aviation promotion, 94
Civil War, 14
civilian flight schools, 129–130
Civilian Pilot Training Program, 130
  Piper J-3 Cubs, 131
Clark Field, 127
Clark, Julia, 59
Clark, Laurel, 347
classified, 255
Clausewitz, Carl von, 259
Clay, Gen Lucius, 217–218
coalition, 257
Cochran, Jacqueline, 161, 162
cockpit, 48
Cold War, 209–210
  aircraft developments, 249–250
  Berlin Airlift, 215–219
  end of, 252
  missile and nuclear developments,
    251–252
Coleman, Bessie, 51, 54, 82–85
  barnstormer, 85
Collins, Col Eileen, 340, 347
Collins, Lt Michael, 332–334, 345
Colonel James Jabara Airport, 206
Colonial Air, 190
colony, 221
Columbia, 338, 342
  accident, 344

combat box formation, 149
combined arms, 143
comets, 294
commercial aircraft, 177
  advances, 174–176
commercial airlines, 104, 182–185
  all-cargo or freight, 178, 185
  deregulation of, 197–198
  first flights, 181
  jets and, 196–199
  regulation of, 181, 199
  transatlantic service, 185
Communication Satellite System, 330
Communist Party, 139
components, 307
Confederates, 21
configurations, 196
Congressional Medal of Honor. *See* Medal
  of Honor
Congreve, Col William, 303
Conrad, Charles, 323, 345
consortium, 195
constellations, 295
Continental, 198
control, 309, 311
control, directional, 10
Coolidge, Calvin, 125
Cooper, Jr., Maj L. Gordon, 314, 320,
  323, 345
Copernicus, Nicolaus, 286–288, 297–298
Corn, Joseph, 90
Cornu, Paul, 50
corps, defined, 129
cosmonaut, 326
court-martial, 127
cowling, 108
crankshaft, 49
Crippen, Robert, 345–346
Crissy Field, California, 99
Croatia, 275
Croix de Guerre, 69
cruise missiles, 251
Cuban Missile Crisis, 229–231
  blockade, 231
  cause of, 229
Cunningham, SrA Jason, 265
Curtiss, Glenn, 44–47
  Aircraft company, 45, 71, 78, 84
  awards, 46
  engines, 45
  Flying School, 59
Curtiss' Wasp, 45
cyberspace, 356–357

D

Da Vinci, Leonardo, designer of
  airscrew, 9
  glider, 10
  helicopter, 9, 112
  parachute, 9
Daedalus, 7
Davis Jr., Lt Col George A., 226
Davis, David R., 179
Davis, Gen Benjamin O., 148
Davis, N. Jan, 347
Davis-Douglas Co., 179. *See also* Douglas
      Aircraft
Dayton Accords, 275
D-Day, 141, 157, 159–160
De Gaulle, Charles, 70
death camps, 138
deep space, 361
Defense Meteorological Satellite Program, 331
Defense Support Program (DSP), 331
De la Roche, Raymonde, 58
Delta Airlines, 198
Delta rockets, 327–328
Demos, 291
Denmark, 139
Department of Commerce, 112
  commercial aviation regulation
      agencies, 181
Department of Defense, 208
Department of the Air Force, creation of, 208
Department of the Army, creation of, 208
Department of the Navy, creation of, 208
Department of Transportation (DOT), 199
Depression, 129, 179
Derby, Lt Col George M., 14
Dern, George H., 134
Desert Storm. *See* Operation Desert Storm
Destiny Laboratory, 349
Deutsch, Henri, 19
directional control, 10
dirigibles, 16, 18–19
  invention of, 18
  rigid, 19
  SC-1 (US Army's first), 45
Discovery, 318, 338
Distinguished Service Cross, 140, 206, 226
Division of Military Aeronautics,
      Secretary of War, 122
dogfight, 74
Doolittle, Lt Gen James "Jimmy" Harold,
      99–100, 151
  Tokyo raid (WWII), 167

Dorand, René, 112
Douglas Aircraft Company, 109, 173.
      See also DC planes
  founding of, 179
Douglas Sr., Donald Wills, 179
drag, 22
Drum, Maj Gen Hugh, 134
Duke, Charles, 345
dwarf planets, 293
dynamic lift, 12

E

Eagle, 332
Eaker, Capt Ira C., 103
Earhart, Amelia, 97–98
  Ninety-Nines club and, 164
Earth Radiation Budget Satellite, 331
Earth, 290
Eastern Air Transport, 67, 182–183
Eastern Airlines, 67, 182–183
Edgeworth-Kuiper Belt, 293
Eichstadt, Konrad Kyeser von, 303
Eighth Air Force, 140
Eisenhower, Dwight D., 95, 146
electric motor, 18
elevator, 33
elliptical, 290, 294
Ely, Eugene, 47
embargo, 165
Emmons, Lt Gen Delos C., 134
Endeavour, 338, 342
engines. *See also* internal-combustion
      engines and steam engines
  Curtiss, 45
  jet, 191–193
  multiengine planes, 48
  radial placement, 49
  ramjet, 353
  reciprocating, 192
  rotary, 49
  tandem placement, 48
  weight, 49
Engle, Joseph, 346
English Channel, Lindbergh
      crossing, 93
enlisted pilots, 72, 154
Enterprise, 338, 342
enthusiasts, 88
epicycles, 287
equator, 98
Erwin, SSgt Henry E., 136
Escadrille Américaine, 65

escadrille, defined, 65
escort, 159
Esnault-Pelterie, Robert, 48
Estonia, 139
Etchberger, CMSgt Richard, 239
Ethopia, 139
Europa, 291
European Space Agency, 332
Evans, Ronald, 345
Evolved Expendable Launch Vehicle
    (EELV), 359
Executive Order 9981, 147
Expedition 1, 348
expendable launch, 327
Explorer 1, 306, 313, 319, 331

F

Fabian, John, 346
Faith VII, 323
falling stars, 295
Fascist, 139
Father of Modern Aviation, 23
Federal Aviation Act of 1958, 199
Federal Aviation Agency, 146
  CAA and CAB takeovers, 199
Federal Express, 185
female pilots and astronauts. *See* women
    in aviation
Ferdinand, Archduke Franz, 63
Fernandez, Capt Manuel "Pete", 225
fighters, 76–77, 152–153
Finland, 139
Firman, Armen, 7
First Air Defense Wing, 146
first stage, 329
Fisk, TSgt Wayne, 242
Fitzgerald, F. Scott, 70
fixed wing, 22
flight simulator, 101
flight, 143
flight, ancient attempts at, 7
flying circuses, 84. *See also* barnstormers
Flying Tiger, 185
Foale, Michael, 347
Focke, Dr. Heinrich, 113
Fogleman, Gen Ronald R., 280
Fokker, Anthony, 74
  as mentor, 83
Fonck, René, 62
Ford Island, 127
Ford Motor Company, 95
Foreign Legion, 65

formation pattern bombing, 149
    combat box formation, 149
Fort Bliss, 307
Fort Myer, Virginia, 102
Fort Sam, Houston, 133
Fortin, Paul, 11
Foulois, Maj Gen Benjamin, 42, 52
    independent air force advocate, 133
France in WWII, 139. *See also* D-Day
Franklin, Benjamin, 18
free market, 197
Freedom VII, 321
freight airlines, 178, 185
French Air Service, 69
French Foreign Legion, 65
French sateen, 34
French-American Aeroplane Company, 56
Friendship VII, 322
Friendship, 97
From the Earth to the Moon, 305–306
Frye, William John (Jack), 184
fuselage, 48

G

Gaffney, F. Drew, 347
Gagarin, Yuri, 326
galaxy, 289
Galilei, Galileo, 291
    contributions, 299–300
    tides, 300
Galileo probe, 331, 342
Galileo. *See* Galilei, Galileo
Galland, Lt Gen Adolf, 165
GAM 63 Rascal, 251–252
Ganymede, 291
Gardner, Dale, 346
Garriot, Owen, 346
Garros, Roland, 74
gasoline-powered internal-combustion
    engine, 18
Gemini V, 323
Gemini VI, 323
Gemini VII, 323
Gemini X, 334
general aviation, 186
General Electric, 191
    missile development, 307
General Headquarters Air Force (GHQ), 134
General Motors Fokker Aircraft Company, 67
Geneva Accords of 1954, 232–233
geocentric, 286
geosynchronous, 290

German Imperial Air Service, 70
Germany in WWII, 139
Gibson, Robert, 347
Giffard dirigible, 18
Giffard, Henri, 18
Gift from the Sea, 96
Glenn L. Martin Company, 110
Glenn, Col John H., 222, 320, 322, 345
gliders, 10, 22–23
    Wright brothers, 33–34
Global Positioning System (GPS), 330, 358
Gnome rotary engine, 49
Goddard, Robert H., 302–304
   rockets, liquid, 304
Goodyear Tire and Rubber Company, 180
Gorbachev, Mikhail, 252
Gordon Bennett trophy, 46
Gordon, Louis, 97
Gordon, Richard, 345
GPS (Global Positioning System), 330, 358
Grabe, Ronald, 346
grades, 123
Graham Bell, Alexander, 46
gravity, 289
Great Circle Route, 96
Great Dark Spot, 293
Great Depression, 129, 179
Great Red Spot, 291
Greece, 139
Greely, Brig Gen Adolphus V., 21
Greenland, 89
Gregory, Frederick, 346
Griffin, Michael, 361
Grissom, Lt Col Virgil I. (Gus),
    314, 320–321, 345
ground effect, 354
Ground Mobile-3 (GM-3), 360
guerrilla warfare, 233
Guest, Amy Phipps, 97
Guggenheim Medal, 107
guidance, 309, 311
Gulf War. *See* Operation Desert Storm
gun, machine, 67, 74
gunpowder, 8
Gusmão, Laurenço de, 16
Gutierrez, Col Sidney, 343, 347

H

hacker, 356
Haenlein, Paul, 19
Haise, Fred, 335, 345
Haiti, 279

Hale-Bopp comet, 294
Hall, 1st Lt Charles, 148
Halley's comet, 294
Halverson, 1st Lt Harry A., 103
Halvorsen, 1st Lt Gail, 219
Harbaugh, Gregory, 347
Harbour Grace, Newfoundland, 97
Harris, Bernard, 347
Hauck, Frederick, 346
Hawley, Steven, 346
Hearst, William Randolph, 51, 88
heavier-than-air craft 16. *See also*
    airplanes, gliders and jets
Heib, Richard, 347
helicopters, 22, 50. *See also*
    Sikorsky, Igor
   civilian use, 114
   development of, 112–113
   military use, 114
heliocentric, 287–288
helium, 18
Hellfire missile, 262
Hell's Angels, 174
Helms, Susan, 347–348
Hemingway, Ernest, 70
Henry E. Erwin Outstanding Enlisted Aircrew
    Member of the Year Award, 136
Henry, Joseph, 20
Henson, W.S., 23
Hero of Alexandria, 191
Herring, Augustus, 32
Herzegovina, 275
Hilmers, David, 346
Hiroshima, 168
Hitler, Adolf, 138
Holocaust, 138
Hoo, Wan, 8
Hooe, SSgt Roy W., 103
Hopkins, 2d Lt Joseph G., 103
horsepower, 18
hot-air balloons. *See* balloons
Hoyt, Capt Ross G., 103
Hsin, Han, 8
Hubbard, Eddie, 107
Hubble Space Telescope, 331
Hughes Aircraft, 172
Hughes Jr., Howard R., 172–175
   and Constellation, 174
   as moviemaker, 174
   and "Spruce Goose", 175
Hughes Toolco, 172
Hughes-Fulford, Mille, 347
Hulbert, Murray, 60

Humphreys, 2d Lt Frederic E., 42
Hundred Years' War, 303
Hungary, 139
Hurricane Andrew, 280
Hurricane Katrina, 280
  helicopter use, 114
Husband, Rick, 347
Hussein, Saddam, 257, 267, 272
Hyakutake comet, 294
hydrogen, 18
hypersonic air vehicles, 352
hypersonic, defined, 352
hypothesis, 287

I

Icarus, 7
Il-Sung, Kim, 221
incendiary bombs, 167
incentives, 108
incompetent, 127
India, 139
induced lift, 12
inertia, 308
infantry, 141
insurgents, 267
interdiction, 145
internal-combustion engine, 19
International Geophysical Year, 312
International Space Station (ISS),
    314, 348–249
international waters, 232
Internet, 356
Io, 291
Iraq, 257
Irish Sea, 93
Irwin, James, 345
isolationist, 141
Italy, 139

J

Jacobson, A1C Elizabeth, 270
James Jr., Gen Daniel "Chappie", 242
Japan, 139
Jarvis, Gregory, 346
Jemison, Mae, 339, 347
Jernigan, Tamara, 347
jet engine, 188, 191–193
jet lag, 196
Jet Pilot film, 174
Jet Propulsion Laboratory, 313, 339
JetBlue, 198

jets, 16, 188–196
  commercial impact of, 196–199
  engines, 188, 191–193
  jumbo, 194
Joint Chiefs of Staff, 270
jumbo jets, 194
jumpsuit, 57
Junkers, Hugo, 77
Juno 1, 313
Jupiter, 291

K

Kaiser, Henry, 174
keel, 19
Kelliher, Herb, 199
Kelly, 1st Lt Oakley, 124
Kennedy, John F., 231
Kepler, Johannes, 298–299
  contributions, 299
Keys, Clement, 182
Khrushchev, Nikita, 231, 312
King of Portugal, 16
King, Rollin, 199
kites, 7–8
Komarov, Vladimir, 327
Korean War, 210
  aircraft used in, 221–222
  cause of, 221
  helicopter use in, 114
Kosovo, 276
Krikalev, Sergei, 347
Kuhn, Thomas S., 288
Kurds, 272
Kuwait, 257

L

Lafayette Escadrille, 65
Lafayette, Marquis de, 65
Lahm, 1st Lt Frank P., 42, 53
Laika, 312, 319
Lance P. Sijan Award, 228
LANDSAT (land satellite), 331
Langley Air Force Base, 24
Langley, Dr. Samuel Pierpont, 24
lateral balance, 46
lateral turns, 32
latitude, 221
Latvia, 139
launch vehicles
  Soviet, 329
  US, 327–328

laws of motion, 12
Le Bourget Airport, 93
Lee, Mark, 347
legend, 8
Legion of Merit, 102
LeMay, Gen Curtis E., 149–150
   Berlin Airlift, 217
Leningrad siege (St. Petersburg), 139
Leonov, Alexei, 326
Leslie's Weekly, 56
Levitow, A1C John, 240
Liberty Bell VII, 321
Libya, 247
Lichtenberg, Byron, 346
lift, 18
   Bernouillian, 12
   dynamic, 12
   induced, 12
   Newtonian, 12
lighter-than-air craft 16. *See also* balloons
    and dirigibles
light-year, 294
Lilienthal, Otto, 23, 33
limited war, 221, 225
Lincoln, Abraham, 20
Lind, Don, 346
Lindbergh, Anne Morrow, 94, 96
Lindbergh, Charles A.
   Anne Morrow, wife of, 94, 96
   barnstormer, 87
   transatlantic flight, 92–94
Listen: The Wind, 96
Lithuania, 139
Lockheed Martin Atlas V, 359
logistics, 134
Londonderry, Northern Ireland, 98
Long Island Airways, 190
Long-Range Raid (WWI), 72
Louis XVI, King of France, 17
Love, Nancy Harkness, 161, 163, 218
Lovell, James, 335, 345
Lowe, Thaddeus, 20
Lucky Lindy, 95. *See also* Lindbergh,
    Charles A.
Lufbery, Raoul, 66
Luftwaffe, 141, 143
   Battle of the Bulge, 165
   blitzkrieg, 145
Luke, 2d Lt Frank, 68
Luna 2 and *3*, 332
lunar roving vehicle (LRV), 335
lunar, 321
Lynn, CMSgt Kevin, 269

M

MacArthur, Gen Douglas, 221
Mach Riders of Nellis Air Force Base, 225
mach, 213
machine guns, 67, 74
Mackay Trophy, 241
Macready, 1st Lt John, 124
Madole, Glenn, 52
mail. *See* airmail service
mainstream, 100
Malta, 145
manned flight, first, 17
Mannock, Edward, 62
Mariner 10, 289
Mars, 291
   space colony, 363
Marshall Plan, 210
Marshall Space Flight Center, 306
Marshall, George, 210
Marsnik, 332
Massachusetts Institute of Technology, 179
materiel, 156
Mattingly, Thomas, 345–346
Maughan, 1st Lt Russell, 124
Maxfield, Lt Col Joseph E., 14
McAuliffe, Christa, 346
McCandless, Bruce, 346
McCool, Willie, 347
McDivitt, James, 345
McDonnell Douglas, 194
McMonagle, Donald, 347
McNair, Ronald, 346
Medal of Honor, 266
   Bennett, Warrant Officer Floyd, 89
   Byrd, Rear Adm Richard E., 89
   Davis Jr., Lt Col George A., 226
   Doolittle, Lt Gen James "Jimmy"
     Harold, 100
   Erwin, SSgt Henry E., 136
   Levitow, A1C John, 240
   Pitsenbarger, A1C William, 238
   Rickenbacker, Edward, 62
   Sijan, Capt Lance, 228
Mediterranean, 145
Melnick, Bruce, 347
mentor, 83
Merbold, Ulf, 346
Mercury astronauts, 314, 320–327
Mercury, 289
metal fatigue, 191
meteorites, 295
meteors, 295

meteroids, 295
milestone, 94
military coup, 279
Miller, Maj Glenn, 157
Milosevic, Slobodan, 275–276
Minh, Ho Chi, 232
Mir, 337
missile defense, 358–359
missiles, 211
  ballistic, 251
  cruise, 251
  defense, 358–359
  GAM 63 Rascal, 251–252
  Hellfire, 262
  intercontinental ballistic missile
    (ICBM), 210
  mission specialist, 318
  Northrup SM 62 Snark, 251–252
  in spacecraft, 327
  submarine-launched ballistic missile
    (SLBM), 210
  surface-to-air (SAM), 229
  warhead, 251
Mitchell, Brig Gen William "Billy", 67
  Army Staff College, 126
  Battle of Saint Mihiel, 71, 74, 78, 123
  campaign for Army Air Service, 78,
    120–121, 123–127
  George Washington University, 126
  Wisconsin Volunteers, 126
Mitchell, Edgar, 345
module, 326
Mohri, Mamoru, 347
Moisant, John, 56
Moisant, Matilde, 57–58
monoplane
  fighter, 77
  first design, 23
  powered, 47
Montenegro, 275
Montgolfier gas, 17
Montgolfier, Étienne and Joseph, 17
Montgomery, John J., 23
moon
  Earth's, 290, 325
  Jupiter's, 291
  Mars', 291
  Neptune's, 293
  Pluto's, 293
  Saturn's, 292
  Uranus', 292
Moon, 1st Lt Odas, 103
Morrow Board, 125

Moseley, Gen T. Michael, 271
motor. *See* electric motor
MQ-1 Predator, 262
multiengine planes, 48
muslin, 38
Mussolini, Benito, 139
Myers, Capt David A., 99
Myers, Gen Richard, 270
myth, 7

N

Nagasaki, 168
nanotechnology, 355
nano-UAV, 355
Napoleonic Wars, 303
NASA's Marshall Space Flight Center, 306
National Advisory Committee for
    Aeronautics, 87
National Aeronautics and Space
    Administration (NASA), 87
  creation of, 313, 319
National Air Lines, 185
National Air Marking Program, 164
National Defense Acts
  of 3 June 1916, 72
  of 1920, 123
National Military Establishment, 208
National Security Act of 1947, 134, 207–208
National Security Council, 208
National Socialist Party, 138
National Transportation Safety Board
    (NTSB), 199–200
NAVSTAR (Navigation Signal Timing
    and Ranging), 330
Nazis, 138
Neptune, 293
Nero, Sgt Ulysses S., 125
  bombadier, 128
  inventor, 128
Netherlands, 139
neutral, 239
New Zealand, 139
Newton, Isaac, 11–12
  laws of motion, 12, 308
  Newtonian lift, 12
Newton, Sir Isaac, 300
Newtonian lift, 12
Newton's laws of motion, 12, 308
Ninety-Nines club, 101, 164
Nixon, Richard, 234, 240
no-fly zone, 272
non-rigid craft, 19

Noonan, Frederick, 98
Norden Mark XV, 132, 156
Noriega, Manuel, 248
Normandy, 159. *See also* D-Day
North American Aerospace Defense
 Command (NORAD), 262
North Atlantic Treaty Organization
 (NATO), 210
 Operation Allied Force, 271, 276
 Operation Deliberate Force, 271, 276
 Operation Deny Flight, 271, 276
 West German acceptance, 243
North Pole flight, 88
North to the Orient, 96
Northern Ireland and Amelia Earhart, 98
Northrop SM62 Snark, 251–252
Northwest, 198
nuclear deterrence, 208
nuclear war, 229

O

Oberth, Hermann, 304–305
observation aircraft, 76
observatory, 297
occupation, 141
Ocker, Sgt William C., 99, 102
 Doris Ocker, widow of, 102
O'Connor, Bryan, 347
Odlum, Floyd Bostwick, 162
O'Hare Airport, 196
Olds, Lt Col Robert, 161
Omlie, Phoebe Fairgrave, 87
On the Revolutions of the Celestial Spheres, 288
Onizuka, Col Ellison, 344, 346
Oort Cloud, 294
Operation Allied Force, 271, 276
Operation Anaconda, 263, 265
Operation Deliberate Force, 271, 276
Operation Deny Flight, 271, 276
Operation Desert Shield, 257–260
 end of, 259
Operation Desert Storm, 257–260
 end of, 259
Operation Eagle Claw, 243–244
Operation El Dorado Canyon, 247–248
 aircraft used, 248, 250
Operation Enduring Freedom (OEF),
 261–262, 271
 unmanned air vehicles (UAVs) and, 355
Operation Iraqi Freedom (OIF), 267–271
 precision weapons used, 268
Operation Just Cause, 248

Operation Noble Eagle (ONE), 262, 271, 358
Operation Northern Watch, 271–272
Operation Overlord, 159
Operation Provide Comfort, 271–272
Operation Provide Hope, 271, 273
Operation Provide Promise, 271, 275
Operation Provide Relief, 271, 277
Operation Restore Hope/Restore Hope II,
 271, 277–278
Operation Rolling Thunder, 234
Operation Shining Hope, 271, 276
Operation Southern Watch, 271–272
Operation Uphold Democracy, 271, 279
Operation Urgent Fury, 245–246
Operation Vittles, 217
Operations Linebacker I and II, 234–235, 238
orbit, 289
orbital flight, 320
Orbital Test Vehicle (OTV), 360
ordnance, 125
Orion, 361–362
ornithopter, 10
Orteig, Raymond, prize, 88, 92
Ostfriesland, 120–121, 123
outrigger, 113
overhaul, 128
Overmyer, Robert, 346

P

PAC-3, 359
Pailes, Maj William, 341, 346
Pan American Airways, 110
 jet service, 188–189
Panama Defense Forces (PDF), 248
parachutes
 first attempt, 7
 first design, 9
paratroopers
 in Operation Just Cause, 248
 in WWII, 159
Parker, Robert, 346
patent, 23, 41
 jet engine, 191
Paul II, Pope John, 299
payload, defined, 307
Payton, Gary, 346
Pearl Harbor attack, 127, 137–138
Pentagon, 261
People Express, 197
perigee, 322
Pershing, Gen John J., 71
Philippine Insurrection, 102

Phillips, W.H., 50, 112
Phobos, 291
pilots, female. *See* women in aviation
Pioneer probe, 331
pioneers, female. *See* women in aviation
Pitcairn Aviation, 182
pitch, 33
Pitsenbarger, A1C William, 238
planes. *See* early airplanes, biplanes,
     monoplanes, or aircraft
Pluto, 293–294
Pluto-Kuiper Express, 294
Poland, 139
Polo, Marco, 8
porthole, 48
Portland Chinese Aero Club, 166
Portugal, King of, 16
Post Office Department, 104
Pourpe, Marc, 66
POW, 228
   Airey, TSgt Paul W., 160
   Robinson, A1C William, 237
   Son Tay POW camp, 242
Pratt and Whitney, 184
precision daylight bombing, 132, 149
precision weapons, 262, 268
   GBU-38, 268
   GBU-39, 268
   smart bombs, 251
Presidential Medal of Freedom, 100, 270
pressurized cabins, 175–176
   Boeing 307 Stratoliner, 176, 184
printing presses, 16
prisoner of war. *See* POW
probe, 331
Project Apollo, 325
Project Explorer, 313
Project Gemini, 324
Project Heavy Green, 239
Project Mercury, 320. *See also*
     Mercury astronauts
propellant, 310
propulsion, 193
   Jet Propulsion Laboratory, 313
   in rockets, 309–310
Ptolemaic system, 295
Ptolemy, Claudius, 286, 295
public awareness of aviation, 84, 86, 90
Pullman sleepers, 183
pursuit aircraft, 129
   first aircraft, 132
Putnam, George, 98
pylons, 56

Q

Quesada, Lt Gen Elwood R. "Pete", 103, 146
   as chief of FAA, 199
   close air support, 146
Quest Airlock, 349
Quick Reaction Force, 265
Quimby, Harriet, 56–57

R

R-7 (8K71), 329
R-7 (8K72), 329
R-7 intercontinental ballistic missile
    (ICBM), 329
radar, 155, 175
   Project Heavy Green, 239
radial engine placement, 49
Raiche, Bessica Medlar, 56
Raiche, François, 56
ramjet, 353
Ramon, Ilan, 347
Rangers, 331
ranks. *See* grades
Reagan, Ronald, 100
   Operation Eagle Claw, 244
   Operation Eagle Fury, 245
reciprocating engine, 192
reconnaissance. *See* aerial reconnaissance
Red Baron, 70. *See also* von Richthofen,
    Baron Manfred
refueling, aerial, 103
Reightler, Kenneth, 347
Reitsch, Hanna, 113
relative wind, 36
Reorganization Act of 1920, 122
Reserve, Army, 92
Resnick, Judith, 346
Resolution 660, 257
Resolution 678, 257
retractable, 108
reusable launch, 327
Revolutionary War, 65
revolves, 289
Rheims Air Meet, 46
ribs, 38
Richmond, Virginia, 182
Richter, 1st Lt J.P., 103
Rickenbacker, Edward, 62, 66–67
   Eastern Airlines, 183
Ride, Sally, 343, 346
rigid craft, 19
   airships, 180

rigid dirigibles, 19
Robinson, A1C William, 237
rocket engine, 307, 309
rockets, 8, 303, 327
  principles of, 307–309
  Saturn, 306
Rodgers, Calbraith Perry, 51, 88
Rodman Wanamaker Trophy, 58
Roman Catholic Church, 286
Romania, 139
Roosa, Stuart, 345
Roosevelt Field, 92
Roosevelt, Eleanor, 161
Roosevelt, Franklin D., 98, 129, 168
Roosevelt, Theodore (Teddy), 16
Rosendahl, Lt Cmdr Charles E., 180
rotary-wing aircraft, 50
rotates, 289
rotors, 50
Rough Riders, 15–16
Royal Air Force (British), 73
  World War II, 140, 145
Royal Naval Air Service, 73
Rozier, Pilatre de, 17
rudders, 18, 36
Runco, Mario, 347
Russia, 139
Russian Revolution, 138
Ryan Aircraft, Inc, 92

S

S.S. Mayaguez, 241
sabotage, 137
safety, civilian, 199–200
Sakigake, 332
Salyut 1 and 7, 337
San Francisco earthquake, 23
San Juan Hill. See Battle of
        San Juan Hill
Santos-Dumont, Alberto, 19
sateen, French, 34
satellites, 211
  communication, 330
  navigation, 330
  observation, 331
  scientific, 331
  Soviet, 332
Saturn 1B, 328
Saturn rockets, 306
Saturn V, 306, 308, 328
Saturn, 292
Saudi Arabia, 257

scheduled airlines, 109
Schirra, Capt Walter, 320, 323, 345
Schmitt, Harrison, 345
Scientific American trophy, 46
Scobee, Francis, 346
Scott, Blanche Stuart, 51, 54
Scott, David, 345
Scott, Gen Winfield, 20
Scout, 328
scramjet, 353
secede, 275
second stage, 329
secretary of defense, first, 208
Secretary of the Air Force Michael Wynne,
        356–357
Seddon, M. Rhea, 347
Sega, Maj Gen Ronald, 341, 347
Seguin, Laurent and Gustav, 49
Selfridge, 1st Lt Thomas, 42
Senate Military Affairs Committee, 133
Serbia, 63, 275
Shaw, Brewster, 346
Shepard, Rear Adm Alan, 320–321, 345
shooting stars, 295
Short brothers, Eustace, Howard
        and Oswald, 48
Shriver, Loren, 346
shuttles, 338
  crew positions, 340
Sicily, 157
Sigma VII, 323
Sijan Hall, 228
Sijan, Capt Lance, 228
Sikorsky Aero Engineering
        Corporation, 114
Sikorsky, Igor, 48, 77
Silver Star, 266
  Fisk, TSgt Wayne, 242
  Undorf, Maj Robert, 241
skids, 39
Skylab, 336–337
Slayton, Maj Donald K. (Deke), 314,
        320, 323, 345
Slick airline, 185
Slovenia, 275
smart bombs, 251
Smith, 1st Lt Lowell H., 103
Smith, Cyrus R., 182
Smith, Fred, 185
Smith, Michael, 346
Smithsonian Institution, 20, 304
solar system, 286–289
solitary confinement, 237

solo, female flight, 55
Solter, 2d Lt Andrew F., 103
Somalia, 277
Son Tay POW camp, 242
sortie, 260
South Africa, 139
South Pacific, 98
South Pole flight, 88
Southwest Airlines, 198–199
Soviet Union, 209
Soyuz 1, 4 and *5*, 327
Soyuz, 326–327, 329
Spaatz, Gen Carl "Tooey", 103, 140
   Air Force chief of staff, 208
Space Act of 1958, 313
Space Command, 314
Space Maneuver Vehicle, 360
space race, 312–314
   moon walk, 333
Space Shuttle, 328
Spacelab, 337–339
Spanish-American War, 14
   Ocker, Sgt William C., 102
spars, 38
spatial disorientation, 99
spectators, 84
speculative, 305
Sperry, Elmer, 100
Sputnik 1, 306, 312, 332
Sputnik 2, 312, 319
squadron, 143
St. Petersburg siege, 139
Stafford, Thomas, 345
stalemate, 71
Stalin, Joseph, 139
stealth aircraft, 255, 267
Stewart, Robert, 346
Stinson family
   brothers, Eddie and Jack, 59
   mother, Emma, 60
   sisters, Katherine and Marjorie, 59–60
stockholder, 172
strafe, 75
Strategic Air Command (SAC), 150, 208
strategic attacks, 72, 141, 146
Strategic Triad, 210
streamlining, 9
stressed skin, 108
Strickland, 1st Lt Auby C., 103
Stringfellow, John, 23
strut, 32
struts, 173
Stultz, Wilmer, 97

suborbital flight, 320
subsidy, 108
Sud-Est Aviation, 194
Suez Canal, 145
Suisei, 332
Sullivan, Kathryn, 346
Sumwalt III, Robert L., 200
sun, 289
sunspots, 299
superpower, 257
surface-to-air missile (SAM), 229
surveillance. *See* aerial reconnaissance
Surveyor 3, 335
swallows of death, 69
Swift-Tuttle comet, 294
Swigert, John, 335, 345
Symington, Stuart, 208
Syndicate for Gyroplane Studies, 112

T

Tactical Air Command (TAC), 146, 202
tactical, 145
tail rotor, 113
Taliban, 261, 263
tandem engine placement, 48
Teddy Roosevelt's Rough Riders.
       See Rough Riders
Telstar 1, 330
Tereshkova, Valentina, 326
Tet Offensive, 234
tethered flight, 113
Thagard, Norman, 346
The Winged Gospel quote, 90
theater, 140
third law, 12
Thirty Years' War, 303
Thor, 328
Thor-Delta, 328
Thornton, Kathryn, 347
Thornton, William, 346
thrust, 22
   in jet engines, 193
Thuot, Pierre, 347
Tibbets Jr., Col Paul W., 168
Tiros 1, 331
Titan II rockets, 327
Titan, 292
   rockets, 327
Titan II rockets, 327
Titian III-E/Centaur, 328
Titov, Vladimir, 347
Tomb of the Unknown French Soldier, 69

Tonkin Gulf Resolution, 232
torque, 50
totalitarianism, 311
Trans World Airlines. *See also*
    Transcontinental and Western Air
    (TWA)
transatlantic flight, 88–89
  commercial, 185
Transcontinental Air Transport (TAT), 183
Transcontinental and Western Airlines
    (TWA), 109, 183–184
  Hughes, Howard R. and, 172–175
  Trans World Airlines, 172
transcontinental, 97
transports, 154
treasonable, 127
Treaty of Versailles, 143
tri-jet, 194
Trippe, Juan, 188–189, 190
Triton, 293
Truly, Richard, 346
Truman, Harry S., 130, 147, 168
Tsiolkovsky, Konstantin Eduardovich, 303
Tunner, Col William, 163
  Berlin Airlift, 217–218
turbine engine, 192. *See also* jet engine
Tuskegee Airmen, 130, 147–148

U

U.S. Airlines, 185
U.S.S.R., 139
U-boats, 63
Undorf, Maj Robert, 241
Union Army, 20
Union (Civil War), 20
United Aircraft and Transport
    Corporation, 184
United Aircraft Corporation, 95, 184
United Airlines, 108, 198
  jet service, 194
United Flight 93, 202
United Nations (UN), 209
  Korean War and, 221, 223
United States Air Service, 65
United States in WWII, 139
United States Naval Academy
  Byrd, Rear Adm Richard E., 89
  Douglas Sr., Donald Wills, 179
Unity, 349
unmanned air vehicles (UAVs), 354
  micro-UAVs, 355
upper stages, 329

Uranus, 292
US Air Force, 122, 134
  in Europe, 150
US Air Service, 65
US Airways, 198
US Army Air Force, 95, 122, 134
US Army Signal Corps, 14
  Aeronautical Division, 52, 122
  Aviation Section, 53, 122
  balloon section, 21
US Coast Guard helicopter use, 114
US global interventions, 1990–2006, 271
US Special Operations Command, 244
US Strategic Air Forces in Europe, 140
USS *Arizona*, 137
USS *California*, 137
USS *Hornet*, 100, 167
USS *Lexington*, 166
USS *Maddox*, 232
USS *New Jersey*, 125
USS *Nimitz*, 243
USS *Oklahoma*, 137
USS *Pennsylvania*, 47
USS *Shenandoah*, 180
USS *Virginia*, 125
USS *West Virginia*, 137

V

V-1 rocket, 305
V-2 ballistic missile, 251, 306
V-2 rocket, 305
van den Berg, Lodewijk, 346
Vanguard, 312–313
Vega 1 and *2*, 332
Venera, 332
Venus, 290
Verne, Jules, 305–306
Veterans Administration, 136
Viet Cong, 233
Vietnam War, 232–242
  aircraft used, 235–236
  cause of, 232
  end of, 235
  helicopter use, 114, 235, 237–238
  POWs, 237, 242
Vietnamese Air Force (VNAF), 233
Villa, Pancho, 128
Vin Fiz, 51
virtual, 356
von Braun, Wernher, 306–307, 313
von Richthofen, Baron Manfred, 62, 70
Voskhod 1 and *2*, 326

Voskhod, 326, 329
Voss, Janice, 347
Vostok, 326, 329
Vostok 1, 326
Vostok 6, 326
Voyagers 1 and *2*, 331

W

Wall Street Journal, 182
Wang, Taylor, 339
War of 1812, 303
warhead, 251
warp, 32
Warsaw Pact, 211
Washington Post, 200
Watt, James, 18
Wayne, John, 174
weapons of mass destruction (WMD), 267
weight, 193
Weighted Airman Promotion System, 160
Western Air Express, 183
Western Allies, 215
Westervelt, George Conrad, 106
Wetherbee, James D., 347
White Sands Proving Ground, 307
White, Ed, 324–325, 345
Whittle, Frank, 191
Wilkinson, TSgt Timothy, 254
Willard, William P., 57
Wilson, Woodrow, 63
    Army Air Service, 122–123
wind tunnel, 35
wings, 7
wing-walking, 86
wing-warping, 32
women in aviation
    Cheung, Katherine Sui Fun, 101
    Clark, Julia, 59
    Coleman, Bessie, 51, 54, 82–85
    de Laroche, Raymonde, 58
    Earhart, Amelia, 97–98
    fashion and, 57
    Ninety-Nines club, 101, 164
    Omlie, Phoebe Fairgrave, 87
    Quimby, Harriet, 56–57
    Raiche, Bessica Medlar, 56
    Reitsch, Hanna, 113
    Ride, Sally, 343

Scott, Blanche Stuart, 51, 54–55
    Stinson, Katherine and Marjorie, 59–60
    Tereshkova, Valentina, 326
Women's Airforce Service Pilots
    (WASP), 161
Women's Auxiliary Ferry Squadron (WAFS),
    161, 163, 218
Women's Flying Training Detachment
    (WFTD), 161, 162
Woodring, 2d Lt Irvin A., 103
Worden, Alfred, 345
World Trade Center, 261
World War I pilots, 65
World War II
    air power's importance in, 141
    causes, 138–139
    Battle of Britain, 140–141, 155–156
    Battle of the Bulge, 164
    Battle of the Coral Sea, 166
    Battle of Midway, 166–167
    Pearl Harbor, 137–138
Wright Brothers, Wilbur and Orville, 30–42
    first manned powered flight, 6, 37
    kites, 32–33
    relationship with US Army, 40–42
    wing design, 34–35
Wright R-3350, 173
Wright Whirlwind engines, 88, 92
Wynne, Secretary Michael, 356–357

X

X-34, 363

Y

yaw, 39
Yeager, Charles "Chuck", 174
    sound barrier and, 213
Young, John, 345–346
Yugoslavia, 139
Yugoslavia, 275

Z

Zarya, 349
Zeppelin, Count Ferdinand von, 19, 73
Zij-i Sultani, 297
Zvezda, 349